Who Put the Rainbow in *The Wizard of Oz?*

Yip Harburg, Lyricist

E. Y. (Yip) Harburg, 1896–1981. (Photo by Barbara Bordnick.)

Who Put the Rainbow in *The Wizard of Oz?*

Yip Harburg, Lyricist

Harold Meyerson and Ernie Harburg

with the assistance of Arthur Perlman

Ann Arbor

THE UNIVERSITY OF MICHIGAN PRESS

First paperback edition 1995
Copyright © by the University of Michigan 1993
All rights reserved
Published in the United States of America by
The University of Michigan Press
Manufactured in the United States of America

Cover design and art *Beth Keillor Hay with Kirsten Neelands*
Cover lettering *Sudee Taormira*
Cover photo *Barbara Bordnick*

1996   1995   4   3   2   1

A CIP catalogue record for this book is available from the British Library.

Library of Congress Cataloging-in-Publication Data

Meyerson, Harold.
   Who put the rainbow in the Wizard of Oz? : Yip Harburg, lyricist /
Harold Meyerson and Ernie Harburg.
      p.   cm.
   Includes bibliographical references and index.
   ISBN 0-472-10482-9 (alk. paper). — ISBN 0-472-08312-0 (pbk. : alk. paper)
   1. Harburg, E. Y. (Edgar Yipsel), 1898–1981.   2. Lyricists—United
States—Biography.   I. Harburg, Ernest.
ML423.H313M5   1993
782.1′4′093—dc20
[B]   93-27444
                                                                                  CIP
                                                                                  MN

To Joseph Meyerson—Whose love of word play and of justice provided just the right schooling for this book—and a good deal else. From Harold

To Anna and Harry and all other unsung heroes who touched us and made us sense an invincible spirit and a common goodness—with love, Ernie

The word *rainbow* never appears in L. Frank Baum's book, *The Wizard of Oz*. It was lyricist Yip Harburg who put it in the film. As he recalled it:

This little girl thinks: *My life is messed up. Where do I run?* The song has to be full of childish pleasures. Of lemon drops. The book had said Kansas was an arid place where not even flowers grew. The only colorful thing Dorothy saw, occasionally, would be the rainbow.

"Over the Rainbow Is Where I Want to Be" was my [dummy] title, the title I gave Harold [Arlen, composer]. A title has to ring a bell, has to blow a couple of Roman candles off. But he gave me a tune with those first two notes [an octave apart]. I tried *I'll go over the rainbow, Someday over the rainbow* or *the other side of the rainbow*. I had difficulty coming to the idea of *Somewhere*. For a while I thought I would just leave those first two notes out. It was a long time before I came to *Somewhere over the rainbow*.

The magic in song only happens when the words give destination and meaning to the music and the music gives wings to the words. Together as a song they go places you've never been before.

The reason is obvious: *words make you think thoughts. Music makes you feel a feeling. But a song makes you feel a thought.* That's the great advantage. To feel the thought. . . . And that's why . . . you can teach more through song and you can rouse more through song than all the prose in the world or all the poems. . . .

Songs have been the not-so-secret weapon behind every fight for freedom, every struggle against injustice and bigotry: "The Marseillaise," "The Battle Hymn of the Republic," "We Shall Overcome," and many more. . . .

Songs are the pulse of a nation's heart. A fever chart of its health. Are we at peace? Are we in trouble? Are we floundering? Do we feel beautiful? Do we feel ugly? . . . Listen to our songs. . . . The lyricist, like any artist, cannot be neutral. He should be committed to the side of humanity.

Yip Harburg

Preface

The 1990 Academy Awards television broadcast closed with an "Over the Rainbow" satellite-feed sing-along from Los Angeles, Moscow, Buenos Aires, Sydney, Tokyo, and London, the producers apparently assuming that if there was such a thing as a global song, "Over the Rainbow" was it. Hundreds of millions of people around the world know "Over the Rainbow" and all the songs from *The Wizard of Oz*. Only a relative handful know that Yip Harburg wrote the lyrics.

In the course of a fifty-year career as one of the leading lyricists of American theater song, E. Y. ("Yip") Harburg wrote the lyrics to some of the most widely known, provocative, and brilliantly crafted songs from the heyday of the Broadway and Hollywood musical. Yip wrote the words for over a dozen classic songs such as "Brother, Can You Spare a Dime?" "April in Paris," "Only a Paper Moon," "Over the Rainbow" (indeed, all the lyrics for *The Wizard of Oz*, as well as the dialogue that integrates the songs and script). He also conceived, wrote the lyrics, and coauthored the books for such notable and innovative musicals as *Bloomer Girl* and *Finian's Rainbow*.

Yet, Yip Harburg is an almost entirely unknown artist to an American public that knows and loves the works he created. An indeterminate small number of people *do* know Yip—as they know Ira Gershwin and Lorenz Hart and Cole Porter (as a lyricist) and Oscar Hammerstein II—that is, as a master lyricist of the age of American theater song. But even those few who know of Yip's talent and his distinctive voice, unique style, and characteristic set of concerns do not know the full range of his work. Yip wrote the lyrics for over five hundred songs (the list is at the end of this book) with over fifty composers (also listed) and over thirty-five "great" songs (included in *The Great Songs Thesaurus*). In this book the life-range of his lyrics have been published for the first time.

Lyricists are certainly less celebrated than their more widely known composer collaborators: George Gershwin, Richard Rodgers, Cole Porter (as a composer), and Harold Arlen. The conventional wisdom—even among cognoscenti of the American musical—is that the composer is the *real* creator of the song and the show; the lyricist is somewhat and somehow secondary. Consider, for instance, the following assessment of musicals of the forties, by the distinguished critic

Brooks Atkinson in his 1970 history, *Broadway*: "Harold Arlen's *Bloomer Girl,* full of comedy and nostalgia, and Burton Lane's *Finian's Rainbow,* full of political satire and comic caprice, helped to redeem Broadway from drudgery." With all due acknowledgment to the prodigious musical achievements of Arlen and Lane, Atkinson's assessment refers largely to Yip, who not only coauthored *Finian's* book (with Fred Saidy) but directed *Bloomer Girl,* and for *both* shows conceived the theme, wrote the lyrics, provided the politics, the satire, the caprice, the comedy, and was their guiding spirit. Indeed, as this book will show, Yip was, after Oscar Hammerstein II, one of the key figures in the transformation of the Broadway musical revues into the musical plays of the forties and fifties and thereafter. Finally, it should be known that Yip Harburg's contribution to the classic film *The Wizard of Oz* went beyond writing all the lyrics; he also rewrote the script for the integration of story and song, wrote all the dialogue in the film's middle 45-minute operetta-like sequence, helped cast Bert Lahr and Ray Bolger, and did the final script edit/rewrite. As with his other shows, Yip gave the film both coherence and charm.

In the years since Atkinson's *Broadway*, theater song has lost even more ground to the rock revolution. Since the seventies, however, there has been a resurgence of interest in and the beginnings of a reevaluation of the songs of the twenties to fifties. This change in status, which has reached the American theater composer, has not quite extended to lyricists. In the early nineties, the Smithsonian Collection of Recordings still refers to "Harold Arlen's 'Over the Rainbow' " in its brochure. This distortion of origin is akin to thinking that a baby is the creation of one parent solely. The problem is that the craft of theater lyric writing in America is invisible. Only a rare few—such as Ira Gershwin, Larry Hart, Alan Jay Lerner, Cole Porter, Stephen Sondheim, and Yip Harburg— become *great* theater lyricists. What these lyricists have lacked is critical appreciation; we hope that this book may help to remedy this lack.

For in reality, a song is a synergy of both music and words; a song only exists in the merger of lyrics and music. A song is a *new* entity with its own properties that neither the lyrics nor the music carry separately. The lyricist and composer can only coauthor a song. Further, no lyric is intended to be read as poetry, divorced from the music. *A lyric is created to be sung.* The lyric and music are jointly crafted to emerge as a single work of art. Printed lyrics are usually banal compared to the beauty of the same words when sung. Yip Harburg's work comes closer than anyone's to being the exception to this rule. His printed lyrics are imbued with poetry and wit, a testament to his beginnings as a poet of light verse. But their analysis in this book also considers the music with which the lyrics are merged.

A great theater song that endures in a global community over decades is a true work of art. But because it enters the public community, and eventually the public domain, it cannot be bought and sold. A song can be sung by anyone, and therefore it does not meet many Euro-American values for an artwork—as songs do among Native American cultures.

In this book we focus on Yip Harburg's songs in shows. For the first time, the full range of Yip's major works (plus a few of his neophyte efforts) appears on the printed page—where, we are confident, they will amuse and inform the reader. Yip was a master of the witty song, in particular of the logic of grammar and rhymes run amok into neologisms, of lines comically overlong or disastrously abrupt: "And lots of things which should be happening—ain't." Like Ira Gershwin and Larry Hart, Yip came out of the light verse tradition so prevalent in the first quarter of the century. Like them, he extended that tradition into the realm of theater song, crafting signature songs for a talent like Bert Lahr and mock-operatic sequences in *The Wizard of Oz* and other shows. We also include a smattering of Yip's light verse and a discussion of those shows on which Yip coauthored the book or shaped the story. Our book is therefore not a conventional biography of Yip, but rather a study of his work and his sensibility: of his career, his craft, his themes, his politics, his composers, and the contexts in which he wrote.

Employing extensive and original interviews with Yip and with some of the composers with whom he worked, especially Burton Lane, Jay Gorney, Johnny Green, Jule Styne, Earl Robinson, and Phil Springer, we will look at the creative and collaborative processes that went into the classic songs, from conception to completion. Yip's worksheets in the E. Y. Harburg Collection at Yale University and his videotaped talks in the E. Y. Harburg Collection at Lincoln Center's Library for the Performing Arts in New York City allow us to look at songs as works in progress, and we include here, for instance, the many couplets that did not make it into the final draft of "If I Only Had a Brain," and early versions of "Brother, Can You Spare a Dime?" that show Yip's attempts to heighten the concreteness and impact of the lyric.

Our aim is not simply to illuminate Yip's work, but to look at Yip as a collaborator with composers Jay Gorney, Harold Arlen, Burton Lane, Vernon Duke, Jerome Kern, Jule Styne, Earl Robinson and the host of others with whom he cowrote songs in a career that ran from 1929 to his death in 1981. The craft of collaboratively created art in song has been largely ignored or ill-understood by the public. This book is a study of the art of song collaboration—building upon Deena Rosenberg's study of the Gershwins, *Fascinating Rhythm,* and on recent books about collaboration, such as Bernard Rosenberg and Ernest Harburg's *The Broadway Musical.* We also discuss the shows and films for which Yip crafted these songs as well as the talents who introduced them: Bert Lahr, Beatrice Lillie, Bobby Clark, Lena Horne, Ethel Waters, and Judy Garland. Arthur Freed and Vincente Minnelli are also part of Yip's story.

Finally, we place Yip and his work in a broader context than those of his circle and his craft—that of the social and political worlds to which Yip responded. Alone among the popular theater songwriters of his generation, Yip wrote songs that consciously refracted and commented on these social contexts; that is one reason his work lends itself easily to analysis. Few American artists in any medium have ventured more outspoken, serious, and satiric statements on society than Yip achieved on the Broadway musical stage of the forties, fifties (while being blacklisted from pictures), and sixties.

Referring on one occasion to the over fifty composers with whom he worked, Yip called himself a "chameleon," whose concerns and voices shifted with each show. In fact, though his work ranged from the indignant "Brother, Can You Spare a Dime?" (with Jay Gorney) to a ballad as poignant as "Last Night When We Were Young" (with Arlen) to a mock-ballad as nonsensical as "If I Were King of the Forest" (with Arlen) to the whimsical "Something Sort of Grandish" (with Lane) to the biting humor of "Free and Equal Blues" (with Robinson), the essential Harburg is plain to see in almost all his work. Behind a lover's Paris, over the rainbow in Oz, or beneath a paper moon, Yip's songs reveal a skeptical but deeply celebratory affirmation of life. They place a great emphasis on the power, both constraining and liberating, of belief, and characteristically convey their point with intelligence and humor.

The lyrics in this book are the work of an intensely free spirit. "Yip was all joy," Burton Lane once said of the lyricist's invariable reaction to a good new melody, and that joy suffuses Yip's work. May this book both inform and delight. For, in Finian's words, it is part of Yipper's "elegant legacy."

Harold Meyerson
Ernie Harburg
Spring, 1993

Acknowledgments

To those of Yip's collaborators who spent considerable time with us and enabled us to know Yip better—Burton Lane, Johnny Green, Dana Suesse, Jule Styne, Earl Robinson, Jay Gorney, Phil Springer, and Ira Gershwin. And to Harold Arlen's tenderness.

To Nick Markovich, who organized a mass of materials over too many years and word processed this book impeccably through many drafts; to Camille Croce Dee, who helped gather the source material; to Fred Carl, who helped with manuscript preparation; to Peggy Brooks and Joan Intrator, who edited, respectively, the first and final drafts; to the copyeditors at the University of Michigan Press and to Joyce Harrison, editor; to Beth Hay, artist for the cover; to Barbara Bordnick, photographer, who caught Yip and his spirit in the first and last photos in this book.

To Deena Rosenberg Harburg, who helped initiate and guide this project and to which she contributed her spirit, ideas, and unflagging zeal toward bringing this book to fruition, and who collaborated in analyzing "Brother, Can You Spare a Dime?"; and to Arthur Perlman, who helped us gather and organize the basic material, including the lyrics and early outline drafts.

Special thanks to Lena Horne for insights into her work with Yip in film and on stage.

To the archivists at the Beinecke Library at Yale Library, the New York University Bobst Library; Bob Taylor and the staff of the Billy Rose Theatre Collection, New York Public Library for the Performing Arts at Lincoln Center; Ken Culkin, Rodgers and Hammerstein Archives of Recorded Sound, New York Public Library; Maryann Chach, the Shubert Archive; Lynn Doherty and Kathy Mets, formerly of the Theatre Collection, Museum of the City of New York; Kristine Krueger, National Film Information Service, and the staff of the Margaret Herrick Library, Academy of Motion Picture Arts and Sciences; Louis Rachow, International Theater Institute; The Northwood Institute; B. J. Bullert; Kathryn L. Beam, University of Michigan at Ann Arbor, Department of Rare Books and Special Collections; Mark Trent Goldberg, The Ira and Leonore Gershwin Trusts; Ned Comstock, Doheny Library, University of Southern California; Madeline Matz, Library of Congress, Motion Picture Division; Will Friedwald; John Fricke; Jim Steinblatt.

Special thanks to Aljean Harmetz, who graciously allowed us copies of her full interview notes with Yip used in her excellent book *The Making of "The Wizard of Oz"*.

To the Musical Theatre Program at New York University Tisch School of the Arts, where many theater artists and writers contributed to much of the background knowledge needed to understand Yip's world and work. This first and still only musical theater writing program at a university in the world was one Yip helped to initiate, where he planned to teach, and where he helped select Deena Rosenberg as the founding chair.

And to the Harburg Foundation, which has continuously funded the writing of this book; and to Marge Harburg and Arnold Corrigan, Foundation board members, who were always encouraging and informative.

And, with love, to Jan Breslauer, who sped the edit, and Miranda Meyerson, who put up with her father's occasional disappearances into the mists of song arcana.

To all—our deep appreciation and thanks.

Grateful acknowledgment is made to the following authors, publishers, and journals for permission to reprint previously published materials:

Columbia University Press for excerpts from *Creators and Disturbers* by Bernard Rosenberg and Ernest Goldstein. Copyright © 1982 Columbia University Press, New York. Reprinted with the permission of the publisher.

CPP/Belwin, Inc., for lyric examples from songs from *The Wizard of Oz* (E. Y. Harburg and Harold Arlen). Copyright © 1938, 1939 (renewed 1966, 1967) Metro-Goldwyn-Mayer, Inc., c/o EMI Feist Catalog Inc.; for lyric examples from "Lydia, the Tattooed Lady." E. Y. Harburg and Harold Arlen. Copyright © 1939 (renewed 1967) Metro-Goldwyn-Mayer, Inc., c/o EMI Feist Catalog Inc.; for lyric examples from "Poor You." E. Y. Harburg and Burton Lane. Copyright © 1941 (renewed 1969) Metro-Goldwyn-Mayer, Inc., c/o EMI Feist Catalog Inc.; for lyric examples from "Life's Full of Consequence." E. Y. Harburg and Harold Arlen. Copyright © 1942 (renewed 1970) Metro-Goldwyn-Mayer, Inc., c/o EMI Feist Catalog Inc.; for lyric examples from "Happiness is a Thing Called Joe." E. Y. Harburg and Harold Arlen. Copyright © 1942 (renewed 1970) c/o EMI Feist Catalog Inc. World rights controlled and administered by CPP/Belwin, Inc., Miami. All rights reserved. Used by permission.

Doubleday for literary examples from *Harold Arlen: Happy with the Blues* by Edward Jablonski. Copyright © 1961 by Edward Jablonski. Reprinted by permission of publisher.

Harcourt Brace & Company for literary excerpts from *World of Our Fathers,* copyright © 1976 by Irving Howe, reprinted by permission of Harcourt Brace & Company.

Harwin Music Company for lyrical examples from *Jamaica*. Lyric by E. Y. Harburg. Music by Harold Arlen. Copyright © 1957 (renewed) Harold Arlen and E. Y. Harburg. All rights controlled by Harwin Music Co. and Glocca Morra Music Corp.; for lyrical examples from "Looks Like the End of a Beautiful Friendship." Lyric by E. Y. Harburg. Music by Harold Arlen. Copyright © 1978 Harwin Music Co.; for lyrical examples from "Promise Me Not to Love Me." Lyric by E. Y. Harburg. Music by Harold Arlen. Copyright © 1978, 1985 Harwin Music Co.; for lyrical examples from "The Silent Spring." Lyric by E. Y. Harburg. Music by Harold Arlen. Copyright © 1963 (renewed), 1985 Harwin Music Co. All rights reserved. Used by permission.

Oxford University Press for literary examples from *Broadway Babies* by Ethan Mordden. Copyright © 1983 by Oxford University Press; and for literary examples from *American Popular Song* by Alec Wilder. Copyright © 1972 by Oxford University Press. Used by permission of the publisher.

PolyGram International Publishing, Inc. for lyrical examples from "Californi-ay." Lyric by E. Y. Harburg. Music by Jerome Kern. Copyright © 1944 (renewed PolyGram International Publishing, Inc. All rights reserved. Used by permission.

Random House, Inc. and Alfred A. Knopf, Inc. for excerpts from *Hard Times* by Studs Terkel. Copyright © 1970 by Studs Terkel. Reprinted by permission of Pantheon Books, a division of Random House, Inc.; and for excerpts from *The Making of* The Wizard of Oz by Aljean Harmetz. Copyright © 1977 by Aljean Harmetz. Reprinted by permission of Alfred A. Knopf.

Warner/Chappel Music, Inc. for lyric examples from songs from *Life Begins at 8:40* (Ira Gershwin, E. Y. Harburg, Harold Arlen). Copyright © 1934 New World Music Company Ltd. (renewed). Rights for the extended renewal term in the United States controlled by WB Music Corp., SA Music and Glocca Morra Music. Rights on behalf of Glocca Morra Music administered by The Songwriters Guild of America. Rights for the world, excluding the United States, controlled by Warner Bros., Inc.; for lyric examples from songs from *Hooray for What?* (Harold Arlen, E. Y. Harburg). Copyright © 1937 Chappell & Co.; (renewed); for lyric examples from songs from *Hold On to Your Hats* (E. Y. Harburg, Burton Lane). Copyright © 1940 Chappel & Co. (renewed); for lyric examples from songs from *Bloomer Girl* (Harold Arlen, E. Y. Harburg). Copyright © 1944 Chappell & Co. (renewed); for lyric examples from songs from *Finian's Rainbow* (E. Y. Harburg, Burton Lane). Copyright © 1946 Chappell & Co. (renewed); for lyric examples from "The Begat" copyright © 1947, 1952 Chappell & Co. (renewed); for lyric examples from songs from *Flahooley* (Sammy Fain, E. Y. Harburg). Copyright © 1951 Chappell & Co. (renewed); for lyric examples from songs from *The Happiest Girl in the World* (E. Y. Harburg, Jacques Offenbach). Copyright © 1961 Chappell & Co. (renewed); for lyric examples from songs from *Darling of the Day* (E. Y. Harburg, Jule Styne). Copyright © 1968 Chappell-Styne, Inc.; for lyric examples from "Let's See What Happens" (E. Y. Harburg and Jule Styne). Copyright © 1967 Chappell-Styne,

Contents

Prologue: Yip on Being a Lyricist

Yip Harburg was the first featured speaker at what became the renowned "Lyrics and Lyricists" lecture series at the Ninety-second Street "Y" in New York City. In his talk, he addressed the conundrums of the lyricist's trade:

The question . . . is—why the anonymity of the lyricist as against the recognition of the composer? To understand the genesis of this small injustice, we must first understand the genesis of the universe and the entire human situation, and this is no problem for me. Since I do most of my thinking in rhyme, let me rhyme it out for you:

> God made the world in six days flat
> On the seventh, He said, I'll rest
> So He let the thing into orbit swing
> To give it a dry-run test
> A billion years went by, then He
> Took a look at the whirling blob
> His spirits fell as He shrugged, ah well,
> It was only a six-day job.

Now where did the Almighty go wrong? His book says, "In the beginning was the Word." But if you remember, the Word was God's and not man's. It was God who said, "Let there be light." Before he uttered those words, the angels kept flying in the dark and heaven must have been one vast infirmary of dislocated wings. Now, God, being omnipotent, surely must have conceived the idea of light long before He created the universe, but not until he found the word for light was he able to negotiate the miracle. Let us suppose that God had only the tune for light. There he stood on the brink of eternity saying, "Da da da da" [to Beethoven's Fifth Symphony]. Well, we would all still be in the dark. But having once put the word to the tune, he commanded, "Let there be light." And there was light.

But did he share the word with man so that man could communicate with his brothers? Alas, no. It was eons before man, too, began to invent language. Man could growl and grunt and groan, yodel and even sing. When he dragged his

Neanderthal bride over the threshhold of his cave his larynx was able to warble a cadenza of joy long before he could say, "Baby, it's cold outside." This perhaps explains why people today can hum a tune, but can't remember the words.

Music, which is an extension of our emotions, comes naturally. It is the vested interest of the heart, a very ancient organ. The word must be worked at and memorized, for it is the vested interest of the frontal lobe, a rather recent development.

So, man finally invented words. And words gave man his finest tool with which to confuse, conceal, obfuscate, and antagonize. And that's where the trouble began and where it's still at—no communication. You have only to read the Bible to know the mess that the ancient world and the Hebrew children were in. Always in danger of disappearing, like most of the ancient tribes, until little David began to sing the songs on his nonelectric harp and found that where the talk-talk failed, the sing-song prevailed. And so did the Hebrew children, who now, after thousands of years of persecution and diaspora are still magnetized and brought together every year by the overwhelming magic of a hymn known as Kol Nidre.

But this kind of magic in song happens only when the words give destination and meaning to the music and the music gives wings to the words. Together as a song they go places you've never been before.

The reason is obvious—*words make you think thoughts. Music makes you feel a feeling. But a song makes you feel a thought.* That's the great advantage. To feel the thought. You rarely feel a thought with just dialogue itself. And that's why song is the most powerful weapon there is. It's poignant and you can teach more through song and you can rouse more through song than all the prose in the world or all the poems.

In 1830, Belgium was in a state of unrest. The kingdom tyrannized. The people cowed. Daniel Oberre was a renowned composer; he was also an archreactionary. Antipeople, promonarchy, pro–status quo. Oberre was conducting an opera . . . in Brussels. It was about an uprising of the hungry peasants of . . . Italy. Eugene Scribe had written a revolutionary lyric for the rebels to which Oberre set a march.

Oberre may not have been for the people, but his music was. Being an artist, he had to write *music to match the lyrics. The song broke up the show.* It shook the theater, brought the audience to its feet, crystallized all the pent-up emotions against the government in general and Oberre in particular. They sang, they shouted. The reactionary composer could not control the audience. He dropped his baton and fled, the audience, in loud pursuit, still singing his song. The song that ignited the Revolution of 1830 in Belgium. The song that Oberre, the opportunist, could not suppress in Oberre, the tunesmith. Oberre was hoisted by his own ballade.

Songs have been the not-so-secret weapon behind every fight for freedom, every struggle against injustice and bigotry: "The Marseillaise," "The Battle Hymn of the Republic," "We Shall Overcome," and many more. Give me the makers of the songs of a nation and I care not who makes the laws.

To be a lyricist you've got to be a euphoric masochist. Only this, I and the lady who shares my bed, board, and thesaurus know. As Marc Connelly once remarked about writing in general, you must prepare to be a daily commuter between heaven and hell. To feel something of the torment of a suitor infatuated with a new idea; fearful of being unworthy of your new love, you're hell-bent to win her. Once you conquer her, you conquer the most formidable of all arts.

A book, a play, a painting must be sought. The song . . . seeks you. What's more, it catches up with you. It is ubiquitous and sinewy. It besieges you in your kitchen, in your elevator, your supermarket, your dentist's chair. It can be dangerous. A song can degrade your culture; debase your language. It can pollute your air and poison your tastes or it can clear your thoughts, refurbish your spirit. It is the pulse of a nation's heart. A fever chart of its health. Are we at peace? Are we in trouble? Are we floundering? Do we feel beautiful? Do we feel ugly? Are we hysterical, violent? Listen to our songs.

The wielder of so sensitive, so eloquent a medium of communication has responsibilities. The lyricist, like any artist, cannot be neutral. He should be committed to the side of humanity. He should be concerned for the rights, potential, and dignity of his fellow man. He should also be able to express these ideals with a proper concern for the rights of the human ear, the potential of the human brain, and the dignity of the English language.

I do not wish to intimate that the lyric writer is a more evolved creator than the composer. The composer is merely luckier; he works in a medium in which the appeal is directly to the emotions. The lyric writer must hurdle the mind to reach the heart.

The greatest romance in the life of a lyricist is when the right words meet the right notes. Often, however, a Park Avenue phrase elopes with a Bleecker Street chord, resulting in a shotgun wedding and a quickie divorce. Music is the relentless censor of the false thought and the wrong word. Maria Malabrand, the celebrated soprano, was warned by her father, the great Garcia, for whom Mozart wrote the part of Don Juan, that you cannot sing a lie and stay on pitch. I almost believe this.

Chapter 1

Roots: Russian, Jewish, New York City

Unless you know your roots, you're a lost soul.—Yip

E. Y. ("Yip") Harburg was born on April 8, 1896, to immigrant Russian Jewish parents on New York's Lower East Side—a year, a city, a lineage that describe the roots not only of Yip Harburg but of American theater song lyrics as well. For Yip, Ira Gershwin, Lorenz Hart, and Oscar Hammerstein, as well as such other notable lyricists as Howard Dietz, Harry Ruby, and Irving Caesar, were all born in New York to Jewish families in 1895 or 1896: a few years in which a new cultural generation arose.

This is an astonishing concentration of major figures in what has always been the small field of lyric writing. A complete consensus list of the great theater song lyricists would surely include these four or five members of the class of '95–96 augmented with probably no more than a few other names: Cole Porter, Alan Jay Lerner, perhaps Dorothy Fields and Frank Loesser—and, another generation later, Sheldon Harnick and Stephen Sondheim. Or consider another measure: in Alec Wilder's *American Popular Song,* a survey of the greatest songs of Broadway, Hollywood, and Tin Pan Alley in the years between 1900 and 1950, of the 162 references to the thirty-eight lyricists listed in the book's index, fully seventy-five are to Dietz, Gershwin, Hammerstein, Hart, and Harburg. Moreover, the generation of '95–96 twice played a seminal role in the history of the medium. It was Larry Hart and Ira Gershwin, after all, who most developed the art of the theater song lyric in the twenties. It was Oscar Hammerstein and Yip Harburg, as we shall see, who pioneered the integrated musical play during the forties.

Some of the reasons for this concentration—but only some—can be set forth in fairly broad strokes. Only New York City children could grow up steeped in all the varieties of theater and popular entertainment that were the foundation for creating that most hybrid of art forms, the American musical. Nor is there anything surprising in their being drawn disproportionately from a Jewish population, as theater during that WASP-dominated period was one of the rare

5

industries open to Jews, in part because it was one of the even rarer industries largely owned by Jews. Beginning with the monopoly control of vaudeville and live theater bookings by producers such as Klaw and Erlanger, to the Shuberts' strong ownership of New York Broadway theaters, to the West Coast film empires originated and run by Jewish moguls, the world of entertainment was dominated at the top by Jews, thus affording Jewish actors, composers, writers, and other talents their career opportunities in the New World struggle for a new life.

As to their date of birth, the lyricists comprise a concentration within a concentration. The years between 1894 and 1899 produced a great many of the primary creators of modern American culture: Faulkner, Fitzgerald, Hemingway, and Dos Passos among novelists; Ford, Capra, and Hawks among filmmakers; Gershwin and Ellington among composers; Astaire and Keaton among performers—a list that only scratches the surface. A distinct cultural generation was defined within very narrow age limits. "Year of birth has more than its usual importance in the case of American writers born between 1891 and 1905," critic Malcolm Cowley notes in *Exile's Return,* his survey of American literary life in the twenties. "They grew up at a time when the literary atmosphere of the country was changing rapidly, with the result that each age group was likely to form its own ideals of what a good novel or poem should be."

Indeed, persons born in the late nineties missed the stylized Victorian era and emerged into the new social consciousness that in 1912 a new magazine, *Vanity Fair,* called the "modern" era. The First World War and the Roaring Twenties catalyzed the fairly rapid transformation of American political, sexual, technological, and literary values. The explosion of older forms of musical entertainment—black, minstrel, vaudeville, English music hall, and light opera—fused into a new American art form called musical comedy. This new form was developed by a vanguard of eager young Jewish sons of immigrants who all resided in New York City, where most of the present Broadway theaters were built between 1900 and 1927, ushering in the contemporary American musical theater.

All the more reason, then, to define with some precision the common cultural heritage and attitude of the lyricists of 1895–96. Yip's early life is in many of its particulars a paradigm of others. With greater or lesser emphasis on any one point, his contemporaries shared his immersion in and access to all forms of theater; his orientation to the commercial arenas of art; his schooling in traditional poetic forms and in the light verse of the period, which fused popular content to classical forms; and his love affair with America and New York City, which was to take the form of a heightened receptivity to a polyglot culture whose sound and music were still to be invented. In other aspects—most notably the desperate poverty into which he was born and the radical politics that he was to embrace—Yip's life was, for his cohort, exceptional.

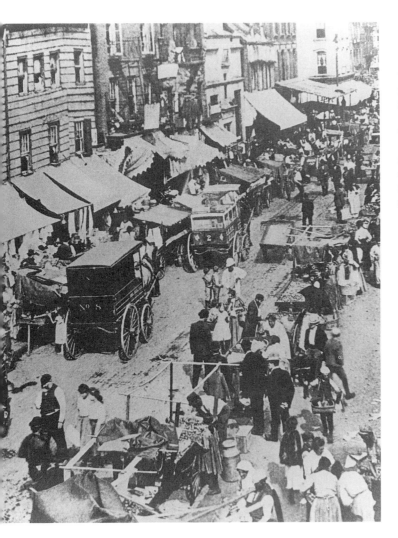

This photo of Hester Street in the Lower East Side of Manhattan in 1899 is from the wondrous book *World of Our Fathers* by Irving Howe, who describes the world where Yip grew up. (Museum of the City of New York.)

The insert shows, *left,* Yipsel and a friend in 1904. (Collection of Harburg Estate.)

Our best and most vivid guide to Yip's early years is Yip himself (largely as quoted in Bernard Rosenberg and Ernest Goldstein's book, *Creators and Disturbers*). But Yip on Yip is not simply autobiography. It is cultural history as well.

> I'm a New Yorker down to the last capillary.
>
> I grew up around Hester and Allen Streets, in the heart of the Lower East Side, which was also the pushcart center of the world. When I was about seven, we moved to Eleventh Street and Avenue C, a sort of borderline between the Irish and the Italians that was just becoming Jewish. Among the kids there was plenty of friction. The enmity was supposedly residential—block by block—but we Jews were always aware that the goyim were after us. Since they came in gangs we formed gangs too. We fought the 14th Streeters who were Italian, we fought the Irish—and both of them fought the Jews.
>
> Our folks didn't know much about all this. A kid was automatically independent at the age of eight, surely by the time he was ten. We were all little fiery Jews with excitement and a sense of compulsion and creativity and a little bit of good male activity.
>
> The street, not the home, was your life. Your parents spoke Yiddish. That alone made you a displaced kid. The older generation of men and women brought their Russian and Jewish culture with them. They spoke no English. Down on the street you were being Americanized, but in a special ghetto way. Parents were very proud of children who spoke English and could interpret for them. This put the parents in an inferior position.

Yip's parents, along with the millions of Jewish émigrés from Russia, had come to New York in the late 1880s. Yip was the youngest of four children (he had two brothers and a sister); but another six had died in childbirth or infancy. Such was the mortality rate of those living in poverty in New York's Lower East Side.

Irving Howe informs us in *World of Our Fathers* that

> a 1908 census of 250 typical East Side families showed that fewer than a quarter of them slept two in a room; about 50 percent slept three or four in a room; and nearly 25 percent, five or more in a room. Toilet facilities were two to a floor at best and foul privies at worst. The clamor of pushcarts, refuse carts and grocery wagons was part of the daily way of life. Perhaps worst was the fear of fire in the wooden slums and the daily assault of smells. . . . Life was abrasive, clamorous. . . . By 1898 the Tenth Ward, only a bit more than half a square mile, bulged with a population of 82,000.

Yip's father and mother (bearing the surname Hochberg) worked in a ladies' garment sweatshop; Yip's sister Anna worked fourteen to sixteen hours a day in the shops; and as a boy Yip also worked in the shops packing clothes. It was one of a stream of odd jobs at which he worked as a youth; another was lighting and damping the gaslights on Broadway. The apartment at Eleventh and C where he spent much of his childhood was a sixth-floor walk-up cold-water flat. He had no bed: he slept on chairs that he and his sister Anna would push together each evening, absorbing (Yip quotes his idol, George Bernard Shaw), "the chill of poverty which never leaves your bones."

Not just the poverty but the divisions between home and street were greater for Yip than they were for his future fellow lyricists and composers, with the one decided exception of Irving Berlin. Hart and Hammerstein and Rodgers were of assimilated German-Jewish stock, the children of professionals, merchants, and entrepreneurs. The Gershwin parents, like the Hochbergs, were recent Russian immigrants, only they had come not from the shtetl but from St. Petersburg. The Gershwins were middle class and had become assimilated to modernity and urban life well before they crossed the ocean.

Among the classic lyricists, then, Yip alone grew up in the changing and contradictory ghetto world of the Russian-Jewish working class, at once traditional and radical, grim and heady. The rituals observed in the Hochberg household were the ancient ones of orthodox Judaism—augmented, however, by the nightly reading of the new socialist *Jewish Daily Forward*. The world into which Yip emerged each morning was one of middle-class aspirations and working-class radicalism. "Jewish socialism," Irving Howe has written,

> was primarily a political movement dedicated to building a new society. . . . [J]ust as international socialism helped to transform the consciousness of humanity, so did Jewish socialism [in America] transform the consciousness of the Jews. . . . Jewish socialism and unionism transformed the *posture* of Jewish life . . . creating a new kind of person: combative, worldly, spirited, and intent upon sharing the future of industrial society with the rest of the world.

It was a posture, a politics, that Yip, virtually alone, would bring to the mainstream American musical.

"The drama of life," Yip recalled,

> was enacted within a context of poverty. You lived from month to month. But youngsters didn't feel the sting of it because everyone else was poor, too. We knew no other way of life, and it didn't mean much to a kid who turned the street into an exciting playground. You could swipe your sweet

potatoes from the grocer, light a bonfire, and eat 'em right there at midnight.

The nickname Yip, well, it's one of those funny things that stick to you for the rest of your life. My people were immigrants. They came from Russia. And *yipsl* was the [Yiddish] term for a squirrel and evidently I was quite a flighty kid. I moved fast and went from one thing to another and I clowned a lot and I sort of was a maverick in the family. They were all frightened people. I tried to lift them up all the time with games and fun and running. And I was very good at athletics; I won all my four prizes for high jumping, for running, for baseball and so the word *squirrel* became part of it, and it was "yipsl" to the kids around the block. . . .

Now, when you've lived in one place all your life like New York and your friends grow up with you in public school and they go with you to high school, well . . . so it was Yippy and Yipianny and then I began writing under Yip.

My parents were Orthodox Jews, though not as strict as the Hassidim. To some extent, they were tongue-in-cheek Orthodox. My father did go to *shul* regularly and I usually went with him. Whatever religious feeling I had evaporated when I was about 15 in the face of a devastating personal crisis. I had an elder brother, Max, twelve years my senior—my hero—my inspiration. He was the first-born. . . . Max became a famous scientist. At the age of 20 he got a B.S. from City College. A superb physicist and mathematician with . . . a master of science degree from New York University and a Ph.D. from Columbia. I remember his having written a thesis on the weight of the earth, news of which was all over the papers.

My parents were mystified. I was a kid; he was my God. Wonderful people started coming to the house—scientists, mathematicians, physicists. It was a world apart. And then, at age 28, he died of cancer. My mother, broken by the shock, died [some years] after. The tragedy left me an agnostic. I threw over my religion. I began seeing the world in a whole new light. My father was shaken, but something in him had to carry on. He had a great sense of humor. I told him I was not going to *shul* any more, "*Papa, Ich gehe nicht.*" We talked in Yiddish. He said, "Well, *sonele,* I don't blame you, I can understand. But I'm an old man. I need insurance."

The House of God never had much appeal for me.

(Years later, in the poem "Atheist," Yip wrote:

Poems are made by fools like me
But only God can make a tree;

And only God who makes the tree
Also makes the fools like me.

But only fools like me, you see,
Can make a God who makes a tree.)

Anyhow, I found a substitute temple—the theater. Poor as we were, on many a Saturday, after services, my father packed me up and told my mother that we were going to *shul* to hear a *maggid*. A *maggid* was a super rabbi who usually came over from Smolna or Slutsk or some unpronounceable place. But somehow, instead of getting to the *maggid* from Slutsk we always arrived at the Thalia Theater where the great Madame Lipsik or Tomashevsky was performing. These excursions were an adventure not only in art but in mischief, for we never told the Mamma. As far as she knew, it was the holy Sabbath, we were out soaking up the divine wisdom of a *maggid*.

Do I remember Tomashevsky? I remember every bit of him. Everything in the Yiddish theater set me afire. The funny plays had me guffawing; they were broad and boisterous. And the tragedies were devastating.

Yip was not alone in viewing the theater as a kind of substitute temple. Irving Howe has written of the early Yiddish theater:

This was a theater of vivid and raw talent, innocent of both art and the pain of immigrant life. It was a theater of primary, unevaded emotions, Jewish emotions that had only yesterday escaped from the prison house of Europe. This theater created an atmosphere of holiday, a secular Sabbath still in touch with received associations of religion. . . . By 1918 New York City had almost twenty Yiddish theaters. The eclecticism of this style was so incorrigible that no European style could survive transplantation intact.

As America transformed the Yiddish theater, so Jews stormed onto the new American stage. Yip witnessed both developments:

The Yiddish theater was my first break into the entertainment world, and it was a powerful influence. Jews are born dramatists, and I think born humorists too. Yiddish has more onomatopoetic, satiric, and metaphoric nuances ready-made for comedy than any other language I know of.

Jewish humor was the basis for so much great vaudeville, my next passion. Whenever I could rake up a quarter, I would spend weekends in the gallery of the Palace Theater watching these most wonderful performers: Al Jolson, Fanny Brice, Willie Howard, Ed Wynn, Bert Lahr.

Memorable times: saving up the quarter, walking maybe five miles to the theater, going up to the "pit" in the third gallery, revelling in the great artist. I was hooked.

Nor was vaudeville the only popular medium in which Yip was immersed:

I was always a kid who loved popular songs. I loved all the Irving Berlin songs. I knew every popular song and I knew how to sing them.

My passion to be an actor was also consuming. Luckily, the public school I attended, P.S. 64, had a lovely stage. When the teachers found that I was a talented reciter and actor, they had me on all the time. . . . I won prize after prize for acting and reciting.

The next great big impact that I remember, which had some connection with my work, was a very sweet lady, a Miss Wiseman, with blonde hair, at Public School 64 on Ninth Street and Avenue C, who took me, took three kids in the class, because we were the top of the class, to see Maude Adams in *Peter Pan*. I've kept this picture of Maude Adams as Peter Pan all this time. And I think that experience had something to do with . . . my love for fantasy.

It is one of the defining characteristics of the class of 1895–96 that as children and young men, the medium to which they were drawn most strongly was theater rather than popular song. Hammerstein, of course, was raised in the theater as the grandson of one of New York's foremost opera *impressarios*. Hart, too, was a child of theater (he was translating German operettas into English for the Shuberts when Richard Rodgers met him); and Ira Gershwin, perhaps even more than Yip, had interests that ran the gamut from contemporary European drama to the most backwater vaudeville house (in his early twenties, Ira reviewed vaudeville acts in a New York–based trade paper).

This early affinity for theater was to shape their subsequent careers. Song for the class of '95–96 was in essence an element of theater. Almost never in their careers—even early on, when the distance between the musical stage and Tin Pan Alley was not so great as it was later to become—did Hart or Hammerstein, Yip or Ira, make the rounds of music publishing houses or enter into song plugging or writing lyrics for jazz bands. They rarely ventured into the world of single popular songs outside the confines of a show or a picture. It is this

Maude Adams, star of the legitimate show, *Peter Pan* (1905), which thrilled Yip's nine-year-old imagination forever and kindled his love for fantasy and works of J. M. Barrie, novelist/playwright. (Collection of Harburg Estate.)

immersion in theater that sets them apart from the majority of their contemporaries, including such major figures as Irving Berlin and Johnny Mercer.

School encouraged Yip's growing affinity for theater:

> I liked school because of the acting, the drama, and the recitation. Basically, I loved the English language, the poetry. We had inspiring teachers. I was a whiz at "The Village Blacksmith," and "The Wreck of the Hesperus." Once I invited my folks to a recitation contest. I won a prize that evening with "Spartacus and the Gladiators." They wept at my "Gunga Din," and Tennyson's "Lady Claire." Those were the beginnings, the roots of my passion for rhymes.

"Those of us who were a little more sensitive," Yip once told Max Wilk, were directing ourselves to the settlement houses, like the Henry Street Settlement [where Yip once took a course from a young social worker named Harry Hopkins—later to become one of the paramount figures of the Roosevelt Administration]. Wonderful places. They took the kids under their wing. I belonged to a literary dramatic club. We were putting on plays, and that excited me.

I had an English teacher—his name comes back to me as though it was yesterday: Ed Gillesper. I'd write something for the school newspaper, or a composition, and he'd . . . say, "Harburg, come up here and read it to the class." I'd read, and there would be twenty-odd kids laughing out loud, and by God, that was really something. I'd tell myself, I want to repeat this experience.

At public school, I began writing verse . . . at an early age. . . . [W]e had a baseball team in Tompkins Square Park and I wrote a song for the bleachers. The Henry Street Settlement House and the Educational Alliance downtown had little newspapers. I wrote poems for the newspapers. P.S. 64 had a [monthly] newspaper and [I] gloried in seeing [my] name in the little print.

There was no place to study at home, a cold-water apartment with no steam heat; the stove was in the kitchen and it was always cold. So my study was the library on Tenth Street, right opposite Tompkins Square Park. . . . It was a fine, warm, clean place, and there were lovely librarians, with blonde hair and blue eyes and elegant accents. The attraction was magnetic. And they put me on to some great books. I devoured the contents of Carolyn Wells' *Vers de Société* and gravitated towards light verse of all kinds. . . . O. Henry . . . made a dramatic impression on me; to this day, I can't write a poem without an O. Henry twist in the last line.

Every immigrant family . . . knew that education would improve their lives. I was aware. I empathized with my father in his sweatshop, my mother at her washing and making hair nets for a living on the Lower East Side. *I always had hope that someday they would be liberated.* It became part of my chemistry—to free them from drudgery.

(Years later, Yip commented:

I am a rebel by birth. I contest anything that is unjust, that causes suffering in humanity. My feelings about that are so strong, I don't think I could live with myself if I weren't honest [about that].)

[I attended] Townsend Harris Hall, a special place which combined high school and college (City College of New York) for seven years, cutting off

Yip at City College of New York, ca. 1915. (Collection of Harburg Estate.)

a year. There were tough competitive entrance exams—you had to be a masochist to attempt to get in—and those admitted were an elite group, real studious kids from the Lower East Side. . . . "Get that degree!" was the aim of life. We were driven. At the same time, the education was terrific.

Yip, the young radical, also recalled that he had trouble with college officials when he started wearing a "soft," nonstarched shirt collar.

My passion for humorous verse and stories goes all the way back. . . . My father . . . delighted in good satire. It was one of his great joys to sit at night and read me funny articles by great Yiddish writers from the columns of the Jewish press—stories by Sholem Aleichem and others that tickled and delighted us both.

Perhaps my first great literary idol was W. S. Gilbert. I adored his light verse. One day at school [this was Townsend Harris in 1910] I pulled out a book of his Bab Ballads and other poems, and the kid sitting next to me showed great and excited interest. His name was Ira Gershwin. We always

Yip *right,* with arm around girl, with his friends ca. 1916, in the Finlay Club, a literary group including Ira Gershwin whose members were all serious writers-to-be and a few friends for a lifetime. (Collection of Harburg Estate; courtesy of Lillian Meltzer.)

sat side by side. He was "G;" I was "H." Ira took a look at the book and said, "Do you know that a lot of this is set to music?" I was incredulous. "There's music to it?"—"Sure is. I'll show you." He invited me up to his house, a "swank" apartment on Second Avenue and Fifth Street, with a Victrola! Compared to most of us, the Gershwins were affluent; Ira had an allowance and money to buy magazines, books and records. He was great about sharing them with me. That first afternoon he played *HMS Pinafore* for me. There were all the lines I knew by heart, put to music! I was dumbfounded, staggered. Gilbert & Sullivan tied Ira to me for life.

Gilbert's satirical quality entranced us both—his use of rhyme and meter, his light touch, the marvelous way his words blended with Sullivan's music. A revelation!

We had something special in common, Ira and I. . . . Soon we wrote for the official high school paper; our column was called "Much Ado." It was an imitation of "The Conning Tower," Franklin P. Adams' column in *The New York World.* . . . In college, at CCNY, we started a column called "Gargoyle Gargles" in the campus paper, and I ran another column called "Silver Lining," in the *Mercury,* a monthly.

For their "Gargoyle Gargles" column the authors signed off as "Yip and Gersh."

"It was the age of light verse," Yip said.

Every newspaper had a columnist like FPA [Franklin Pierce Adams] who attracted contributors, and each contributor had a nickname. Fred Saidy [future Yip collaborator] was Frederique, GSK was George Kaufman. It used to be exciting to open up the papers.

What makes Adams's column significant today is that he did not write it alone. On the contrary, he encouraged all available talents to contribute, and "The Conning Tower" became the finishing school for a generation of American humorists. Adams discovered George S. Kaufman, Robert Benchley, Dorothy Parker (who said of Adams, "He raised me from a couplet"). Other up-and-coming contributors included E. B. White and James Thurber, playwright Morrie Ryskind, poets Louis Untermeyer and Newman Levy, future lyricists Howard Dietz, Dorothy Fields, and Yip. Whether or not Adams ran their material, though, the future theater lyricists wrote in the style of his column.

For many New York high school and college students of the teens and early twenties, for Yip and Ira at Townsend Harris, for Hart and Ryskind at Columbia, the columns had a special magic. They synthesized a mastery of the city with a mastery of the language; they offered a way to combine street smarts with book learning; they conferred an elite status, an *insider* status, on the very sort of writers they were endeavoring to become. In the New York of 1920, Scott Fitzgerald later wrote, Adams's column was the one "forum for metropolitan urbanity." For the children of immigrants, contributing to that forum was a confirmation of their assimilation, mobility, talent. "When Adams accepted things of mine," Yip told Max Wilk, "and I saw my name in his column, along with Marc Connelly's or Dorothy Parker's—well, it gave me such a lift I felt I could conquer anything!"

The ascendancy of the columns made the study of poetic composition particularly compelling to the class of '95–96. The English curricula of elite high schools and colleges still stressed a rigorous training in classical poetic forms—forms that appeared daily in the most widely read columns in New York. "We were well-versed in all French forms," Yip once recalled, "the ballad, the triolet, the rondo, the villanelle, the sonnet. We were highly disciplined. We were never permitted to use an oricular rhyme or a tonal rhyme like *home* and *tone.*" Within a few years, though, this was a curriculum that the most advanced English students, electrified by the revolution in poetry led by Eliot, Pound, and the later Yeats, would have reason to regard as thoroughly outmoded. But through the end of the First World War, the classical forms were still—indeed, *newly* —relevant, and Yip, Ira, and Larry Hart in particular mastered them all.

Asked on one occasion to list the influences on his work, Yip responded with what he considered a universal syllabus for the aspiring lyricist. "My roots are Shakespeare," he said, "Wordsworth, Shelley, Shaw: the English language. If you want to write songs and you don't know A. E. Houseman, if you don't know Dorothy Parker, Frank Adams, [Chicago columnist and light versifier Bert L.] Taylor, [W. S.] Gilbert, you cannot begin to be a good lyric writer." The list confirms Malcolm Cowley's observation that what constituted the ideal novel or poem to any cohort of writers of the twenties reflects the tastes and standards of a brief moment in an epoch of change. The list may not be quite the transhistoric recipe for good song lyrics Yip claimed it to be. But as an account of the utmost historic specificity, linking together wildly dissimilar writers whom the class of '95–96 studied and absorbed, it illuminates not where song lyrics come from, but, rather, some of the origins of American theater song. (In fact, the black songwriters of the so-called coon songs of this period also contributed a folk/colloquial language to the lyrics of the time that heavily influenced the development of American lyrics.)

For it was not just the classic poetic forms that had begun to seem old-fashioned to some by the midtwenties. To writers just a few years younger than Yip and his contemporaries, the world of Adams and the columns no longer exercised their peculiar fascination. A generational rift had occurred with Adams planted firmly in the camp of the old. FPA had no use for the poetic innovations of postwar literature; in the early twenties, he used the "The Conning Tower" to ridicule e.e. cummings, *The Waste Land,* and the avant-garde literary magazine, *The Dial.* Fitzgerald's *This Side of Paradise* and its focus on postwar youth appalled him. He refused to come to terms with the new world and the new literature that emerged in the wake of the war. "As early as 1921," a recent biographer notes, "FPA's standing as arbiter and mentor to youth began to erode." Ironically, Adams and his work were never more popular than in the twenties; indeed, the case can be made that his column helped bring into being an audience for the musical theater that by 1930 Ira Gershwin characterized as "lyric conscious." But the sway that FPA and his column had held over many of the best and the brightest of New York's adolescent writers had been broken.

The fleeting mystique of light verse can best be measured by the obscurity surrounding those "Conning Tower" contributors—Newman Levy and Sam Hoffenstein, to name only two—who stayed within the field. Adams's better known protégés moved on from "The Conning Tower" to make their reputations as playwrights, prose humorists, and lyricists. Among these, the lyricists owed him the most. A classically rigorous light verse provided Yip and his peers with a training they were to put to use in theater song, a medium not sufficiently developed during the teens to command their full involvement and allegiance. Later, as lyricists, Yip, Ira, and Larry Hart invariably would insist that the music be written first; then they would write their lyrics to fit the notes, calling upon the metrical discipline and rhyming virtuosity with which their training in light verse had provided them. Adams's contribution, at bottom, was to have invested that training with a status and romance that spurred them on.

In 1916, Ira dropped out of CCNY—an option open to a middle-class Gershwin, perhaps, but definitively closed to a desperately poor Harburg. "He [Ira] didn't have the fears that we had," said Yip,

> the insecurity. It would have been death for me to leave college in my sophomore year.
>
> When Ira left college, I suffered on with the goddamn trigonometry and differential calculus. But I did take some very good courses in Shakespeare with a professor named Coleman. Another teacher who influenced me greatly was Professor William Bradley Otis. He recognized something in me and made me wait after school one day, saying, "I want you to continue writing, especially humorous pieces." I began submitting little poems for publication. A magazine called *The Parisian* was the first to buy a poem from me, for ten dollars. After that came *Judge* and *Puck,* ten dollars, fifteen dollars, here and there. It was evident that you couldn't make a living this way. At that point I never thought of writing poems as a career. As for songs, I had no idea how they were written, let alone that they could mean anything to me.

Yip's nonabsorption in songs at the time of his college graduation, 1917, is entirely understandable. It wasn't just that he and the class of '95–96 had not yet found their métier. The fact is that their métier, that of theater song lyricist, had not yet been invented.

In part, the problem was that the music wasn't ready yet. With the definite exception of Hammerstein, all of them were to find as their collaborators men younger than themselves. In Yip's CCNY graduation year, George Gershwin was nineteen, Richard Rodgers fifteen, Harold Arlen twelve, Burton Lane five. The new urban sound of theater song, with its complex rhythms and its blue harmonies adapted from black and Jewish music, still lay ahead. For the present, theater song meant European style operetta, the genre in which Hammerstein apprenticed himself, or the brash, unsophisticated numbers of vaudeville and revues.

There were, of course, exceptions. Since 1914, Jerome Kern, lyricist P. G. Wodehouse, and librettist Guy Bolton had been producing a series of pioneering, miniature book musicals at the tiny (299 seat) Princess Theater. The form was new, but the spirit and setting, while present day, were still far removed from the polyglot sidewalks of New York. Irving Berlin's work was New York to the core, but it was not yet theater song—defining, instead, the upper limit of what vaudeville and revue could offer.

Two beliefs united the class of '95–96: they loved popular song, and they knew that song lyrics could be better. On the day in 1919 when he first met Larry Hart, Rodgers was to recall, Hart lit into popular lyrics. "His theories," wrote Rodgers, "and they were countless, began with his disdain for the childishness of the lyrics then being written for the stage. He felt that writers were afraid to approach adult subject matter and that the rhyming in general was elementary and often illiterate."

However, creating a more sophisticated song lyric would take some time. Ira and Hart were to spend a number of years working their way into the theater and learning to write songs with, in Hart's case, the boy genius he had stumbled upon, or, in Ira's case, the one living in the next room. But apprenticeship was a luxury Yip could not afford; as he saw it, there was never really any alternative to going into business. As the soon-to-be Lost Generation of novelists and poets flocked to Europe to drive ambulances or fly planes, Yip finished college. Within a few months, a peculiar opportunity arose that combined overseas travel with a well-paying job, and Yip jumped at the chance to have a well-paying job and to avoid being drafted into the First World War—a war he firmly opposed.

As Yip told Deena Rosenberg:

> Some big alumnus came along and offered me a job in South America [in Uruguay]. I went and after I got down there the war started here, but I was working for the Swift Company, and that was considered part of the war effort.
>
> It was the first time I was able to support my mother and father, which was what I wanted. They were poor, pathetic people and I felt awfully guilty

Yip, *top* (*right*) and *third from left* (*below*) and friends in Uruguay, 1917–20, one of whom became friend-for-life. Here Yip learned Spanish and the guitar, supervised several hundred factory workers, wrote plays, and was "becoming a man." (Collection of Harburg Estate.)

about them. I was able to send back money. I became a big shot down there. I got to be head of a department and I was written up in all the papers, so I was for the first time becoming a man. And I realized this was important for me. Because I was a frightened little kid all the time, and I began feeling like a man, real grown up. I had the image of my father always in mind. They [my parents] frightened me that they were loose screws in the world and that I would be like that too. This trip helped me to grow up.

When you're alone in a foreign country and you have to work for yourself, you become a man damned quick. Also the experience. I began feeling the triumph of being a leader, of making decisions, of having five hundred people under me and being a big shot. I stayed another year after the war finished. Two years. I was afraid to come back, afraid of not getting a job. I had such a good job down there.

I kept in touch with the Finley Club [a writing group started in college]. My friends and Ira's . . . were all together. . . . I would write them poems back home, and I was even writing poems for the *Montevideo News* in English. It was an English paper, so I became sort of a top guy in the English community there. Then we put on some American plays. I was a very good actor and we put on some three-act plays. You can't imagine when you're living in an isolated country where the handful of Americans are all homesick and you give them an American show. You become like Merlin. And so wherever I went I was always given respect—no matter if I was a lost kid in space.

I thought I was going to write light verse, and I thought I'd write short stories, because I felt the urge to do that and I knew that something happened every time I wrote one of those things—that it was overcoming all obstacles, insecurities, all fright. It was my one foot on the threshhold of life.

[But on returning from Uruguay in 1920] I went into business because I didn't think you could make money at versifying. I had to support my mother and father. I was established in . . . the electrical appliance business, by a colleague of mine, Harry Lifton. Harry got the capital. He liked me. . . . [W]hen Harry Lifton, go-getter extraordinaire, said, "C'mon, let's go into business," I went along with him.

It was the boom period of the twenties and we started to make money in appliances. For seven years we went up and up and were worth about a quarter of a million by 1929. But I never stopped contributing to the different columns. To Don Marquis in *The Sun.* To Frank P. Adams when he was in *The World* and in *The Evening Mail* and in *The Herald-Tribune.* In fact, my name appeared many times . . . somewhere, with a poem.

Some of Yip's work reflected the classical poet turned businessman (note the classic rhyme pattern):

FRENCH FORMS FOR COLLECTION DEPARTMENTS

Form I. Reminder Triolet.
Dear madam. We beg to make mention
Of Charge Account 8602.
With your very kind condescension,
Dear Madam, we beg to make mention
Of a payment which slipped your attention,
And which is TWO weeks overdue.
Dear madam, we beg to make mention
Of Charge Account 8602.

Form II. Delinquent Rondeau.
Dear Customer, 'tis with regret
That we must write this second let-
Ter re Account 8602
Which now is FOUR weeks overdue.
Since we've had no response as yet

Take notice that our terms as set
Down in our Contract MUST be met.
We too have bills to pay like you
Dear Customer.

Our price is low. Our service bet-
Ter than your dollar bill can get
In any store. So kindly do
Not force us to begin to sue.

P.S.
Treat this request not as a threat
Dear Customer.

In 1923, Yip entered into what was to be a rocky marriage with the Boston-born Alice Richmond. At this time, Yip changed his name from Irwin Hochberg to Edgar Y. Harburg. The Y stood for "Yip." Two children, Marge and Ernest, were born during the middle twenties.

Most of Yip's poems that have come down to us from the twenties are like his subsequent earliest song lyrics: competent, amusing, and in the zeitgeist style of light verse. "Cupid's Boomerang" could have been written by Dorothy Parker:

> If his eyes are twinkling tears
> Let love whisper in your ears.
>
> If his heart is beating fire
> Wrap youself in sweet desire.
>
> If his words are charms that sing
> Let your senses swoon and swing.
>
> If his arms are bold and strong
> Run, sweet girlie, run along.

In some of his twenties poems, though, the distinctive characteristics of the master lyricist–to-be peek fleetingly through the conventional forms. In "Definition," Yip pursues the logic of the suffix and the momentum of the rhyme into the realm of neologism—a realm where he was later to become king:

> One he loves, two he loves,
> He's a bigamist.
>
> Three he loves with all his heart,
> He's a trigamist.
>
> Four he loves, five he loves,
> A polygamist.
>
> And if six he casts away,
> That's a pigamist.

"The Eternal Urge" compresses into the aphoristic style of the columns the spirit that was later to suffuse "When I'm Not Near the Girl I Love, I Love the Girl I'm Near," and numerous other Harburg contemplations:

> In the Spring a young man's fancy
> lightly turns to thoughts of love,
>
> and in Summer—and in Autumn—and
> in Winter—see above.

Throughout the twenties, Yip recalled,

> I'd see Ira every week, several times a week, sat with him. He was
> beginning to write with George. Ira liked to have me around. When Ira
> began writing words to George's music in the twenties, I became aware of
> lyric writing as a possible profession.
>
> Business or no business, my first love in those heady days was still the
> theater. I went to all the musical shows and all the straight shows—and
> devoured them. The variety was staggering. There were something like
> sixty or seventy shows a season. There was a burst of enthusiasm, fresh-
> ness, and new writers experimenting with new things. Rodgers and Hart,
> the Gershwins, Cole Porter, Kern and Hammerstein came on the scene
> with a whole new kind of song and show, far removed from Tin Pan Alley,
> more literate, more sparkling. As for straight theater, suddenly you be-
> came aware of all the exceptional imports—Ibsen, Shaw, Chekhov,
> Molnar. Plus Americans like O'Neill. I depended on the theater for my
> spiritual life. I attended every show I could get into. . . . For me business
> was a sideshow. And I thought I'd be able to sell the business in another
> few years and become a writer. But heaven was ahead of me, and that
> beautiful depression of 1929 came along and knocked the hell out of my
> business. I found myself broke and personally in debt for about fifty
> thousand dollars, my name on all sorts of contracts that I had never read
> or cared to. All I had left was my pencil.

In interviews in his later years, Yip stressed time and again his antipathy to
business, his love of songwriting, his gratitude to the 1929 crash. "We made a
lot of money and I hated it," Yip told Max Wilk. "I hated every moment of it."
"I was relieved when the Crash came," he told Studs Terkel. "I was released.
Being in business was something I detested. When I found that I could sell a song
or a poem, I became me, I became alive. . . . When I lost my possessions, I found
my creativity. I felt I was being born for the first time."

Beyond question, of the two lives Yip had been leading—that of published
poet and theater aficionado, and that of New York electrical appliance
businessman—he greatly preferred the first to the second. And now, the choice
was no longer necessarily between the life of the starving artist and that of the

successful entrepreneur. Since the midtwenties, Ira and Hart and now Cole Porter had demonstrated that the kinds of talents Yip possessed could be put to use in musical theater and be richly rewarded in the process. But pressures to remain in business came from the office ("I'd signed a contract saying I wasn't going to spend any time except on the business," he told Max Wilk. "The guys who put up the money for the business probably figured I'd go off and neglect it") and from home (where his wife, according to Yip's sister Anna, urged him to stay the course while the money was good). The crash ended the pressure.

Yip was to detail to a succession of interviewers what happened next:

> I immediately got hold of Ira and I said, "Ira, I think I'd like to be a songwriter from here on. I'm through with business." And he said, "You should have done it a long time ago." But as I was fearful, he said he'd put me in touch with a composer and gave me a five hundred dollar check, enough to see me through for three or four months. I sent my wife and two kids off to California, assuring them, "I'll break into this new business somehow." I rented a little back room four flights up in a house on Eighty-fifth Street, from a Russian friend, Lala, living with her mother.
>
> Meanwhile, Ira had called [composer] Jay Gorney, recommending a fellow classmate. Luckily, Jay's lyricist, Howard Dietz, had just teamed up with a new composer, Arthur Schwartz, and Jay needed a new collaborator. He asked who I was. Ira answered, "Well, he hasn't written song lyrics, but you'll know him from 'The Conning Tower.' He signs himself 'Yip.'" To which Jay responded, "Oh, Yip from 'The Conning Tower'!" Ira made a date for me. I worked at the Sterling Watch Company in the daytime and wrote with Jay at night.

It is, all in all, a remarkable story. Our general assumption is that the major events of history—crash, war, depression, civil unrest—affect the major artists of any given period in a fairly uniform fashion: the depression turned artists leftward, Vietnam sharpened the artistic community's quarrel with America, and so on. But for Yip, the crash had personal significance unequaled virtually anywhere in the American artistic world. One searches in vain the list of his contemporaries among novelists, filmmakers, songwriters, playwrights, for just one besides Yip whom the crash ruined, drove out of business and into a new and, for a time, shaky life—not to mention into his ultimate métier. Among all the American artists whose faith in the system was eroded by the depression, only Yip had actually had his life shattered by the fall of the market—and only Yip was so rudely disenthralled with the system and freed from its routine. As had happened before, with his brother's death, a faith that had been weak to begin with became impossible to sustain at all.

Midlife conversions from business to art are rare in the lives of American artists. Yip used the language of religious conversion in describing his switch: "I was released. . . . I became me, I became alive. . . . I felt I was being born." Perhaps the closest parallel to Yip's story is that of Sherwood Anderson, the writer who served as a beacon for so many of the novelists who were Yip's contemporaries. As Anderson told it, he was trapped, like Yip, in a business he hated; like Yip, he yearned to get out and write; like Yip, though without benefit of the crash, he walked away from it all one day—pausing in the middle of dictating a letter, donning his jacket, and departing the office forever. Like Yip, he moved from comfortable circumstances to a little back room; like Yip, he lived apart from his wife and children; like Yip, he was in his midthirties (he was thirty-six; Yip was thirty-three).

There is one last point of similarity between Yip's story and Anderson's. Neither one may be entirely accurate.

For in fact, both Anderson's and Yip's narratives described breaks much cleaner and neater than they actually were. Anderson did walk away one day in 1912, though it was not entirely a conscious protest: he suffered a nervous breakdown, and two more years were to pass before he left home and business. In Yip's case, his songwriting began with a series of scripts and lyrics he ghosted for a monthly radio show, "The Ever Ready Radio Hour," which was on the air throughout 1929, and the first of which was broadcast that February. His collaboration with Gorney began with this February show. In July, Earl Carroll's *Sketchbook* opened on Broadway with three songs by Yip and Jay. In October, a full ten months after Yip got together with Gorney to write his first songs, the market crashed.

How much of Yip's account, then, is accurate? That his wife and children moved to California while he stayed in New York is confirmed by his children, though to what degree this was a consequence of financial reversal and to what a consequence of a crumbling marriage is difficult to determine. That Yip lost his fortune at the end of the twenties is certainly true, and that hard times followed upon the reversal is confirmed by several sources. "I met Yip through Ira Gershwin," composer Burton Lane recalls. "Yip was scrounging around in those days. He was living in a club. He had a little room there. This was in the late twenties." How late in the twenties remains unclear. If Harburg and his partner Harry Lifton went under before the crash, Yip's story would hold up save in that one particular: it would be his own business collapse, not the general one that followed soon enough, that precipitated the change. "Harry Lifton encouraged him to do light verse writing while he was still with the firm," Yip's daughter Marge says. In this account, Yip would have spent 1929 with one foot in each identity: a difficult situation that the crash mercifully terminated. "The Crash," Marge Harburg continues, with hindsight, "gave him his permission to write."

Whatever the circumstances of the sea change in Yip's life, one fact becomes persistently clear: for all his later talk of how liberating the changeover seemed, it had to have been an anxious, even harrowing, period. Cut adrift from his family, heavily in debt, unable still to make the total break with the hated world of business (even in Yip's own account, he worked in a watch company by day and wrote with Gorney only by night), living in greatly reduced circumstances— all this, whether in early 1929 or late 1929 or mid-1930, was the background against which, as Yip was later to quip, "I had my fill of this dreamy abstract thing called business, and I decided to face reality by writing lyrics"—for musical theater.

Chapter 2

Yip's Apprenticeship: Becoming a Lyricist

They each have something different to offer you, which gives you a new dimension and a new inspiration. Burt [Lane will] open up a certain sense of satire. Harold [Arlen] opens up a certain sense of emotion. One is an extrovert and one is an introvert. They both turned me into what they are, and so I am I don't know what. Too complex for everything.

In 1929, when Yip began writing lyrics, the theater song lyric we associate with the musical stage between the First and Second World Wars was only four or five years old. Ira Gershwin had begun writing regularly with George in 1924. In tandem with Richard Rodgers, Larry Hart reached Broadway one year later with the first of the *Garrick Gaieties*. Ira and Hart were in the vanguard of a new kind of lyricist. "The musical theater scene was quite a few steps removed [from Tin Pan Alley]," Yip noted.

> The people writing for it were well-equipped. Most of them had college training, and had some experience at least with college shows. . . . The musical comedy writers were completely literate. Mostly, the guys writing songs for Tin Pan Alley were close to illiterate grammatically, but they had a sense of showmanship and an ear for what the people liked.

The new-style song lyrics were part of a broader revolution in American culture. In 1924, the year that the brothers Gershwin hit Broadway as a team, Edmund Wilson noted in the *New Republic* that a sea change had overtaken American comedy. In place of the comedies of George Ade and George M. Cohan, with their brash businessman heroes, a new kind of comedy, more critical of the business culture, was coming to Broadway via such talents as George S. Kaufman. The year 1925 marked the debut not only of Rodgers and Hart but also of the *New Yorker,* the magazine that proclaimed itself "not for the little old lady in Dubuque." Between the traditional high culture and mass culture audiences, a third stratum had arisen out of the growing educated urban middle class. It formed the base for what Ira by decade's end would term a

29

"lyric-conscious audience." It welcomed the wit and wordplay of the new lyricists, encouraged them in their war on what Hart termed "the brutally cretin aspects of our culture."

The new model song came almost as a shock to Yip, opening a realm of possibility that had not hitherto existed. "It was your music and Larry's lyrics which first sparked the fire that eventually became this writer's flame fatale," Yip wrote Richard Rodgers in the sixties. "The impact of your very first songs was an explosion that shook the rhymes out of my psyche and changed my life from what might have been pedestrian routine to exciting creativity." "Larry Hart was a brilliant lyric writer," Yip said on another occasion. "He broke a lot of ground. He took the sentimentality out of sentiment. I felt a kinship with many things he did." But for all his affinity with the new song lyrics of Ira Gershwin, Larry Hart, Cole Porter and others, Yip the novice lyricist was not yet capable of comparable efforts.

"To make the transition from verse writing to song writing is like a leap from Peter's foot to Satan's knee, or from Satan's foot to Peter's knee," Yip once told an interviewer.

> It's an altogether different medium. Verse writing is an intellectual pursuit. You sit home with a book; you are quiet; you absorb the thought; you chuckle to yourself. A song done in a theater is an emotional explosion. At the end of it you expect applause. You've got to move an audience, not only with the words, but with the emphasis on the music. . . . When I saw what Ira and Larry Hart were doing, I thought, "That's what I'd like to do."

Yip and Ira

It is clear that Ira Gershwin was Yip's true mentor in learning the new craft of setting words to music. When the two inseparable souls of Yip and Ira temporarily took different occupational paths in the decade of the twenties—Ira to lyricist, Yip to business (and light verse)—it was Ira's (and Larry Hart's) art that Yip emulated and studied at first hand. It was Ira who urged Yip to take the leap into lyric writing, loaned him money, and introduced Yip to Jay Gorney and Burton Lane and later to Vernon Duke. Ira also cowrote Yip's first lyric to Duke's music, and later cowrote the lyrics with Yip to *Life Begins at 8:40,* with music by Harold Arlen. We know that Yip and Ira spent endless hours discussing and viewing the new American musical comedies and theatrical shows at their height in New York City in the twenties. They analyzed the works, the lyrics, the players, even as Ira's success bloomed in this new career. This deep boyhood-

For Yipper —
One (if not the)
of my oldest and
most talented
friends,
With affection
and admiration —
Ira

Yip met Ira and George Gershwin about 1910 and they became life-long companions; Ira and Yip were each born in 1896 and each had an early passion for light verse and lyrics. Ira (left) and George Gershwin appear here in a well-known photo from the thirties; unfortunately no extant photo shows the three friends together. The inscription bears an' unusual number of superlatives for the low-keyed Ira. (Collection of Harburg Estate.)

based rapport and close friendship as colleagues lasted for the rest of their lives. Ira exerted an important abiding influence in Yip's apprenticeship and in Yip's later development as a mature lyricist.

The leap from Peter's foot to Satan's knee took Yip several years to complete. There was nothing exceptional, though, in the length of Yip's apprenticeship. Ira had been writing lyrics for six years before he and George connected on *Lady, Be Good!* in 1924. Hart had been writing with Rodgers for five years (and for some additional years before Rodgers came along) before the *Gaieties*. In his book, *Lyrics on Several Occasions,* Ira suggests that a period of development and adjustment was all but inevitable for the fledgling lyricist:

> Given a fondness for music, a feeling for rhyme, a sense of whimsy and humor, an eye for the balanced sentence, an ear for the current phrase, and the ability to imagine oneself a performer trying to put over the number in progress—given all this, I would still say it takes four to five years

collaborating with knowledgeable composers to become a well-rounded lyricist.

In Yip's case, apprenticeship lasted three-and-one-half years.

Why should the art of lyric writing demand such an extended apprenticeship? Sarah Schlesinger, a lyricist and teacher, told us:

> The evolution of a lyricist's craft, intuitions, and aesthetic powers is one of the least understood aspects of musical theater. *Theater lyric writing* is a technically precise and intellectually complex art form which not every poet or prose writer can master. As lyricists approach a new lyric they begin with an infinite number of possibilities that must be crafted to fit an unforgiving *matrix* of minuscule proportions—often no more than eighty words long. The refrain of Yip's lyric "April in Paris" is only 65 words long.
>
> Within this controlled and concentrated form, there lies tremendous power. It is the lyricist's job during his apprenticeship to learn to harness that power by filling the matrix with (1) fresh lyrics that match (2) the metrical pattern and (3) structure of the music, (4) have perfect rhyme, (5) serve the dramatic situation, (6) grow from character, (7) follow a dramatic progression, (8) reflect the lyricist's point of view, and (9) satisfy the technical demands of the human singing voice. A good song is a small masterpiece.
>
> The challenge of becoming a lyricist involves not only perfecting individual writing skills but also learning to be an effective collaborator, one of the most demanding of human relationships. Not only must lyricists find a way to transfer their intent into the minds of their listeners, they must make their message heard and understood in tandem with their musical collaborators. The theater lyricist must also be collaborating with the book writer of a musical, as well as directors, actors, designers, and producers who impact the lyric-writing process.
>
> Although lyricists employ many of the same tools as poets, the demands of their craft are significantly different. While lyrics and poetry both employ meter, rhyme, and sound, it is music which constrains and propels the theater lyric, shaping its form as well as its content with melody, harmony and rhythm.

Yip and Jay

While Ira served as Yip's mentor to the craft of writing lyrics, so Jay Gorney served as mentor to Yip's learning about the music that goes with lyrics. During a Hawaiian vacation in 1976, Yip wrote a letter to Gorney, the composer with whom he had written his first lyrics some forty-seven years earlier. "We met," Yip wrote,

> and through your experience and expertise, a light versifier became a lyricist. No mean feat that—since Dorothy Parker and Frank P. Adams tried to make that transition without success. What might have happened had they had your guidance is an interesting conjecture.

Gorney was eight months younger than Yip, but until he was ten, he had lived in Bialystok, Russia, moving then with his family to Detroit. Like Yip, he had graduated from college (University of Michigan) in 1917; like Yip, he was later to join the radical Left. Unlike Yip, he had stayed in school for several additional years and become an attorney. However, after a college career devoted at least in part to producing musicals and leading jazz bands, the practice of law in Detroit seemed dull and relatively unremunerative. After one year, Gorney abandoned both Detroit and the law to try songwriting in New York. He had been at it for nine years before meeting Yip, during which time he had written songs for an Eddie Cantor musical, authored the score for the 1927 musical hit *Merry-Go-Round,* and become musical supervisor at Paramount's new all-talkie studio in Astoria, Queens.

Yip's first work with Gorney was uncredited. Gorney and Henry Souvaine had been commissioned to turn out weekly hour-long musicals for CBS radio's "Ever Ready Radio Hour." Beginning in early 1929, Yip scripted and wrote the (now missing) lyrics for three of the shows. The first of these, aired on February 19, was entitled, "The Mayor of Hogan's Alley," and included a suitable inaugural song for a Lower East Side alumnus: "New York Is Full of Aliens." "Now that I read these scripts," Yip was to write in the annotations to his collection at Yale University, "I am grateful for the anonymity."

But Yip's work with Gorney was not confined to the radio. "We wrote a dozen or so songs together, right off the bat," Yip recalled.

> Just then, Earl Carroll had a new theater with a turkey in it called *Fioretta,* which flopped. Jay and I caught him on the rebound and played him our songs. "Great," he said, "these'll make my new revue." The show was called *Sketch Book*—an immediate hit.

Earl Carroll's Sketch Book opened July 1, 1929, with Yip and Jay receiving top billing among the show's songwriters for the three songs they had contributed. There then followed the names of the thirteen other songwriters who had work in the show. Broadway revues of the period typically consisted of a series of quite distinct sketches, songs, dances, and specialty numbers

Jay Gorney, composer and mentor to Yip, at the piano, Yip, *right,* and Bobby Connolly, choreographer for several of Yip's early shows and *The Wizard of Oz,* appear with the dancers on the set of the Universal film *Moonlight and Pretzels,* 1933. (Courtesy of Sondra Gorney.)

apportioned among the show's comics, singers, dancers, and chorus girls. The revue could be, and frequently was, a chaotic format. It was, however, a format that afforded the fledgling songwriter a reasonable chance to place a couple of songs (seldom more) in a show—particularly inasmuch as there were more than forty such shows a season during the twenties, and most of them flopped.

Gorney's position at Astoria also enabled Yip to embark on songwriting for pictures. Among the talkie features Paramount turned out at Astoria in 1929 were two that featured Helen Morgan, whose performance of the Kern-Wodehouse "Bill" in *Show Boat* two years earlier had elevated her to coequal status with Fannie Brice as chanteuse supreme of the wronged woman torch song. For *Roadhouse Nights* (which also featured the nightclub act of Clayton, Jackson, and Durante—their only appearance on film), Gorney and Harburg authored the Morgan lament, "It Can't Go on Like This." For the Rouben Mamoulian film *Applause,* they composed another Morgan ballad of true-blue self-abuse: "What Wouldn't I Do for That Man?" These numbers are about as far removed as possible from what was later to become the quintessential Harburg song. In subject matter, attitude, tone, development (or lack thereof), rhyme, wordplay, and use of metaphor, they stand light-years from Yip's later work. But here we look at one of them, "What Wouldn't I Do for That Man?" precisely because it illustrates the problems Yip faced in developing his craft and in finding a suitable musical milieu and material. This is not where Yip was headed, but it was most certainly where he came in.

WHAT WOULDN'T I DO FOR THAT MAN?
(excerpt)

Verse.

Life was blind to me
Now it's kind to me
Love has opened my eyes
Since it came to me
Life's a game to me
With the sweetest surprise
I never knew how good it was to be
A slave to one who means the world to me

Chorus.

I loved that man from the start
And way down deep in his heart
I know he loves me, heaven knows why
And when he tells me he can't live without me
What wouldn't I do for that man?

He's not an angel or saint
And what's the odds if he ain't
With all his faults I know we'll get by
I'll be so true to him he'll never doubt me
What wouldn't I do for that man?
If I could only rest my weary head
On his shoulder
I'd close my eyes right there and wish
I'd never grow older

I'll never leave him alone
I'll make his troubles my own
I'll love that man like nobody can
I'm just no good when his arms are about me
What wouldn't I do for that man?
Oh, what wouldn't I do for that man?

Clearly, this is not "what Ira and Larry Hart were doing." The most striking aspect of "What Wouldn't I Do?" is how old-fashioned it was by the standards of 1929. The very genre belonged to the prewar era, to the larger-than-life vaudeville melodramatics of Brice and Sophie Tucker ("Bill," in fact, had been composed in the teens, too). Those melodramatics—including, in the second chorus, a two-line pause to allow the singer, presumably overcome, to recompose herself—are brought right into the song.

This was the problematic terrain on which Yip began his work. The lyric must remain necessarily "artless": the authenticity of the singer's voice takes precedence over any felicities of expression—except that the singer's voice comes encased in genre conventions and clichés, which Yip simply reproduces. Some of this is a function of the song's *success:* Yip and Jay had tailored the song to Morgan's stage personality, with its inherent strengths and limits. Even within those limits, though, the lyric falls short. The rhyming is pedestrian. Metaphor is altogether missing. The lyric, like the music, does not build at all, indeed, subsides into repetition. Lyrically and musically, the drama in the song's final stanza is no more developed than the drama of the song's first lines: there is no forward motion here, merely variations on a basic theme. This is a rather undifferentiated and low form of song life: a snippet from any portion of the song can represent the whole.

On one level, this catalog of shortcomings encapsulates almost everything Yip was to overcome within a few years' time. They are endemic, that is, to his period of apprenticeship—but not only to that. They are endemic as well to almost all the music to which he was setting words during that period: and with one notable exception, it is only when Yip is given first-rate music during this period that he creates first-rate lyrics. His apprenticeship, so to speak, is overdetermined: the crudeness of musical expression inhibits—or at minimum, delays—the development of his verbal expression.

"I had never heard that kind of music before," Yip once said of his first exposure to Harold Arlen. "I was writing with Jay Gorney and we were writing in the Jerome Kern vein." Gorney's music and that of Yip's many other apprentice-period collaborators sounds not only pre-Arlen but pre-Rodgers and pre-Gershwin. Beyond question, Yip learned a great deal about songwriting in his early years with Gorney and *thirty* other composers: about verbal economy, about which vowel sounds can be held easily by singers and which not, about tailoring the song to the singer. But internal rhyme is often a function of melodic or even harmonic variation; metaphor, of the mood of the music; and narrative thrust, of the unfolding of the music. Here, with rare exceptions, a lyricist can go no farther or faster than the composer. Here, many of Yip's beginner lyrics grind to a halt.

In writing a song, Yip believed that the music invariably had to precede—and thereby lay the groundwork for—the words. "A great song requires a great melody that comes right out of the heart and brain of the composer without any constriction imposed by a lyric," he once said.

The composer has to more or less feed you. Feeding him an idea, a title, is fine, but usually if you give him a complete, immutable lyric first, he'll start underscoring and usually a banal melody results. A great song requires a great composer, and a great composer brings out the best in a lyricist: the melody acts as a discipline on his wit and invention.

The problem was that the converse is also true: an undistinguished melody seldom fosters a sparkling lyric.

There were, of course, other limiting factors in Yip's apprentice years besides the music. He was much less free than he would later be to dictate the subject matter of his songs. Some of his early efforts are English versions of foreign songs. ("My Fortune Is Love" renders a German tango [!] into English.) Some were assignments to set lyrics to preexisting melodies. Some had to be composed to order on immediate deadline. "When you're doing musical comedy," Yip once said,

> you often want to move on to the new things, so you write—"perform"— quickly and get through with it. The temptation is to take the easy way out. I did that sometimes, especially when I was starting out and didn't have a standard to overcome. Now that I can't afford it, I won't do that unless my brain runs dry.

Yip certainly did not exculpate himself for his early shortcomings as a lyricist. "Early songs used in pictures or written to tunes for publishers," he notes in his collection at Yale. "Terrible! How did I ever dare go into songwriting? Must have been desperate."

Here then are some examples of an as yet unmastered craft. We start with the second stanza of "Some Night When the Moon Is Blue," which puts end-line rhymes on otherwise unaccented syllables:

> Though love has neglected me
> I'll look for you patiently
> Some night, some night, when clouds are few
> And the moon is blue.

"It Can't Be Real" shows Yip still having difficulty fitting the words to the music without resorting to stilted contractions:

> It can't be real
> It makes me feel
> 'Twas done for sympathy.

But even when Yip had passed through his 'twas and 'twould period, metaphor and narrative development remained a problem. The story of Yip's apprenticeship is the story of how a lyricist evolved from "It Can't Be Real" to "April in Paris" in a little more than two years—and with a multitude of composers.

Composer Hopping

From almost the very outset of his songwriting career, Yip began composer hopping. Yip worked with more composers than any lyricist of comparable stature; only Johnny Mercer comes close. ("When I'm not near the composer I love," he told Morley Safer on the television program *60 Minutes* in 1978, "I love the composer I'm near.") In a career extending over 50 years, Yip worked with 48 composers on 376 songs published and registered at ASCAP. (See table 1.) The list does not include those collaborations on songs that went unpublished—such as his short-lived efforts with Kurt Weill many years later, or with those composers not with ASCAP.

Yip had a stock answer when asked about his wandering work habits:

> Being a very eclectic guy, I always liked trying a new style, whether it was a sad social comment like the Dime song or something like "Lydia, the Tattooed Lady" for a zany fellow like Groucho Marx. *I'm a chameleon.* I love putting myself into everyone else's shoes—and each composer lends me a pair.

In fact, though, there lurked beneath the chameleon a very solid identity, whose concerns and motifs would in time find expression in songs by very different composers. If there was a chameleon period in Yip's career, though, it was his apprenticeship. Between 1929 and 1934, Yip wrote with thirty-one different composers before settling into a long-term partnership with Harold Arlen. A number of these—with whom Yip worked only once or twice—were not nearly so accomplished as Jay Gorney. Of the twenty-two composers with whom Yip wrote before his first song with Arlen, only two, Arthur Schwartz (with whom Yip wrote only one song during this period) and Vernon Duke, could be said to have developed into major songwriters. Yip's progress as a lyricist, then, unfolded at two different speeds: incremental, as he learned his craft with journeyman composers, and fast-forward on those occasions when the music called forth greater efforts.

Part of the incremental process involved keeping a notebook. Yip had an ever-present scrapbook of jottings of turns of phrases, wordplays, couplets, and so forth. He was daily, constantly on the qui vive for such scraps. One of the early

TABLE 1. Yip's Composers and Number of Songs Published with Yip and Registered at American Society of Composers, Authors and Publishers (ASCAP)

Composer	First Year of Collaboration	Lifetime Total
1. Jay Gorney	1929	30
2. Frank Tours	1929	2
3. Sammy Fain	1929	23
4. Henry Souvaine	1929	2
5. Phil Cohan	1929	1
6. John W. (Johnny) Green	1930	8
7. Vernon Duke	1930	25
8. Peter de Rose	1930	1
9. Arthur Schwartz	1930	5
10. Ralph Rainger	1930	1
11. Milton Ager	1931	1
12. Oscar Levant	1931	3
13. Hugo Riesenfeld	1931	1
14. Lou Alter	1931	1
15. Mario Bragiotti	1931	1
16. Robert Stoltz	1931	1
17. Werner Heyman	1931	1
18. Igor Borganoff	1932	1
19. Joseph Myer (Meyer)	1932	2
20. Emmerich Kalman	1932	1
21. Juan Llasas	1932	1
22. Raoul Moretti	1932	1
23. Harold Arlen	1932	111
24. Richard Myers	1932	1
25. Lewis Gensler	1932	11
26. Senia Pokrass	1933	3
27. Dana Suesse	1933	2
28. Roger Edens	1933	2
29. Morgan Lewis	1934	1
30. Jean DeLettre	1934	1
31. Maria Grever	1934	1
32. Franz Waxman	1935	1
33. Karl Hajos	1935	1
34. Will Irwin	1937	1
35. Herbert Stothart	1938	1
36. Burton Lane	1940	42
37. Carl Sigman	1941	1
38. Earl Brent	1942	2
39. Margery Cummings	1942	1
40. Jerome Kern	1943	11
41. Earl Robinson	1944	9
42. Nick Acquaviva	1959	1
43. Jacques Offenbach	1961	24
44. Milt Okun	1964	5
45. Jule Styne	1967	15
46. Ann Sternberg	1969	2
47. James Van Heusen	1978	1
48. Phillip Springer*	1979	12*

*Not listed with ASCAP

memories of his then nine-year-old son was attending a movie (*The Awful Truth* with Cary Grant and Irene Dunne) at which Yip was laughing uproariously (and the people nearby casting withering glances)—and suddenly, Yip took out a pencil, turned on its light, and scribbled words onto a small pad, still laughing— a true collector. "A good lyric writer," Yip once said, "has ideas stacked away. You store away titles, maybe one word you like. The creative process is haphazard and elusive. You must know how to structure, to edit. You must be a good cabinetmaker." Some pages from Yip's 1930 notebooks, now held at Yale University, contain possible song titles and lyric lines:

Using hearts for stepping stones
It's the old Adam in me
Even free, love is expensive
Don't let the rain be your waterloo
I'm not a highbrow—but lately I've been writing sonnets to your eyebrow
When my head is on their shoulder—they smoulder
I envy your lipstick
He's a swell sensation—leaves nothing to the imagination
Let me be charmed—let me find illusion in your arms
Beauty's only skin deep—but that's deep enough for me (I'm no cannibal)
He: What do you think of evolution?/She: It's a good idea but can they
    enforce it?

And rhymes:

let your virtue/desert you
wedlock/deadlock
gaze meant/amazement
don't know what wrong or right meant/excitement

The First Hit Song

One of the notebook lines soon was worked into one of Yip's first hits. The song was "I'm Yours," and the composer a twenty-two-year-old Harvard graduate who had recently come to work at Astoria: Johnny Green. Green was to go on to a career as one of Hollywood's most notable composer-arrangers and conductors, but it was right at the outset of his career that he composed his best-known songs, among them "Body and Soul." He and Yip coauthored eight in their Astoria days.

"Yip bedazzled me with his use of words," says Green.

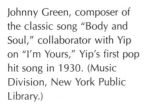

Johnny Green, composer of the classic song "Body and Soul," collaborator with Yip on "I'm Yours," Yip's first pop hit song in 1930. (Music Division, New York Public Library.)

What Yip was not nearly so adroit with in those days, as he later became, was music per se [though at that point, Yip played the banjo, harmonica, and guitar]. Yip came in with the title, "I'm Yours." We wrote it for that kooky little featurette, "Leave It to Lester." He asked me if I liked the title, "I'm Yours" and I said, "Yeah, it's a lovely title. There's such simplicity, there's such directness about two words, 'I'm Yours.' What more can you tell a woman? That spells to me the diatonic scale." He says, "What is that?" I said, "You know it."—"No, no."—I said, "It's just what it sounds like: going up the scale. I would like to come up with a melody based on that kind of simplicity." He said, "Give me a for-instance." I said, "Like this," and—I'm not exaggerating—I went [plays the opening musical phrase of "I'm Yours"] and I said, "Now a mutation of that, but going down." He said, "That's it! Don't go any further." I didn't say it, Yip said it. He then said, "That's diatonic?" I said, "It's diatonic as hell."

I'M YOURS

Verse. Ever since we parted with
The love we started with
I just can't erase you from my mind
Really, it's regrettable
You're non-forgettable
Every place I go your face I find
What would night time be with every star away?
What is life to me when you are far away?

Chorus. Ask the sky above
And ask the earth below
Why I'm so in love
And why I love you so?
Couldn't tell you tho' I try, dear
Just why, dear
I'm yours

When you went away
You left a glowing spark
Trying to be gay
Is whistling in the dark
I am only what you make me
Come take me
I'm yours

How happy I would be to beg and borrow
Or sorrow
With you
Even tho' I knew tomorrow
You'd say we were thru

If we drift apart
Then I'll be lost alone
Tho' you use my heart
Just for a stepping stone
How can I help dreaming of you?
I love you
I'm yours!

It was Yip who had identified the first strain and the counterstrain. He had begun to cultivate what his last collaborator, Phil Springer, was to call his "infallible ear" for a good tune. The tune in this case was much more lively than those of the other composers with whom he had been working: a sprightly, stepwise melody that is then varied a few notes higher. The lyric, though, tends to be only a livelier version of Helen Morgan self-sacrifice. It restates more than it progresses, and the lyric to the release is particularly unoriginal. In 1930, Yip had not yet freed himself from the love-song conventions he was soon to transcend. Still, this is the only published song in which Yip used the words "I love you"—a phrase he (like Ira) would eschew in all his later lyrics.

Nineteen thirty was also the year Yip began working with Vernon Duke, though it was not until 1932 that the two began writing together regularly. The following year Yip coauthored only one song with Duke, two disappointing songs with Oscar Levant, several one-shot interpolations and English renderings. Nineteen thirty-one was also the year of the German tango. It was the year of an altogether standard bit of musical/lyrical boosterism in response to the growing depression: "It's in the Air," with music by Lou Alter and lyrics cosigned if not cowritten by producer (and would-be lyricist) Billy Rose. An excerpt suggests Rose might have coauthored the lyric after all:

> It's in the air!
> It's all over town!
> It's in the air!
> There's no talking it down
> And everywhere
> For plain citizen brown
> Skies are blue and pastures are green!
> Stocks showing up!
> Steel going up!
> No slowing up now.

1932: Breakthrough

The song's optimism, of course, was not only totally unfounded, it was negated by the decline in show business no less than in steel. The following year, 1932, marked a nadir in the number of Broadway productions: the money—both to produce shows and to see them—was disappearing fast. Yet despite the decline in Broadway musicals, 1932 was Yip's breakthrough year. He authored all the lyrics to three revues: *Ballyhoo of 1932* (with music by Lewis Gensler) that spring, and *Americana* (with music by six different composers) and *Walk a Little Faster* (with music by Duke) that fall. Yip had more songs on Broadway than any other songwriter in 1932. But the breakthrough wasn't merely quantitative. It was, by year's end, qualitative as well.

Ballyhoo of 1932 was no classic, but one song was revived years later by Lena Horne, which she described as the "very basic lyrics of Yip Harburg." It opened with

> Thrill me
> With a kiss that's vicious
> With a love delicious
> Though it's all fictitious . . .

Ballyhoo gave Yip the opportunity to develop his comic lyric writing. The show's star was Willie Howard, a great Yiddish-accent comic of the Broadway stage. It was through revues that Yip became the foremost comics' lyricist of his time. In his first show, the *Sketchbook,* he had contributed one number for Eddie Cantor. *Ballyhoo* allowed him to craft material for Howard (who prompted Yip to such couplets as, "Oh, she don't like Greyhound buses / so she'll come with six white husses"). Later that year, he was writing for Bea Lillie and Bobby Clark. He would in time write for Ed Wynn and Groucho Marx, and in his last revues, he provided the definitive material for Bert Lahr. Around talents such as these, he learned to construct entire evenings of entertainment.

"The revues were built around two or three people," he recalled.

> You had a Bea Lillie or a Fannie Brice and a Bert Lahr and a Willie Howard and you knew where you were at. They were giants. They were intrinsically great. All they had to do was put their foot in front of the footlights and you laughed. Their bodies were humorous. Their bodies were articulate, everything about them was. They were the invisible line that kept the whole thing together. We'd wait for them to come out; they were the connecting link. And with that as an invisible thread you could do anything.

(In the seventies, Yip, trying to write a revue of his songs, observed, "They don't make them like that any more.")

Yip's next show, *Americana,* lacked the connective thread of a comic star but had in its place a satiric sensibility commenting on the altogether bleak current events of 1932. The sensibility was that of the show's librettist, J. P. McEvoy. As Yip recalled it:

> *Americana* had a theme. J. P. McEvoy was a great satirist. . . . It was just before Roosevelt, and the theme was the Forgotten Man. The very first

speech [of Roosevelt's campaign] was that this had been a country of the Four Hundred—the people who had the money, but we had forgotten one thing, the Man, the Forgotten Man, the fellow who fights your wars, who works the lathe and the mills, and he made the Forgotten Man phrase the current popular slogan. So we opened the show with that idea.

I had an opening chorus; I wrote the opening chorus with Vincent Youmans, who took the money and disappeared. He got a ten-thousand-dollar advance, which was terrific at the time . . . and all I could get out of him was the opening chorus, and then he disappeared and nobody ever heard from him. I had to get the show on in two months. It wasn't written. It wasn't anything. They had the theater all sewn up. So I said, "I'll have to get composers," so I got Jay Gorney and I got Harold Arlen, who was unknown, and Burton Lane. I said, "Just throw me three tunes." That's what they did, and I think we got a nice, funny score out of it.

But there was nothing slapdash about Yip's approach to *Americana;* he quickly settled into the painstaking routine he was to follow for the duration of his career. To a considerable degree, he was energized by the show's political and aesthetic aspirations. "It was the first such show with social comment," he once said. Charged with writing all of *Americana*'s lyrics, and all the lyrics for a new show with Duke opening two months later, Yip brought in a twenty-three-year-old budding lyricist as reinforcement on two of *Americana*'s songs. Decades later, Johnny Mercer would recall what he had learned from the experience:

Yip Harburg taught me about that [taking pains in lyric writing]. He's a terrific writer. . . . God, he'll sit in a room all day and he'll dig and he'll dig and he'll dig. And it shows. . . . Yip was a big influence in teaching me how hard to work. Sometimes we'd get a rhyming dictionary and a Roget's and we'd *sweat.*

Yip's lasting achievement on *Americana* involved, as we shall see, a good deal of perspiration, but it began in a burst of inspiration. "I was walking along the street," he told Studs Terkel,

and you'd see bread lines. The biggest one in New York City was owned by William Randolph Hearst. He had a big truck with several people on it and big cauldrons of hot soup, bread. Fellows with burlap on their shoes were lined up all around Columbus Circle, and went for blocks and blocks around the park, waiting.

There was a sketch in *Americana.* . . . In the sketch, Mrs. Ogden Reid of the *Herald-Tribune* was very jealous of Hearst's beautiful bread line. It

This Associated Press photo from 1932 was captioned, "In strange contrast to the dazzling bright lights of Broadway [the Times Square District] New York City and the well-clad, well-fed throngs that flow past them, hundreds of hungry men stand shivering nightly waiting their turn for a sandwich and a cup of coffee." One-quarter of American workers were unemployed. Yip and Jay Gorney's song, "Brother, Can You Spare a Dime?" was the anthem of the Great Depression and remains a world classic. (AP/Wide World Photos.)

was bigger than her bread line. It was a satiric, volatile show. We needed a song for it.

On stage, we had men in old soldier's uniforms, waiting around. And then into the song. We had to have a title. And how do you do a song that isn't maudlin? Not to say: my wife is sick, I've got six children, the Crash put me out of business, hand me a dime. I hate songs of that kind. I hate songs that are on the nose.

The prevailing greeting at that time, on every block you passed, by some poor guy coming up, was "Can you spare a dime?" or, "Can you spare something for a cup of coffee?"

I thought that would be a wonderful title. . . . I was writing with Jay Gorney at the time and he had a tune and the tune had a lyric. It was a torch song and it went this way [to the tune of the opening lines of the chorus of "Brother, Can You Spare a Dime?"]:

> I could go on crying
> Big blue tears
> Ever since you said we were through
> I could go on crying
> Big blue tears. . . .

I said, "Jay, is this lyric wedded to this tune?" And he said, "Well, we can get a divorce if you have the right tactics." I said, "I've got a title for it: 'Brother, Can You Spare a Dime?'"

The music Gorney had composed with its original lyric might have gone unnoticed. By 1932, though, Yip's ability to hear new meanings in music had been sharply honed. It was a key component of his lyrical ability throughout his career but never did it contribute to such a transformative leap as it did here.

The anecdote attests to the inspiration, but Yip's worksheets attest to the perspiration. During the writing, he toyed with turning the song into a satiric attack on the superrich, on John D. Rockefeller in particular. He wrote:

> Once you drilled an oil well
> Made it gush
> How Socony did climb
> Once you drilled an oil well
> Now I'm flush
> Brother, here's a brand new dime.

And then, in the same vein:

> Say, I'm making millions
> While you exist
> Help me make life sublime
> Help me be a great philanthropist
> Brother, here's a brand new dime.

Essentially, though, Yip's worksheets show the song moving toward ever more concrete serious imagery. "I once fought a man," he begins one stanza, but it lacks the tactile immediacy of the other stanzas; he drops it. He writes, "The mills of the east and west / The forges of the north and south," but he abandons the representative for the specific. He changes phrases and the order of words within phrases:

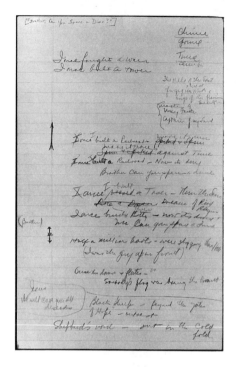

Page from sketches for the lyric to "Brother, Can You Spare a Dime?" Notice word change from "I once built a railroad" to "Once I built a railroad." (Reproduced from the E. Y. Harburg Collection, the Yale Collection of the Literature of the American Musical Theatre, Yale University Library.)

Once I built a railroad—made it run
Spiked and spun against time
Once I built a tower to the sun—

Like a dream of

Once the drums and flutes

Black sheep—beyond the gates of hope

Shipbuilder's voice—out in the cold/fold

Years later Yip explained:

I grew up when America had a dream. And its people a hope. . . . Whether we were struggling against the shackles of slavery or the shackles of scarcity, the hope was there.

In 1930 the dream collapsed. The system fell apart. The people were . . . not in revolt. This was a good country, on its way to greatness. It had given our immigrants more freedom, more education, more opportunity than it had ever known. What happened? We were baffled, bewildered, and the bewildered, baffled man sang:

BROTHER, CAN YOU SPARE A DIME?

Verse.

They used to tell me
I was building a dream
And so I followed the mob
When there was earth to plough
Or guns to bear
I was always there
Right on the job

They used to tell me
I was building a dream
With peace and glory ahead
Why should I be standing in line
Just waiting for bread?

Chorus.

Once I built a railroad,
Made it run
Made it race against time
Once I built a railroad
Now it's done
Brother, can you spare a dime?

Once I built a tower
To the sun
Brick and rivet and lime
Once I built a tower
Now it's done
Brother, can you spare a dime?

Once in khaki suits
Gee, we looked swell
Full of that Yankee Doodle-de-dum
Half a million boots went sloggin' thru hell
I was the kid with the drum

Say, don't you remember?
They called me "Al"
It was "Al" all the time
Say, don't you remember
I'm your pal
Buddy, can you spare a dime?

"In the song," Yip told Studs Terkel,

> the man is really saying: I made an investment in this country. Where the hell are my dividends? . . . It's more than just a bit of pathos. It doesn't reduce him to a beggar. It makes him a dignified human being, asking questions—and a bit outraged, too, as he should be.

The outrage—Yip and Jay's outrage—is grounded in a particular Marxian precept: that labor is denied the full reward for its work. "[I was] well aware at that time," Yip said,

> of what was wrong with our whole economic system: that the man who builds, the man who creates, is not always the man who gets the profit. He's always working for the man who sells him. So that bewildered person in the street is now saying, I built the railroad, I built the tower, I went to war for this country. Why are my hands empty? And I think what made that song popular and great, and why it's lasting now, is that it's still asking the universal question of why does the man who produces not share in the wealth?

Thus, Yip's first great lyric is no mere lamentation, but a carefully modulated cry of anger that arose from Gorney's musical cry of pain. Gorney brought to the song boyhood memories of the shtetl (including an attack by cossacks on his village) in Russia. The music that Jay wrote for his torch song is drawn from a lullabye in his Russian-Jewish musical roots. Rhythmically and melodically it sounds like a Jewish chant. The opening phrase of the chorus progresses up the first five notes of the minor scale (fig. 1); critic Deryck Cooke has written that this melodic motif sounds a universal feeling of pain, a protest against misfortune, while the lyric cries out, in Yip's words, the "baffling plaint" of the oppressed everywhere.

Fig. 1.

Yip's challenge in crafting the lyric for "Brother" was much like the challenge confronting the street-corner panhandler: to establish that character's individuality and the moral and political basis of his claim. In so doing, Yip appropriated a subtle lyric-building technique at which Ira had excelled for some time. It is a slow escalation of the degree of intimacy and self-revelation on the part of the character—a task accomplished by movement towards direct address, from third person ("*they* used to tell me") to first ("once *I* built a railroad") and then to second ("Say, don't *you* remember"), which then at the final moment brings the listener and singer directly together, "*I'm your* pal."

The lyric to the verse in "Brother" starts with the distant, generalized "they"—a society and its ideology that the singer once believed in. "They used to tell me" is conversational, in past tense, as if the singer is going to tell us a story that no one tells him any more. The lyric to "They used to tell me [I was]," coupled with the falling minor chord, feels ominous and hooks us in. Few American theater or popular songs of the time began so emphatically in a minor key, and even fewer remained in minor in the chorus. Indeed, this was an American soul song.

The story, it is soon clear, encompasses everyone—from those in a pastoral setting, "with earth to plow," to those in the military "with guns to bear." The internal rhymes—where, there, earth, bear—help the listener to remember, along with the singer, that they were told, and believed, they were "building a dream with peace and glory ahead." The music is made more emphatic by the bold upward melodic leap on the words "[buil]ding a [dream]," as if to say it makes no sense to suddenly "be standing in line"; the word *line* goes up to the highest note in the song thus far, and resolves on an even higher one—the tonic, the home note the song has been seeking—on the word "*just* [waiting for bread]." The contrast between plowing and bearing arms, and standing and waiting is as baffling and poignant to the singer as it is outrageous: "If I did all this, what am I doing here?"

The music to the verse is appropriate for a quest gone awry. The melody moves downward and then leaps up by increasing intervals without ever coming to a musically restful stop. The music to the chorus, by contrast, usually proceeds one step at a time, appropriate for the more concrete tasks the lyric recounts.

We know from the verse that the singer had sought the American dream, and that the dream has been shattered. In the chorus, the nature of that dream is made at once more specific and more idealistic: "Once I built a railroad"—the ascending minor scale culminating in the high tonic on "road"—"made it run" (the reality), "made it *race against time*" (the vision of glory). This is immediately paralleled and underlined in "Once I built a tower" (the reality) "to the sun" (another vision of glory). The singer then drops from the sun to the breadline.

The bridge (the middle countermelody section in the chorus) also draws us further in, this time to the "Great" war, when everyone was filled with patriotism and "looked swell" right before (another promise lost) we went "sloggin' thru hell." The steady beat of boots in the chords accompanying the first two lines sets up the rise to glory ("full of that Yankee Doodle-de-dum") in the third line, before the disturbing discordant harmonies of "sloggin' thru hell" returns us to earth. Then, in the next line the singer as an individual rises out of the collective, to a rising, pleading melody line, "I was the kid with the drum." This is immediately followed by "Say, don't you remember," with the word *say* falling on the highest note of the song, demanding that we listen.

The lyric is a masterpiece of economy. Each of the three main stanzas ("Once I built a railroad . . . ," "Once I built a tower . . . ," "Say, don't you remember . . .") of the chorus are first-person narratives that culminate suddenly in a direct appeal to the listener: "Brother, can you spare a dime?" Slowly, cumulatively, the listener (like the man or woman solicited for the dime) is drawn into the singer's story. In the final stanza, the level of listener implication is raised: the whole passage is by direct address. The panhandler shares a past with us, he has a name, he is our pal—and the steadily growing intimacy culminates with the substitution of "Buddy" for "Brother" in the song's last line.

Further, the entire narrative weight of the collapse in the first two stanzas is placed on a three-note, three-syllable line, "Now it's done." Yip prepares us for the line by underscoring the separateness of the three-note figure when it first appears three lines earlier in each of the first two stanzas. He creates a distinct, subjectless clause to accompany the figure ("Made it run") and gives it emphasis by repeating the first two words in the following line. All of this also serves to set up the song's climactic assertion of commonality and interdependency in the last repetition of the three-word figure: "I'm your pal." But now the feeling of connectedness between the singer and the listener is charged by the unexpected musical leap from the low notes of the preceding "Say, don't you remember" to the highest notes of the song on the words, "*I'm* your *pal*." The music and lyric together make us feel the quiet desperation of the singer.

As they unfold, the narrative and the emotion grow in intensity as they have not in any previous Harburg song. The moral and political urgency Yip wanted to convey in "Brother" sped the development of his craft and propelled him to a much higher standard for lyric writing.

Before "Brother" could reach the stage, however, it had to pass the inspection of *Americana*'s producers, the notorious Shubert brothers. Yip recalls:

> The Shubert brothers were an empire. There was Jake Shubert and Lee Shubert and they owned practically 80 percent of all the theaters in New York City and they were brothers for about seventy years and they hadn't talked to each other for about fifty. They lived apart . . . and when either

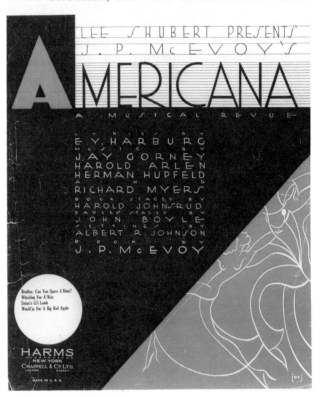

The song sheet for "Brother, Can You Spare a Dime" in 1932. The song was almost thrown out of the show and attempts were made to ban it from radio networks, but records by Bing Crosby and Al Jolson were enormously popular. In 1992 Tom Waits sang its current version, an anthem for the homeless and unemployed in the late eighties and early nineties. The song has been chosen as a theme by the National Coalition of the Homeless for its annual national fund-raising efforts. (Collection of Harburg Estate; courtesy of Sondra Gorney.)

of them wanted to do a show, it was understood that they would want the other to collaborate.

So, Lee was doing this show and he liked the song, "Brother, Can You Spare a Dime?" and he sent a message over to Jake to come over to listen to the song. That was the contract they had, that they would verify each other's songs. But since they didn't speak to each other, they had no hot line, and the medium was not the message, but the young boy who sent the message. . . . "Tell him to come over and listen to a song." And J. J. came over and Lee said, "Tell him to listen to this song. It's about the depression." And J. J. sat there and he said, "All right, tell him I'm listening."

Jay sat down at the piano and I sang that song with all the feeling of a man who was bankrupt, and after we got through, Jay looked at him and Lee looked at him and J. J.'s face was sour. First of all, they each hoped the other would have a flop every time they were doing something. They were competing with each other and Lee said, "Ask him, does he like it?" J. J. said, "Tell him I don't like it." Lee said, "Ask him why not." J. J.'s face fell; it hadn't far to fall, and he said, "Tell him I don't like it because I just don't like it." At this point Lee really went out of his mind, and he hadn't far to go, and he said, "Ask him why not!" J. J., pulling himself up to his full dictatorial height, "because it's too sorbid!" [*sic*]. But Lee was the senior partner and we got it in and the rest is history.

When *Americana* opened on Broadway on October 5, 1932—at the bottom of the depression, with nearly one-quarter of the work force unemployed, and only one month before the Hoover-Roosevelt presidential election—"Brother" stunned its audience. It was the first theater (or film, or pop) song to treat the wreckage of the depression seriously. Very few Tin Pan Alley or musical theater songs had dealt with the depression at all, and they had done so in the manner of the Billy Rose-y 1931 "It's in the Air" —a halfhearted attempt to cheer the depression away. Indeed, the integration of social and personal message in "Brother" was without precedent in the American musical theater of 1932 (with the very partial exception of "Ol' Man River").

Newspaper reviews of revues seldom if ever devoted any space to the discussion of song content: revues (and their reviews) were about the comics and the dancers and the scenery. Not so *Americana*'s reviews: "The Messrs. Gorney and Harburg have written something so stirring it will run away with the whole show," wrote Gilbert Gabriel in the *New York American,* "and maybe with a couple of charity drives and social revolutions too, if they don't watch out." Calling the song "plaintive and thundering," Brooks Atkinson in the *Times* said it "has expressed the spirit of these times with more heart-breaking anguish than any of the prose bards of the day." The *Herald-Tribune* began its review with a discussion of "Brother"; *Theater Arts Monthly* contended that it "deflates the rolling bombast of our political nightmare with far greater effect than all the rest of Mr. McEvoy's satirical skits put together"; and *Variety* found it the only praiseworthy element in the show.

"Brother" became an instant hit and a political event. "Everyone picked up the song," Yip told Terkel.

> Bands were playing it and records [including enormously popular ones by Bing Crosby and Al Jolson] were made. [With the election approaching] the Republicans got pretty worried about it. Some of the network radio people were told to lay low on the song. In some cases, they tried to ban it from the air. But it was too late. The song had already done its damage.

In the annals of thirties song, "Brother" stands virtually alone. With the exception of Harry Warren and Al Dubin's "Remember My Forgotten Man" from *The Golddiggers of 1933*, and a handful of others, Broadway, Hollywood, and mainstream pop song steered clear of dealing with the major social reality of the decade. At the mass level, song was an escape; at the elite level, at the level of the Gershwins and Rodgers and Hart and Porter, it was, even when serious, focused on the personal at the expense of the social. Yip's achievement in "Brother" was to have personalized the social, to have encapsulated the destruction and upheaval of the depression in an individual story. He had imposed the theme twice: first, on Gorney's inspired torch song/lullabye and second, on an industry that declined to acknowledge the propriety of social concerns as song subjects. At each instance, he had triumphed.

But the show, as *Variety* and *Theater Arts Monthly* both suggested, was not an unqualified success. With the exception of "Brother," one song with Duke and his initial song with Arlen (see chap. 3), the score—cobbled together with six composers—was not altogether distinguished. Such was not the case for Yip's next show, though, which opened a scant two months and two days after *Americana*. It was called *Walk a Little Faster*, and in it he and Vernon Duke became major songwriters.

Yip and Duke

The first great composer with whom Yip worked, and the one who provided the material with which Yip evolved from a journeyman to a master lyricist, was Vernon Duke. This on-again, off-again collaboration with Duke was to last only four years, 1930–34, and it was to prove a difficult relationship for both. Nonetheless, it is largely within the twenty-five songs Yip wrote with Duke in those four years that Yip's lyrical genius takes shape. He becomes fluent in internal and multisyllable rhyme; he becomes at ease with metaphor; he learns to build both comic and dramatic lyrics; he learns—and transcends—narration.

"I met Vernon Duke through George Gershwin," Yip told Max Wilk:

> Vernon had just come over from Europe. He was Russian—his real name was Vladimir Dukelsky—and he was very far advanced in his music. Very serious composer. As Dukelsky, his symphonic works were performed in concert halls. In Europe, he'd worked with Diaghilev, writing ballets, and he was very avant-garde for this period. . . . George Gershwin was very impressed with Duke's music.

American theater songwriters of Harburg's generation came disproportionately from Jewish refugees from Czarist Russia: Gorney and Berlin arrived as young children; the Gershwins and Yip were born here shortly after their parents had arrived. Duke, by contrast, was an ethnically Russian, upper-class refugee from the new Soviet Union of the Bolsheviks. While still in his early teens, he had

Vernon Duke (*below*), composer of the classic "April in Paris" (1932), with whom Yip (on the beach) had a tempestuous but fruitful partnership over a few years. Lena Horne recalled Yip as "the liberator" and Duke as "the sophisticate." (Collection of Harburg Estate; Music Division, New York Public Library.)

received a more rigorous music academy training than any of his American counterparts. His precociousness extended to his facility for new American music: he grew conversant with Gershwin's earliest songs, for instance, while in Turkish exile during the Russian Civil War. He became a friend and semiprotégé of Gershwin's while living in New York in 1922–23. By 1924 he was in Paris, where, at age twenty, he composed a successful ballet for Diaghilev. He returned to New York to stay in 1928, on the heels of his first musical show (in London) and the premiere of his first symphony (in Paris, with Serge Koussevitsky conducting).

"It was at Ira's," Duke wrote in *Passport to Paris,* an autobiography in which he displays a marked antipathy to Yip,

> that I met stocky, aggressive E. Y. Harburg, then writing with Jay Gorney, who started him off on his lyric writing career. I was shown a song the two had just written for the *Earl Carroll Sketch Book* entitled "Kinda Cute"— it was just that—and I returned the compliment by playing a half-dozen tunes, one of which struck Ira and Harburg as a possible hit. They began "writing it up" then and there, and the ultimate result was "I Am Only Human After All," which resulted in my signing a Harms [music publishing] contract a few months later.

So began a highly improbable, highly productive partnership between a street-smart Jewish socialist and a cosmopolitan White Russian social-striving fashion plate who emerges from his own autobiography as an effete elitist. For a time, the unlikely duo seemed to thrive on their differences. Indeed, Duke once commented that he couldn't write with the urbane Howard Dietz because the two were too similar in outlook. By contrast, he wrote,

> no two people were less alike than Richard Rodgers and Lorenz Hart, than George and Ira Gershwin, than (the classic example) Gilbert and Sullivan; yet they complemented each other, the qualities lacking in one were abundantly present in the other and vice-versa—therein lay the reasons for the success of their teamwork.

In later years, Yip was to tell Max Wilk that a similar dynamic energized the team of Duke and Harburg:

> Vernon brought with him all of that Noel Coward/Diaghilev/Paris/Russia background. He was a global guy with an ability to articulate the English language that was very interesting. A whole new world for me. He could drive you crazy and he could also open up a new vista. Maybe it was a

little chi-chi and decorative, but with my pumpernickel background and his orchid tunes we made a wonderful marriage.

Maybe we were a strange mixture. We didn't compromise with each other. I applied the every-day deep-down things that concerned humanity to his sense of style and grace, and I think it gave our songs an almost classic feeling, along with some humor. We came together at a certain point, and for a while it was fine. He satisfied my sense of light verse and the need for sophistication.

Lena Horne years later would describe this odd couple as "the sophisticate" and "the liberator."

Duke brought melodic sophistication and unprecedented harmonic complexity to Broadway, but there was seldom if ever a European sound to his music (in contradistinction to Gorney's). "His absorption of American popular music writing was phenomenal," Alec Wilder once wrote, and such (non-Harburg) Duke hits as "Taking a Chance on Love" and "I Can't Get Started" (with Ira) surely confirm Wilder's judgment. So do the smattering of songs Yip wrote with Duke before they teamed up for *Walk a Little Faster* in the autumn of 1932.

Walk a Little Faster was the height of Broadway sophistication. It was produced by Courtney Burr, who had produced Cole Porter's *50 Million Frenchmen* in the previous year. The sketches were by S. J. Perelman, just returned from Hollywood and his work on the Marx Brothers epic, *Horse Feathers*. Boris Aronson, just arrived in America from Europe, was engaged to do the sets; Albertina Rasch was the choreographer and Monty Woolley the director. Burr had asked Duke if he wished to do the songs with Dorothy Parker. Duke insisted on Harburg.

Walk starred two of the stage's great comics: the offbeat Beatrice Lillie, and a little man with spectacles painted on his face who was, in Brooks Atkinson's words, "the greatest of the running clowns"—Bobby Clark. Clark, as always, appeared in tandem with his stooge, Paul McCullough. The ballads were to be entrusted to "honey-haired and honey-voiced" (Duke's description) Evelyn Hoey.

Walk provided Yip with his first major opportunity to write witty material. "That's when I discovered I could write comedy songs," he told Max Wilk. "That really titillated me the most—the comedy, the satirical idea." Clark and McCullough, Duke recalled, had a hilarious opening number in "That's Life," a kind of two-four strut, and "I recall Bobby running across the stage arm in arm with McCullough, singing through his cigar and taking it out of his mouth every so often to bark at Harburg and myself, 'You're making it tough for me, boys!'"

"That's Life" is a number tailored to Clark's running style, comically collapsing human existence into woefully inadequate summations:

THAT'S LIFE

That's life
St. Peter blows on his horn
And so you wake up one morn
Find that you're born
That's life

That's life
You buy a pair of long pants
For that fraternity dance
Bingo! Romance.
That's life

You go to school and learn La Paloma
And Greek for corn on the cob
Then you get your diploma
And you're right in line for that Fuller Brush job

That's life
You're right on top of the heap
You get a swell penthouse cheap
Walk in your sleep
That's life

That's life
You go along in the red
Just when you're getting ahead
Bingo! You're dead.
That's life.

"Greek for corn on the cob" shows Yip's growing capacity to tailor the lines to the comic. In its cheerfully inept misappropriation of culture, it is pure Bobby Clark.

The wit in the *Walk* score was not confined to the comics' songs, however. "Speaking of Love" is built around a series of three-syllable internal rhymes that are set to the highest (somewhat mock-melodramatic) notes of their stanzas. It is the first song in which Yip achieves comic development through steadily more witty and farfetched rhymes, pushing over into neologisms. Here are some stanzas:

SPEAKING OF LOVE
(excerpt)

Speaking of love
Give me a frank account
How is your bank account?
Speaking of love

Speaking of love
When you're through courting me
Who'll be supporting me?
Speaking of love

Speaking of love
I'd become passionate
If there's some cash in it
Speaking of love

Speaking of love
I'll be your nincompoop
Just be my income-poop
Speaking of love.

(Whether Yip had yet mastered the art of successful neologism is another question: in her review Dorothy Parker took him to task for "income-poop.")
"I liked Vernon's facility," Yip told Max Wilk.

> He was fast and very sophisticated, almost too sophisticated for Broadway. *Walk a Little Faster* had some very smart stuff in it. In fact, that's when I bounced out of the bread-and-butter stage into sophistication. My light verse background popped up to reinforce me, and I could write much easier with Vernon than I could with some of the others. It was light, and airy, and very smart.

As to the one masterpiece of *Walk*'s score, Yip's and Duke's accounts agree on little other than that the song's genesis was a Boris Aronson model for a set of Paris.
Aronson, said Yip,

> was in love with Paris. He came to Paris by way of Kiev when Stalin got in. And he designed one of the most beautiful, sensitive sets that ever was seen, and, of course, the producer calls the lyric writer in and says, "We need a song for that set."

The music to "April in Paris," Duke claimed in his 1955 autobiography, *Passport to Paris,*

> was written . . . in New York at . . . "West Side Tony's." . . . After auditioning some particularly untalented girls, we all repaired to Tony's; the "we" consisting of Dorothy Parker, Evelyn Hoey, Robert Benchley, Monty Woolley, Johnny McClain, Burr, and myself. . . . After several double scotches we all got pretty sentimental, the Scotch reminding us of Miss Hoey's tartan skirt in her Paris number, the mention of the number inevitably leading to Paris, how wonderful it was in the spring and how vile Manhattan was at that time of year. . . . The rest went off in true class-B musical picture fashion. . . . "My kingdom for a piano!" . . . The ever obliging Tony ventured the information that an old and wretched upright was at my disposal on the second floor [Duke then composed the tune in a burst of inspiration]. . . . I then proceeded to "ham it up," telling all and sundry that I had just given birth to a masterpiece that was certain to "make the show."

Now the Harburg version:

> So I went down to Cook's Tours and got some brochures to see what it [Paris] was like. Most people think I was at the Cafe de Jou-Jou looking at the Eiffel Tower when it was written, but I was really at Lindy's looking at the marquee of the Winter Garden. Anyhow, I find that writing songs of places I haven't been and people I haven't seen are the most exciting, because, after all, beauty is what you in your spirit and imagination invest in a place or a person.

The music was written in Tony's, the lyrics in Lindy's. Yip does not figure in Duke's account nor Duke in Yip's. This was not the warmest of collaborations. And in this instance, it produced a masterpiece.

APRIL IN PARIS

Verse.

April's in the air,
But here in Paris
April wears a diff'rent gown
You can see her waltzing
Down the street

The tang of wine is in the air,
I'm drunk with all the happiness
That spring can give
Never dreamed it could be so
Exciting to live

Chorus.

April in Paris
Chestnut in blossom
Holiday tables under the trees

April in Paris
This is a feeling
No one can ever reprise

I never knew the charm of Spring
Never met it face to face
I never knew my heart could sing
Never missed a warm embrace
Till,

April in Paris,
Whom can I run to?
What have you done to
My heart?

"It is immediately clear," Alec Wilder has written, "that melodically and harmonically this was an extraordinary beginning for a song in 1932 or any other year." The music of the chorus's opening, writes Wilder, "must have been a hair-curler for its first audiences."

Just melodically and harmonically? What about lyrically? This is emphatically not the way song lyrics speak, either. The lyric begins without context. The first stanza of the chorus is not a sentence—declarative or interrogatory or exclamatory or direct address or any of the ways in which song lyrics characteristically unfold. It is something quite different: sheer imagery, a catalog of images.

It is also, in fact, a brilliant, almost haikulike, solution for Duke's at once sweeping but parsimonious tone poem—so lush in harmony, but with so few notes in the melody. Narrative would be fearfully constricted in these passages. The best lyrical evocation of this kind of music, Yip concludes, is to keep the lyric purely imagistic throughout the first stanza. This is a telegraphic imagism: the singular form of the word "chestnut" creates a forest of blossoms (and, alas, is usually rendered in plural form by singers). "April in Paris" begins almost as a French symbolist song, Yip playing Mallarmé to Duke's Debussy.

The propulsive motion, musically and lyrically, in "April" is towards the revelation of the emotion behind these initial images. Yip's first definition is deliberately distanced and generalized: "This is a feeling / No one can ever reprise." In the release, the emotion is not merely identified; it is personalized. The harmonies become less exotic. Yip anchors the release around the word *never;* he opens with "never missed the charm of spring" and closes the release with "never missed a warm embrace"—using the sounds *m* and *s* to suggest the warmth to which the lyric alludes.

First-person narration, strikingly absent from the lyric to this point, inaugurates the release, progressing from commentary on a lover's Paris (the charm of spring) to his/her personal interaction with it (never met it face to face) to his/her emotional state (my heart could sing) to romance and its perils (never missed a warm embrace). Each line of the release lyric, that is, carries us one step at a time from "April"'s imagistic beginnings towards its immediate and personalized conclusion.

The last stanza, musically and lyrically, is a piece of astonishing virtuosity. The lyrics are constructed around two emotional questions (a trademark of Yip's lyrics: "Brother, Can You Spare a Dime?" "Over the Rainbow," and "How Are Things in Glocca Morra?" all conclude with questions). After restating the front phrase, Yip and Duke jointly and hugely raise the emotional stakes. Duke sweeps the melody line dramatically upwards, then again, paralleling the front phrase, but higher, to a resolution at the top of the octave. Yip moves the lyric in equally bold fashion. "Whom can I run to?" begins with the shock of correct grammar and moves immediately to an unexplained dread that underlies all the imagery. The immediacy and urgency of this line, so sudden, so near the end of the song, propels the song into unknown terrain. The last line is that rarity in song lyrics: a genuine climax. The fear—and, reading backwards, the emotions and the images—are explicated and decoded. The movement from imagery to generalized feeling to personalized feeling has taken one final step: to direct address in question form where the answer is implied. "April in Paris" burrows inward. Its subject, we learn only at its conclusion, is the cry of hearts everywhere: "What have you done to . . . my heart?"

The *Walk a Little Faster* score is miles from Helen Morgan. It is very much *like* "what Ira and Larry Hart were doing." But "April in Paris" is not what Ira and Larry Hart were doing. It is not like what Duke and Harburg did in any of their other work. Sweeping and concise, enraptured and apprehensive, mysterious and resolved, art song and pop song, Tony's and Lindy's, "April in Paris" is unique—and a masterpiece of American theater song.

For all that, *Walk a Little Faster* barely made it into New York. At its Boston tryouts, the songs were very well received, with reviewers noting the "modernisms" in the music. The problem was the book, which did not work at first and which then went through the usual revisions and contortions. (One evening, Perelman, Harburg, and Duke returned to the theater twenty minutes after the conclusion of intermission to find that the show was over: that night's revision had been to cut the second act to fifteen minutes.)

Walk limped into New York with its book still unfixed and its songs suddenly muted: on opening night, Evelyn Hoey, who was to perform the ballads in general and "April in Paris" in particular, had contracted laryngitis. *Walk* ran for 119 performances, with the backers, though not the writers, receiving checks. Only when threatened with a lawsuit did producer Burr settle up with Harburg, Duke, and Perelman.

But "April in Paris" refused to die. Music critic and Gershwin biographer Isaac Goldberg praised the piece in an essay in the *Evening Post*. Singer Marian Chase sang it nightly at New York's Surf Club. Eventually the song was recorded, and in short order became a hit. By 1935, Universal Pictures had asked Yip to produce a film musical around the song.

In the autumn of 1932, through his work on "Brother, Can You Spare a Dime?" and *Walk a Little Faster,* Yip joined the ranks of master lyricists. Public acknowledgment came soon after. On Sunday, January 8, 1933, the *New York Times* profiled "the Lyrical Mr. Harburg" as "a member of the newer school of lyric writers who are giving Broadway audiences these days a series of rhymes somewhat more intelligent than 'June' and 'moon.'" Private acknowledgment came even earlier. On November 18, 1932, as *Walk* was opening in Boston, Yip received a telegram from one of its score's enthusiasts. "Heard some of your lyrics the other day," it read, "and I hope they'll be as successful as I think they will be." It was from Larry Hart.

Chapter 3

Review of Revues

It's a Barnum and Bailey world
Just as phony as it can be
But it wouldn't be make believe
If you believed in me.

Walk a Little Faster was actually the second play on which Yip had worked to open on Broadway during the first week of December 1932. Four days earlier, on December 3, *The Great Magoo,* a play by Ben Hecht and Gene Fowler, premiered to indifferent reviews and soon closed after eleven performances. The play contained one song, a work that producer Billy Rose had commissioned from Yip. For the music, Yip turned to a young composer with whom he had written but one other song: "Satan's Li'l Lamb" in *Americana.* The composer was Harold Arlen, and he was to become Yip's most celebrated and enduring collaborator.

"Harold and I met through Earl Carroll," Yip recalled.

> He contributed some songs to the 1930 *Vanities,* so I met him backstage. [Arlen and lyricist Ted Koehler composed most of the songs for that revue, in which Yip and Jay Gorney had several songs as well.] Harold had a big hit then called "Hittin' the Bottle." I liked his stuff; it was rather new. It was sort of a challenge to me, an enigma. I thought he had something that approached George Gershwin. They really weren't the same, but he had a typically American approach. It was away from the Viennese derivation of the Kerns and the other writers, and I took a shine to that gutsy, earthy [quality]. It was a combination of Hebrew and black music, which I seemed to have a great affection for.

Arlen's early life could have served with only slight alteration as a model for the story of *The Jazz Singer.* Arlen grew up in Buffalo, where his father, Samuel Arluck, was the Jewish community's preeminent cantor. Word of the cantor's virtuosity spread well beyond upstate New York (at one point, he was offered a national concert tour of liturgical music). More remarkably, by Arlen's own account, his father's chanting anticipated the new sounds of jazz. Arlen recalled playing some of the earliest Louis Armstrong recordings and marveling how Armstrong's riffs could so closely resemble Cantor Arluck's interpolations. In later years, the cantor would work some of his son's compositions—"Stormy Weather," "My Shining Hour"—into his synagogue chanting.

In his midteens, the jazz-struck Arlen formed a band, the Buffalodians, for which he was the lead singer. By his early twenties, Arlen had settled in New York, where he supplemented his singing gigs by doing arrangements for jazz bands. In 1929, the twenty-four-year-old Arlen was working as rehearsal pianist for the new Vincent Youmans musical, *Great Day,* when composer Harry Warren was struck by one of Arlen's extended riffs. It was, Warren insisted, a song; and he introduced Arlen to lyricist Ted Koehler, who set words to it. The song was "Get Happy"—and Arlen and Koehler were launched as a team.

Though they occasionally interpolated songs into Broadway revues, Arlen and Koehler worked primarily at Harlem's legendary Cotton Club, where they turned out two shows a year from 1930 through 1934. Writing for such talents as Ethel Waters, Cab Calloway, and a very young Lena Horne, the Arlen-Koehler team produced such standards as "I've Got the World on a String," "Stormy Weather," "Between the Devil and the Deep Blue Sea," "Ill Wind," as well as more specialized material such as Calloway's "Wail of the Reefer Man." By the fall of 1932, when Rose came to Harburg with his request, Arlen had already established himself as one of the most jazz-oriented, musically sophisticated, innovative composers in the business. The song submitted to Rose further enhanced his reputation—as it did Yip's, notwithstanding Rose's claim to coauthorship of the lyric.

"Billy Rose was a producer at the time," Yip recalled.

> I was a neophyte at the time. He was doing a show called *The Great Magoo* . . . and it needed one song. It was about a barker in a Coney Island joint. They wanted a song for that barker, a man disillusioned with the world, and he had finally fallen in love. He called me up and said, "Do you have any kind of a song that would fit that situation?" Harold had a tune. He had the whole tune. And I got an idea—there's a guy who sees the lights of Broadway, thinks the whole world is that, that the moon is a paper moon, everything is a Barnum and Bailey world. So I got a title and fitted the first two lines: "Say, it's only a paper moon / Floating over a cardboard sea." Harold and I brought it to Billy Rose, and he said, "Gee, that's great. Let's sit down and do it." When Billy Rose said, "Let's sit down and do it"—he's the producer of the show; he's paying you an advance; you're a neophyte; what are you going to do? You sit down.

To arise with:

IT'S ONLY A PAPER MOON

Say, it's only a paper moon
Sailing over a cardboard sea
But it wouldn't be make believe
If you believed in me

Yes, it's only a canvas sky
Hanging over a muslin tree
But it wouldn't be make believe
If you believed in me

Without your love
It's a honky-tonk parade
Without your love
It's a melody played
In a penny arcade

It's a Barnum and Bailey world
Just as phony as it can be
But it wouldn't be make believe
If you believed in me.

Yip's worksheets at Yale reveal that he had at some earlier point ventured a similar lyric:

> It's all confusion
> It's all unreal
> This sad illusion
> Of brick and steel
> I'm in a city
> Beneath a cardboard sky.

These lyrics, of course, did not fit the tune Harold produced—either literally or in spirit—or Rose's dramaturgical requirements. They attest, though, to the image bank on which Yip drew when Harold gave him the music.

Like much of Arlen's work, "Paper Moon" is painstakingly loose and buoyant. It begins three of its four stanzas with octave leaps, which Yip eases into with apparently casual conversation: "*Say,* it's only a paper moon," and "*Yes,* it's only a canvas sky." The lyric moves from concrete illustrations in the first two stanzas to a more direct statement of a cosmology in the last, but the language remains vivid, colloquial, conversational: in character with the barker, in no way pretentious. It is, writes Alec Wilder, "a very innocent lyric."

Only, it's not. In fact, "Paper Moon" is not only an illustrious beginning for the Arlen-Harburg collaboration. It is also the first of Yip's songs to concern itself with the power of illusion, conviction—if we take Yip's word for it, even ideology. It was far from an innocent lyric, Yip insisted in a 1961 manuscript:

> Eugene O'Neill took five hours to say in *The Iceman Cometh* that man cannot live without illusions. My own belief is that man cannot live *with* them. Politically, they can be disastrous, and musically, they are just as capable of thwarting human happiness. . . .

> A songwriter's responsibility when all is said and done is to know himself and to know the world he lives in. When he observes, "It's a Barnum and Bailey world / Just as phony as it can be," as I did several years ago, he should faithfully report his findings in song, not bury them under a pious platitude or a happy grin.

To New Left acquaintances of the sixties, Yip apparently carried his interpretation one step further. "Paper Moon," he told sociologist Richard Flacks, was about nothing less than systemic mystification: how belief in a system, a world, is all that ultimately sustains it.

But Yip was also willing to put a more conventional spin on his interpretation of the lyric. "There's a saving grace called love," he told Max Wilk while discussing the song in the early seventies. "Without it, life is all a honky-tonk parade." But then Yip adds, "In other words, it's not make-believe as long as someone believes it."

In this vein, Yip invested "Paper Moon" with an almost cosmic romanticism:

> I think everybody, not only every artist, but every person who thinks, is confronted with two things in his life—his drive to be related to the universe, but that's a hard thing because there are so many stars and it's very hard to grasp that relationship. So his next best thing is to be related to humanity, but there are a lot of people and that's hard too.
>
> But, if he can identify himself, and relate really with one other person, he will relate with all of humanity and he will relate with all the universe.

Yip's paradoxical attitude toward illusion and belief—whether they are "disastrous" or "a saving grace"—constitutes a deep and unresolved tension that was to suffuse his lyrics for the duration of his long career. Inescapably, American song lyrics at some point mean love song lyrics ("I'm in the *romance* business!" songwriter Frank Loesser used to shout). Beginning with "Paper Moon," though, Yip produced a series of ballad lyrics that depicted belief and romance as arbitrary constructions. Many of the images that recur in Yip's work—that old devil moon, April, spring—are harbingers not only of enchantment but simultaneously of entrapment and artifice. Throughout the thirties in particular, Yip's ballad lyrics are characterized by this paradoxical double vision. They are less love songs than songs about love and its complexities.

On more than one occasion, Yip claimed his work had a particularly close affinity to that of Larry Hart. Between the cynicism of Cole Porter and the sentimentality of Oscar Hammerstein, Hart and Harburg created worlds of deep ambivalence towards romance and belief. "Larry Hart had few observable illusions," Yip wrote in the early sixties. "Yet his 'Funny Valentine' and 'It Never Entered My Mind' are touching, bitter-sweet odes that describe perfectly the true condition of love, as opposed to the moonlight-drenched variety." If "My Funny Valentine" and "With a Song in My Heart" are Hart's "April in Paris," then his "Falling in Love with Love" or "I Wish I Were in Love Again" are his equivalents of Yip's "Fun to Be Fooled" or "Old Devil Moon." Yip's ambivalence is more politicized, of course: where Hart describes self-delusion, Yip is at some level also describing ideology; where Hart affirms the need to love, Yip also affirms the need to believe.

In mid-1933, Yip reteamed with Vernon Duke on what was to be their last collaboration, the new edition of the *Ziegfeld Follies*. This was to be the first *Follies* since Ziegfeld's death in 1932. In control of the show were the omnipresent Shubert brothers, to whom Ziegfeld's widow, Billie Burke (later Glinda, the

Good Witch of the North in *The Wizard of Oz*), had sold the rights to the name for a paltry one thousand dollars.

In the spring of 1933, Duke writes in his autobiography, "Harburg and I were summoned by Lee Shubert to help with the score of his proposed new edition of the *Ziegfeld Follies*. This was again to be an 'assembled' score, although originally most of the songs were by Lou Alter and Arthur Swanstrom." By the time the show finally opened (January 4, 1934), five composers had songs in the show and Duke had well over half. The lyrics to all of them came entirely from Yip.

This last go-round for the Duke-Harburg team proved particularly stormy. By the autumn, they had ceased working together. Moreover, Lee Shubert had cut some of their songs and inserted those of other teams. The Shuberts' new director, John Murray Anderson, insisted on the reinstatement of the Harburg-Duke songs, though, and even managed to bring the two together to create a few more. In his autobiography, Duke was to depict Yip as explosive and emotional, terms that Duke's other collaborators characteristically applied to Duke himself. (Even the tactful Ira Gershwin called Duke "my excitable friend," and Duke's collaborations seldom lasted more than one show.) By the time the *Follies* opened, Harburg and Duke were clearly looking for other partners.

The first post-*Ziegfeld Follies* starred one of Ziegfeld's greatest stars, Fanny Brice, along with Willie and Eugene Howard; it also featured the dancing talents of a young Buddy Ebsen. Unfortunately, Brice's contract stipulated that her songs were to be written by her husband, Billy Rose, so Yip was precluded from writing for the grand mistress of the American-Yiddish malapropism.

Yip and Duke composed two notable songs for the *Follies:* "What Is There to Say?" and "I Like the Likes of You." "What Is There to Say?" is a relaxed but precisely crafted ballad.

WHAT IS THERE TO SAY?

Verse.

Darling, pardon my confusion
But are you an optical illusion
And if not, then what on earth
Are you doing to me?

If my speech is willy nilly,
It's because I cannot gild the lily
I should love to sing your praises
But phrases and words are silly. . .

Chorus.

What is there to say?
And what is there to do?
The dream I've been seeking
Has practic'lly speaking
Come true

What is there to say?
And how will I pull through?
I knew in a moment
Contentment and home meant
Just you

You are so lovable
So liveable
Your beauty is just unforgivable
You're made to marvel at
And words to that effect
So,

What is there to say?
And what is there to do?
My heart's in a deadlock
I'd even face wedlock
With you.

Yip's lyric begins, both in the verse and the chorus, with protestations of verbal ineptitude, even a mild panic ("How will I pull through?"), but this is neither a stammering song (like "I Like the Likes of You") or a song of genuine romantic confusion and disorientation (like "April in Paris"). In each of the main-strain stanzas (one, two, and four), the title protestation is set to a rising, but not urgent line. The lyric builds around a succession of escalating two-syllable rhymes that call attention to themselves first by their digressive content ("practic'lly speaking"), then by their somewhat forced character (moment/home meant) and finally by encapsulating the song's tone in one line and resolving the tension in the next ("My heart's in a deadlock / I'd even face wedlock"). The sense these lines convey is that of a tenuous mastery of the situation and the emotion, with both music and rhyme more complex—and showing off about it, too—than in the stanzas' front phrase. (The deadlock/wedlock rhyme had first appeared in Yip's workbooks in 1930.)

"I Like the Likes of You" is the most relentlessly inarticulate of Yip's songs of love-struck inarticulation, a subject he first addressed in his 1930 song with Gorney, "How I Wish I Could Sing a Love Song." It was performed in the *Follies* by a young singer named Brice Hutchins, soon to change his name to Bob Cummings—and the song projects the kind of likable, stammering, somewhat befuddled character Cummings was to portray. It was one of Ira Gershwin's favorite lyrics.

I LIKE THE LIKES OF YOU

Verse.   Lady, last Saturday, or was it yesterday?
I was rehearsing a speech
Really, I think it's a peach
Hope you don't think it a breach
Of, recognized etiquette
I'm from Connecticut
You see the state that I'm in,
I mean I'm in a mess,
What was that speech
Oh yes . . . yes . . .

Chorus.   I like the likes of you
I like the things you do
I mean, I like the likes of you

I like your eyes of blue
I think they're blue, don't you?
I mean, I like your eyes of blue

Oh dear, if I could only say what I mean
I mean, if I could mean what I say
That is, I mean to say
That I mean to say that

I like the likes of you
Your looks are pure de-luxe
Looks like I like the likes of you.

I LIKE THE LIKES OF YOU

FROM THE MUSICAL PRODUCTION
"ZIEGFELD FOLLIES"

WORDS BY

E. Y. HARBURG

MUSIC BY

VERNON DUKE

PRICE 60 CENTS
IN U.S.A.

HARMS
INCORPORATED
New York

Some early hit songs that Yip and his composers created in revues from the early thirties: "Only a Paper Moon," "April in Paris," "What Is There to Say?" "I'm Yours," and "I Like the Likes of You." (Last two songs, Music Division, Library of Congress; others, Collection of Harburg Estate.)

"Like the Likes" shows Duke and Harburg working together in top form. The fifth line of the verse returns us to the melody of the first line, but it returns set against a minor and agitated harmony, as the lyric veers into panicked nonsense ("recognized etiquette / I'm from Connecticut"). The main strain of the chorus sets a bouncy tune to a lively rhythm, and the chorus repeats that strain (this is an AABA song) as the singer becomes mired ever deeper in repetition. "The release," Alec Wilder has written, "has a marvelous slithery idea and sticks to it by repeating it twice more with shifting harmony." Actually, the release descends in half-step intervals, as the singer works and reworks his sentence to try to get it right, as he feels more and more deflated and unable to formulate his thought. Both musically and lyrically, the release suggests sinking in quicksand.

For the lyric, Yip adopted a rigorously simple vocabulary and rhyme scheme. This is a song of obvious end-line rhymes. The chorus is comprised entirely of one-syllable words, with the single exception of "de-luxe" (pronounced as "de-looks"). Ira Gershwin beamed at the lyric's craft.

The *Follies* opened to favorable notices, which focused, as usual, on the show's top comics, Fanny Brice and Willie Howard. Music and lyrics got short shrift from the critics, though among at least some reviewers, there was a growing awareness that Duke's complex music demanded more attention than they were able to pay.

The end of the Harburg-Duke collaboration also coincided with the final dissolution of Yip's first marriage. Characteristically, he turned to light verse as one means of dealing with his turmoil:

MASTER OF HEARTS

Splintered hearts for mending
    Would need a plaster cast
And Time, perhaps, unending—
    I thought, in years gone past.

But practice finds me able
    To mend—and time to spare—
With moisture and gum label
    The deepest kind of tear.

Yip found some solace in the company of his coworkers. By 1934, he had become a member in good standing of the elite fraternity of theater songwriters. It was a community, Yip contended, that held its members to high standards of creativity. "I write for my peers," Yip once said,

In fact, our tribe of songsmiths always wrote for our peers. We were very much ashamed of ourselves if we wrote anything clichéd, if we took an idea from another person. By "our tribe," I'm talking about Cole Porter, Ira Gershwin, Hart, Dietz, all those people who got together every week, usually at George Gershwin's house, and we would more or less compare the things we were working on.

All the songwriters got together regularly at the Gershwins in the twenties and thirties. Something like Fleet Street in Samuel Johnson's time—an artistic community where people took fire from each other. We'd hang around George's piano, playing our latest songs to see how they went over with the boys. We were all interested in what the other fellas were up to; we criticized and helped each other. There was great respect for each other's work and the integrity of our own music and lyrics. Sometimes, we would hear a whole great score before a show opened, a new Gershwin show, or Rodgers and Hart. We ate it up, analyzed it, played it over and over. You wouldn't dare write a bad rhyme or a clichéd phrase or an unoriginal or remotely plagiarized tune, because you were afraid of being ripped apart by your peers. This continuous give-and-take added to the creative impulse. It worked as incentive, opened up new ideas, made it necessary to keep working and evolving.

Everyone you could imagine came to the Gershwin parties on weekends, not only songwriters, but all kinds of people—performers, critics, actors, novelists, choreographers—the likes of Moss Hart, Oscar Levant, Harpo Marx. Wherever the Gershwins happened to be living, whether on Riverside Drive or in Beverly Hills, when we all went out west writing for the movies, their house was always crammed with creative people. Those were exciting, inspiring days.

They grew more exciting when, early in 1934, the Shuberts asked Yip to do the lyrics for what was to be their smartest revue—a witty, innovative show in the tradition of *The Garrick Gaieties* and *The Bandwagon.* The production was entrusted to director-designer John Murray Anderson, who brought the show off, Yip later said, "with wonderful charm, wonderful scenery, such lovely costumes . . . such great taste." It was, Yip recognized at the outset, an unusual opportunity—a show that mixed the wit and critical spirit of the smaller revues with the budget and spectacle of the larger ones. It was also, Yip recognized, a tremendous amount of work in a relatively short time. Having just completed all the lyrics for the *Ziegfeld Follies,* an exhausting assignment, it was more than Yip was willing to tackle all by himself. He thus recruited as colyricist his writing partner from his school days, Ira Gershwin.

Yip approached Ira knowing that Ira uncharacteristically had time on his hands: brother George had embarked on what was to prove the two-year project of writing *Porgy and Bess,* in which initially Ira was not supposed to participate. Yip's other collaborator was not so easy to pin down. He wanted Harold Arlen to do the music, and Arlen viewed it as a major opportunity—to solo on a major revue, to work with Ira and Yip, to leap from the Cotton Club to Broadway. "This show really meant something," Arlen was to say in later years. The problem was, it also meant severing his partnership with lyricist Ted Koehler—a task to which, in time, the gentle Arlen steeled himself, and wrote Koehler a letter suggesting that they split. The three-way collaboration was on. "We got together every night at nine or ten o'clock," Yip recalls (as Ira recalled it, Yip was characteristically a couple of hours late),

> and worked till four o'clock in the morning with Harold at the piano, and it was joyous. George was busy writing *Porgy and Bess.* He had a penthouse across the street on Seventy-second Street. Ira lived on the north side of the street and George lived on the south. We would get together at George's place [and he would play] what he was doing on *Porgy and Bess* and we would play him what we were doing on *Life Begins at 8:40* [the name of the Shubert revue]. They were glorious days.

For Yip and Ira, the collaboration had the aspect of a reunion. "Ira had a Wodehousian lightness, a funny point of view," said Yip.

> He had a delightful sense of whimsy. Working together was like doing a crossword puzzle—one making up one line one day, the other making up the next line the next day. Ira and I have a similar sense of humor. He shies away from sentimentality.

For Arlen, though, the show marked a sudden and total immersion in a new kind of lyrics. "Yipper is a Gilbert and Sullivan lover," Arlen once said.

> This means a torrent of lyrics. I had to adapt myself to his kind of thinking and find a way to please myself at the same time. Working with him didn't limit me—that is, I didn't have to set lyrics. We really collaborated.
>
> Ira is very much like Yip. . . . [M]an, they sure gave me an interesting time!

In Arlen, Yip found a composer whose commitment to innovation and abhorrence of the familiar rendered superfluous any peer group pressure to rise above the routine. "Harold was the most fastidious and demanding-of-himself [composer]," Yip said,

> that you could find anywhere. He threw everything out. He was frightened of everything sounding like something else. He's got many great tunes that

he won't release. . . . He works with discipline and passion. He will labor on one phrase, sometimes for weeks, exploring every musical possibility with the patience of a chess champion.

Characteristically, Arlen would find his main themes away from the piano. Like Yip, he carried a notebook with him at all times to jot down his (in this case, musical) ideas; like Yip, he then spent hours developing them. By the time he went to work with Yip and Ira, Arlen's musical innovations had begun to jell into a distinct pattern. The Arlen song was distinguished by a structural freedom (some of his most notable efforts are far longer than the standard thirty-two bars), by melodic leaps (such as the octave leap which began "Paper Moon" and "Over the Rainbow"), by an affinity for the blues. His insistence on unusual melodic patterns was another distinctive feature: George Gershwin once pointed out to Arlen that there are no repeated musical phrases in the opening stanza of the "Stormy Weather" chorus—a genuine rarity in song craft.

From the outset, Arlen's work with Yip was to take him far afield from the blues, and Yip testified on more than one occasion to Arlen's versatility. "Even though he's known as the pope of all the blues," Yip said, "he can jump at the whole gamut and into the most delicate of madrigal music." The score for the Shubert revue took Arlen from the familiar world of ballads, production numbers, and torch and rhythm songs to the newer terrain of comic parody numbers, patter songs, mock marches, and extended send-ups of opera. "It was a completely perfect score for a show," said Ray Bolger, who starred in it. "It was the freshest score that had been on Broadway in a year."

If there was a unity in the revue, it was a unity of tone and approach. "Ira and I had a point of view," Yip recalled. "We were going to write a satiric show and more or less cover the field. We weren't focusing on one thing. . . . We started off by kidding the theater. The fact that we called the show *Life Begins at 8:40* [curtain time then was 8:30 P.M. for Broadway theaters] already tells you that we had tongue-in-cheek." The title was Ira's suggestion, a play on Walter Pitkin's then-popular book, *Life Begins at 40.*

8:40 began by calling attention to its framing as a show, to all the conventions to which it was about to adhere. "We had this big Munich clock on stage," Yip told Max Wilk,

and out of that clock come all of the characters that would appear in the revue: the husband, the lover, the wife, and blues singers, and comedians, and dancers, and so on. And in the words for the opening, we said:

> At exactly eight-forty, or thereabouts
> This little play world
> Not of the day world
> Comes to life.

Lacking a story line, the Broadway revue was at least latently anti-illusionary: it was a comic's medium, allowing for acknowledgment of and interplay with the audience, for running commentary in comedy and song on the show itself. *8:40* was particularly insistent upon its proclamation of artifice and illusion and emotional imagery. In that regard, even with Ira's participation, the themes and ideas sound distinctly Harburgian.

Perhaps the most familiar terrain for Arlen in *8:40* was the slow, rocking urbane blues he composed for Ira and Yip's witty lyric, "Will You Love Me Monday Morning as You Did on Friday Night?" One stanza of a later chorus anticipates the post–sexual revolution lyrics of such current lyricists as Sondheim:

> Since I met you I'm not the same
> And by the way, what is your name?
> And will you love me Monday morning
> As you did on Friday night?

The double vision of the Harburg love song achieved its fullest expression in the nearest song to a straight ballad in the *8:40* score: "Fun to Be Fooled." If there is a quintessential Harburg love song of the thirties, it is this, crafted with Ira.

FUN TO BE FOOLED

Verse.

Spring is here,
I'm a fool if I fall again
And yet I'm enthralled
By its call again
You say you love me
I know from the past
You mean to love me
But these things don't last

Fools rush in
To begin new love affairs
But tonight
Tonight, my dear who cares?

Chorus.

Fun to be fooled
Fun to pretend
Fun to believe
Love is unending
Thought I was done
Still it is fun
Being fooled again

Nice when you tell
All that you feel
Nice to be told
This is the real thing
Fun to be kissed
Fun to exist
To be fooled again

It's that old devil moon
Having its fling once more
Selling me spring once more
I'm afraid love is king once more

Fun to be fooled
Fun to pretend
This little dream
Won't end.

Alec Wilder notes that with the exception of the Arlenesque octave leaps in the release, Arlen has composed a ballad of "Kern-like" directness and tranquillity. In fact, the interaction of music and lyrics is considerably more ironic and quietly disturbing than Kern's major ballads. The chorus is comprised of short musical phrases built around the tonic and the dominant notes, against which Yip and Ira have set short phrases almost in a child's language: fun to be fooled, fun to pretend. In both music and lyrics, the fourth lines of the first two chorus stanzas ("Love is unending" and "This is the real thing") come, as it were, wrapped in quotes: the treatment here is purposefully, visibly conventional; it approaches deliberate schmaltz. Indeed, in the second stanza, the lyric grows almost patronizing toward this level of belief: "Nice" is not merely descriptive, it is also a rather curt and dismissive evaluation of the emotional/mental state under description.

In the release, the lyricists summon Yip's symbols of romance—spring and that old devil moon—to do double duty as agents of entrapment and illusion. The sales pitch is made plainly visible ("Selling me spring once more")—but the sale is transacted nonetheless.

"Harold is a very, very melancholy person," Yip once told Max Wilk. "Behind every song Harold writes is a great sadness and melancholy. Even his happy songs. You take a song like his rousing hit, 'Get Happy.' Sing it slowly. Examine it. It's *painful.*" In fact, in both the sparseness and descending character of its main phrases and the un-Kern-like blue notes of its last lines in several stanzas, "Fun to Be Fooled" is uncommonly subdued and contemplative for ballad music. Both music and lyrics are balanced somewhere between the exultation of a love song and the resignation that comes with believing that love is an illusory state. The song, Yip once said, was "an extension of the same idea" as "Paper Moon." In "Fun to Be Fooled," he explained,

> I was saying life is all being fooled, we are all being fooled by it, but while it's happening it's a lot of fun. I think it's a lot of fun. I think it's a lovely excursion and I'm glad I got a ticket for this short cruise, and that's all.

The other boy-girl songs of *8:40* were more comic in spirit. Of their generation of lyricists, Ira and Yip were the two who most extensively practiced word alteration, and it was nearly inevitable that their show together would contain one such effort. Writer of "'S Wonderful," Ira was King of Contractions; Yip, who was later to pen "Would You Be So Kindly?" and "Something Sort of Grandish," was the Sultan of Suffixes. Together, they turned out "You're a Builder Upper," a comic account of a love relationship that is all too true to life:

YOU'RE A BUILDER UPPER

Verse.

When you want to, you are able
To make me feel that I'm Clark Gable
Then, next minute, you make me feel
I'm something from the zoo

First you warm up, then you're distant
Never knew a girl so inconsistent
I'm a big shot, at half past one
And so-and-so by two

Heaven forgive you for your sins
Keeping me on needles and pins!

Chorus.

You're a builder upper,
A breaker downer
A holder outer
And I'm a giver in-er
Sad, but true, I'm a sap-a-roo, too,
Taking it from a taker-over like you

Don't know where I'm at-a
I'm just a this-a
Then I'm a that-a
A taker on the chin-er
My, my, my, what a weaky am I
To love you as I do

Just when I'm ready to sob
You hand me a throb
And ev'rything is hunky dory
And that's my story
Open your arms
And I'm a stooge for your charms

You're a builder upper,
A breaker downer
A holder outer,
And I'm a giver in-er
Sad, but true
I love it, I do
Being broken by a builder upper
Like you.

"Two very interesting guys," Arlen called Yip and Ira, "always experimenting with words. Using the language, twisting it, bending it." Harold's music for "Builder Upper" twists and bends, too, jumping nervously in the verse, and then ending the first stanza and the entire song with a note that begins on the dominant and slurs upward one step to the sixth tone. It's an abrupt and jagged conclusion, rather like ending this off-balance song in midair.

The most enduring comic-romantic song from *8:40*, however, is a quiet soft-shoe duet whose rhymes and wordplay build slowly toward an antic conclusion and whose story is rooted in depression realities:

LET'S TAKE A WALK AROUND THE BLOCK

Verse.

I never travel'd further north
Than old Van Cortlandt Park
And never further south than the Aquarium
I've seen the charm of Jersey City
But, first let me remark
I saw it from the Empire State Solarium

But I've been putting nickels in the
Postal Savings Bank
And when those nickels pile up,
We can toddle off in swank
And I don't mean an ordinary Cook's tour
I mean a "Cabin De Luxe" Tour

Chorus.

Some day we'll go places
New lands and new faces
The day we quit punching the clock
The future looks pleasant
But, at present,
Let's take a walk around the block

You're just the companion
I want at Grand Canyon
For throwing old blades down the rock
The money we have'll
Go for travel
Meantime, let's walk around the block

Gangway! We'll begin
When our ship comes in
You'll sit on my lap
All over the map

To London in Maytime,
To Venice in playtime,
To Paris in time for a frock
To Boston in bean-time
Darling, meantime,
Let's take a walk around the block

Second Chorus.

In Winter at Christmas
We'll visit the isthmus
And see how they lock up a lock
And then in Caracas
On a jackass
We'll take a ride around the block

I give you my promise
We'll visit St. Thomas
And then at the Virgins we'll dock

She.

The Virgins can wait, sir,
It grows late, sir,
Let's take a walk around the block

Both.

Onward to Cathay
Then to Mandalay
Then Vladivostok
Where Bolsheviks flock

We'll send the folks cables
Accumulate labels
Buy souvenirs till we're in hock
Right now we are flat in
Old Manhattan
Let's take a walk around the block.

Music critic and Gershwin biographer Isaac Goldberg wrote of Harold Arlen and his score for *8:40,* "His aim is at once to achieve a singable, quotable tune that shall not be too easily predictable." "Walk around the Block," with its surprising melodic turns within the tight confines of a necessarily laid-back soft shoe, exemplifies Arlen's technique. It also exemplifies Ira and Yip's understanding of the form. A quiet song, it requires a slow-building lyric. The comedy takes off only with the high note of the last stanza of the first thirty-two bars (that is, the high note of the last A stanza in what is an AABA song). It is on that note that they place the "bean"—"To Boston in *bean*-time." Thenceforth, for the second thirty-two bars, the rhymes and comedy grow more improbable and insistent.

8:40 had more than its share of insistent comedy in any event. The show marked a breakthrough not only for Yip and Harold but also for its lead comedian and star, the great comic Bert Lahr. To some considerable degree, the breakthroughs were interlinked. In Arlen and Harburg, in Yip most particularly, Lahr found writers capable of expanding his comedy into a travesty of social propriety. In Lahr, Yip found an incendiary comic capable of blowing pretense to smithereens. Born in New York to an immigrant Jewish family just one year before Yip, Lahr joined with Yip to make a formidable team—two New York street kids determined and supremely able to lampoon a pompous and hoity-toity culture.

Lahr came to *8:40* with an expansive comic vocabulary of expressions, noises, and gestures developed over decades in burlesque and vaudeville. "Bert Lahr . . . starts in burlesque," Yip once recalled.

> Billy Watson's Beef Trust, as some of them were called, was built around some gal coming out and doing a striptease, but between the striptease, you had to make those people who are less than common denominator laugh out loud belly laughs. That was the kind of training that Bert Lahr got. They'd go around from city to city and they built their act up. They would be doing one joke for about five weeks until it was a terrific laugh. . . . By the time they got here, that joke was developed.

From these at once exacting and humble beginnings, Lahr developed a character that he took with him into his first Broadway shows. From 1928 through 1933, Lahr starred in a series of Broadway musicals in which the dominant creative talents were those of the songwriting team of DeSylva, Henderson, and Brown. The Lahr character in these shows applied a manic energy to a kind of free-floating buffoonery. "When DeSylva, Henderson and Brown were writing for him," Yip told Lahr's son and biographer, the critic John Lahr,

They saw Bert as the low-down comic, the average "gnong-gnong" guy. He was the patsy . . . a semi-idiotic guy who always gets things wrong. I understood Lahr in a different way. . . . I took him out of the burlesque and gave him intelligent lyrics. And the juxtaposition was terrific. His whole visage was that of a clown. With Bert Lahr in the position of Caruso, you got your fun right off the bat. . . . When you get a good clown like Bert Lahr, you can destroy so many foibles in the social system if you give him the right word.

Life Begins at 8:40 featured as its main event, then, the collision of Bert Lahr with proper society. Working with Lahr, Arlen and Yip created songs and scenes for the nouveau bon vivant. One such was "C'est la Vie," a song Lahr performed with *8:40*'s other stars, Ray Bolger and Luella Gear. Lahr told his son John, "I said to Yip, 'I'd love to do something with an Inverness Cape.' It gave him his idea for his song and sketch on the bridge. Being known as a low comedian to do something that was directly opposite made it funny." Yip's scene had Lahr and Bolger stationed on a Parisian bridge, planning to leap into the Seine over their failed love affairs—with, it turns out, the same girl. Enter the girl herself (Gear) who tells them: "You do not understand. I tell you I do not love you because I love you each so much and if I tell one, I hurt the other." She has just come, however, from the film *Design for Living*, in which a ménage à trois lives happily ever after, and she suggests they give it a try. Concluding the verse with a rejection of conventional morality:

> Duets are made by the bourgeoisie—oh
> But only God can make a tri-o

they proceed into a lilting waltz complete with a bilingual pun. (These are the last three of five stanzas):

> C'est la vie
> Sans souci
> In a sweet little hide-out for three
> Breakfast will be set
> Tête a tête a tête
> We'll wake up and have crepes suzette.

> C'est la vie
> C'est la guerre
> C'est la vie, c'est la guerre,
> Sailor, beware!
>
> Oh what fun
> Three hearts beating as one
> C'est la vie, c'est la vie, c'est la vie.

It was a particularly appropriate song for *8:40* in light of the creative ménage à trois that produced its songs.

The defining moment for the new Lahr, though, was the solo concert that Yip and Harold devised for him. It was something of a defining moment for Arlen and Harburg too. Arlen had grown up hearing his father's recordings of Caruso and John McCormack and leading concert singers of the day; Yip, memorizing contemporary third-rate poets of the Joyce Kilmer/Edgar Guest variety. Now Lahr strode onto the concert stage with a song modeled loosely after "Ah, Sweet Mystery of Life." For all concerned, it was payback time.

"Things" (that is the name of the song, just "Things") cannot be separated from Lahr's performance, and his son John has written a running account in his biography of his father, *Notes on a Cowardly Lion,* from which we print excerpts:

> Lahr came on stage in a tuxedo and sporting a brown hairpiece that brought his hairline, like a dorsal fin, to an abrupt point on his forehead. A piano player sat beside him, elegantly poised for the recital. Lahr turned graciously to the small audience on the stage and began:
>
> "Ladies and Gentlemen, the first number of my second group was written in a little garret on the left bank of Giaconda Canal and is entitled 'Things,' simply 'Things.'"
>
> Lahr's pinky shoots up to his tooth. He vibrates his finger like a tuning fork in the side of his mouth. His teeth are straight and clenched tight as if he were holding on to some terrible truth.
>
> > When I was but a little lad
> > I used to think of things
> > The only joy I ever had
> > I had because of things.
> > But now that I'm to manhood grown,

> Fond memory always brings
> The utter, utter, utter
> Loveliness of things.
>
> Let others sing of Mandalay
> Let others sing of trees,
> Let others sing of Mother,
> And the busy, busy beeeeezzz . . .
> But I'm happier far than a million kings are
> When my soul sings of things.

Chorus.   Things, sweet happiness of things.
> Things that ease the rocky way,
> Things that look at God all day,
> Things, sweet misery of things.
> From birth bed to the grave,
> Aren't we all to them a slave
> What makes all the ocean wave
> Things (ah, ah), things (ah, ah, ah) . . .

Inspired by Lahr's trills, the pianist essays his own cadenza. Lahr glares at him.

> When the frost is on the punkin',
> And the sun in the west is sinkin',
> Can't you hear those paddles chunkin' . . .

His wig rebels again, falling completely over his face. His hands grope in front of his nose trying to locate the hair that has covered his eyes. He finally gets hold of it and tries to smooth it in place. He tries the last line again.

> Lickity split and to beddy for things
> Fit as a fiddle and ready for things . . .

When he says "ready," he winks at a woman in the front row of the stage audience.

> You can have your smoke pipe rings,
> Your Saratoga Springs,
> But give me . . .
> Give me . . .

The saxophone drones on. Lahr, determined to finish the song despite the orchestra, throws his hands up in despair, "Oh, go home!" And in a crescendo of baritone lyricism, he finishes emphatically,

> Give me things!!

"He fussed and fumed to get gimmicks into 'Things'," Arlen told John Lahr. "It was an endless game for him, until he finally got as many laughs out of it as possible."

"Things" preceded by one year the Marx Brothers' like-minded assault on proper culture, *A Night at the Opera*. (In fact, however, opera singing and concert song is the one aspect of opera that the Marxes *don't* go after in their picture.) It also preceded by one year Gershwin's *Porgy and Bess*. By the midthirties, a new, ascendant urban culture—off the sidewalks of New York— was able and confident enough to seek to supplant or to savage an older, duller, more homogenous culture—and Yip, Harold, and Bert were at the head of the pack.

"No one could write for [Bert] better than E. Y. and myself," Arlen told John Lahr, and Lahr concurs. "Many outstanding writers," he observes,

> created material with Lahr in mind—S. J. Perelman, Abe Burrows, George S. Kaufman, William Saroyan—but none came as close to his buffoonery as Arlen and Harburg did. And although the Arlen-Harburg collaboration [with Lahr] would not go beyond 1939, their special material for Broadway and *The Wizard of Oz* remained Lahr's trademark.

8:40's finale was an extended mock-operetta entitled "Beautifying the City" that dealt lightly but in a partisan vein with local and national politics, and that managed to reprise most of the evening's songs in the bargain. Lahr played the heroic Dictator LaGuardia, who enters to a classic Gilbert and Sullivan fanfare from the chorus.

> He gave the city class-o
> There's dancing on the mall
> He introduced Picasso
> To the boys at City Hall
> Delancey Street has flowers
> The Bowery has no bums
> With chromium-plated showers
> He has beautified the slums.

To which Lahr responded with the appropriate patter song:

I'm Dictator Fiorello
I'm a many-sided fellow
When you look at me you almost see Napoleon!
I love music. I'm artistic.
I'm a statesman pugilistic
As a brain I'd even take Professor Moley on!

(In *Of Thee I Sing* three years earlier, Ira had rhymed Napoleon with simoleon.)

In the finale, numbers are reprised in new contexts. The Taxpayers Association sings "Fun to Be Fooled"; Bolger, as deposed Mayor Jimmy Walker, explains his return from exile with "Walk around the Block"; and the scene concludes with a revision of "Builder Upper" into a paean of praise for LaGuardia. A deep affection for both LaGuardia and Roosevelt suffuses this final number, as it was to suffuse Yip's lyric to "God's Country" in *Hooray for What?* three years later. "It was a real people's country," Yip told Deena Rosenberg: politically, the New Deal was the April and the spring in which Yip believed.

In "Beautifying the City," Ira was returning to the extended mock-operatic form of which he had demonstrated himself the master in the political trilogy (*Strike Up the Band, Of Thee I Sing, Let 'Em Eat Cake*) he had created with his brother and George S. Kaufman and Morrie Ryskind. It was a new form for Yip, and one he was not to have cause to use again until he had to set a scene in Munchkinland. "Beautifying the City" was the sum total of Yip's preparation for the extended comic musical sequences of *Oz*.

"We tied up the whole show" with "Beautifying the City," Yip told Deena Rosenberg; in fact, over half a dozen numbers are reprised in full or in part. At the final curtain, then, the delicate mix of self-referential reprises and political commentary, of artifice and lampoon, heightened *8:40*'s satiric, political, anti-illusionary—in a word, Harburgian—character. Yip and Gersh had replayed their college days, but this time as Broadway sophisticates.

Life Begins at 8:40 opened on August 27, 1934, to generally rave reviews. Critics focused first and foremost on Lahr, with the most perceptive among them, Brooks Atkinson and John Mason Brown, noting the transformation in his comedy ("The Quieter and Even Funnier Bert Lahr" was the title of a Brown piece that ran a few days after the opening). The authors had the unusual experience of having one of their songs, "Things," singled out as the high point of the evening's comedy. A recurrent theme of the reviews was the "smartness" of the evening, a quality a number of critics chose to demonstrate by praising or quoting the lyrics. One critic went so far as to define the Harburg touch:

Harburg's arrival on the musical comedy and revue scene several years ago added a new vigor to lyric writing. To the old requisites, the need for laughs and tears in the lyrics of a popular song, he added a sly satiric and social note. Harburg made an old idea new to the musical stage by pointing out that the vices and foibles of a people may be twitted out of existence. . . . He managed to sneak in several numbers which had a strong satiric and social import and which somehow got under the skin of his audiences.

Arlen's music came in for relatively little notice, a consequence perhaps of the paucity of ballads in *8:40*. "Fun to Be Fooled" was the nearest thing to a ballad in the entire score, and while there were no songs with an "April in Paris" intensity (or "Stormy Weather," for that matter), nothing in the script or set called for it. What the *8:40* score demonstrated, rather, was Arlen's freshness and versatility. They were qualities Yip prized in a composer. "Harold was one of the rare guys," Yip later said, "who had the facility to go that long range from fun to high misery or comedy or whatever it is we have now and make the tune fit the idea. Harold is so great on his own. He really has genius qualities."

For a while, the composer hopper had settled down. Of the fifty-one published songs Yip was to write between 1935 and 1939, all but six were written with Harold Arlen.

Chapter 4

Give My Regards to Broadway

Let's pretend
That this moonlight and music
Is never to end

Let's deny
That we're here
In a fly-by-night world
'Neath a fly-by-night sky

Let's not ask
Of romance
Do our hearts stand a chance
Let the fiddle unravel the riddle
And on with the dance!

In the midthirties, Broadway musicals moved to Hollywood—first and foremost through its songwriters.

In large part the precipitating cause was money. Musical production dried up on Broadway during the toughest years of the Depression. Where the boom years of the late twenties had seen more than forty musicals produced in a season, the bust years of the early thirties saw the number of musicals per year cut to roughly a dozen (which was one reason why the competition to insert songs in revues was so fierce). In Hollywood, by contrast, the production of musicals remained fairly constant after Warner Bros. *42nd Street* helped revive the genre in early 1933. The pay was steadier and higher. Songwriters may have traded in their prestige and autonomy for the income, but in the midthirties, the Astaire-Rogers musicals offered a format that was clearly comparable to the best Broadway had to offer. Besides, Yip noted,

> a songwriter needed hits to get his degree in ASCAP. For that, chances were much better in films. The New York critics looked down on them. Broadway was the snob literary Park Avenue, and Hollywood, skid row. But for a while, especially during the Astaire/Rogers period, Hollywood was making some great pictures with a wealth of great songs. Kern, Berlin, DeSylva, Henderson, and Brown were out west.

So were Yip and Harold—though initially, not working together. When Yip traveled to Hollywood in late 1934, it was not just to write songs, but to produce a picture for Universal Studios based around the song "April in Paris." (Yip's organizing talents from his early executive training in business had begun to increase the scope of his film and theater work.) Arlen was on the same train, bound west to do a picture with Ted Koehler; George S. Kaufman was on the train, too, for initial work on the project that was to become *A Night at the Opera.* Yip's producing stint turned into a frustrating experience: Universal was the studio that had the greatest difficulty weathering the depression, and after a number of months, the "April in Paris" project became a casualty of the studio's financial reorganization.

Yip had had his initial doubts about moving west in any case. In the early thirties, he had sent a mock–Andrew Marvell pastoral to a lady friend who was urging him to come west:

> Your sweet intoxicating clime
> Is causing reams of bootleg rhyme.
> Your earth is rich and that's a cinch
> But is it worth two grand per inch?
> Your fruits I hear profusely grow,
> But have you seen our pushcart row?
> I'm for your birds and morning dew
> But then I like my borsht soup too.

By the midthirties, Yip's fears of exile from the land of borscht and pushcarts were assuaged by the influx of his New York peers; and he too had fallen under the spell of the rich earth and California sun. "Socially, we were a refugee colony of New Yorkers," Yip recalled.

> We were doing well. Life was luxurious. I had never lived in a house with a garden around me. Sunshine, sunshine, every day, everywhere. Shorts, tennis, golf, swimming, kumquats. Refugees? Like hell.

"So you've learned to like California!" Ira Gershwin wrote Yip from New York in January of 1935. "What's new about that?"

"Last Night When We Were Young"

Early 1935 found Yip also writing a story for a Warners Dick Powell musical, *Broadway Gondolier,* which, unlike the "April in Paris" project, went into production. It also found him hosting Arlen in his house for a time. Arlen arrived with what was even by his standards a difficult piece of music to which he had been unable to get a lyricist to respond. Arlen had composed the piece before

Harold Arlen, *seated,* and Yip lived together in Lawrence Tibbitt's home in Beverly Hills, where they created the classic song "Last Night When We Were Young" (1935). The song was later recorded by Judy Garland and by Frank Sinatra. (Courtesy of Lillian Meltzer.)

leaving New York, where he had played it for George Gershwin and his musical adviser, William Daly. Gershwin was preoccupied with *Porgy and Bess* at the time, but Daly considered the piece and said that he didn't understand it: an astonishing assessment from one of the nation's leading musical intellect. Yip takes up the tale from there:

> [Harold] wrote this beautiful melody. . . . When he had it finished, he never showed it to me. He showed it to me about a year later because he had showed it to Jerome Kern. Jerome Kern had said, "I think the song is a little too esoteric for popular consumption." Then he showed it to George Gershwin. He played it for George. And George said, "Harold, why do you get so complicated? People can't sing these songs." Then he gave it to Johnny Mercer and Johnny Mercer said, "I don't think I could write a lyric to that." [Arlen could have that effect on people. At one Hollywood party in the midforties, a somewhat inebriated Mercer came up to Arlen and told him that he really didn't understand his music. At that point, the two had already written "Blues in the Night," "One for My Baby," and

other standards. Arlen was flabbergasted.] Arlen never told me about these things and he gave it to me. My particular psyche happened to be on his vibe at that time and the title and lyric came out of the tune completely. I was so moved by it.

What Yip came up with initially was a first line that could serve as a title as well: "Last Night When We Were Young." "The juxtaposition of those two phrases is almost a whole world of philosophy," Yip said,

and when you get that, I don't know where it comes from. I wish I knew. I'd get a lot of them if I could. But I suppose the tune opened it up. When I heard that tune [he hums the front phrase] the whole pathos of the human situation, of the human race, is in that musical phrase. Old Harold gave it to me. I rode in on the coattails of his genius.

This was the lyric Yip fashioned:

LAST NIGHT WHEN WE WERE YOUNG

Last night when we were young
Love was a star, a song unsung
Life was so new, so real, so right
Ages ago, last night

Today, the world is old
You went away and time grew cold
Where is that star that seemed so bright
Ages ago, last night

To think that Spring had depended
On merely this, a look, a kiss
To think that something so splendid
Could slip away in one little day break

So now let's reminisce
And recollect the sighs and the kisses
The arms that clung
When we were young
Last night.

"Last Night When We Were Young," writes Alec Wilder, "goes far beyond the boundaries of popular music. . . . It is written with such intensity that it gives the illusion of being a song of great range, whereas it is only one step beyond an octave." Wilder attributes the illusion to the "unrelieved tension engendered throughout"—primarily by the suspension of a melancholy melody over a disquieting and ever-shifting harmony. Indeed, the harmony as much as the melody creates the musical tension and propels the music forward— something highly unusual in popular song. The melody, as in "Fun to Be Fooled," is comprised chiefly of short, often descending, phrases, which Yip sets with short lyrical phrases.

The first line of the lyric lays out the theme and tone of the piece: this is a song of sudden, transformative loss. In the first two stanzas, the loss is registered imagistically: time grows cold, stars grow dim. The release confronts us squarely with the subjectivity and fragility of spring: this is the other side of "Fun to Be Fooled." Spring is not being sold again; and without it, the world is abruptly disenchanted. Yip also responds to the rising musical intensity of the release (octave leaps and dissonant harmonies) with a more complex rhyme scheme: two-syllable rhymes in lines one and three (depended/splendid), and internal rhymes in lines two (this/kiss) and four (away/day)—all features that are absent from the shorter phrases of the other stanzas.

The final stanza moves from metaphor to more literal physicality. What remains, the last stanza insists, is remembrance only, and the memories grow steadily more physical and intimate—from sighs to kisses to arms that clung. The lyric ends with an inversion of the first line, a poetic technique Yip had learned decades earlier, which here fits the music and the despondent mood.

If Yip heard a meaning and a lyric where others had not, it was in part because the music must have recalled a similar line he had used in a poem seven years earlier. The spirit of the poem is quite different from that of the song, but the line, which concludes the poem, clearly had taken on a life of its own. The poem was entitled "Maturity," and it was printed in one of the columns in 1928.

> When I was young, a woman's tear
> Found me a trembling cavalier
>   Whose heart, aflutter, left its shrine
>   To help absorb the [illegible] brine
> Her whimper was a well-aimed spear
>   That splintered on my sturdy spine
>   Like thunder light upon a pine
> I waited on her whims with fear
>   When I was young.

> Ah Time! No cultivated leer
> Can now reshape this bard's career
>   No female pout can undermine
>   This heart grown stout with wisdom's wine
> What used to be—was all—last year
>   When I was young.

In Yip and Harold's canon, "Last Night" is without parallel. It moves beyond Arlen's usual blues into something more painful, less remediable, and Yip responds with a picture of that disillusioned world he would occasionally recommend in theory, to recoil from, if this song is any evidence, in practice. To Yip this is the nearest thing to a Kaddish in the Arlen-Harburg songbook: it is a song about death—of romance, of belief. It is the only lyric Yip ever wrote about losing love irrevocably and came after his first wife had left him, his father had died, and his business had collapsed.

It was also a manifestly difficult song for a listener to apprehend. When Yip and Harold's Beverly Hills landlord, opera star Lawrence Tibbett, sought to insert the song in one of his pictures, the studio balked. The same thing happened years later to Judy Garland and Frank Sinatra—though in time, all three recorded the number and it acquired a following among musical cognoscenti. Years later, *New York Times* critic Stephen Holden wrote that listening to Sinatra's rendering of the song "is to be transported for a moment to the center of the earth and to feel the deepest loneliness."

Forays into Films

In September 1935, with Yip's Universal deal up in smoke and Harold's picture with Koehler completed, Harburg and Arlen signed a one-year "for hire" contract with Warner Bros. Warners was not famous for its respect of songwriters: longtime Warners composer Harry Warren used to tell the story of his confronting a musical ignoramus producer who had rejected one of his songs, and asking him what gave him the right to judge. "Because you're standing *there*," the producer answered from behind his desk, "and I'm sitting *here*."

Though the films on which Arlen and Harburg were to work in their year at Warners were routine programmers, the team turned out a succession of good songs. *The Singing Kid* brought them the opportunity to do a picture with Al Jolson, for whom they wrote "You're the Cure for What Ails Me" and "I Love to Sing-a"—this last, one of Yip's suffix songs, in which he appended a closing short *a* sound to every song cliché he could pile on. The chorus begins:

> I love to sing-a
> About the moon-a and the June-a
> And the Spring-a

and concludes in fine Jolson fashion:

> I love to wake up with the South-a
> In my mouth-a
> And wave the flag-a
> With a cheer for Uncle Sammy
> And another for my mammy
> I love to sing.

Stage Struck, a typical Dick Powell-Joan Blondell backstage programmer, featured a love song set in a natural history museum and thus afforded Yip the chance to write a Darwinian-Shavian life force romancer. Harold composed a deadpan lilting foxtrot, and Yip's lyric turned on the bracketing of the evolutionary saga within the overripe clichés of romance magazines: an inspired comic juxtaposition.

FANCY MEETING YOU

Verse.
> The more I look at you
> The more it seems to me
> That you and I were friendly once
> Way back in history
> You're so familiar to me
> My heart just seems to know
> We've been brought together again
> Out of long ago

Chorus.
> It can't be true
> Just fancy meeting you
> Remember when the world began
> I was your prehistoric man?
> The dawn broke . . .
> And like two lovesick fish in the sea
> We awoke!
> And love climbed up our family tree
> When hearts are true
> What's a million years or two?
> It paid to wait for old man fate
> To lead us out of the zoo.
> It all goes to prove what downright love can do
> Fancy, fancy meeting you!

"It was a great period," Arlen told Max Wilk.

> Maybe it was the accident of us all working there because of the Depression. Practically every talent you can name . . . Jerry Kern, Harry Warren, the Gershwins, Dorothy Fields and Jimmy McHugh, Oscar Hammerstein—even Berlin, although he didn't stick around. . . . We were all on the weekly radio Hit Parade. If we weren't first, we were second; if we weren't second, we were fourth. A sensational period.

The fraternity of lyricists, which had nourished Yip in New York, came west, too. An anecdote Saul Chaplin related to Wilk shows the fraternity in action. In arranging the music for the 1944 Gene Kelly musical *Cover Girl* (score by Jerome Kern and Ira Gershwin), Chaplin discovered he needed some comic patter for Kelly and comic Phil Silvers. He called on Ira for the additional lyrics, only to find a gathering straight out of the Gershwins' New York assembled in Ira's house.

> I went there and sitting around were E. Y. Harburg, Marc Connelly, Leo Robin, Arthur Schwartz, and the late Oscar Levant. I spoke to Ira and Ira said to the group, "Listen, don't leave—we need two lines for this thing." So I played it. Well, the joke lines started coming from all these talented guys so fast you could not believe it. Harburg had literally dozens of them. There were so many coming from them all it became a contest of their own prowess instead of what I needed.

And Return to Broadway

Nor was it impossible to break away to do at least some work on a Broadway show. In April 1936, Yip received a telegram from fledgling Broadway director Vincente Minnelli, then planning yet another Shubert revue, *The Show Is On.* "I am now getting together my own revue to go into rehearsal in late August," he cabled. "I would give anything if you and Harold could work on it with me, but I suppose it's impossible for you to get away for that long—or is it?"

Yip soon received a letter from his New York–based attorney, Abe Berman, advising him in no uncertain terms against coming to New York for a show. Hardly any musicals were succeeding on Broadway, Berman pointed out; and the money was in Hollywood. Yip and Harold compromised: they wrote two specialty numbers in Hollywood and sent them back east.

In fact, Minnelli cobbled together *The Show Is On* from a series of one-shot contributors. The program read like a songwriters' all-star game: besides the two songs from Arlen and Harburg, there were a number of songs by Vernon Duke and Ted Fetter, one by George and Ira Gershwin ("By Strauss"), one by Rodgers and Hart, one from Schwartz and Dietz, another from Hoagy Carmichael and Stanley Adams, and contributions from three other songwriters as well, for a grand total of fifteen.

Yip and Harold's contributions were comic specialty numbers for the show's stars, Bert Lahr and Bea Lillie. For Lillie, they authored a number called "Josephine Waters," in which Lillie did her impression of Josephine Baker. For Lahr, it was concert time once more. When they had finished the piece, they cut a record (Arlen by then could do a more than passable Lahr) and mailed it east. Lahr recognized it as the best material he had ever received. It was entitled "Song of the Woodsman," and again, we excerpt from John Lahr's biography of his father:

> When the curtain came up, it uncovered an unlikely woodsman. Lahr was posed preposterously next to a scrawny tree with an ax in his hand. He wore a checkered hunter's shirt and a toupee matted on his head. He began raising both hands delicately to his chest and then unleashing an outrageous sound.

> > The day's at the dawn
> > And the dawn's on the morn
> > The morn's on the corn
> > And the corn's on the cob

> ["I was parodying part of Browning's 'Pippa Passes,'" Yip told John Lahr.]

> > The year's at the Spring
> > And the day's at the morn
> > The hillside's dew-pearled
> > The lark's on the wing
> > The snail's on the thorn
> > God's in his heaven—
> > All's right with the world!

> He stops to let the logic of the lilting words sink into his own befuddled brain.

> > All's right with the world.
> > All's rah-rah-rah-rah-rah-rah-rah right with the world.
> > O, a woodsman's life is the life for me
> > With an all wool shirt 'neath an all wood tree
> > For the world is mine where 'ere I stand
> > With a song in my soul
> > And an a-a-a-a-a-a-a-ax in my hand

Lahr strikes an operatic pose.

> For I chop and I chop and I chop
> Till the sun comes up
> And with every stroke the welcomes ring
> When my truest friend, my ax I swing
> What care I if the stocks should drop
> Long as I can chop, chop, chop, chop.
> Songs were made by fools like me
> But only a baritone, a very bari-baritone
> Can sing while the tall trees flop
> So let me chop, chop, chop, chop, chop, chop.

He backs away from the tree and shoulders his papier-mâché ax, swinging boldly at the tree.

> Heave-swing! Heave-swing!

As he swings, a barrage of wood pelts him from the wings.

> Heave-swing! Heave-swing!

A second barrage—and while Lahr is trying to protect himself, he knocks his wig off. After a frenzy of fumbling, he restores it atop his head—sideways—and returns, earnestly, to the song.

> There's no stoppin'
> Me or Chaliapin
> When we're choppin' a tree
> When we're choppin' a tree.

Fussing with his wig, eyes aflutter, he begins softly—

> What do we chop when we chop a tree?
> A thousand things that you daily see.
> A baby's crib, the poet's chair,
> The soap box down at Union Square,
> A pipe for Dad, a bat for Brother,
> An extra broom for dear old Mother,
> Pickets for the fence, buckets for the well,
> Poles for American Tel & Tel,
> Cribbage boards for the Far West Indies,
> Toothpicks for the boys in Lindy's,
> Croquet balls for you and me—
> That's what we chop when we chop a tree.

His voice rises in passionate declamation—

Whadda we chop when we chop God's wood?

And then, reverently—

> Guns to protect our womanhood,
> The better mousetrap, the movie mag,
> The mast to hoist our country's flag,
> Handles for the Fuller Brush,
> Plungers for the obstinate flush
> Comfort seats, all shapes and classes
> For little lads and little—lasses,
> Modernistic beds built just for three
> That's what we chop when we chop a tree.
> Heave - swing! Heave - swing!

He tenses up to receive the onslaught from the wings. Nothing comes. Again—

> Heave-swing! Heave-swing!

He covers his head, and when nothing happens, he looks in disgust at the stagehands and continues—

> For I chop and I chop and I chop

At the crescendo of his song, his arms dramatically outstretched, he is bombarded again. He cowers, but struggles on—

> Till the sun comes up
> There's no stoppin'
> Me or Chaliapin
> When we're choppin' a—tree.

"Bert is precisely the opposite of that lip-smacking romantic instinct," Yip told John Lahr. "He was exploding the pompous baritone. I couldn't write those words for anyone else. 'Choppin' and Chaliapin,' for instance, is Bert Lahr language."

Yip spent some of November 1936 back east as *The Show Is On* struggled through its out-of-town tryouts in Boston and Philadelphia: his previous work with Lahr and Lillie and his track record with revues had led Minnelli and the Shuberts to recruit him as a "show doctor." Apparently, his medicine worked: *The Show Is On* opened in New York that December to highly enthusiastic reviews. Yip and Harold again had the unusual experience of having their song acclaimed as the evening's comic high point.

Yip brought a unique combination of attributes to the writing of comics' songs. The chameleon qualities of "the best little actor on the Lower East Side," as he once called himself, served him brilliantly when it came to writing for comics. In the same sense in which we can say Fred Astaire collaborated not only with his dance partners but with the great songwriters of his age, Yip collaborated not only with his composer partners, but with the great comedians of the Broadway stage.

Hooray for What?

Yip's month with *The Show Is On* clearly whetted his appetite to return to Broadway. Since 1935, he had been working on an outline for a musical that he intended to be to international politics what *Of Thee I Sing* had been to domestic politics. The story concerned a small-town inventor-chemist who unintentionally finds the formula for a death gas, which world powers proceed to scramble after madly. Initially, Yip conceived the project for Victor Moore (the forlorn Vice-President Throttlebottom of *Of Thee I Sing*) as the inventor. A subsequent draft was written for Clark and McCullough, stars of *Sing*'s predecessor, the 1930 *Strike Up the Band,* though McCullough's suicide in 1936 terminated that idea. By early 1937, Yip had interested the Shuberts in the project, to star in this incarnation a major Broadway comic whose radio career had taken him away from the stage for the past four years. It was a natural, all agreed, for Ed Wynn.

Yip's intent on the project, which he titled *Hooray for What?* was clear from the outset. By the midthirties, Yip, like millions of his countrymen, was watching with horror and apprehension the rise of fascism and the spread of conflict overseas. One widespread reaction to the coming crisis was a surge of antiwar sentiment across the nation. College students took the Oxford Pledge, proclaiming their intention never to fight in a war. A populist groundswell arose against munitions manufacturers, and a popular revisionist account of the First World War that held those manufacturers accountable took hold in some precincts of both the American Left and the American Right.

Yip once said he started thinking about *Hooray for What?* after seeing a photo of Basil Zaharoff, one of the munitions magnates, in the paper. Yip explained the story line:

> It was about a funny inventor, Ed Wynn, who always invented crazy things, and one of the things he invented was—well, at that time we didn't have the atom bomb—but it was a gas that he invented. . . . But he didn't want to release it to the world because it was so violent that anybody having it could conquer the world. . . . He was a very simple, charming, lovable, soft-hearted human being, who had an apple orchard, and he was trying to invent an insecticide that wouldn't kill the worms.

While working on this insecticide, not to harm worms, this soft-hearted man, through his experiment, invents a gas that makes people leapfrog, makes cows turn purple, give red milk, and things like that. And so the ammunition company that's making poison gas descends on him; they think they've got a great man who will give them something. They've found out that he has a gas that will be so terrible that whoever had it could conquer the world. He won't give up that gas; he keeps it in a football.

And somehow or other some spies get hold of it, and each country's spy sells it to another country. . . . So now everybody's got the gas, and everybody thinks they're the only ones who have it, . . . and we have a wonderful symbolic theme—we had three nations' balloons blown up on full-stage. One was Hitler, one was Mussolini, and one was Hirohito. And we had voices coming out of the loudspeaker: "We have the gas. . . ." But what they didn't know was that one of the spies copied the formula backwards and instead of 2MO, it came out M20, so they got laughing gas instead. When they let it loose on the soldiers, they all began to laugh. . . . The Germans began kissing the Russians and the Russians began kissing the Japanese. . . . And that was the end of the show.

But several factors combined to create a somewhat different show than the one Yip had originally intended. Crucial to *Hooray*'s transformation was its conversion into an Ed Wynn show. Wynn's persona, that of an indomitable naïf in a scheming world, was suited perfectly to the demands of the plot, but Wynn's innocent comedy invariably dominated any show in which he starred. By the estimate of one critic, Wynn held the stage for fully three-fourths of *Hooray*.

Much of the book, which the Shuberts entrusted to the team of Howard Lindsay and Russel Crouse (the team who later wrote the hit *Life with Father*) working from Yip's outline, sought to fuse Wynn's innocence to the evening's broader themes: at one point, talking to European diplomats about their war debts, Wynn says, "Don't you know that if you fellows miss a couple more payments, America will own the last war outright?" But much of the book was simply pure Wynn shtick, a collection of outrageously bad puns, non sequiturs, and sight gags whose relation to the show's broader concerns was tenuous. It made for a delightful evening in the theater, but not one so tightly integrated as *Of Thee I Sing*.

Singing, in fact, was the other part of the Wynn problem for Yip and Harold: *Wynn did not sing at all*. The music for *Hooray*, then, would not include any comic's songs or any of the kind of extended comic sequences Arlen and Harburg had shown themselves capable of in *8:40* and would again in *Oz*. Still,

Hooray for What? (1937) was an antiwar musical comedy farce which Yip conceived, helped produce, and write against the background of rising fascism and militarism in Europe and Japan. Strangely, one of the songs, "In the Shade of the New Apple Tree," landed Yip and Arlen the job as songwriters for *The Wizard of Oz.* (Collection of Harburg Estate.)

despite the limitations imposed on the project, *Hooray* was a watershed in Yip's career. It was *his* project—conception by Harburg, politics by Harburg, lyrics by Harburg, script shaped if not exactly written by Harburg. In both Yip's career and in Broadway musical history, *Hooray* was a transitional work, a midpoint between the comedians' revues on which Yip started work as a lyricist and the full-blown political book musicals he was to create in the forties.

With *Hooray,* Yip embarked on an early version of the bicoastal life. For the duration of the thirties and throughout the forties, he would maintain his primary residence in Los Angeles, near the security of studio contracts, but travel back to New York as the opportunities for shows arose. "I shuttled to New York at least every two years to do a show," he said.

> My heart, my big heart, was where the real tinsel blazed—Broadway. The cynosure, the center of all sophistication, was still New York. The goal, the dream, was the Broadway show. Those of us who came back periodically to the stage were always honored, envied, and rewarded. In the movies, the target was the mentality of a 12-year-old.

Yip and Harold's leave-taking for New York to work on *Hooray* was an uneasy one, however. In the weeks before their departure, they had seen a frightening and bewildering deterioration in the condition of their friend George Gershwin, who was then suffering from the final stages of an as yet undiagnosed brain tumor. When they left on July 4, George moved into Yip's Beverly Hills house, the better to escape what was commonly believed to be the psychological pressures he was under. One week later, he was dead, and Yip and Harold had lost not only a close friend but perhaps the central figure of the tight little world of songwriters from which they drew so much sustenance.

Inasmuch as Yip had conceived *Hooray for What?* it is surprising how little of the score actually attempts to deal with the show's main themes. In fact, only *Hooray*'s first song, the title song, conveys the story line's antimilitaristic politics. "Hooray for What?" bites somewhat more deeply than the rest of the score or book, where the attack is confined to the war lust of diplomats and armament kings. Here, it is mass jingoism—not only German and Italian, but American—that is at issue. The song is set within an Indiana town meeting that decides to run Wynn out of town on a rail for his chemical experiments. These are themes touched on nowhere else in the evening. But in *Hooray*'s opening scene, and in "Hooray for What?" we are back if only momentarily in the politics of the original 1927 *Strike Up the Band,* the Kaufman-Gershwin show that never made it to Broadway because of a book that was then judged too savage in its send-up of American wartime politics.

HOORAY FOR WHAT?
(excerpt)

Hip-hip, hooray
Hip-hip, hooray
Hooray for what?
We don't know what,
It's just hooray.
For there's no better way
To enjoy such a beautiful day,
Than to get up and get out in the open
And shout hooray.
Throw out your chest,
Throw up your hat,
Another strike—another war,
Can come from that.
If you can yell out loud in a crowd,
You're a great patriot,
Come along, shout hooray, for what!

All.	Where on Earth would Hitler be today
	How would Mussolini rule and sway?
Man.	What would happen to La France
	Or to this mighty U.S.A.?
All.	If it weren't for the fellow
	Who believed in Lux and Jello,
	And would give his life to bellow,
Man.	Hip-hip!
All.	Hooray!
Man.	Hip-hip!
All.	Hooray!

Hooray for what?
We don't know what.
It's just hooray.

"Hooray for What?" is an old-fashioned American antiwar song emerging from a late-thirties surge for peace and isolationism. A truer representation of the more celebratory spirit that prevailed on the left during Roosevelt's second term is Yip's lyric to *Hooray*'s other political song, "God's Country." While some of its lyrics can be taken as mildly contemptuous of the objects of pop culture veneration (from Popeye to Gypsy Rose Lee), it is preponderantly patriotic in tone, contrasting in particular the Roosevelt/LaGuardia regimes with those of European fascist and Communist governments.

GOD'S COUNTRY
(excerpt)

Hi there neighbor, going my way?
East or west on the Lincoln Highway
Hi there Yankee,
Give out with a great big thankee
You're in God's country

Where grass is greener—timber taller,
Mountains bigger—and troubles smaller
Hi there chappie,
Look over the sea, be happy
You're in God's country

A hundred million rooters can't be wrong
So give a hand—give a hand
Give a cheer for the land,
Where smiles are broader—freedom greater
Every man is his own dictator
Hi there Yankee,
Give out with a great big thankee
You're in God's—God's country

We've got no Mussolini—Got no Mosley,
But we've got Popeye and Gypsy Rose Lee
Hi there Yankee, give out with a great big thankee
You're in God's country
Let's drink a toast to Uncle Sammy,
Jessel's mother and Jolson's mammy;
To Benny's Jello and a guy called Fiorello,
In La Gu-a-rd-ia's country

A hundred million rooters can't be wrong
So give a hand—give a hand,
We've got no Trotsky—got no Stalin,
But we've got Freddie and Gracie Allen,
Hi there Yankee
Give out with a great big thankee,
You're in God's country. . . .

Love its highways—love its alleys,
Its Rocky Mountains and Rudy Vallees.
Hi there neighbor you don't need sword or sabre,
Here in God's Country.
Just wave that flag for Aimee Semple,
Coca-Cola and Shirley Temple?
You Cohen and you Biddle,
Hats off for Rubinoff's Fiddle.
You're in God's Country.

A hundred million rooters can't be wrong.
So give a hand—give a hand,
Where wheels are whirling, whistles blowing,
Milk and honey are overflowing.
Hi there neighbor,
Cheer up Capital and Labor,
You're in God's Country.

Where smiles are broader—freedom greater,
Every man is his own dictator,
And what's more, we are
So happy to have F.D.R.
Running God's country.

Unfortunately, it was *Hooray*'s book, not its score, that carried the attack against the rising war lust in Europe. The score, though, did contain one of Yip and Harold's liveliest rhythm and wordplay numbers, "Buds Won't Bud."

BUDS WON'T BUD

Verse.

When your world goes to pieces overnight,
Something's wrong, something's wrong
When you don't know your left shoe from your
   right
Something's wrong, very wrong
When the clock sips tea
As your head strikes three
And you feel like you're in a Walter Disney dream
Something's wrong with this entire scheme . . .

Chorus.

Buds won't bud
Breeze won't breeze and
Dew won't dew
One and one ain't even two
When the love you love
Won't love you

Buds won't bud
Chicks won't chick
Nicks won't nack
Black is white and white is black
When the love you love
Won't love back.

On account there's no accountin'
When you can't have the one you like
All your troubles just keep mountin'
And the world is on a sit-down strike

'Cause buds won't bud
Breeze won't breeze and
Dew won't dew
One and one is eighty-two
When the love you love
Won't love you

Second Chorus. Buds won't bud
Breeze won't breeze and
Crow won't crow
Eenie meenie's minus mo
When the love you love
Says "heigh ho"

Buds won't bud,
Notes won't note and
Knots won't knot
T's won't cross and
I's won't dot
When the hope you hope
Goes to pot

On account there's no accountin'
When you can't bring your dream about
All your troubles keep on mountin'
And the world is just a big black-out

'Cause buds won't bud
Breeze won't breeze and
Dew won't dew
C.O.D. is I.O.U.
When the dream you dream
Won't come true.

"Buds Won't Bud" had a history that extended well beyond the confines of *Hooray for What?* and illustrates Yip's tenacity with what he considered a good lyric. For Yip not only would insert his lyrics into otherwise neglected melodies, as with "Brother, Can You Spare a Dime?" He also would recycle some of his favorite lyrics that had languished in obscure songs that had not taken off. "You're the Cure for What Ails Me" was initially a 1930 lyric to a Gorney tune; in 1936, Yip reworked it to a new tune by Arlen, which Jolson performed in *The Singing Kid.* "Buds Won't Bud" went through *two* previous incarnations. It began life as "You Didn't Do Right by Me," to music by Dana Suesse, in the 1932 revue, *Ballyhoo.* It next resurfaced in altered fashion as "Cause You Won't Play House," to music by Morgan Lewis, in the revue *New Faces of 1934.* Suesse, for one, had no trouble with Yip resetting the song he had initially written with her. "It's not a very good tune, really," she said of the 1932 effort. "It's just a throwaway tune. It's the lyric that's darling."

In the 1932 version, the lyric differs from its final incarnation in its more normal beat and its greater reliance on explanatory sentences.

You Didn't Do Right by Me (1932)	Buds Won't Bud (1937)
The buds won't bud	Buds won't bud
The dew won't dew	Breeze won't breeze
One and one ain't even two	Dew won't dew
And the cuckoo clocks refuse to coo	One and one ain't even two
'Cause you didn't do right by me	When the one you love won't love you.
The buds won't bud	Buds won't bud
The seeds won't sprout	Chicks won't chick
The daisies all grow inside out	Nicks won't nack
And this thing called love's a Big washout	Black is white and white is black
'Cause you didn't do right by me	When the love you love won't love back

The Arlen version has a much more intricate rhythm, allowing Yip to produce a more immediate, sustained wordplay lyric. Arlen also permits him to drop the deadweight article *the* from the start of the line—and the revised Arlen-Harburg first line is so musically and lyrically arresting that, as with "Paper Moon," the title shifted from the stanza's last line to its first.

Hooray's most notable songs fall in the category of the Arlen-Harburg cautionary songs about love. "Down with Love" is one of Arlen's upbeat and somewhat offbeat rhythm songs. Yip's comical-lyrical assault on love begins with the standard paraphernalia—"Flowers and rice and shoes"—and quickly turns its attention to love-song rhetoric and love songs themselves ("Down with songs / That moan about Night and Day"). (The lyric and music were reinterpreted years later in the seventies by Barbra Streisand.)

DOWN WITH LOVE

Verse.   You, sons of Adam, you, daughters of Eve,
The time has come to take your love-torn hearts
Off your sleeve
Look, look about you
What do you see?
Love-sick, love-lorn, love-wrecked, love-worn
Boo-hoo-manity
There'll be no peace on earth until this curse
Is wiped off from this love mad universe
Are we mice or men? Can't you see the light?
Come you fellow victims, let's unite.

Chorus.   Down with love
The flowers and rice and shoes
Down with love
The root of all midnight blues
Down with things
That give you that well known pain
Take that moon and wrap it in cellophane

Down with love
Let's liquidate all its friends
Moon and June and roses and
Rainbow's ends
Down with songs
That moan about night and day
Down with love
Yes, take it away, away

Away, take it away
Give it back to the birds and the bees
And the Viennese

Down with eyes romantic and stupid
Down with sighs
Down with Cupid
Brother, let's stuff that dove
Down with love!

Yip's final lyrical comment on both life and love had an Arlenesque musical sound, even with an unconventional popular song structure (AAAB). The second verse, linking love to the suspension of other beliefs, is pure Yip:

LIFE'S A DANCE
(excerpt)

Let's pretend
That this moonlight and music
Is never to end
Let's deny
That we're here
In a fly-by-night world
'Neath a fly-by-night sky
Let's not ask
Of romance
Do our hearts stand a chance
Let the fiddle unravel the riddle
And on with the dance!

And Then, the Consequences

Hooray for What? went through substantial reconstruction in its pre-Broadway tryouts. Between its Boston opening on October 30, 1937, and its Broadway opening on December 1, 1937, choreographer Agnes de Mille and featured player-singers Kay Thompson and Hannah Williams were replaced. While the show never abandoned Yip's initial thematic impulse (indeed, Wynn gave interviews comparing the show to Kurt Weill's contemporaneous antiwar musical, *Johnny Johnson*), it was reshaped to include more and more of Wynn's unrelated antics.

Either because of or despite all the changes, the end result was a smash hit. The New York critics celebrated Wynn's return to the stage after his exile on radio. Yip's lyrics received considerable notice too: "Harold Arlen's felicitous score," wrote John Mason Brown, "is accompanied by E. Y. Harburg's bright lyrics." "A leisurely contemplation of them [Yip's lyrics]," wrote Sidney Whipple in the *Brooklyn Eagle*, "will reveal, we are sure, some extraordinarily joyful rhymes and considerable reason as well."

In one sense, *Hooray for What?* was the prototype for such later, more fully developed and distinctive Harburg musicals as *Finian's Rainbow* and *Flahooley.* With *Hooray,* Yip formulated his central strategy in creating a musical: the more serious and controversial the issue under discussion, the more fantastical and farcical that discussion must be. In *Hooray,* Yip was not yet in a position to give final shape to the fantasy—reflecting the still-embryonic nature of the book musical and of Yip's still quite limited power. Nonetheless, however cursorily, *Hooray* looked at the gathering war clouds in Europe and subjected the powers behind them to fantastical ridicule, and the show was a major commercial success. If Yip needed to reinforce his belief in the practicality of fantasy, *Hooray* provided all the evidence he needed.

Serendipitously, *Hooray* also played a key role in convincing a fledgling Hollywood producer that Yip and Harold were the right pair for a fantastical musical film he hoped to make. What convinced him in particular was one last song that Yip and Harold had written for *Hooray*. The song was at once hip and sentimental, a balance struck even in its title: "In the Shade of the New Apple Tree."

IN THE SHADE OF THE NEW APPLE TREE
(excerpt)

Verse.

A lot of leaves have fallen,
A lot of grass has grown,
In the apple orchard
Your granny once had known

Rouge your lips, sweet lady,
Light your cigarette,
Fly through the sky,
For no matter how you try
To change all nature, yet . . .

Chorus.

Underneath that shady apple tree
You recall a picture dear to me
Your dress is another's
But your smile is still your mother's
In the shade of the new apple tree

Though you bob your hair and show your knee
Though the world is new and fancy free
And the old moon's above you
And the words are still "I love you"
In the shade of the new apple tree

Gone are all the bonnets and bows
That set one's heart aflame,
Gone are the hoops and the bustles and the skirts
But a kiss is still the same

Hey, nonny oh, fortunately
There'll always be you and me
In the shade of the new apple tree.

"It's a sophisticated country song, if such can be," Alec Wilder has written. "And it's a delightful rollicker. It surprises the listener by not returning to the expected main strain after the release, though it does repeat the last phrase of it at the close." What "Apple Tree" combines is Arlen's swinging looseness—complete with octave leaps and a complex rhythm—with a gentle harmony and lightly nostalgic lyric.

It was apparently just what Arthur Freed had been looking for. A songwriter under contract at MGM, Freed had been energetically lobbying studio head Louis B. Mayer to let him produce musicals. Mayer had finally consented, though for his initial effort, Mayer apprenticed Freed to then-producer Mervyn LeRoy. Freed had his property in mind, too: a children's classic, the rights to which he had just persuaded Mayer to buy from Samuel Goldwyn. For Freed, "Apple Tree" was both swinging in a commercial sense and old-fashioned in accord with the needs of the picture. It somehow managed to express both the family values that MGM promoted and a hipness suitable for an age of swing.

Until *Hooray* had premiered, Arthur Freed had been considering Jerome Kern for the upcoming picture. "In the Shade of the New Apple Tree" changed his mind. "That song," Arlen told Max Wilk, "got us *The Wizard of Oz*."

The Scarecrow (Ray Bolger), the Tin Man (Jack Haley), and Dorothy (Judy Garland) with
Toto meet the Cowardly Lion (Bert Lahr) in the forest. Yip Harburg's lyrics for the character
of the Cowardly Lion masterfully portray the dilemma of a lion who needs "de noive."
Harburg and Arlen had created highly praised songs for Lahr in two earlier Broadway
musical revues; and it was Yip who got Lahr the role of the Lion. (Turner)

Chapter 5

The Wizard of Oz: Broadway in Hollywood

The basic laws of genuine fantasy are far more rigid than the laws that govern an ordinary screenplay, and *The Wizard of Oz* gained its indestructibility by adhering to these laws. As Harburg and Arlen accepted this assignment, I had no fears. Less experienced men might well have tried to reduce the movie to a "whimsy" level. Any kind of patronizing condescension in tone, *even unintentional,* is fatal to a project of this nature. Fantasy must appeal to the adult in all children, and the child in all adults, or it is neither fish, fowl nor good red herring. This may seem like a needless word of warning in your ear; but the major battles during the making of *Oz* were all at this level; and there were times when it looked as if we were fighting a losing battle against simple incomprehension.

—Noel Langley, screenwriter for *The Wizard of Oz*

"*You* got the job?" Jerome Kern asked Harold Arlen a bit incredulously upon learning that MGM had selected Arlen and Harburg to write the score for *The Wizard of Oz.* "There were plenty of other major songwriters who were damned unhappy and shocked when they'd heard that we'd gotten it," Arlen told Max Wilk, "because they'd all been sitting around, waiting for that job."

Oz was regarded in Hollywood songwriting circles as a project worth waiting for. The film was intended as MGM's riposte to Disney's critical and commercial triumph, *Snow White and the Seven Dwarfs,* and the studio had made clear that it would spare no expense to bring L. Frank Baum's children's novel to the screen. *Oz* would be shot in what was still the fledgling Technicolor process, making it one of the first feature-length live-action musicals to be filmed in color. It was budgeted at just over $2 million (it eventually came in at $2,777,000); the Astaire-Rogers *Top Hat,* by way of comparison, had cost $620,000 when it was filmed three years earlier. *Oz* was to be the costliest picture MGM had essayed in years. Moreover, Yip told Aljean Harmetz (author of the excellent history, *The Making of "The Wizard of Oz"*), MGM didn't really anticipate making its money back: "Once a year," said Yip, "they did a loser for prestige." *Oz* was to be Metro's prestige loser of 1939.

119

In the end, of course, it proved to be a good deal more than that: a harbinger of the new, integrated musical that was to emerge in the forties; one of the most enduring fantasies ever filmed; an almost universally known monument of American popular culture. It was, as Aljean Harmetz argues persuasively, more the product of the studio and the studio system than of any one individual. And yet, besides L. Frank Baum, if there is one person preeminently responsible not just for the charm of the musical but for its coherence, it is Yip.

Yip's impact on *Oz*, in turn, was largely due to the backing he received from Arthur Freed, perhaps the most sympathetic producer for whom Yip was ever to work. In actuality, Freed's role on *Oz* was that of an uncredited associate producer. The credited, and more than nominal, producer was Mervyn LeRoy, an aging boy-wonder director at Warner Bros. whom Louis B. Mayer had brought to MGM in hopes that LeRoy could fill the void created by the death of production chief Irving Thalberg. But as a stranger to both film producing and musicals, LeRoy chafed in his new role and would return after a few years to directing.

Freed had been a successful journeyman lyricist under contract at Metro with his partner, composer Nacio Herb Brown (the Allan Jones–Kitty Carlisle songs in *A Night at the Opera* are theirs). He had also become extremely close to studio head Louis B. Mayer, and it was either at Freed's insistence or LeRoy's (depending on who told the story) that Mayer purchased the rights to *Oz* from Samuel Goldwyn. It was surely at Freed's insistence that Mayer granted Freed's wish to become a producer by assigning him to the picture as a kind of musical associate to LeRoy. In consequence, though, the power behind *Oz* was fragmented from the start. Freed was not allowed to produce by himself, as he desired; LeRoy was not allowed to produce and direct, as he desired. In *Oz*, it seems Freed had total control over only one talent decision—the selection of the songwriters.

Freed and Yip had never met when Freed decided to hire the team of Arlen and Harburg for the *Oz* score, but Freed was thoroughly conversant with their work. On one level, the selection of Arlen and Harburg was not surprising: of the lyricists capable of sustained comic writing in the vein *Oz* required, Yip headed the pack. In 1938, Ira Gershwin was still recovering from the shock of his brother's death, and Larry Hart, for all his brilliance, did not spring to mind as a lyricist for children. *Hooray for What?* had provided whatever evidence Freed required that Arlen and Harburg were capable of sustaining comedy and sentiment. "Arthur had sensed my love of whimsy," Yip told Harmetz. "And he was right. He told me to read *The Wizard of Oz*. I read the book and loved it. It was my sort of thing."

"Harburg had a great sense of fantasy in his lyrics," Freed told John Lahr. Indeed he did—beginning with *Oz*. At the time Freed hired him, Yip had demonstrated his capacity for dealing with serious material in a whimsical and farcical manner, for lyrics of a childlike playfulness, for sentiment that was devoid of sentimentality. That was enough to commend him for the project. If Freed was able somehow to intuit that Yip possessed, beyond those qualities, an aptitude for fantasy, then the credit is all Freed's, for Yip had yet to work in a fantastical vein. (More likely, Freed's comment to Lahr is perfect twenty-twenty hindsight.)

It wasn't that Freed and Yip were on the same political wavelength; far from it. "He was a flag waver of the first order," Yip told Harmetz.

> He was a reactionary and he detested everything I stood for. But that didn't stop him from respecting me artistically. After I was blacklisted, he tried like hell to get me back. . . . He had a real feeling for musical things. Underneath the crude, brusque exterior was that lovely, sensitive feeling for music and lyrics. What Freed felt [about Yip's work] was that it had a poetic value. The average producers, commercial fellows in pictures, didn't refer to it that way. [They'd say,] "You write college stuff."

Yip's affinity for *Oz* ran deeper than his love of whimsy or his previously unexercised capacity for fantasy—deeper, in fact, than Yip himself may have realized at the time. For it was *Oz* that put Yip in touch with the political parable cloaked in fantasy—a form in which Yip was to do his most personalized work in the years to follow. As Henry Littlefield surmised in his 1964 article in *American Quarterly*, L. Frank Baum's novel provides a political allegory for grown-ups neatly encased within a fairy tale for children. Baum wrote *Oz* in 1900, amid the wreckage of the failed Populist movement of the nineties. As Baum saw it, the potential coalition of farmers (the Scarecrow) and urban industrial workers (the Tin Man) had been subverted by the political chicanery of financial interests and the shortcomings of the Populists' own leaders, most particularly presidential candidate William Jennings Bryan—the model, alas, for the Cowardly Lion. Littlefield suggests that Dorothy's dispatching of the wicked witches (the forces of finance); befriending the Scarecrow, Tin Man, and Lion; and exposing the wizard (the federal government) as a powerless humbug was Baum's fairy-tale version of a political transformation he devoutly wished.

Yip never gave any indication that he (much less Arthur Freed, Mervyn LeRoy, et al.) was aware of the particulars of Baum's subterranean politics. The cottage industry of Baum scholarship that unearthed the politics of *Oz* did not yet exist in 1938 (and may never have come into existence at all had the film not given the book renewed life). But *Oz* has broader politics to which Yip was acutely attuned, as two of his most crucial interventions on the project attest. While Yip had no reason to suspect Baum intended the death of the Wicked

Witch of the East to symbolize an eclipse of eastern (i.e., Wall Street) financial interests, he responded to her death and the subsequent celebration of the Munchkins by excising a spoken scene and supplanting it with an exultant mini-operetta. "Ding-Dong, The Witch Is Dead" is among other things a song of liberation in the form of a comic production number. Similarly, it was Yip who authored the dialogue in the scene near the conclusion of the film in which the wizard, stripped of the appearance of magical powers, grants the wishes of Dorothy and company with altogether worldly responses. The wizardry of *Oz* was only a paper moon; Baum has the exposed wizard say, "I have been making believe." *Oz* provided Yip with the first of his happy endings involving demystification to which he would turn again in subsequent musicals in which he was more in control of crafting the story.

Ultimately, *Oz* defined Yip no less than Yip helped define *Oz*. The lyricist for Munchkins was to become the lyricist for leprechauns and genies and the author of shows of fantasy and magic that ended as parables of magic explained and humans empowered. Arthur Freed was right: *Oz* was most definitely Yip's "sort of thing." But Baum's book became Yip's musical.

An Integrated Score

Yip's initial and most critical contribution to *Oz* was his suggestion that the picture have a fully integrated score—that is, song and dance, far from interrupting the plot (as was common practice), would actually be the medium through which plot unfolded and character was delineated. It was a daring proposal. In 1938, only a handful of musicals on Broadway (chiefly, the Kern-Hammerstein *Show Boat* and the Gershwin-Kaufman-Ryskind *Of Thee I Sing* political trilogy) and in Hollywood (chiefly, Ernst Lubitsch's *One Hour with You,* the Rouben Mamoulian–Rodgers and Hart *Love Me Tonight,* the Rodgers and Hart–Lewis Milestone *Hallelujah, I'm a Bum,* the Rodgers and Hart *The Phantom President,* and the Mamoulian-Kern-Hammerstein *High, Wide, and Handsome*) had taken this form. (Mamoulian's *Oklahoma!* was yet to come, in 1943.) Moreover, none of these shows or films (except the 1937 *High, Wide, and Handsome*) had been made after 1933. The pseudorecitative, the versified speech that Ira Gershwin had realized on stage and Larry Hart on the screen, was thought of as incompatible with the more naturalistic style of the more recent Astaire-dominated musical screen—that is, when it was thought of at all.

Only, *Oz* was not to be a naturalistic film in any event; if it was to work, it required a nonnaturalistic style. Accordingly, Yip told Harmetz, when he suggested the integrated score ideas to Freed, the associate producer "accepted the integrated concept quickly and was very encouraging."

But the creation of an integrated musical film required a much more comprehensive coordination of song, script, casting, direction—all the elements of the film—than was usually the case. The common denominator in virtually all the earlier integrated musicals was that they were made by a powerful producer-director—Lubitsch, Mamoulian, Milestone—who controlled every aspect of the film's development. On *Love Me Tonight,* for instance, Mamoulian commissioned and received the Rodgers and Hart songs before anyone had begun work on the script, and he then supervised the script's development around the score.

But there was no such figure on *The Wizard of Oz.* There was a producer, new to both producing and to musicals; there was an associate producer, also new to producing and with circumscribed power; and both were working on other projects at the same time. No director was assigned to the picture until shortly before the actual shooting commenced; then, it required four directors to bring in the finished product. Eleven separate writers would work on the screenplay.

This was not the most promising of terrains on which to attempt an integrated musical, but Yip soon found that Freed was willing to entrust more and more responsibility to him in order to realize the picture's potential. Fortuitously, Yip and Harold were signed on to the picture at a rather early date, May 19, 1938. The shooting script was not finalized until October 10, by which time Yip had become the script's editor as well as the lyricist.

Some of Yip's growing power over the script and the picture was implicit in the very notion of integration. Early on, Yip excised the scene of Dorothy's arrival in Munchkinland and substituted the operetta. Indeed, both scenes of social exposition, Munchkinland and the arrival in the Emerald City, are carried entirely in song. The dance sequences also flowed from the song sequences, and, like Bert Lahr and Ray Bolger, the dance director, Bobby Connolly, had also worked with Yip many times ever since Universal's film *Moonlight and Pretzels* in 1933.

More of Yip's growing responsibility was a function of the proliferation of screenwriters. Among the eleven writers who took a crack at *Oz* were Herman J. Mankiewicz (who later scripted *Citizen Kane*), Herbert Fields (who had written the librettos to a number of Rodgers and Hart Broadway shows), and Yip's fellow light-versifier Samuel Hoffenstein (who had a cowriting credit on *Love Me Tonight*). *Oz's* primary screenwriter, though, was a young Englishman named Noel Langley. Langley had finished a first draft of the script around the time Arlen and Harburg came aboard, revised it through late spring and early summer, and then had his material rewritten in a more domesticated vein (e.g., the "There's no place like home" ending) during midsummer by the team of Florence Ryerson and Edgar Allen Woolf.

Langley did not take kindly to the revisions; he made it clear to Freed and LeRoy that if the revisions stayed in, he wanted out. But it was neither Freed nor LeRoy who decided between Langley and the Ryerson-Woolf team; it was Yip.

"Harburg supported Langley's versions," Harmetz writes. "And Arthur Freed both respected and trusted Harburg." "In the end," Langley told Harmetz, "Harburg became so militant that Freed supported him. If it hadn't been for Harburg going to Freed and blowing his top . . ."

As had been the case with *The Show Is On* and *Hooray for What?* Yip had become the "show doctor" on *Oz,* and the editor of all the scripts. Freed gave him the screenplay drafts, Yip told one radio interviewer, and

> it was an acrostic, a crossword puzzle. I said to Arthur Freed, "Give me time and let me think the thing out musically and lyrically. Let me write a score for the thing that will tell the story and then we will hang some of the best scenes on to that score. Now, that was a completely maverick way of working, but I thought it was the musical feel that was going to swing this show.

The story and characters, of course, as in all well-integrated musical plays, led the way for the songwriters.

Yip's goal of an integrated musical involved shaping the script around the songs. "Songs seem simple," he told Harmetz.

> They're not. The process of putting music in is very intricate. One function of song is to simplify, to take the clutter out of too much plot and too many characters, to telescope everything into one emotional idea. You have to throw out the unnecessary. And lots of things not in the script have to be invented to make the songs work.

"I knew how to change plot around to make the plot fit the songs," Yip told Harmetz. Yip was also a master of how to "set-up" or lead the way into a song.

> I liked a lot of things Langley had, and threw the other stuff out. I threw out the Munchkin sequence and lyricized it, the whole ten minutes in rhyme. Never done before or since. I edited the whole thing and brought back Langley's story, which was simpler. And added my own.

"Harburg's only screen credit on *The Wizard of Oz,*" Harmetz concludes, "was 'Lyrics by E. Y. Harburg.' But the final shooting script is actually his blend of Ryerson, Woolf, and Langley" and Yip's own writing, which included the transitions; the Wizard's speech bestowing brains, heart, and courage; the lines for Bert Lahr and Frank Morgan, which appear in the rough drafts of his lyrics and were reset in the script; and all the dialogue that "set-up" the songs.

In the judgment of Harmetz, "Harburg had been allowed to manipulate the script with a freedom that had been given to no other lyricist." And M. P. Hearn, who edited the screenplay of *Oz* on the occasion of its fiftieth anniversary, has written:

> Although he received no screen credit for his considerable contribution to the screenplay, Harburg was brought in to work out a compromise from the various drafts. . . . Harburg's revision therefore was a judicious blending of Langley with Ryerson and Woolf as well as additional dialogue of his own.

Casting

Nor were the lyrics and script the full extent of Yip's creative participation. *Oz's* songs are crafted to particular performers, and Yip was given a major say in the casting process. Not coincidentally, the Lion, the Scarecrow, and the Tin Man had all worked with Yip before: Bert Lahr on *Life Begins at 8:40* and *The Show Is On,* Ray Bolger in *8:40,* and Buddy Ebsen (the original Tin Man before he was hospitalized by a costume-induced infection) in the 1934 *Ziegfeld Follies.* ("I wanted Buddy very much," Yip told Harmetz.)

"Harburg promoted Lahr for the part of the lion," John Lahr writes in *Notes on a Cowardly Lion.*

> As a lyricist who could imitate his sound, he began ad-libbing his lines from the script to the producers. " 'Put up your dukes! Put up your paws!' Can you imagine Bert doing that?" LeRoy and Freed liked the idea.

> "I wanted him for the part of the Cowardly Lion [Yip told John Lahr] because the role was one of the things that *The Wizard of Oz* stands for: the search for some basic human necessity. . . . Call it anxiety, call it neurosis. . . . When the Cowardly Lion admits that he lacks courage, everybody's heart is out to him. He must be somebody who embodies all this pathos, sweetness, and yet puts on this comic bravura. Bert had that quality to such a wonderful degree."

Yip also lobbied heavily to cast W. C. Fields in the part of the wizard. Of the bogus awards ceremony near the picture's end, Yip told Harmetz,

> I wrote this scene for W. C. Fields, not Frank Morgan. Can't you just hear Fields saying his lines with that inimitable delivery? I demonstrated the part to Louis B. Mayer and others with all the passion of my schoolboy experience. Thank you, P.S. 64.

Indeed, a great deal of the wizard's part was crafted for Fields and left essentially unaltered in the final script—the balloon ascension material, for instance, builds on running gags in any number of Fields's pictures.

The Politics of Integration

At the time he came to *Oz,* Yip was familiar with the earlier Mamoulian/ Lubitsch/Rodgers and Hart efforts at integrated film musicals. "The trouble was," he told Harmetz, "those stories didn't give the lyric writer enough leeway. This story did." But unless leeway is defined as a setting in fantasy, the stories in the Rodgers and Hart pictures in particular afforded Larry Hart remarkable leeway. The leeway Yip experienced in *The Wizard of Oz* had little to do with the story and everything to do with the peculiar power vacuum into which he had been thrown.

The Wizard of Oz stands alone among American film musicals as the one integrated production that was *not* primarily the product of a producer-director. Producer-directors were not common at MGM, where control of the picture was vested more nebulously in "the studio." Until 1936, there was nothing nebulous about the MGM system: at the center of a system of rotating writers and directors and talents appearing and vanishing from a project was the head of production, Irving Thalberg. "What makes the unity?" a bewildered foreign visitor to the studio asks Monroe Stahr, Scott Fitzgerald's fictionalization of Thalberg in *The Last Tycoon.* "I'm the unity," Stahr replies.

With Thalberg's death in 1936, MGM sought to give primacy to the studio's individual producers, the vast majority of whom, however, lacked the creative vision and knowledge to impose a distinctive touch on their pictures. Yip's leeway on *Oz* was an accident of timing in the post-Thalberg vacuum: Freed was not yet powerful enough to call the shots nor experienced enough to know what all those shots should have been; LeRoy had the power Freed lacked but had even less relevant experience than Freed. Yip by no means controlled *Oz:* his songs were cut from the picture's last half-hour, he loathed the ending, he was ultimately powerless in the postproduction battle over whether to cut "Over the Rainbow" from the picture. But *Oz* remains the only movie in film history where the lyricist provides, not just the spirit, but the unity. In Harmetz's assessment,

> *Love Me Tonight* achieved its unity through the outline in Rouben Mamoulian's head. *An American in Paris, Singin' in the Rain, Meet Me in St. Louis* would achieve their special unities through Arthur Freed oversee-ing the sensibilities of such directors as Donen and Minnelli. In *The Wizard of Oz,* it was Harburg's involvement with a script "which allowed a song to lead everywhere. All a director had to do was follow the lyrics."

Throughout his career, the scope of Yip's responsibilities grew and changed with the changes in the musical. From his apprenticeship through his work at

Rehearsal for the "Good News" radio program, June 29, 1939. Among the participants, *standing, left to right,* Bert Lahr, Ray Bolger, MGM executive L. K. Sidney, Yip, composer/conductor Meredith Willson, music publisher Harry Link, and, seated at the piano, Judy Garland and Harold Arlen. (Courtesy of Edward Jablonski.)

Warner Bros. in 1937, he was a lyricist only, on revues, on essentially bookless shows—though by the time of *The Show Is On,* he was considered sufficiently conversant with the entire form to be called in as a show doctor. On *Hooray for What?* and *The Wizard of Oz,* he functioned not merely as lyricist but as overall editor—but these were transitional shows, part star-based, part book musicals, and his own control on each project was tentative and limited.

In 1938, though, Yip's rising authority and musical expertise coincided with changes in the musical genre and changes in MGM's musical pecking order and vested him with uncommon influence over *The Wizard of Oz.* Aljean Harmetz is right to assert that *Oz* is the studio's film more than it is any one individual's, but it owes some of its cast, and its coherence and its unity—not to mention its lyrics—to Yip. And unity—as explained through the ages from Aristotle to Coleridge to Frank Rich—is what distinguishes a true work of art.

The Score

In the Harburg Collection at Yale University library is a bound copy of *The Wizard of Oz* score inscribed by Arlen: "For Yip—Ran across this score some time ago—knowing it's the kind of job you'd like to do, thought you'd be interested in looking it over—Harold."

The *Oz* score is not only remarkably distinctive; it is remarkably unified, dramaturgically as well as musically. The entire social exposition of *Oz*, everything we see in Munchkinland at one end and the Emerald City at the other, is carried in musical numbers (the two longest numbers in the film: "Ding-Dong, the Witch Is Dead" and "The Merry Old Land of Oz"). Both numbers are abruptly terminated by the Wicked Witch of the West (the first time, appearing in a puff of smoke; the second time, skywriting "Surrender Dorothy" over the Emerald City), the truncation of a production number being the very height of antisocial behavior. Moreover, within the overall distinctiveness of style of the *Oz* score, the lyrics to the songs for the Scarecrow, Lion, and Tin Man ("If I Only Had a Brain/Heart/Nerve," and "If I Were King of the Forest") have their own distinct lyrical characteristics: these are the lyrics of comic neologisms and deliberately forced rhymes.

Virtually all of Yip and Harold's material is concentrated within the middle 45 minutes of a 101-minute picture, the only exception being "Over the Rainbow." From the initial appearance of the Munchkins to the conclusion of Lahr's "If I Were King of the Forest," eleven musical numbers (including the three reprises of "We're Off to See the Wizard") are performed—a number of them scarcely over a minute's duration, the Munchkin operetta stretching to six minutes, ten seconds. In all, 43 percent of this time—effectively, the middle forty-five minutes in *Oz*—is taken up by musical numbers. This is an uncommonly high percentage of time to be devoted to numbers, particularly inasmuch as the numbers contain a good deal of narrative-related singing and rather little dancing. (By way of comparison, film and dance critic Arlene Croce calculates that *Follow the Fleet* and *Roberta,* two Astaire-Rogers films, each devote 29 percent of their running time to the numbers.)

As far as Yip and Harold were concerned, more of *Oz* should have proceeded in this manner. "The Jitterbug," which ended up on the cutting room floor, was the one number in which the four singing principals would have performed together, and Arlen and Harburg also sought to reprise "Ding-Dong" upon the death-by-melting of the Wicked Witch of the West. ("She met her fate / We liquidate-d her.") But for the middle forty-five minutes, *Oz* unfolds primarily through song and production number—virtually in comic operetta.

The Signature Song

Oz begins, of course, with the one song not set in *Oz*, surely, the most widely known song Yip and Harold together or with others ever wrote. Though "Over the Rainbow" was the first song in the picture, it was actually the last to be written and the last to be filmed. Nothing on "Over the Rainbow" came easy, Yip told the audience during one of the Ninety-second Street Y lyricists' evenings:

> You always have trouble writing a ballad. Of course, I was writing for a situation of a little girl who was desperate, had never seen anything beyond an arid Kansas where there was no color in her life; there were no flowers [according to Baum]. It was all brown and sepia and at a moment when she was troubled in a childish way, she wanted to escape in a song of escape—where could she go? The only thing colorful that she's ever seen in her life was the rainbow.

> *The book had no reference to a rainbow.* In fact, it gave the makers of the picture, the producers, the director, the idea of having the first part done in routine everyday black and white, so that when she got over the rainbow, she got into a colorful Munchkinland. So I had that idea in mind: of a little girl wanting something, a place somewhere that was over that rainbow and I told Harold about it and we went to work on a tune.

Arlen and Harburg agreed that the ballad should be "a song of yearning," Yip told Harmetz. "Its object would be to delineate Dorothy and to give an emotional touch to the scene where she is frustrated and in trouble." Only, Arlen could not get the music for that emotion, that situation. "I can't tell you the misery that a composer goes through when the whole score is written but he hasn't got that big theme song that Louis B. Mayer is waiting for," Yip told the Y audience. "The contract was for fourteen weeks and we were on our fourteenth week. We didn't get paid after the fourteenth. He surely sweated it out, but he couldn't get a tune."

The melody finally came to Arlen as he was out driving with his wife. As Arlen biographer Edward Jablonski recounts it,

> He and Anya had decided to drive to a movie at Grauman's Chinese Theater—that is, Anya drove, the composer was too nervous with anxiety about the ballad he hoped to find. They had reached the spot where the original Schwab's drugstore was located, on Sunset Boulevard, when the "broad, long-lined, melody" came to Arlen; he jotted it down in the car. "It was as if the Lord said, 'Well, here it is, now stop worrying about it!'"

Sheet music cover, front and back, for "Over the Rainbow." (Collection of Harburg Estate.)

"He called me," Yip told the Y. "It was twelve o'clock at night and he said, 'Please, please, come right over. I've got the tune.'" (This was not so exceptional as it may sound: Yip and Harold generally worked at night on *Oz* so that Yip could play tennis and Harold golf during the daytime. Writing the score may have been fraught with anxiety, but the working conditions were nothing to complain about.)

"I ran to meet him at home," Yip wrote in 1973.

> He approached the piano with the usual blue-eyes-toward-heaven ritual and played the first eight bars of "Over the Rainbow." My heart fell. He played it with such symphonic sweep and bravura that my first reaction was: "Oh, no, not for little Dorothy! That's for Nelson Eddy." Harold, always sensitive, never aggressive or defensive, was shattered. His Hill-crest [Country Club] suntan suddenly took flight. I was miserable. I confess with head bowed low: the song almost suffered extinction by me while it was still aborning.

"For two weeks after," Yip told the Y audience,

> without money from Metro, he was still working on that tune. Finally, he called me over and said, "I *feel* this tune; this is a great tune. Now you must write it." When a composer like Harold says that, then you've got to, as Willy Loman's wife says, pay attention.
>
> When Ira and George were working on a thing, and they met an impasse, they'd always call me or call Harold. So I called in Ira. I said, "Ira, Harold's got a tune here and here's the situation," and I told him. I was too involved emotionally to analyze the thing, to put my finger on it to communicate it to Harold. But Ira, being a third person, was more clearheaded and less involved. He said, "Harold, play that tune with a little more rhythm." Harold sat down and said, "What do you mean? This way?" [When] he played, the thing cleared itself up for me, and Ira said, "See, it's the way Harold's playing it." Harold and I were both too intense to have figured that thing out. I said, "Ira, you're right, that's fine."
>
> Next Harold couldn't get a middle. Well, Harold had a little dog, Pan, a silly little dog, who ran away. Harold had a little whistle for him that went like this [whistles middle tune—"Someday I'll wish upon a star"]. I said, "Harold . . ." This is the crazy life we lead. This is the way songs are written.

It was an almost automatic thing for Arlen to do. "We'd instinctively give each other clues about what we were thinking," Yip recalled nearly forty years later. "I'd incorporate his ideas into my lyrics. He'd incorporate my ideas into his music."

Yip remembered bits and pieces of what had happened when Arlen then left the ballad in his hands. "The girl was in trouble," he told Harmetz,

> but it was the trouble of a child. In *Oliver,* the little boy was in a similar situation, was running away. Someone thought up a song for him, "Where is Love?" How can a little boy sing about an adult emotion? I would never write "Where is Love?" for a child. That's analytical adult thinking, not childish thinking. This little girl thinks: *My life is messed up. Where do I run?* The song has to be full of childish pleasures. Of lemon drops. The book had said Kansas was an arid place where not even flowers grew. The only colorful thing Dorothy saw, occasionally, would be the rainbow.

> "Over the Rainbow Is Where I Want To Be" was my title, the title I gave Harold. A title has to ring a bell, has to blow a couple of Roman candles off. But he gave me a tune with those first two notes [an octave apart]. I tried *I'll go over the rainbow, Someday over the rainbow* or *the other side of the rainbow.* I had difficulty coming to the idea of *Somewhere.* For a while I thought I would just leave those first two notes out. It was a long time before I came to *Somewhere over the rainbow.*

Yip then wrote the dialogue leading into the song:

> *Aunt Em.* Now, Dorothy dear—stop imagining things . . . you always get yourself into a fret over nothing. You just help us out today and find yourself a place where you won't get into any trouble!

> *Dorothy.* Some place where there's no trouble . . . do you think there is such a place, Toto? (*dreamily to herself*) There must be. Not a place you can get to by a boat or a train. It's far far away . . . (*music starts*) Behind the moon . . . Beyond the rain.

OVER THE RAINBOW

Verse [not
sung in film].

When all the world is a hopeless jumble
And the raindrops tumble all around
Heaven opens a magic lane

When all the clouds darken up the skyway
There's a rainbow highway to be found
Leading from your window pane
To a place behind the sun
Just a step beyond the rain

Chorus.

Somewhere over the rainbow
Way up high
There's a land that I heard of
Once in a lullaby

Somewhere over the rainbow
Skies are blue,
And the dreams that you dare to dream
Really do come true

Someday I'll wish upon a star
And wake up where the clouds are far behind me
Where troubles melt like lemon drops
Away above the chimney tops
That's where you'll find me

Somewhere over the rainbow
Bluebirds fly,
Birds fly over the rainbow
Why then oh why can't I?

If happy little bluebirds fly
Beyond the rainbow
Why oh why can't I?

"What makes Harold Arlen, and a few more people like Arlen, the geniuses they are," Yip once said, is

> dramatic feel, which is more than just songwriting. It's got to be something that moves an audience, either to laughter or to tears. Anything in between is placid and becomes a pop song. . . . One person is born with a sense of dramaturgy, another not. That's what makes the difference between the great musical comedy writers and those that write pop songs.

The dramaturgy of "Over the Rainbow" lies in the fact that it *is* a song for Nelson Eddy as well as for little Dorothy. The octave leap with which Arlen begins the front phrase, and the other graceful leaps of the first sixteen bars situate this song of yearning in emotional overdrive from the start. The challenge facing Harold and Yip was to balance the power of that emotion against the poignancy and delicacy of its childish context. Even Arlen's front phrase begins to address that task, as the leaps grow smaller in lines three and four of the first stanza. These in turn prepare the way for the "little whistle" of the release.

Yip's lyric follows a similar progression. *His* front phrase needed to stress the yearning, the distance suggested by Arlen's octave leap. He started out, he once noted, with long vowels:

> You have to work for sound and the emotion of the tune. For example, for "Over the Rainbow" I was given a tune which, for the first part, I couldn't use consonants. I couldn't write, "Say Bud." It wouldn't sing. You have to use open vowels. "Somewhere o-ver the rainbow. . . ." The "o" comes right in—that is an important part of the writing. So, on top of the playfulness of words, on top of the meaning and the poetry, the sound has an importance.

> Somewhere ōver the rāinbōw
> Wāy up hīgh
> or: Skīes are blūe

But in the third and fourth lines of the first stanza, long vowel sounds vanish. As Arlen's leaps subside, the long vowels are supplanted by short (notably, "a," "of," and "once," which Yip employs as an ordering if subtle internal rhyme). The stanza concludes with the song's first clearly child word: *lullaby.* The child words are concentrated, though, in the more musically childlike release.

The final testimony to Yip and Harold's struggle to reconcile "Rainbow"'s power with its context is their decision to bring back the release to end the song. "Rainbow" has an AABAB' structure—as if Arlen and Harburg feared throwing the song out of balance by ending with the main phrase.

There is, of course, no neat division between a child's song and an adult's, and in many of the masterpieces of twenties and thirties theater song, a childish wistfulness lurks as a subtext. "Someone to Watch over Me" and "The Man I Love," for instance, contain a child's yearning for security within the lyrics of adult romantic yearning. Yip's analysis of Dorothy's "childish thinking" further serves, however inadvertently, to illuminate the extent of the overlap. "This little girl," he told Harmetz, "thinks, 'My life is messed up. Where do I run?'" Is the final stanza of "April in Paris," then, with its sudden and melodramatic "Whom can I run to?" an example of childish thinking? A great many ballads, in fact, work on an emotional level in which childish emotions underpin an adult context. If "Over the Rainbow" is one of the precious few songs introduced by a child to become a grown-up hit and an enduring classic, it is precisely because it balances so elegantly the childish context with a great emotional force.

The final element in "Rainbow"'s balance is its singer. Judy Garland was a sixteen-year-old playing a child when she played Dorothy. (She had been discovered in 1934 by Burton Lane in a downtown Los Angeles theater as one of a trio called the Gumm Sisters. She was signed to an MGM contract and given a succession of minor parts before she was cast as Dorothy.) She brought to the song's emotion far more authority than any twelve-year-old could have, without any sacrifice of a child's innocence. One winces at the thought of Shirley Temple, MGM's first choice for the part, tackling the song. King Vidor's direction of the scene also seems premised on a realization of the need for balance between adolescence and childhood: Dorothy swings on the wheel of a harvester and eventually sits on its seat, as if she wishes to leave but cannot—but she concludes the song glancing at, then playing with, then embracing Toto.

For Yip, the ballad was also significant for adding one more image to his personal collection. There are rainbows in earlier Harburg lyrics, but they are characteristically only songwriting conventions (indeed, in "Down with Love" from *Hooray for What?*, "rainbows ends" are among the pieces of romantic detritus to be discarded). In *Oz*, though, the rainbow is Yip's invention—his metaphor for dreaming, his device to propel a black-and-white consciousness into color, the most colorful thing, he realized, that Dorothy had ever seen. After *Oz*, the rainbow was no mere rhetorical device for Yip, but a complex symbol of human aspiration. In later years, Yip sometimes called himself a "rainbow hustler."

When Dorothy crosses over into Oz, the film shifts not only from black and white to color but also from prose to poetry, speech to song. "I loved the idea of having the freedom to do lyrics that were not just songs but *scenes*," Yip told Max Wilk.

It gave me wider scope. Not just 32-bar songs, but what would amount to the acting out of entire scenes, dialogues in verse and set to Harold's modern music. All of that had to be thought out by us and then brought in and shown to the director so he could see what we were getting at. Things like the three Lullaby girls and the three tough kids who represented the Lollipop Guild. And the Coroner . . . it wasn't in the book.

It was in the film, with all dialogue and lyrics by Yip:

Dorothy. But, if you please, what are Munchkins?

Glinda. The little people who live in this land. It's Munchkinland. And you are their national heroine, my dear . . . (*To Munchkins*) It's all right. You may all come out and thank her. [She starts singing in a conversational tone so that it is hard to realize, at first, that a number has begun.]

> Come out
> Come out
> Wherever you are
> And meet the young lady
> Who fell from a star
>
> She fell from the sky
> She fell very far
> And Kansas she says
> Is the name of the star

Munchkins.
> Kansas she says
> Is the name of the star

Glinda.
> She brings you good news
> Or haven't you heard
> When she fell out of Kansas
> A miracle occurred . . .

Dorothy.
> It really was no miracle
> What happened was just this
> The wind began to switch
> The house to pitch
> And suddenly the hinges started to unhitch
> Just then the witch
> To satisfy an itch
> Went flying on her broomstick
> Thumbing for a hitch
> And oh, what happen'd then was rich

Munchkins.	The house began to pitch
	The kitchen took a slitch
	It landed on the wicked witch
	In the middle of a ditch
	Which was not a healthy sitch-uation
	For a wicked witch
	Who began to twitch
	And was reduced to just a stitch
	Of what was once the wicked witch
A Munchkin.	We thank you very sweetly
	For doing it so neatly
2nd Munchkin.	You killed her so completely
	That we thank you very sweetly
Glinda.	Let the joyous news be spread:
	The wicked old witch at last is dead!
Munchkins.	Ding dong! The witch is dead
	Which old witch?
	The wicked witch
	Ding dong, the wicked witch is dead
	Wake up, you sleepy head
	Rub your eyes,
	Get out of bed
	Wake up, the wicked witch is dead
	She's gone where the goblins go,
	Below, below, below, yo-ho
	Let's open up and sing
	And ring the bells out
	Ding dong, the merry-o
	Sing it high,
	Sing it low,
	Let them know the wicked witch is dead
Munchkin Mayor.	As Mayor of the Munchkin city
	In the County of The Land of Oz
	I welcome you most regally
	But we've got to verify it legally
	To see
2nd Munchkin.	To see
Munchkin Mayor.	If she

2nd Munchkin.   If she

Munchkin Mayor.   Is morally, ethically,

2nd Munchkin.   Spiritually, physically,

Both.   Positively,
Undeniably,
Absolutely
And reliably
Dead.

Coroner.   As Coroner
I must aver
I thoroughly
Examined her
And she's not only merely dead.
She's really most sincerely dead.

Mayor.   Then this is a day of independence
For all the Munchkins and their descendants.
Yes, let the joyous news be spread
That the wicked old witch at last is
Dead!

Munchkins.   Ding dong! The witch is dead
Which old witch?
The wicked witch
Ding dong, the wicked witch is dead

Wake up, you sleepy head
Rub your eyes,
Get out of bed
Wake up, the wicked witch is dead

She's gone where the goblins go,
Below, below, below, yo-ho
Let's open up and sing
And ring the bells out
Ding dong, the merry-o
Sing it high,
Sing it low,
Let them know the wicked witch is dead.

Lullabye League   We represent the Lullabye League
Munchkins.   The Lullabye League

	The Lullabye League
	And in the name of the Lullabye League
	We wish to welcome you to Munchkinland.

Lollypop Guild	We represent the Lollypop Guild
Munchkins.	The Lollypop Guild
	The Lollypop Guild
	And in the name of the Lollypop Guild
	We wish to welcome you to Munchkinland.

All Munchkins.	We welcome you to Munchkinland
	Tra la la la la
	Tra la la
	Tra la la
	Tra la la la la la

| *Mayor.* | From now on you'll be history |

| *1st Munchkin.* | You'll be hist— |

| *2nd Munchkin.* | You'll be hist— |

Mayor.	You'll be history.
	And we will glorify your name
	You will be a bust

| *1st Munchkin.* | Be a bust |

| *2nd Munchkin.* | Be a bust |

| *Mayor.* | In the Hall of Fame |

Munchkins.	Tra la la la la
	Tra la la
	Tra la la
	Tra la la la la laaaaaaaa

[Wicked Witch of the West appears in red smoke
and spoken dialogue resumes]

The Munchkinland operetta is more formally ambitious than anything Yip
was to undertake in his later Broadway shows—in part because it comments
upon a social formality and order that was fading from the American scene. The
sequence isn't simply musicalized speech; it's musicalized speeches—of mayors
and council members, union leaders and the heads of ladies' auxiliaries, coroners
and soldiers. Indeed, the integrated operettas of the late twenties and thirties—
the *Of Thee I Sing* trilogy; *Hallelujah, I'm a Bum; The Phantom President;* and

Yip, Ira, and Harold's "Beautifying the City" sequence from *Life Begins at 8:40*—dealt disproportionately with public and political rituals. They were send-ups of the conventions of straight society, of the hollow rites of—the precise targets varied—small town/old style/WASP/bourgeois establishments. It was a form that more or less was played out by 1933, perhaps because for the first time there was a national establishment, the New Deal coalition, from which the Gershwins and Harburg no longer felt estranged. The integrated musicals of the forties are largely devoid of the kind of public ceremony that was the basis of their thirties counterparts. In Munchkinland, the comic send-up of recital, speech, and ceremony that Yip and Ira and Hart derived from W. S. Gilbert is revived one last time— necessarily, in a fantasy context.

The send-up is a gentle one, of course. The operetta, like a number of songs in Yip's later shows, is a day-of-deliverance celebration: politics, as far as Yip was concerned, at its apogee, not its nadir. Both the celebration and the comedy revolve around the number of ways the witch can be said to be dead. The lyric begins to run gently amok when Yip starts placing normally unstressed syllables on emphasized notes: "Which was not a healthy *sitch*-uation for a wicked witch." It settles down to a study of how many ways death can be adverbialized: completely, sweetly, neatly, legally, morally, ethically, spiritually, physically, positively, undeniably, absolutely, reliably—culminating with "not merely" and "sincerely." The establishment is smothering fact with ceremony, treating death as if it were policy—but it is a little people's establishment; it is withal a celebration, and Yip's laughter is finally more empathetic than derisive.

The rough drafts of "Ding-Dong" in Yip's collection at Yale are almost identical to the finished product, with the notable exception of one couplet:

> She really went and blew a fuse
> There's nothing left of her but shoes.

Three weeks before the filming ended, director Victor Fleming asked for a song to end the Munchkinland sequence, as Dorothy sets out for the Emerald City down the Yellow Brick Road. Yip and Harold wrote the following song for the Munchkins.

Verse.   Follow the yellow brick road
                         Follow the yellow brick road
                         Follow follow follow follow
                         Follow the yellow brick road
                         Follow the rainbow over the stream
                         Follow the fellow who follows a dream

> Follow the yellow brick road
> Follow the yellow brick road
> Follow follow follow follow
> Follow the yellow brick road

Chorus.   We're off to see the wizard
> The wonderful Wizard of Oz
> We hear he is a whiz of a wiz
> If ever a wiz there was
>
> If ever, oh ever, a wiz there was
> The Wizard of Oz is one becoz
> Becoz becoz becoz becoz becoz
> Becoz of the wonderful things he does
> [Musical phrase without lyrics]
> We're off to see the wizard
> The wonderful Wizard of Oz.

Not all of the printed lyric is sung in the film. The difference is in the second stanza of the verse, which in the picture is reduced to:

> Follow the yellow brick
> Follow the yellow brick
> Follow the yellow brick road.

Yip was to recycle the printed stanza, though, in a later song of questing: "Look to the Rainbow" in *Finian's Rainbow*.

The first songs written for *Oz* were the "If I Only Had a Brain/Heart/Nerve" triptych. Indeed, Arlen had written the music in 1937, at which time it was intended for *Hooray for What?* under the title "I'm Hanging on to You." The song was dropped from the show, however, and as was so often the case, Yip judged the tune suitable in another context—here, to his character songs in *Oz*.

Yip's worksheets at Yale for these songs are particularly rich and enjoyable. Many couplets that did not make it into the final lyric are played with in these pages, like the Scarecrow's:

> Know the wherefore and the whyness
> Of the wetness and the dryness
> If I only had a brain.
>
> And to you, my darlin' Dorothy,
> I'd be Bergen, not McCarthy
> If I only had a brain.

I would be no sweet potato
I would think out things like Plato

It would be the farmer's daughter
Not the horse I'd lead to water.

I could save any nation
With orations on inflation

Oh, I'd never have to stagnate
I'd be a mental magnate

As well, Yip wrote introductory verses to the three character songs. The Scarecrow's runs:

Verse.   Said a scarecrow swingin' on a pole
To a blackbird sittin' on a fence
"Oh, the Lord gave me a soul
But forgot to give me common sense"—
If I had an ounce of common sense—

Chorus.   I could while away the hours
Conferrin' with the flow'rs
Consultin' with the rain
And my head I'd be scratchin'
While my thoughts were busy hatchin'
If I only had a brain

I'd unravel ev'ry riddle
For any individdle
In trouble or in pain

Dorothy.   With the thoughts you'd be thinkin'
You could be another Lincoln
If you only had a brain

Scarecrow.   Oh, I could tell you why
The ocean's near the shore
I could think of things
I never thunk before
And then I'd sit
And think some more

> I would not be just a nuffin'
> My head all full of stuffin'
> My heart all full of pain
> And perhaps I'd deserve you
> And be even worthy erv you
> If I only had a brain.

The first stanza anthropomorphizes in a way entirely appropriate to a talking scarecrow in a magic land—who soon, though not conferring with flowers, will be arguing with apple trees.

Again, the lyric in the film deviates from Yip's printed lyric in the two penultimate lines, which in the film go:

> I would dance and be merry
> Life would be a ding-a-derry.

For the Tin Man's song, Yip's verse ran as follows:

Verse.

> Said a tin man rattling his gibs
> To a strawman sad and weary-eyed
> "Oh, the Lord gave me tin ribs
> But forgot to put a heart inside"
> Then he banged his hollow chest and cried—

Chorus.

> When a man's an empty kettle
> He should be on his mettle
> And yet I'm torn apart
> Just because I'm presumin'
> That I could be kinda human
> If I only had a heart.

> I'd be tender, I'd be gentle and awful sentimental
> Regarding love and art
> I'd be friends with the sparrows
> And the boy that shoots the arrows
> If I only had a heart.

> Picture me a balcony
> Above a voice sings low
> "Wherefore art Thou, Romeo?"
> I hear a beat
> How sweet!

> Just to register emotion
> Jealousy, devotion,
> And really feel the part
> I'd stay young and chipper
> And I'd lock it with a zipper
> If I only had a heart.

Yip's workbooks for the Lion's song shows that he was also writing spoken dialogue for Lahr—and possibly that some lines that ended up in the script began as lyrics. "Look at the bags under my eyes," he has Lahr saying. "Haven't slept—afraid of the clock." And:

> I can't fall asleep
> Because I'm afraid to count sheep.

There are couplets that never made it in:

> I could be as good as others
> Good enough for Ringling Brothers.

And couplets that made it after alteration:

> And defeat with equal prowess
> Any moose or any mou-esse.

And lines that never made it to full couplets, but whose intent is clear even in fragmentary form:

> _____wrestle
> They'd never call me Cecil.

The verse (not in the film) goes as follows:

> Said a lion, poor neurotic lion
> To a miss who listened to him rave
> "Oh, the Lord made me a lion, but the Lord
> Forgot to make me brave"
> Then his tail began to curl and wave—

Yip wrote an entire AABA song for Lahr:

Yeah, it's sad, believe me, missy
When you're born to be a sissy
Without the vim and verve
But I could change my habits
Never more be scared of rabbits,
If I only had the nerve

I'm afraid there's no denyin'
I'm just a dandylion
A fate I don't deserve
But I could show my prowess
Be a lion, not a mow-ess
If I only had the nerve

Oh, I'd
Be in my stride
A king down to the core
Oh, I would roar the way I never roared before,
And then I'd rrrrwooof
And roar some more

I would show the dinosaurus
Who's king around the foress'
A king they better serve,
Why with my royal beezer
I could be another Caesar
If I only had the nerve.

But in the film, the song is shortened to:

Yeah, it's sad, believe me, missy,
When you're born to be a sissy
Without the vim and verve
But I could show my prow-ess
Be a lion, not a mow-ess
If I only had the nerve

I'm afraid there's no denyin'
I'm just a dandylion
A fate I don't deserve
I'd be brave as a blizzard

Tin Man.   I'd be gentle as a lizard

Scarecrow.	I'd be clever as a gizzard
Dorothy.	If the wizard is a wizard Who will serve
Scarecrow.	Then I'm sure to get a brain
Tin Man.	A heart
Dorothy.	A home
Lion.	The noive
All.	We're off to see the wizard The wonderful Wizard of Oz.

The shortening of Lahr's song may have had something to do with balancing Lahr, Bolger, and Haley's screen time, since Lahr was later to have another solo, "If I Were King of the Forest," to which some of Yip's lines from his draft for "Nerve" would be relocated (dinosaurus / foress'). The longer version is also sacrificed, though, to an ending that establishes the characters' camaraderie. Actually, the three character songs balance individuality with interrelationship. They share distinct characteristics beyond their music—lyrics that drop final *g* and veer into neologistic rhyme. These are distinct but kindred voices, star turns that turn into a ceremony of bonding. (Indeed, Arlen and Harburg had considered developing the entry into Lahr's woods—"Lions and Tigers and Bears"—into a full-fledged song, but it would have lessened the building impact of "Brain / Heart / Nerve" performed in succession.)

"If I Only Had a Brain / a Heart / the Nerve" moved the procession to the deadly poppy field. But, helped by Glinda's snow, the quartet approached the Emerald City, to a background song (the music for which was composed by Herbert Stothart along with Arlen):

OPTIMISTIC VOICES

Ah,
You're out of the woods,
You're out of the dark,
You're out of the night,
Step into the sun
Step into the light

Keep straight ahead for
The most glorious place
On the face of the earth
Or the sky

Hold onto your breath
Hold onto your heart
Hold onto your hope
March up to that gate
And bid it o-pen

They're out of the woods
They're out of the woods
They're out of the woods . . .

You're out of the woods,
You're out of the dark,
You're out of the night,
Step into the sun
Step into the light,
March up to that gate
And bid it open,
Open . . .

Yip and Harold had started on an entrance song to the Emerald City, "Horse of a Different Color," when they realized that "The Merry Old Land of Oz" already was their entrance song. (Yip's workbooks demonstrate his usual methodical approach at work in "Horse"; he begins listing colored animals: yellow dogs, purple cows, and so on.)

THE MERRY OLD LAND OF OZ

Verse. [Not in film]. There's a garden spot, I'm told
Where it's never too hot and
It's never too cold,
Where you're never too old,
Where you're never too thin or tall
And you're never, never, never too
Too, too anything at all

Oh! You're not too mad and
You're not too sane
And you don't compare and
You don't complain
All you do is just sit tight
'Cause it's all so, so, so
Downright right

Chorus.   Ha, ha, ha!
Ho, ho, ho!
And a couple of tra-la-las
That's how we laugh the day away
In the merry old land of Oz

'Bzz, 'bzz, 'bzz,
Chirp, chirp, chirp
And a couple of la-de-das
That's how the crickets crick all day
In the merry old land of Oz

We get up at twelve
And start to work at one
Take an hour for lunch
And then at two we're done
Jolly good fun

Ha, ha, ha!
Ho, ho, ho!
And a couple of tra-la-las
That's how we laugh the day away
In the merry old land of Oz.

Tailors.   A pat pat here
And a pat pat there
And a couple of brand new straws
That's how we keep you young and fair
In the merry old land of Oz

Metal Polishers.   A rub rub here
And a rub rub there
Whether you're tin or bronze
That's how we keep you in repair
In the merry old land of Oz

Beautician.	We can make a dimple smile out of a frown
Dorothy.	Can you even dye my eyes to match my gown?
Beautician.	Uh-huh
Dorothy.	Jolly old town
Beauticians.	A clip clip here
	And a clip clip there
	We give the roughest claws
Lion.	That certain air of savoir faire
	In the merry old land of Oz
Dorothy and Friends.	Ha ha ha
	Ho ho ho
	Ha ha ha ha
Lion.	Haw
Dorothy and Friends.	That's how we laugh the day away
	In the merry old land of Oz
	That's how we laugh the day away
	With a ha ha ha
	Ha ha ha
	Ha ha ha
	Ha ha ha
	Ha ha ha
	Ha ha ha
	In the merry old land of Oz
	Ha ha ha
	Ha ha ha . . .

"Merry Old Land" shows the deftness with which Yip and Harold had by now come to use Lahr. Among the four supplicants to the wizard, Lahr is the tag. "Then I'm sure to get a brain / a heart / a home / da noive," they sing back in the forest, the camera, following the lyric, panning across to Lahr's cross-eyed mugging. In "Merry Old Land," we have another tracking sequence that goes from Scarecrow to Tin Man to Dorothy to Lion, in which the four are spruced up for their appearance before the wizard. The Scarecrow and Tin Man have no lines here, Dorothy just a couple of words, and the Lion is given the lines, "That certain air / Of savoir faire" to mangle in his best Bronxese. They then proceed sequentially with laughing lines ("Ha ha ha / Ho ho ho"). Lahr is given the final "Haw," which he somehow manages to turn into a laugh line. With Lahr, Arlen and Harburg could now perform minimalist no less than maximalist art.

Maximalism, in any event, was just around the corner. It was the last of Arlen and Harburg's mock concert songs for Lahr: "If I Were King of the Forest."

Lion.

If I were King of the Forest
Not Queen, not Duke, not Prince
My regal robes of the forest
Would be satin, not cotton, not chintz

I'd command each thing
Be it fish or fowl
With a woof and a woof
And a royal growl

As I'd click my heel
All the trees would kneel
And the mountains bow
And the bulls kow-tow
And the sparrows would take wing
'F I, 'f I, were king

Each rabbit would show respect to me
The chipmunks genuflect to me
Tho' my tail would lash
I would show compash
For ev'ry underling
'F I, 'f I, were king, just king

All.

Each rabbit would show respect to him,
The chipmunks genuflect to him

Scarecrow.

And his wife would be Queen of the May

Lion.

I'd be monarch of all I survey
Monarch of all I survey
Mah-ah-ah-ah-ah-ah-ah-ah-ah-narch
Of all I survey

Dorothy.

Your majesty, if you were king
You'd not be afraid of anything?

Lion.

Not nobody, not nohow

Tin Man.

Not even rhinocerous?

Lion.

Imposserous.

Dorothy.

How about a hippopotamus?

Lion.

I'd thrash him from his top to bottomamus

Dorothy.

Supposin' you met an elephant?

Lion.	I'd wrap him up in cellophant
Scarecrow.	What if it were a brontosaurus?
Lion.	I'd show him who's king of the fores'
All.	How?
Lion.	HOW?
	Courage!
	What makes a king out of a slave?
	Courage!
	What makes the flag on the mast to wave?
	Courage!
	What makes the elephant charge his tusk
	In the misty mist or the dusky dusk?
	What makes the muskrat guard his musk?
	Courage!
	What makes the Sphinx the Seventh Wonder?
	Courage!
	What makes the dawn come up like thunder?
	Courage!
	What makes the hottentot so hot?
	What put the "ape" in apricot?
	What have they got that I ain't got?
All.	Courage!
Lion.	For courage is the thing of kings
	With courage I'd be king of kings
	And the whole year round
	I'd be hailed and crowned
	By ev'ry living thing
	'FI, [If I]
All.	'Fe, [If he]
Lion.	'FI,
All.	'Fe,
Lion.	'FI were king!

Here again, the version in the film is somewhat shortened, the cut coming in the last stanza (perhaps the reference to king of kings was thought somewhat irreverent). In his workbooks, Yip tries out a range of fanciful formulations before winnowing down the lyric:

> The chipmunk wants his chip
> Mongoose—mong
> Muskrat—musk
>
> Jaguar
> What a wag you are
>
> Mongoose
> Make him dance the Tongoose

Like "Things" and "Song of the Woodman," "King of the Forest" attacks in equal measure the pretensions of the concert stage and the inanities of Edgar Guestian poetry. The progression from mountains bowing and bulls kowtowing to sparrows taking wing permits Lahr to move from grand roaring to dainty fluttering. In the spoken ode to courage, sound totally eclipses sense. The passage begins with the evolution from king to slave, moves quickly into rhetoric for its own sake (the flag, the sphinx, and the dawn), and finally into prefix deconstruction (the hot Hottentot, the ape in apricot).

Like the Munchkin operetta, "King of the Forest" attacks a culture that was already being eclipsed by a newer, less pretentious, more polyglot style. Lahr would continue to send up opera (he was an uproarious Siegfried in 1951's *Two on the Aisle*), but concert song would no longer be a resonant target. After *Oz*, Arlen and Harburg concentrated on book shows, while Lahr, his talents at once too anarchic and too great to confine within most musical librettos, remained chiefly with revues. "King of the Forest" was their last song together, though the three were frequently in search of a project they could jointly undertake. On his deathbed in 1967, Lahr kept talking about an updated version of *A Midsummer Night's Dream* he wanted Yip and Harold to write for him.

"I am always disappointed when I see the picture," Yip once said,

> because they deleted several songs at the end of the picture and they made it a chase and I feel the loss of music there; they should not have done that. Several songs were taken out at the end of the picture which should have been in—it would have been a much better picture.

The most painful cut was the one major song and dance for all four principals—a number that had taken five weeks to film and cost eighty thousand dollars to produce. En route to the castle of the Wicked Witch, Dorothy and company were attacked by Jitter Bugs—insects of Yip's devising. But "The Jitterbug" was squashed on the cutting room floor.

In fact, "King of the Forest" is the last number in Oz. A reprise of "Ding-Dong" on the occasion of the Witch of the West's death was vetoed; so was a reprise of "Over the Rainbow."

Yip hated the film's ending, grafted on to the picture by the combined forces of Woolf and Ryerson, Freed and LeRoy, and Mayer himself. "The picture didn't need that 'Home, Sweet Home,' 'God Bless Our Home' tripe," Yip told Harmetz. And yet, Yip's contributions to the penultimate scene—contributions not to the score but to the script—are the most purely Harburgian elements in Oz. What Yip produced was a happy end without magic—the dream affirmed but the illusion exposed.

In Yip's workbooks for Oz, there is a testament he has written—whether intended as lyric or as a printed title to precede the film is unclear—which established Oz as a symbol of Utopia and a metaphor for belief.

> Behold your dream as it gleams in the sun
> Every beam is a jewel that shines for a deed well done.
> Look high! There's a magic make-believe in the air.
> And oh! If you can still use a dream, take your share.
> A more enthralling vision of a wish-come-to-life never was
> So here's to the hearts that believe and belong
> In the land of Oz.

But *Oz* concludes, of course, in a tableau of demystification: the exposure of the wizard as a humbug. When the wizard is found to be the quintessential W. C. Fieldsian carnival con man and balloon ascensionist, he grants the wishes nonetheless. In the book, though, the wizard's gifts were both prosaic and still a bit magical.

As Harmetz notes,

> In Baum, the Wizard has provided the Scarecrow with a head full of pins and needles, the Tin Man with a chest full of red silk heart, and the Lion with a drink that had only to be swallowed to turn to courage. In most of the scripts, the Scarecrow, Tin Man and Lion had discovered they had *always* possessed the brains, heart, and courage for which they had been searching.

Yip's rewrite of the scene affirmed his belief in the power of appearances and illusion. "I devised the satiric and cynical idea of the Wizard handing out symbols," he told Harmetz, "because I was so aware of our lives being the images of things rather than the things themselves." Yip wrote:

> *Wizard of Oz. (To Scarecrow)* Why, anyone can have a brain. That's a very mediocre commodity. Every pusillanimous creature that crawls on

the earth or slinks through slimy seas has a brain. Back where I come from we have universities, seats of great learning, where men go to become great thinkers. And when they come out they think deep thoughts. And with no more brains than you have. But, they have one thing you haven't got, a DIPLOMA. Therefore, by virtue of the authority vested in me by the Universatatus Committeatum E Pluribus Unum, I hereby confer upon you the honorary degree of Th.D.

Scarecrow. Th.D.?

Wizard. Yes, that's Doctor of Thinkology. . . . (*To Lion*) As for you, my fine friend, you're a victim of disorganized thinking. You are of the unfortunate delusion that simply because you run away from danger, you have no courage. You are confusing courage with wisdom. Back where I come from, we have men who are called heroes. Once a year they take their fortitude out of mothballs and parade it down the main street of the city. And they have no more courage than you have. But, they have one think that you haven't got. A MEDAL. Therefore for meritorious conduct, extraordinary valor, conspicuous bravery against wicked witches, I award you the triple cross. You are now a member of the Legion of Courage.

Lion. Ha. Ha. Shucks folks, I'm speechless. Ha. Ha.

Wizard. (*To Tin Man*) As for you, my galvanized friend, you want a heart. You don't know how lucky you are not to have one. Hearts will never be practical until they can be made unbreakable.

Tin Man. But I still want one.

Wizard. Back where I come from, there are men that do nothing all day but good deeds. They are called phila-a-a . . . yes . . . Good deed doers. And their hearts are no bigger than yours. But, they have one thing you haven't got. A TESTIMONIAL. Therefore, in consideration of your kindness, I take pleasure at this time in presenting you with a small token of our esteem and affection. (*Presents a watch*) And remember, my sentimental friend, that a heart is not judged by how much you love, but by how much you are loved by others.

Yip bracketed the scene, though, with a few more lines that did not make it into the picture. The wizard was to have introduced the awards ceremony with the following interchange with Dorothy:

Wizard. I can't produce something out of nothing. But I can do better than that. I can produce *illusions* [emphasis in original]. I can't produce a chicken out of an egg, but I can do something better. I can make you think [I can], and that's better than the real thing.

Dorothy. But we don't want any of your nasty illusions. We want the things you promised—the real thing.

The awards ceremony then proceeds as it was to be filmed—at the conclusion of which, with the appropriate abracadabra, the Wizard pulls a chicken out of the air and, then, pure Yip:

Wizard. The chicken was always there. All I did was make you see it.

Dorothy then asks the wizard if he has any magic to get her back home, and he avers he can get her there not by magic but by balloon—not before, however, Dorothy reprises what was to have been a somewhat altered "Over the Rainbow:"

Wizard. But you wanted to be over the rainbow.

Dorothy. But now I want to be on the other side.

What is difficult to understand is that these scenes came from the same pen that wrote the ode to Oz as a symbol of belief. Oz takes Yip's profound ambivalence toward faith and conviction one step further than "Paper Moon," "Fun to Be Fooled," and "Last Night When We Were Young." A Harburg happy ending, and we will see it again in *Finian's Rainbow*, strips away illusion and affirms its power at one and the same time. (It's almost as though a Marxist had written the last scene to *The Tempest*.) It's a complex and heady brew. One can imagine its effect on Freed, LeRoy, and Mayer was to make them cling even more insistently to the timeworn verities of "There's no place like home."

As *Oz* went into previews, Freed, LeRoy, and Mayer had other decisions to render on Yip and Harold's work. The major battle was over whether to retain "Over the Rainbow," which some of L. B. Mayer's fluglemen argued was slowing down the film. The first preview, Yip told Harmetz, was

unbearable. You were always working with people who knew nothing, working with the ignominy of ignorance. Those ignorant jerks. Money is power. Money rules the roost. The artist is lucky if he can get a few licks in.

As Yip recalls (though Harmetz doubts the accuracy of his memory on this point), Victor Fleming was among those calling for "Rainbow"'s end. "Mr. Fleming walked into the office," Yip recollected, and he said, "I'm sorry to say that the whole first part of that show is awful slow because of that number, 'Over the Rainbow.' We gotta take it out." Now, when a man like that comes in, who doesn't talk but makes pronunciamentos, you've got to listen. Mervyn LeRoy, who was the producer of the picture, suddenly regressed to the little Mervyn Levine again, and the song was out of the picture.

Harold and I just went crazy; we knew that this was the ballad of the show; this is the number we were depending on. We decided to take action. We went to the front office; we went to the back office; we pleaded; we cried; we tore our hair. Harold ran to *shul*. There wasn't a god around who could help us. Finally, Arthur Freed went to Louis B. Mayer and pleaded with him. Louis B. Mayer was a strong arm man when it came to humanity, but when it came to songwriters he was quite sentimental.

People were sentimental with songwriters because they always thought that maybe if they die, they'll write a song about them. You remember when Caruso died, they had a song, "They needed a songbird in Heaven, so God took Caruso away." Well, this could have made a good song: "They needed a God in heaven, so they took L. B. Mayer away." Anyhow, L. B. Mayer was very kind to Arthur Freed and said, "Let the boys have the damned song. Get it back in the picture; it can't hurt." So the song went back in the picture and of course you know what happened.

In Arlen's account to biographer Edward Jablonski, the battle was even more protracted. "Rainbow," said Arlen, was excised after each of the three previews, and on each occasion, Freed would go to Mayer and "argue it back into the film."

The Opening

Oz opened in August of 1939 in New York City to immense (if studio-generated) publicity, huge crowds, and mixed reviews. Most of the middlebrow magazines were not overly enthusiastic. *Newsweek* praised the "magnificent sets and costumes" and enjoyed the trick photography. *Time* thought it "a Broadway spectacle" with a final sequence "as sentimental as 'Little Women.'" Yet the *Time* reviewer was captivated by the fantasy: "As long as 'The Wizard of Oz' sticks to whimsy and magic it floats in the same rare atmosphere of enchantment that distinguished Disney's 'Snow White.'"

Most of the serious critics thought it dreadful. Otis Ferguson wrote in *The New Republic*:

> "The Wizard of Oz" was intended to hit the same audience as "Snow White" and won't fail for lack of trying. It has dwarfs, music, Technicolor,

freak characters and Judy Garland. It can't be expected to have a sense of humor as well—and as for the light touch of fantasy, it weighs like a pound of fruitcake soaking wet.

Russell Maloney in the *New Yorker* was hardly more friendly. Maloney labeled the film "a stinkeroo . . . which displays no trace of imagination, good taste, or ingenuity," although he found "Bert Lahr, as the Cowardly Lion, funny but out of place."

Of the few respected critics who were completely won by the film, Frank S. Nugent, writing in the *New York Times,* was the most important.

> Not since Disney's "Snow White" has anything quite so fantastic suc-
> ceeded half so well. . . . It is all so well-intentioned, so genial, and so gay
> that any reviewer who would look down his nose at the funmaking should
> be spanked and sent off, supperless, to bed.

At the Academy Awards ceremony held on February 29, 1940, the big winner was *Gone with the Wind;* but Yip and Harold won an Oscar for "Over the Rainbow" as the best song, and another Academy Award went to MGM musical director Herbert Stothart for best score. (Today the score award would go to Stothart, Arlen, and Harburg.)

Yet *Oz* confirmed the fears of the MGM front office that it would be their prestige money loser of the year. *Oz* did not go into the black for ten years— until its first theatrical rerelease in 1949. And then, virtually by accident, it became a national institution.

What turned the trick was television. In 1956, CBS-TV entered into negotiations with MGM for the rights to *Gone with the Wind.* MGM turned CBS down cold—but as a consolation prize, offered CBS the rights to *Oz* with the option of rescreening nine more times. Millions of households tuned in to *Oz* in 1956 and then continued to tune in year after year. Each successive airing received extraordinarily high ratings, so that by 1975, *Oz* had the eleventh highest rating of any film ever shown in prime time—and the twelfth, the fourteenth, the sixteenth, the thirty-second. . . . Its ratings read like a ranking of Ted Williams's seasonal batting statistics. Its 1982 airing was estimated to have been seen by *49 percent of all American children.* On its twenty-fifth annual airing in 1983, it was the ninth rated show on network television that week, beating out *Gone with the Wind,* which finished sixteenth. By 1983, *Oz* had taken in six million dollars at theater box offices, and thirteen million dollars in payments from CBS and NBC to MGM. As of this writing, *Oz* is pushing thirty re-airings on network prime time. No other show of any nature has been rerun in prime time more than ten times. In essence, CBS and NBC turned *The Wizard of Oz* into the first video cassette.

E. Y. ("Yip") Harburg, lyricist (left), and Harold Arlen, composer, are honored at the Oscar ceremonies on February 29, 1940, for creating the song, "Over the Rainbow" for *The Wizard of Oz* (1939). (Collection of Harburg Estate.)

Over time, *Oz* became one of the few pieces of American culture that effectively everyone knew. It wasn't until the third or fourth airing, Margaret Hamilton told Aljean Harmetz, that she became aware of the film's rising recognition, and that she was achieving a celebrity level she had never before attained or anticipated. "I hadn't realized what an impact the picture makes on children all over the world," Yip told Harmetz in the midseventies, "until the last six or seven years." To a generation that had grown up on television, *Oz* was filled with easily invocable (because universally understood) symbols. Harmetz traces the *Oz* references through Watergate editorial cartoons and Doonesbury. Two more recent incidents attest to its ongoing ubiquity: first, a postgame clubhouse ritual on the 1988 world champion Los Angeles Dodgers was second baseman Steve Sax's recital of Lahr's "Courage" speech from "King of the Forest." Second, while watching a televised press conference announcing (prematurely and falsely, alas) the sale of Eastern Airlines from the hated Frank Lorenzo to Peter Ueberroth, the pilots and machinists on strike against Eastern

At the climax of *The Wizard of Oz*, Dorothy (Judy Garland) liquidates the Wicked Witch of the West (Margaret Hamilton) by throwing water on her. To Yip this act was symbolic of all struggles against tyranny and he wanted to reprise at this point the universal song, "Ding! Dong! The Witch Is Dead" but was overruled. (Turner Entertainment.)

broke into a spontaneous chorus of "Ding-Dong, The Witch Is Dead"—a story that doubtless would have delighted Yip.

As *Oz* became an institution, it also underwent some critical reevaluation. The process began during its first theatrical reissue in 1949, when, as Harmetz notes, the critics who had seen it first as children welcomed it back with affection and praise. More recently, critical histories of the film musical have tended to upgrade the picture in general and the Arlen-Harburg score in particular. In Ethan Mordden's *The Hollywood Musical*, *Oz* makes the short list of films with the greatest musical scores, and Mordden argues that Yip, chiefly on the basis of his work on *Oz*, should be considered the movies' greatest lyricist. "Harold Arlen and E. Y. Harburg's songs do what few film scores have been able to do so far," Mordden writes. They "set a style that works for one picture and will never work for anything else." *Oz*, says Mordden, "stands as one of the most original and distinctive documents of American art . . . midway between the eccentric 1930's and the normalized 1940's."

It is indeed a "midway" work. It preserves the vaudeville genius of a Lahr within the newly built confines of a book musical; it marks a leap forward for Yip towards the integration of lyrics and libretto and constitutes one last parting (if gentle) shot at the targets of the twenties, at the operas and poetry and stultifying propriety that a Babbitt bourgeoisie had force-fed Yip and his peers while they were growing up. "I think that the pervading idea inside of me," Yip told Harmetz, "is that we live in a world that should be full of pixified fun, you know, flowers, buds. It's my way of laughing at people who are serious and pompous and not seeing the playfulness of life, and doing it through language." In this regard, Oz is Yip's farewell, fonder than he may have realized, to the culture of pomposity against which so much American comedy and art had been directed in the early twentieth century.

The acclaim for Oz was not only belated, it was surprising. Oz may have been a major production from Hollywood's poshest studio, but it aimed after all to be a kids' picture. George Cukor, the most talented of MGM's in-house directors, removed himself from the picture a mere four days after being assigned to it: this was not a serious project. "When I wrote *Finian's Rainbow,*" Yip told Harmetz, "I knew it was important . . . right away. . . . It contained economic and social ideas in fantasy form. Universities were charmed by it immediately. But *The Wizard of Oz* was just for children." Both Arlen and Harburg were to admit to Max Wilk that the success of Oz stole quietly upon them. "I knew 'Over the Rainbow' was a strong song," said Harold, "but I never knew its true strength until afterwards." "We were just doing work, earning a living, and liking what we were doing," said Yip. "We never thought of posterity."

In fact, both Oz's rise to the status of world cultural touchstone and the renewed attention to Harold and Yip's score came too late to have a significant impact on their careers. Yip was already blacklisted from pictures when Oz was first aired on television.

Chapter 6

From *Oz* to New Musical Theater

Life's full of consequence
That old devil, consequence
Life's always full of funny quirks. . . .
It's consequences that irks

MGM's yellow brick road next led the team of Arlen and Harburg from Oz to Marx. Their first post-*Oz* assignment, the Marx Brothers' film *At the Circus,* gave Yip the chance to craft a lyric for yet another great comic. "I've worked with some of the greatest voices of my time," Yip once said,

Jolson, Garland, Lena Horne: but my favorites were Bert Lahr and Groucho Marx: Bert Lahr because he sang the "Woodchopper's Song" that I wrote for him in *The Show Is On* so beautifully; Groucho for "Lydia, the Tattooed Lady." That song was thought to be risqué and we had a hell of a lot of trouble over it. The song went like this:

LYDIA, THE TATTOOED LADY

Lydia, oh, Lydia
Say, have you met Lydia?
Oh, Lydia, the tattooed lady
She has eyes that folks adore so
And a torso even more so

Lydia, oh, Lydia
That "encyclopidia"
Oh, Lydia, the queen of tattoo
On her back is the Battle of Waterloo
Beside it the wreck of the Hesperus too
And proudly above waves the red, white and blue
You can learn a lot from Lydia

La la la, la la la
La la la, la la la
She can give you a view of the world in tattoo
If you step up and tell her where
For a dime you can see Kankakee or Paree
Or Washington crossing the Delaware

Oh, Lydia, oh, Lydia
Say, have you met Lydia?
Oh, Lydia, the tattooed lady
When her muscles start relaxin'
Up the hill comes Andrew Jackson

Lydia, oh, Lydia
That "encyclopidia"
Oh, Lydia the champ of them all
For two bits she will do a mazurka in jazz
With a view of Niag'ra that no artist has
And on a clear day you can see Alcatraz
You can learn a lot from Lydia

La la la, la la la
La la la, la la la
Come along and see Buff'lo Bill with his lasso
Just a little classic by Mendel Picasso
Here is Captain Spaulding exploring the Amazon
And Godiva, but with her pajamas on
La la la, la la la
La la la, la la la
Here is Grover Whalen unveilin' the Trylon
Over on the West Coast we have Treasure Islan'
Here's Nijinsky a doin' the rhumba
Here's her social security numba

At this point [Yip continues] the song was censored; this was 1939 and censorship was at its full height—no sweaters on the screen, they were too erotic. We were told that we'd have to cut it out of the picture. Harold and I were mad, we went to the censorship office [but had no luck]. Finally, we got an idea for how to save the song. We put in a final verse to legitimize the song, which went like this:

> La la la, la la la
> La la la, la la la
> Oh, Lydia, the champ of them all
> She once swept an Admiral clear off his feet
> The ships on her hips made his heart skip a beat
> And now the old boy's in command of the fleet
> For he went and *married* Lydia.

"I tried to get as near to Gilbert and Sullivan as possible for 'Lydia,'" Yip once recalled, "both in the rhyming scheme and the verbal juggling. . . . I had gone to [Groucho's] house many times, on nights when he had Gilbert and Sullivan evenings. He would gather us there, play complete operas, and sing along with them." Writing vehicles for comics was much on Yip's mind in 1939. At year's end, Yip was attempting to enroll Ira Gershwin as his colyricist in a projected Broadway show featuring comic Joe Cook, but Ira was not interested.

Return to Broadway Again

In the end, Yip was to do the show anyway—without Ira, without Joe Cook, even without Arlen. "Harold went off with Johnny Mercer on some other films," Yip recalled. "He felt he needed a change and so did I—so I teamed up with Burt Lane on the score of *Hold on to Your Hats*."

When *Hold on to Your Hats* opened on Broadway in the autumn of 1940, both *Time* and the *World-Telegram* called it an "old-fashioned musical comedy," and with good reason. It was conceived by producer Alex Aarons as an old-style comic vehicle—the kind of show *Hooray for What?* had evolved into—and it became more so as it was rewritten to the talents of its eventual star, Al Jolson. Aaron's idea of a show, Burton Lane was to comment, was to package a star and songs in the mode of his great twenties shows, which had featured the talents of the Astaires and the Gershwins. "He had a great appreciation for quality in music," Lane said. "Books, no. He had no conception of a libretto for a show. He grew up at a time when . . . you did a show for a star. The one we were aiming for was Jack Haley."

The book on *Hats* was by every account nothing memorable—a comic tale of a radio singer starring in a Lone Ranger–type show who is brought west to a dude ranch to dispatch assorted comic bad men despite his fear of horses and guns and all manner of action paraphernalia. The script was by radio gag men Matt Brooks and Eddie Davis and was touched up by Aarons's original twenties librettist, Guy Bolton. Yip and Burt had already journeyed east to continue their work on the show when Haley bowed out upon discovering Aarons had virtually no funds to front the project. They then were already back in Hollywood when the word came that Jolson had agreed to do the show—and fund some of it himself.

The conversion of *Hats* into a Jolson vehicle made the show at one and the same time a theatrical event and a bit of a relic. *Hats* marked Jolson's first appearance on Broadway in nine years. The unrivaled in-person magnetism Jolson exuded on stage had not worn well in the cooler media of radio and the screen; his return to the stage ensured that *Hats* would be one of the season's high points. By the same token, though, no star more outshone his own shows than Jolson. In a Jolson show, the star would invariably discard the book to converse directly with the audience and abandon the score to perform old numbers with which he was identified.

"At the end of the show, he lowers the curtain," Lane remarked of the standard Jolson vehicle,

> opens his shirt, loosens his tie, and says, "Folks, you ain't heard nothin' yet." And he proceeds to do a medley of old songs that have nothing to do with the show—all the old standards: "April Showers," "California, Here I Come," and whatever the hell the songs were. He'd spend half an hour, and [the audience] would forget the score.

But whatever vestiges of control the show's authors attempted to exert over its star vanished completely when Jolson himself became the show's producer and primary backer—coming up with 80 percent of *Hats'* budget himself and supplanting Aarons entirely.

Jolson was not the only member of the *Hats* cast for whom Harburg and Lane tailored material; another was Yiddish-dialect comic Bert Gordon, who played an improbable Tonto to Jolson's incongruous Lone Ranger. The evening's show-stopper, the comic trio "Down on the New Dude Ranch," which Jolson, Gordon, and Martha Raye sang and danced, featured lines for Gordon in which Yip played with deliberately forced rhymes, both in and out of dialect:

> We are going back to husses
> Nature don't like Greyhound busses
> Down on the new dude ranch
> Men are a little more tender there
> Friends are a little more friender there
> And every girl has a little more gender there
> Down on the new dude ranch.

The dude ranch's cowboys offered their own lament in Yip and Burt's "Way Out West Where the East Begins." Here's an excerpt:

Oh, it's no wonder we're gee whizzy
'Stead of ridin' steers we're busy
Being western aphradiziacs
To each rich bitch
Who, with all her swell divorces
And the products she endorses
Doesn't even know a horse's
Saddle from a switch.

In another *Hats* number, a comic duet for Jolson and Raye, Yip runs amok with a suffix, a device he was to return to in *Finian*'s "Something Sort of Grandish," again with Lane. The song here is "Would You Be So Kindly," in which the inexorable logic of the adverbial form moves from everyday words in the first chorus to contractions and neologisms as the song progresses. As Jolson and Raye's comic passion mounts, it is the language that they heedlessly trample.

WOULD YOU BE SO KINDLY?

Lone Rider.   I'm not so hot on my I.Q.,
But that's okay
I've got to tell you I like you,
And that ain't hay
I'm not so bright, not so sharp,
Not so smooth on the sizzling phrase
And so I ask you in my own curioso ways—

Chorus.   Oh, would you be so kindly?
To treat me not so blindly
Oh, would you be so kindly?
Lady, please?
Oh, would you be so sweetly?
To sweep me off my feetly
I'm asking you discreetly
On my knees
Oh, would you be so gently?
To say that you'll be true
And say it sentiment'ly
Just like in "Tea for Two"
Oh, would you be so cutely?
To love me absolutely
Because to put it brut'ly
I love you

Mamie.   Oh, would you be so quaintly?
To hold my hand more daintly
And not to be so saintly
With your kiss
Oh, would you be so nicely?
And not so cold as icely
It's better versa vicely
Just like this

Lone Rider.   Oh, would you be so freely?
And not so shy and coy
And sit upon my kneely
Just like in Sonny Boy?
Would you be so divinely?
To say that you'll be minely
So I could tell you fin'lly
I love you

Mamie.   Oh, would you be so frankly?
So frankly I'll be thankly
To tell me pointly blankly
You'll be mine

Lone Rider.   Oh, would you be so madly?
To say you can be hadly
For goodly or for badly
Rain or shine

Mamie.   Oh, would I be too freshly?
To ask you to my room
I'm only blood and fleshly
And you're so love in bloom

Both.   Like Annie Oakley
You're okey dokely
This ain't the bunkly
To be so kindly
Oh, won't you be so kindly to me?

The main love ballad from *Hats* was "The World Is in My Arms." "It was never a hit," Burt Lane has commented, "but has become a standard." It anticipates later, less conventional Harburg lyrics where the tension between searching and finding, questing and settling down is not so easily resolved. (The song is revived—beautifully—by Michael Feinstein on a 1993 Elektra Nonesuch release, *Michael Feinstein Sings the Burton Lane Songbook*, Vol. 2, Elektra Nonesuch 9 79285-2.)

THE WORLD IS IN MY ARMS

Verse.

My the world was big just a day ago
For just a day ago who,
Who would ever dream I'd be dancing with you

Every star was far just a night ago
And just a night ago, too
I seemed so all miscast
Just getting nowhere fast—

Chorus.

Here was I, a gypsy
Looking for a world to roam in
Now the world is in my arms

No more aimless searching
For a place to feel at home in
For the world is in my arms

Tropical seas, Florida skies
Mexican hills
Here in your eyes

When I see you smile
I see the sunsets of Geneva
What's that magic in your charms?
When I hold you
I hold the world right here in my arms.

Yip even managed to work one political number into *Hats*—a satiric rouser that Jolson put over with terrific verve:

There's a Great Day Coming, Mañana

There's a great day coming, mañana
With a wonderful, wonderful dream
Everybody we're told
Will be rolling in gold
We'll be out of the doldrums, mañana

There'll be beer and pretzels, mañana
There'll be strawberries floating in cream
All your skies'll be blue
All your cares'll be few
All your Fords'll be Buicks, mañana

There'll be high times
Pie-in-the-sky times
So come you mourners
And pick your plums
There's a great day coming, mañana
If mañana ever comes

There's a great day coming, mañana
With a wonderful, wonderful dream
We'll have chocolate fudge
And no one to begrudge
When we balance the budget, mañana
There'll be glory glory mañana
All our glorious dreams'll come true
Income tax'll grow small
Billy Rose'll grow tall
Gypsy Rose'll take all off, mañana
Father Divine
And Amy Semple
Are in their temple
And beating drums
For that great day coming, mañana
If mañana ever comes

Second Chorus. There's a great day coming, mañana
We'll be wealthy and ready to share
Here's your ace in the hole
Guys from off o' the dole
Will be paid to play polo, mañana
There'll be hallelujah, mañana

There'll be brotherly love in the air
Florida will love Cal
Ruby's gonna love Al
Martin Dies'll kiss Stalin, mañana

There's a great day coming, mañana
We'll be Aryans walking on air
We'll be Nordic and fair
With blue eyes and blond hair
We'll be living on ersatz, mañana
There'll be beer and pretzels, mañana
With bicarbonate soda to spare
There'll be glasses to clink
And tequila to drink
Everyone'll be stinkin', mañana

Mister Hitler and Mister Goering and Mussolini
Are beating drums
For that great day coming, mañana
But mañana never comes

"Living on ersatz" indeed: beer and pretzels is about as organic as "Mañana"'s paradise deferred ever becomes—in sharp contrast to the natural imagery that suffused Yip's more serious ballads.

Reviews of *Hats* were universally favorable, praising the score and the humor of the performances: Brooks Atkinson called it "one of the funniest musical plays that have stumbled onto Broadway for years." Mainly, though, they welcomed Jolson back to Broadway. The reviews made clear that this was above all a Jolson show: "At about 11:10," wrote critic John Mason Brown, "he happily discarded the book and began singing some of the songs he has made famous." To thunderous applause, he sang "April Showers," "Sonny Boy." "Swanee."

Lost in the shuffle was the Harburg-Lane score. "I have heard from many sources," Ira wrote Yip soon after the opening, "that the reason your score isn't selling as well as it might is because when Jolson goes into his medley one is apt to forget the earlier songs whether they are by Harburg-Lane or Beethoven-Goethe." "The power of Jolson over an audience," George Jean Nathan noted when *Hats* opened, "I have seldom seen equalled"— and, he might have added, the power of Jolson over the creators of his shows. Yip and Burt returned to California, where they soon produced an appropriate song for their Hollywood homecoming: "The Movies Gonna Get You If You Don't Watch Out."

Tinsel Town

For the next three years, the movies most surely got Yip. He returned to Los Angeles, remarried (to Edelaine Gorney), and had a house built in Brentwood (by one of the rare black architects on the West Coast, Paul Williams). There, he worked with Lane and Arlen on a succession of largely forgettable pictures: *Babes on Broadway, Panama Hattie,* and *Ship Ahoy* with Lane; *Rio Rita* and *Kismet* (no relation to the later stage musical) with Arlen. Now and then, there were songs to be interpolated into other pictures as well: over one such song in Yale's Harburg Collection, Yip was to write, "A dreary lyric written to order for some dreary MGM picture." However, Yip and Burt could not be totally tuned out.

Burt Lane said about a song with Yip for *Ship Ahoy:*

> He avoided clichés like the plague, and he was always searching for a new way to say "I love you" and was very successful at it. I wrote a song with him very shortly after *Hold on to Your Hats* at Metro which turned out to be the first time Frank Sinatra sang as a single rather than with the Dorsey orchestra, and I think it's one of the most endearing lyrics Yip ever wrote. It was for a picture called *Ship Ahoy* [1942] starring Red Skelton, and the song is called "Poor You."

POOR YOU

Verse.

I'm sad for anybody walkin' about
Who's missed all the thrills I've been thru
I'm sad for anybody who hasn't found out
Just what your caresses can do
And that's why I'm "espeshly" sad for you

Chorus.

Poor you
I'm sorry you're not me
For you will never know
What loving you can be

Poor you
You never know your charms
You never feel your warmth,
You're never in your arms.

When it is you I'm kissing,
I pity you constantly
You don't know what you're missing
For you're only kissing poor me

> Poor you
> You'll live your whole life thru
> And yet you'll never know
> The thrill of loving you.

The early forties saw Yip working with some notable new collaborators. With composer Arthur Schwartz, Yip produced the score for the musical film *Cairo*. And in 1944 he initiated a short-lived collaboration with a giant of American music, Jerome Kern.

The project that united Harburg and Kern was *Can't Help Singing,* a Universal Deanna Durbin vehicle that proved to be second-drawer Kern and second-drawer Harburg. For Yip, working with Kern was an exciting but difficult experience. For one thing, he had trouble deciphering Kern's compositions when Kern played them for him on his piano. As he once told radio interviewer Jonathan Schwartz,

> Jerome Kern was not a very good player. In fact, I had to listen to the tune many times before I could get it. He was always mechanically figuring out the tune, and that's very hard on the lyric writer. The lyric writer likes to hear the thing done as if it were done orchestrally. Lane is very good that way.

So good, in fact, that Yip would bring Kern's piano parts to Lane and ask him to perform them so that he could grasp the music more clearly. Lane, however, came to detect some incompatibility between the Harburg and Kern schools of songwriting. Lane recalled:

> I don't think it was on purpose, but Yip would suddenly add notes. He'd come in with a lyric and there were always ifs and ands and buts that weren't there originally. I would try to accommodate him because I always feel that if a writer has a wonderful line, don't spoil it. I was very flexible. But when he was doing a picture with Jerry Kern, Yip used to come over to the house with Kern's piano part and say, "Would you play this for me?" I said, "Sure." He'd throw a line at me. I said, "You've added a syllable. You better not fool around with Kern." And he had to learn exactly what Kern put down.

Besides the title song, which became a hit, and a song entitled "More and More" (also a hit), the score to *Can't Help Singing* contains one "lyric-fun" number—the song "Californ-i-ay."

CALIFORN-I-AY

Verse.

There are poets who sing
Of that mythical Kingdom of Arcady
But alack! And unfortunately
They're not up with the times

For there isn't a thing
In that second-hand Kingdom of Arcady
That compares with the sun or the sea
Of that gold-spangled coast
Pardon us if we boast
When we toast:

Chorus.

Californ-i-ay
Where each plum and each prune
Is as big as the moon
Californ-i-ay
Where December comes dolled up like May
Where the rain doesn't rain
It just drizzles champagne
Californ-i-ay
Where romance is the theme of the day

From San Pedro to Fresno,
No maiden there says "No" when love is nigh
For in gay Californ-i-ay
Ev'rything's tremendous,
Titanic, stupendous
The ocean is better
And bluer and wetter
The mountains are higher
The deserts are dryer
The boys have more shekels
The girls have more freckles
Californ-i-ay
Oh, without it there's no U.S.A.

Yip and Kern did not work together after *Can't Help Singing;* whether their collaboration would have continued had Kern lived longer—he died in the following year—is impossible to surmise. Kern had not worked with a lyricist like Yip since he had worked with P. G. Wodehouse in the memorable Princess Theater shows three decades earlier. His reputation was that of a rather inflexible composer when it came to accommodating his lyricist, and precious few Kern songs except for several with Dorothy Fields contain the kind of verbal pyrotechnics we have come to associate with such lyricists as Harburg, Gershwin, or Hart.

Yip's first song with Kern preceded *Can't Help Singing* by one year, and like his first forties song with Schwartz (they had written one song in 1934), it was written for a political benefit. The Schwartz song, for which Ira Gershwin and Yip wrote the lyric in one evening, was entitled "Honorable Moon," and was conceived and performed for an event benefiting United China Relief. (Yip received a letter of thanks from Madame Sun Yat-Sen.) Yip's initial song with Kern, "And Russia Is Her Name," was performed (by tenor Allan Jones) at a 1943 Hollywood Bowl gala benefiting Russian War Relief.

Yip was long accustomed to composing lyrics for political benefits; the difference was that during the Second World War, those benefits were held for causes that coincided for a time with official government policy. Like many on the political left, Yip suspended a measure of his normally critical spirit in deference to the war effort. All songwriters active during the Second World War, of course, perforce wrote songs in support of the effort. Yip actually wrote relatively few, but one—"The Son of a Gun Who Picks on Uncle Sam," to music by Lane—captures faithfully the wartime nationalism and suspension of class politics that suffused much of the American Left in the war years.

THE SON OF A GUN WHO PICKS ON UNCLE SAM

Verse.

I hate war and war hates me,
And all you sailors hate the sea
The soldiers all hate reveille
Of that I am convinced
But no matter what or whom we hate
We're mighty glad to liquidate
When someone knocks the ship of state
I don't get it!
Well for inst.

Chorus.

The army hates the bloomin' sight of the navy
And how the navy hates the bloomin' marines
But the army and the navy and marines'll take a slam
At the son of a gun who picks on Uncle Sam
Oh capital may take a wallop at labor
The C.I.O. may slug the A.F. Of L.
But the A.F. Of L. and the C.I.O.
Are ready to take a wham
At the son of a gun who picks on Uncle Sam

Though our melting pot may boil red hot
With a thousand diff'rent types
Though we lefts and rights may have our fights
We all stand pat on the no good rat
Who belittles the Stars and Stripes

Oh, Florida may love to roast California
Republicans may roast the old Democrats
But a hundred and thirty million strong
Are ready to roast the ham
Of the one who picks on Uncle Sam
Of the son of a gun who picks on Uncle Sam.

But Yip was ultimately and mercifully an imperfect tribune for the wartime popular front. In spirit, Yip's best political songs are critical, not celebratory; he was ultimately more comfortable assailing than praising the political order. In arms against the system, Yip is a poet; at ease in the system's arms, he is uncomfortable.

And only at the height of the popular front's embrace of things American did Yip become sufficiently acceptable to become, however briefly, a Hollywood musical producer. In 1943, Yip produced the MGM musical *Meet the People* from the successful stage musical by Jay Gorney and Henry Myers. Even then, his temperament remained that of a rebel; Harburg never went gently into the studio night. He reminisced once with Max Wilk about his days at MGM:

I had trouble all the time at Metro, with executives. They'd call me in and say, "Now, look, we want a show here that has no messages. Messages are for Western Union. We like your stuff, but you're inclined to be too much on the barricades. Let's get down to entertainment." Sam Katz, Arthur Freed . . . they were always worried about me. But I always felt my power. They had to have me. If they wanted funny songs, there weren't too many around that could do them. If they wanted songs with some kind of class and quality—well, there weren't too many guys around like Larry Hart and the Gershwins. There were just a few of us, maybe five or six. I figured, hell, if they wanted me, they'd have to endure my politics.

My wife thinks it was because I was liked—and she maintains I have a certain spell-binding charm, with men especially. Now that I look back on those days, I think she may be right. They were all frightened of my ideas, but they all liked me. All of them, even Louis Mayer. Maybe it was some

Yip and Harold Arlen were the songwriters for the historic first all-black film musical for general audiences, *Cabin in the Sky,* which starred talented performers who had been barred from such films during the thirties. During the Second World War, the U.S. government induced the Hollywood moguls to aid wartime racial unity; this trend ended with the war, and harsh racial film stereotypes again appeared. (Note: typical of media hype, the authors are not mentioned in the publicity.) (Collection of Harburg Estate.)

sort of chemistry. I was never a wheeler-dealer, never a businessman *per se,* and they always thought I was a pretty poetic sort of guy and not a conspirator.

Cabin in the Sky

In 1943, the same year as his short-lived career as a producer, Yip took on an MGM assignment that called for a poet. He teamed up with Arlen for his only memorable post-*Oz* picture, *Cabin in the Sky,* from the Broadway show of the same name.

Cabin in the Sky was a film of firsts—the first film for a mass, not exclusively black audience that showcased and starred black talent; the first film to be directed by Vincente Minnelli, later to be acknowledged as a master of the film musical. Part of *Cabin*'s value today is as a record of stellar performers denied access because of racism to the great mass of contemporaneous pictures: the film featured Ethel Waters, Lena Horne, Eddie "Rochester" Anderson, John Bubbles, and Rex Ingram, not to mention Louis Armstrong and Duke Ellington. In form, *Cabin in the Sky* somewhat resembled Marc Connelly's *The Green Pastures,* a musicalized morality play/folk tale. The film was to be an adaptation of the 1940 Broadway musical hit by poet John Latouche and Yip's old collaborator, Vernon Duke.

Yip had been approached initially to do the lyrics for the Broadway show. He declined the offer, for reasons he subsequently explained:

> Vernon Duke had written a beautiful score. He couldn't write bad music, but he was a concert composer—like "April in Paris," you couldn't have a more beautiful tune. His domain was writing these smart, charming, sophisticated songs. When he brought the show to me and wanted me to do it with him on Broadway, I felt he was wrong for the music and I turned it down. And he got mad at me and never talked to me again for a long time. . . .
>
> By some serendipity, while I was working at MGM, they bought the product and wanted to make a picture of it. And Freed, who was a very knowing producer of musicals, came to me and said, "This show needs some Southern songs, and hasn't got any." I said, "I know. That's why I turned it down." He said, "Would you do it?" I said, "Well, I've always loved the property. Let's do it." And I got Harold and we rewrote the score for *Cabin in the Sky.*

There was no doubt in Yip's mind, or anyone's, that Arlen was the right composer for *Cabin.* Arlen, after all, had begun his career as composer of the Cotton Club revues; Ethel Waters had once called him "the Negro-est white man" she had ever known. As Yip himself once noted,

> Arlen's hallmark is his synthesis of Negro rhythms and Hebraic melodies. They make a terrific combination, a fresh chemical reaction. George Gershwin did this too, in his own brilliant way. Gershwin and Arlen created a new sound in American theater music by combining black and Jewish elements.

Curiously, though, for all of Yip's earlier work with Harold, it was not until *Cabin* that the two of them had the opportunity to work together on songs for black performers. Even here, they eschewed a straight-out blues number in the manner in which Arlen clearly excelled. Ted Koehler and Johnny Mercer were Arlen's blues men. For Arlen, work with Yip meant comic songs, theater songs, production numbers, and ballads. Yip's personal exuberance and his politics did not make him the man for Arlen's blues.

Arlen and Harburg were not asked to compose a new score from scratch for *Cabin;* indeed, some of Duke and Latouche's songs had already become standards: the title number and the exhilarating "Taking a Chance on Love" in particular. None of the Duke-Latouche songs are either musically or lyrically in the black idiom, though, and Harold and Yip produced five songs to fill this gap. Of these, three are included in the picture: "Li'l Black Sheep," "Happiness is Jes' a Thing Called Joe," and "Life's Full of Consequence." As performed by the Hall Johnson Choir, "Li'l Black Sheep" comes across like a song composed by the Negro-est white man in America; it is crafted to sound like the most traditional and backwater of black church music, mixing song and shout.

"Life's Full of Consequence," however, is a comic duet performed by Eddie "Rochester" Anderson and his seductress, Lena Horne. Yip was delighted writing for Eddie's raspy voice and wary mien. Trying to be a faithful husband and not succumb to Lena's blandishments, Eddie sings "Consequence" with wide-eyed terror and to a heavily accented and plodding beat, as if he is oh so deliberately backing away from something he wants oh so much.

LIFE'S FULL OF CONSEQUENCE

Verse.   Oh life's full o' honey and life's full o' wine
          Oh life's full o' song and ev'rything fine
          Life is simply reekin' with raisins and riches
          It's packed with pleasure but the only hitch is

Chorus.
He.   Life's full of consequence
          That ole devil consequence
          He takes all the frivol out of fun
          When you got the candle lit
          At both ends
          The scandal it
          Creates always keeps you on the run

          Just when you're weakenin'
          Fate sends the deacon in
          Crash! And your pash
          Ain' worth an ounce
          'Cause den come the consequence,
          That ole devil consequence
          Flings you back with a bounce
          It's consequences what counts

She.   Life's full of consequence,
              But who's scared o' consequence?
              Let's sip the honey while it's sweet
              We could be messin' 'round
              But you is digressin' 'round
              While I'm tossin' nature at your feet

              Why don't we mosy 'round?
              You could be cosy 'round
              A gal who could sprinkle you wid spice

He.   But how 'bout the consequence,
              That ole devil consequence
              I've been burned more than twice
              And I ain't payin' the price

              Just when you're cashin' in
              Boom! Comes the rationin'
              Life's always full of funny quirks
              But worst is de consequence,
              That ole devil consequence
              That's the wrench in the works
              It's consequences that irks.

In "Consequence"'s original verse, Yip attributed all manner of temptation to the Lord:

              De Lord made women
              De Lord made wine
              De Lord made song
              And everything fine
              To ensure all dis
              He furnished five senses
              And den provided de consequences

But if the censors in the Breen office were not about to let "Lydia" slip by them, they had even less inclination to allow Yip to introduce his pantheist and hedonist god to the viewing public: on the screen, "Consequence" appears sans verse (and the song ends with "I ain't payin' the price" sans the last stanza).

"Consequence" is the first in a series of Harburg songs whose titles center around one-word abstract nouns—"T'morra" in *Bloomer Girl* and, still later, *Finian's Rainbow*'s "Necessity" and *Jamaica*'s "Incompatability." In each of these songs, some man-made creation intervenes to undo nature's noble handiwork and inhibit men and women from following their natural impulses. Georgia Brown (Lena Horne) may be an agent of Satan in the screenplay of *Cabin in the Sky*, but in the lyric for "Consequence" she is a smashing advertisement for Yipper's god of nature—a deity we will see a great deal of before the forties are done.

Cabin's other Arlen-Harburg song ended up as the smash hit of the picture, but it began life as an unset tune in Arlen's trunk. It was nonetheless a tune Yip remembered, and one he thought was right for *Cabin*.

As Yip told the story:

> Harold had a tune. He had it for a long time. And he was not proud of it. . . . A reverse situation took place here than with "Over the Rainbow." Here, he had a tune that he never wanted written out. He thought it was too ordinary, and I'd always loved that tune. I'd always begged him to write it, and when we got to *Cabin in the Sky*, I said, "Will you dig that tune out of the trunk?" And he did. And when I said, "Happiness Is a Thing Called Joe" for that tune, for the first time he began liking the tune, and he let me use it. And he was going to throw it away. Harold had a lot of tunes that he threw away that I would love to resuscitate.

It was not, of course, an ordinary tune—there is nothing ordinary about first-rate Arlen—but it was a quiet tune, a tune of small steps and deceptive simplicity, disguising some unusual melodic turns (as Alec Wilder has noted, the song's "first ending" on the line "all I need to know" comes on D for a song in C: nothing routine about that.) To it, Yip set these words:

HAPPINESS IS A THING CALLED JOE

Verse.

Skies ain't gonna cloud no mo'
The crops ain't gonna fail
Caught a bluebird by the toe,
A rainbow by the tail,
A certain man with eyes that shine
Voodoo'd up this heart of mine

Chorus.

It seem like happiness is jes' a thing called Joe
He's got a smile that makes the lilac wanna grow
He's got a way that makes the angels heave a sigh
When they know little Joe's
Passing by

Sometime the cabin's gloomy an' the table bare
Then he'll kiss me an' it's Christmas ev'rywhere
Troubles fly away an' life is easy go
Does he love me good,
That's all I need to know
Seem like happiness is jes'
A thing called Joe
Little Joe,
Mm, mm, mm,
Little Joe.

"Joe"'s lyrics are of a piece with its music, and both fit perfectly the character who sings them and the circumstances of her life. "Joe" put into the idiom of theater songs the love ballad of a religious woman in the rural black south a half-century ago. Her associations and Yip's poetic image are with the difficult material conditions of life—the gloomy cabin and bare table—and to those forms of this-and-other-worldly glory which fill her life: lilacs, angels, Christmas.

Moreover, as Arlen's deceptively simple melody is filled with subtle variations, so Yip's deceptively simple lyric is structured rather rigorously around internal rhymes and assonance (the repetition of vowel sounds). A great many of Yip's songs are so structured; it is "Joe" that he once chose as the object of his illustration of the technique. "There was something I tried to do with that song," he said,

> which most laymen probably would never know about. When you're writing a song, where the rhyme falls makes it either hard or easy to remember. There are certain tricks that the skilled lyric writer has to make a song memorable, provided it doesn't become mechanical and the hinges don't stick out. In other words, you want to rhyme as many places as you can without the average ear spotting it as purely mechanical—which is a thing not known now [in rock lyrics] at all. What I mean is this: you take a stress syllable:

> > It seem like happi*ness* is *jes'* a thing called Joe
> > He's got a *smile* that makes the *li*lac wanna grow
> > He's got a *way* that makes the *a*ngels heave a sigh

> See all the internal rhymes?

> > Sometime the *ca*bin's gloomy *an'* the table bare

> That *and* is rhyming with *ca* whether you know it or not. It's difficult to do, but once you accomplish it, it makes a song live, makes it easy to remember, and if the ideas are good, the whole thing begins to sparkle and take on four new lives instead of one.

From "kiss" and "Christmas" to "fly" and "life," internal rhymes suffuse "Joe" and echo the accents on Arlen's notes.

Other images mark "Joe" as a distinctly Yipper lyric: the bluebirds and rainbow of the verse. In *Oz,* a young girl seeks fulfillment in some undiscovered country far from her farmhouse home. "Joe" is the song of an older rural woman, black and poor, who knows the limits of her options: her rainbow, her bluebird, is her man.

Evalina (Celeste Holm) meets Jeff (David Brooks) in the hit show *Bloomer Girl* (1944). Yip asserted this was the first time on Broadway that feminists helped change the values of a slave-owning man to belief in freedom for all—including blacks and women. Agnes de Mille's vanguard ballet added high meaning to the show's subtle allusion to peace. (Billy Rose Theatre Collection, NY Public Library)

Chapter 7

Bloomer Girl and the New Musical

Till finally there comes this revelation
T'morra is the curse of civilization. . . .

Utopia, Utopia,
Don't be a dope
Ya dope ya
Get your Utopia
Now.

Bloomer Girl: Yip's First Vintage Show

In May of 1943, playwright George S. Kaufman wrote Yip to ask if he and Harold would be interested in doing a musical to a book whose outline he sent along. Arlen and Harburg considered the project but passed on it; besides, they were becoming immersed in work on another new show. "Harold and I have been intrigued by an idea for a musical which has the scope and quality we talked about in our last correspondence," Yip wrote Kaufman in July. "It has the freshness of *Life with Father* and the brashness of *Of Thee I Sing*. Also, it is away from *Oklahoma!*, which has spurred a new race of men all mega-lomaniacally bent on duplicating same."

It was an ironic assessment of the project that was to become Yip and Harold's next Broadway musical, *Bloomer Girl*. Like *Of Thee I Sing*, it was a political show, and, like *Life with Father*, it was a period show. But with nearly half a century's hindsight, its most notable claim may be that it was the first post-*Oklahoma!* musical to consolidate and build upon the formal revolution that *Oklahoma!* had begun.

Conventional wisdom tends to view *Oklahoma!* as the great break point in American musical history. Before *Oklahoma!*, with a few such notable precursors as *Show Boat, Of Thee I Sing, Porgy and Bess, On Your Toes*, and *Pal Joey*, musicals were either revues or star vehicles. *Oklahoma!* inaugurated the era of the musical play, where music, dance, book, performance, and sets were all integral elements in the telling of the tale (integrated by an unusual director, Rouben Mamoulian).

But musicals did not magically evolve overnight from one species to the next. Upon its opening on March 31, 1943—and for the subsequent 18 months, until the opening of *Bloomer Girl* in 1944—*Oklahoma!* remained the only musical play on Broadway. Yip manifestly did not consider himself one of the new race of men attempting to duplicate *Oklahoma!*. His aim was considerably more unusual and important than that: in this formative period, he was the one person working in the American musical theater besides Oscar Hammerstein (and, in another vein, Kurt Weill) with the talent, ambition, and drive to create musical plays.

In part, it was a matter of experience. Yip did not come entirely cold to the form. *Hooray for What?* in its initial conception had been a fledgling musical play; *The Wizard of Oz* had been the first of the new, unified movie musicals that were to come from MGM in the forties—and on each, Yip's contribution went well beyond the lyrics. In part, it was a question of politics. Yip very definitely had something to say, something that could sustain a play as well as a song (indeed, an overabundance of subthemes and plots was to characterize Yip's librettos).

What Yip, along with his librettists, Fred Saidy and Sig Herzig, brought to the art of the musical play was a sense of satire and penchant for political comment. Yip was attempting to carve out an area between the satirical operettas that George S. Kaufman, Morrie Ryskind, and the Gershwins had written in the early thirties, and the largely apolitical but integrated musical of Mamoulian, Rodgers and Hammerstein.

With *Bloomer Girl* Yip took full charge of a show for the first time and was "the muscle" behind it. His credits were for lyrics and staging the production, but really he was everywhere—from selecting and guiding the librettists to battling over the choreography with Agnes de Mille. It was an ambitious effort, and one that helped prepare him for *Finian's Rainbow.* As author Ethan Mordden remarks in his book, *Broadway Babies:*

> Could the [satiric and political show] observe Hammerstein's integrated composition? E. Y. Harburg proved that it could. . . . The musical play presented the truth of the world; so musical comedy must recapture the dream. Harburg was whimsical, idealistic, and leftist; he saw Hammerstein's plan as a chance to reconcile the fun of the musical with the tetchy honesty of theme.

Thus, when *Oklahoma!* broke through, Yip was ready—and by decade's end, he stood second only to Hammerstein among those who had transformed the American musical stage.

In the assessment of musical historian Stanley Green,

No other writer has appreciated [the growing importance of the libretto and librettist] more than E. Y. Harburg. Starting as a writer of sophisticated lyrics for revues in the early Thirties, he soon moved away from revues to concentrate his attention on book musicals. . . .

Because of his deep concern with every phase of a production, Harburg was able to make his musicals more totally an expression of his own personality and point-of-view than were the composers with whom he worked. Rather than merely setting words to melodies or blocking out the rudiments of a story to hold the songs together, more often than not he was the motivating force behind each production. More particularly, in the case of Harold Arlen and Burton Lane, *he was able to furnish composers with concepts that helped them turn out their most successful efforts.* [emphasis added]

The idea for *Bloomer Girl* did not originate, though, with Yip or Harold or with producers John Wilson or Nat Goldstone or with the credited librettists, but rather with a couple active in the Hollywood radical circles in which Yip moved: Dan and Lilith James. Lilith's idea, her husband Dan recounted, was to focus on "the perversities of Fashion to dramatize the early struggles of the Women's Rights movement."

Yip outlines the perversity in question:

Lilith James had come across a costume with a bloomer, and when she went back into research she found that the bloomer was a creation of a woman named Amelia Bloomer. Amelia Bloomer was a fighter for women's suffrage, the women's rights movement. She was a contemporary of Susan B. Anthony. She decided the symbol of women's place in society was the hoopskirts they were wearing.

The hoopskirt was an abominable torture chamber for women. Most of them weighed fifty to seventy-five pounds; they had all sorts of whalebone and everything else. For the sake of the style, women were all victims of it. Amelia thought—and very wisely so; she was ahead of Madison Avenue— that if she just talked women's rights to women, it would be in one ear, out the other. But if she said, "Get rid of those heavy hoopskirts; wear bloomers like men; let's get pants; let's be their equal," that they understood.

According to Dan James, Lilith also developed the principle character, Amelia Bloomer's niece, Evelina. The Jameses then wrote what by Dan's account was a complete first draft and by Yip's simply an outline; in either case, James allowed,

Fred Saidy, *left,* began writing with Yip for the 1944 hit *Bloomer Girl;* then they became close partners co-writing the book for *Finian's Rainbow* and several more shows. Fred's wit was as sharp but gentler than Yip's; they collaborated for many years. (Collection of Harburg Estate.)

"It failed to satisfy our lyricist, E. Y. Harburg and Harold Arlen, the composer." By mutual consent, Yip called in Fred Saidy and Sig Herzig, the two screenwriters whom he had employed on the MGM film *Meet the People,* and reshaped with them a story that they then put in book form. Herzig had worked on the books of a number of Broadway revues and movie musicals. *Bloomer Girl* was Fred Saidy's first stage show. A literate writer with a background in journalism and light verse, he had only recently begun screenwriting, but thenceforth he loomed large in Yip's career, coauthoring with Yip the books to most of his subsequent musicals (*Finian, Flahooley, Jamaica, The Happiest Girl in the World*).

Bloomer Girl concerns the political activities of Amelia (renamed Dolly) Bloomer and the effect they have on the pre–Civil War family of her brother-in-law, hoopskirt king Horace Applegate, and his feminist daughter, Evelina. Evelina is the youngest and only remaining unmarried Applegate daughter; her older sisters are all married to company salesmen, and as *Bloomer Girl* begins, Horace is trying to unify business and family by encouraging his chief Southern salesman, Jefferson Calhoun, to court Evelina. On the eve of the Civil War,

Bloomer Girl centers around Evelina's tutelage of Jeff in matters of gender and racial equality. Evelina, Dolly, and the other feminists of Cicero Falls not only campaign against Applegate's hoopskirts and sexism but also stage their own version of *Uncle Tom's Cabin* and conceal a runaway slave—Jeff's own manservant, Pompey. It was, said Yip, a show about "the indivisibility of human freedom."

Bloomer Girl interweaves the issues of black and female equality and war and peace with the vicissitudes of courtship and pre-Civil War politics. Like *Oklahoma!* the show was steeped in Americana, but it was at no point an escapist entertainment. "There were so many new issues coming up with Roosevelt in those years," Yip once said, "and we were trying to deal with the inherent fear of change—to show that whenever a new idea or a new change in society arises, there'll always be a majority that will fight you, that will call you a dirty radical or a red."

Bloomer Girl was written against the background of the Second World War and of the two great wartime demographic shifts in America: the move of southern blacks north and west into the industrial work force, and the move of women out of the home also into that work force. If the book gives equal weight to both struggles, the songs place greater emphasis on the struggle for racial justice. In terms of the writing of the show, this may have been a consequence of Arlen's special affinity for black music; but in terms of the show's social context, it is surely a consequence of the capacity of Yip's political antennae to pick up the vibrations of the time, as well as his lifelong fight against racism. For the black entry into the industrial work force was in large measure an achievement of the fledgling civil rights movement: Franklin Roosevelt had ordered defense work integrated only after black leader A. Phillip Randolph had threatened a civil rights march on Washington; and the entry of blacks into factories and northern cities was an issue of considerable struggle within some unions and fought, on more than one occasion, bloodily in the streets.

The entry of women, by contrast, was a consequence of government policy that came from the top down; the women's movement was far too weak and unformed during the war years to amount to an independent pressure group. In showcasing the cause of blacks, then, *Bloomer Girl* was a daring and topical show. In showcasing the cause of women to the considerable extent that it did, it was a prophetic show, twenty-five years ahead of its time.

Bloomer Girl was also a wartime show. It begins with Applegate's daughters lamenting the absence of their salesmen husbands on the road all year; and concludes as the Civil War breaks out with an Agnes de Mille ballet on the suffering of war. Just how dramatic this particular subtext would become was, as we shall see, a matter of considerable dispute between Harburg and de Mille.

Underlying *Bloomer Girl*'s overt politics were a number of themes with which Yip had dealt in some of his earlier songs and that were to become characteristic of his work as its scope expanded with the advent of the musical play. The new form gave Yip an entire score to develop his imagery and ideas, and there is, indeed, a theme and a body of imagery that Yip varies from song to song throughout *Bloomer Girl*'s score. It is the theme of natural rights, which Yip contrasts repeatedly with socially created constraints. From the struggles of black Americans to be free, to the struggles of men and women to relate, to the American hope for peace in the world, Yip's lyrics appeal for justification to the doctrines and images of natural law. *Bloomer Girl* is set in Lincoln's time and it contains references to the Roosevelt presidency, but the politics of its lyrics are Jeffersonian.

Bloomer Girl's songs are also unified and distinguished by their period setting, an achievement that is equally Arlen's and Harburg's. Arlen, Yip once said,

> was never concerned with the sociological things. He kind of left that up to me; he thought it was sort of an idiosyncracy of mine. But he was intrigued with the period; with the skirts, with the charm of the music of the time. Harold had such great range, but he was getting to be known for "Blues in the Night" and "Stormy Weather." So he was happy to get the opportunity to jump out of that and into a new medium of old Americana, which was really a spin-off from the English madrigal. I think he wanted to get out and be known for something else, and here he had his chance.

Finally, *Bloomer Girl* moved Arlen and Harburg to another level of theater song, where the interconnections between song and story were closer and more all-encompassing than they had ever been before. For Yip, it was a challenge he was eager to take, toward which he had been moving since the outset of his career. Writing theater songs, he once insisted, was a very different task from writing popular songs outside the context of a show.

> It's quite a different medium, because onstage, you must realize, you are constrained and you are in a tight bondage of plot and character and choreography and lighting and a chorus line that wears hoopskirts, probably, and can't make the right exit. . . . A song on a stage is a scene, a tight scene. In fact, it is the climax to a situation.

> To write a song which you listen to and is not supposed to do anything but soothe you or put you at ease is one thing. But when a song is supposed to emotionalize you, to either make you sad or make you laugh, so that at the end of the song you want to explode with applause, that's hard.

> A song must have not only a life *in* the show, but it also must go out and have a life outside the show so that people who don't know the situation,

don't know what's going on, will still sing that song on the outside. . . . It is your advertising. One good hit song makes a show. Two good hit songs or three makes a real hit.

Bloomer Girl's first song fills both the needs of the plot and the demands of the world outside the show. (*Bloomer Girl* has fifteen songs; we shall look at ten of them.) The opening song, "When the Boys Come Home," is sung by Applegate's daughters, awaiting the return home of their traveling salesmen husbands—but it is preceded in the book by reference to the imminence of civil war. For an audience filled with parents, wives, and sweethearts waiting for loved ones to come home from the war, the opening song therefore had particular resonance (and the song is reprised at the final curtain with specific reference to the Civil War):

WHEN THE BOYS COME HOME

Verse.	Stitch stitch, pray and sleep
	Men must work and women must weep
	Twas ever thus since time began
	Woman, oh woman, must wait for man
	Stitch stitch, tie the strings
	This is the sorry scheme of things
	And only one song keeps hearts abeat
	And only one thought makes waiting sweet
Chorus.	When the boys come home
	The clouds will trip lightly away, away
	The clouds will trip lightly away
	When the boys come home
	We'll all be as merry as May, as May
	We'll all be as merry as May
	There'll be drums and trumpets, tea and crumpets
	Out on the Village Green
	A silver moon for that reunion scene
	Oh what joy
	When the boys come home
	The glorious sound of the tramping feet
	Will echo down the winding street
	That leads to a lane where lovers meet
	And may it prove so sweet, so sweet
	That they will never more roam
	When the boys come home!

"When the Boys Come Home" begins with an invocation and quiet subversion of tradition. Though the chorus deals with the emotions of reunion, the verse—sung by Evelina's unemancipated sisters (in a letter, Yip called them "namby-pambies")—goes beyond mere waiting to lay out the whole passive "sorry scheme of things" that was women's lot. Arlen's music for the verse is stately, proper, traditional; Yip's lyric seems so on first hearing but has a quiet bite: note the equation of prayer with sleep in the song's (and the score's) very first line. Indeed, the verse lyric, we later discover, sharply counterpoints later lyrics in the show: it justifies through tradition and superstition a social order that subsequently is undermined by songs with very different kinds of justification.

Both Arlen and Harburg use "When the Boys Come Home" to create a genteel and gently oppressive world, and to introduce the audience to upper-class Cicero Falls in the spring of 1861. The song is a waltz—deliberately somnolent in the verse, quite exultant in the chorus. It is the first of three waltzes in the score (the others are "The Rakish Young Man with the Whiskers" and "Sunday in Cicero Falls"); period production numbers—in hoopskirts, no less—demanded of Yip and Harold a number of waltzes. One consequence is an unusual-sounding score. As Ethan Mordden was to note in *Broadway Babies,*

> *Bloomer Girl*'s score—as a whole it sounds carefully dated, yet other than the inclusion of an unusual number of waltzes, Arlen uses little pastiche. . . . In other words, if Arlen is writing of and for 1944, and within the conventions of musical comedy, why is his sound so . . . well, alien?

In part, the answer lies in the subtle alienation effect Yip and Harold achieve in this number. The joy Yip has his "namby-pambies" express at the homecoming of their salesmen husbands from selling hoopskirts is entirely conventional; indeed, an obvious appropriation of the "joy and rapture" lyrics of W. S. Gilbert's many maidens. Only in the song's penultimate lines do the "personal" lyrics become subtly political, in the lines, "And may it prove so sweet, so sweet / That they will never more roam." These are sung solo in what is otherwise an ensemble number. This is, however, still a song within the conventions of commercial Broadway theater, and its apparent direction still is towards the more personal and emotional.

But the sound is alien because there is nonetheless a distancing effect at work here, nowhere more so than in the bridge. In the lines,

> There'll be drums and trumpets, tea and crumpets
> Out on the Village Green
> A silver moon for that reunion scene

Arlen's music is at its most lilting, but filled with very un-nineteenth-century shifting harmonies (more than any other lines in the show, these sound like a Rodgers waltz), while Yip's lyrics depict an exultant but then genteel and ultimately artificial scene. The lines work both ways, then: as conventional sentiment expressed by conventional characters; but the "silver moon" hanging over the scene suggests the paper moon that once hung over Yip and Harold's cardboard sea.

Bloomer Girl's odd fusion of old and new sounds continues into its second number, the comic-romantic duet "Evelina," which, however improbably, proved to be the show's biggest commercial hit. The song climaxes the first meeting of the amiable Jefferson Calhoun with a wary Evelina, who knows her father views this courtship as good for business, but is duly concerned about Jeff's intentions.

As an admirer of her Aunt Dolly, Evelina is not the sort to acquiesce quietly to her father's matchmaking. When Jefferson Calhoun arrives and tries to charm her in song, she is suitably cynical:

EVELINA

He.   Evelina, won't ya ever take a shine to that moon?
                Evelina, ain't ya bothered by the bobolink's tune?
                Tell me, tell me how long
                You're gonna keep delayin' the day
                Don't ya reckon it's wrong
                Triflin' with April this way?
                Evelina, won't ya pay a little mind to me soon?
                Wake up! Wake up!
                The earth is fair, the fruit is fine
                But what's the use of smellin' watermelon
                Clingin' to another fellow's vine?
                Evelina, won't ya roll off that vine and be mine?

She turns the tables on him, singing her own version of the song:

She.   Evelina, won't ya ever take a shine to that moon?
                Our lives would be a perfect hitch
                'Cause you're so handsome, I'm so rich
                Evelina, ain't ya bothered by the bobolink's tune?
He.   I'd be content with only you

She.	And just a chambermaid or two
	Tell me, tell me how long
	You're gonna keep delayin' the day
	Don't ya reckon it's wrong
	Triflin' with finance this way?
He.	Evelina, won't ya pay a little mind to me soon?
	Wake up! Wake up!
She.	The trap is set, the pickin's fine
He.	But what's the use of smellin' watermelon
	Clingin' to another fella's vine?
	Evelina, won't ya roll off that vine and be mine?
Both.	Roll off that vine and be mine.
	Roll off that vine and be mine.

In "Evelina," the kidding of convention that was present in "When the Boys Come Home" becomes a bit less concealed—and not simply because the second chorus turns into a duet linking love and money. As with "Boys," there is a gentle send-up of convention here, beginning with the end-line rhyming of "moon" with "tune." It is appropriate to a song sung in the mid–nineteenth century, but it cannot be played straight in a theater song of 1944. And "Evelina," as Alec Wilder noted, sounds like an old-fashioned song—and a forties song.

In fact, "Evelina" is an old-fashioned melody undercut by a blue note and a forced rhyme. The keys to the song are the rhymes for "Evelina" and the notes on which they fall. The rhymes, in order, are "shine to," "mind to," and "vine and." None of these, of course, are real rhymes, unless they are broken down just to rhyming for the one syllable. But they are not meant to be heard in that separated fashion. They come over two-note phrases accompanying the last two notes in "Evelina;" and in singing "Evelina," in the chorus's last line, the final syllable is stressed by stretching it into something of a Southern call—as if calling someone in from the field to the Big House.

More important, though, "shine" and "mind" fall on the highest notes in their lines, and they are blue notes—flatted, suggestive of sexuality, and clearly not of the period in which the song to that point seems set. Modernity and sexuality have been dropped into a gentle ballad, and Yip responds with an appropriately loose rhyme. Yip's worksheets for "Evelina" show that initially, the internal rhyme was not situated on the blue note. At first, Yip wrote (the word on the blue note is italicized):

Evelina, there are blossoms shinin' *under* that moon
and
Evelina, June is shinin' through that *jubilee* moon,

only later realizing the internal rhymes fit best on the blue note.

The blue note appears in only one other place in "Evelina," under the second "Wake up," again underscoring its sexual connotation. The wake-up call then leads into a series of natural images of earth, fruit, watermelon. At this stage, in this song, the imagery is invoked in a light, almost comic, manner: the characters have just met, and the song is a gentle, almost soft-shoesy number. There is no great intensity here, but the groundwork is being laid for later ballads where the emotional stakes are higher.

The song's coda—"Roll off that vine and be mine"— summarizes its spirit. Evelina and Jeff sing it together, in old-fashioned harmony, but nineteenth-century musical formality is refracted through a more modern, sensual, amused lyric.

As a liberated woman of 1860, however, Evelina has other matters besides courtship and love (she is beginning to fall for Jeff) to attend to. She is helping her Aunt Dolly publish a suffragette newspaper, helping thereby to undermine her own father's business. When Jeff comes to retrieve Evelina from Dolly Bloomer's clutches, he is given a little consciousness-raising, complete with Agnes de Mille's choreography and Yip's lyrics:

IT WAS GOOD ENOUGH FOR GRANDMA
(excerpt)

Verse.
Grandma was a lady
She sewed and cleaned and cooked
She scrubbed her pets
And raised her tots
The dear old gal was hooked!
She stitched her little stitches
Her life was applesauce
The thing that wore the britches was boss.
She had no voice in gov'ment
Bondage was her fate
She only knew what love meant
From eight to half past eight
And that's a hell of a fate!

Chorus.   It was good enough for grandma
That good old gal
With her frills and her feathers and fuss
It was good enough for grandma
Good enough for grandma
But it ain't good enough for us!

When granny was a lassie
That tyrant known as man
Thought women's place
Was just the space
Around a frying pan
He made the world his oyster
Now it ain't worth a cuss
This oyster he can't foister on us.

We won the revolution
In 1776
Who says it's nix
For us to mix
Our sex with politics
We've bigger seas to swim in
And bigger worlds to slice
Oh sisters, are we women or mice?

Look twice before you step on
The fair sex of the earth
Beware our secret weapon
We could stop giving birth
Take that for what it's worth . . .

It was good enough for grandma
That good old gal
With her frills and her feathers and fuss
It was good enough for grandma
Good enough for grandma
But it ain't good enough for us!

It is a witty lyric that at times conveys real anger—though that, too, with wit. (Note the line "The thing that wore the britches was boss," where the unspeakable thing does not merit the dignity of the article *the* before "boss.") "Grandma" is a serious argument within a comic song—upbeat, snappy, and suffused with funny rhymes: the music, however, lacks the bite of the lyrics.

Bloomer Girl's next song, by contrast, was conceived as a serious argument within a serious song. The lyric shifts from light verse to poetry, the music from comic march to ballad, the subject from women's rights to a subject that the most enlightened forties audiences considered of greater gravity: the status of blacks. For Dolly Bloomer is concerned not only with women's rights but also civil rights; her headquarters is a way station on the Underground Railroad.

Evelina persuades Jeff to help hide a trunk containing a runaway slave. When the trunk is opened, out steps none other than Pompey, his own slave. "How could you do this, Pompey?" demands Jeff. And the runaway slave explains:

Hubert (Bil) Dilworth sings "The Eagle and Me," a civil rights song from *Bloomer Girl*, 1944. It was revived in the late eighties by Lena Horne, who sang it with a more urgent rhythm and stronger emphasis on the idea of freedom. (Collection of Harburg Estate.)

THE EAGLE AND ME

Verse.
What makes the gopher leave his hole?
Tremblin' with fear and fright
Maybe the gopher's got a soul
Wantin' to see the light

That's it oh yea, oh yea, that's it
The scripture has it writ
Betcha life that's it

Nobody like hole
Nobody like chain
Don't the good Lord all aroun' you make it plain?

Chorus.
River it like to flow
Eagle it like to fly
Eagle it like to feel its wings against the sky

Possum it like to run
Ivy it like to climb
Bird in the tree and bumble bee
Want freedom in Autumn or Summer time

Ever since that day
When the world was an onion
'Twas natch'ral for
The spirit to soar and play
The way the Lawd wanted it

Free as the sun is free
That's how it's gotta be
Whatever is right for bumble bee
And river and eagle is right for me
We gotta be free
The eagle and me.

"The Eagle and Me" occupies a transitional place among what we might term the "black plight" songs of the American theater; that is at once its distinction and its limitation. There had been serious ballads for black characters on the musical stage before that had dealt with the legacy of racism: "Ol' Man River" and Irving Berlin's "Suppertime" come to mind. But both "Ol' Man River" and "Suppertime" are lamentations that take the oppressed black condition as a given, as does the Gershwins' *Porgy and Bess*. Also, "Ol' Man River," "Suppertime," and *Porgy and Bess* are works of the twenties and thirties. "The Eagle and Me" is a ballad of the forties, when, for the first time, a nascent civil rights movement was beginning to direct public attention to the possibility of curtailing institutional racism. A lamentation would no longer suffice, and "The Eagle and Me" is not a song in the same vein as its predecessors. It is, rather, the first theater song of the fledgling civil rights movement.

The challenge before Arlen and Harburg, then, was in large part one of tone. The tone of "Ol' Man River," "Suppertime," and *Porgy and Bess* is tragic but far from agitational: these songs ask people to grieve and persevere but not explicitly to change. Arlen and Harburg and history came together on "Eagle" at a point past mere grieving; the songwriters opted instead to make a case for racial justice. What they created was a light but serious song: Mordden calls it "an amiable hymn to freedom." It was an assignment that evoked one of Yip's richest lyrics.

Like "April in Paris," "The Eagle and Me" moves from an imagistic beginning to a personal conclusion. It begins in the verse with the humblest of associations—the gopher seeking the light—and a rather conventional justification, though certainly one appropriate to a nineteenth-century black character: biblical sanction. In the chorus, though, the sanction of scripture becomes the universals of Darwin and Newton. The first sections of the chorus contain images of nature and the physical world; the striving for freedom is linked with some universal life force, some basic natural law. Of all the images, that of the eagle is given special emphasis, partly by virtue of repetition, partly by its vividness of imagery. There is an almost palpable sense of freedom conveyed by the eagle's feeling his "wings against the sky," enhanced by the alliteration and long vowels on the stressed and longer notes in the words *flow, fly, feel, sky.*

Yip got credit for directing and for the lyrics of the Broadway success *Bloomer Girl* (1944) while infusing the show with its triple themes of feminism, antiracism, and peace. (Collection of Harburg Estate.)

The shock of the lyric comes in the bridge. In one line Yip turns the song into something of a moral creation epic; he moves the basis for freedom beyond the merely natural to the cosmological. The line has its ardent admirers. "My favorite lyric line," Stephen Sondheim said on Jonathan Schwartz's radio show in 1977,

> is from "The Eagle and Me," and it is, "ever since the day when the world was an onion." And that seems the essence of what Yip Harburg could do as, for lack of a better word, a poet. . . . What it is, is a resonant line that implies a whole ethos. But it's such an exhilarating and terrific line and it just sits there and lands so perfectly. It just feels so good.

It was a line that had circled a long time before landing. "A good lyric writer has ideas stacked away," Yip once said. "You store titles, maybe one word you like." The onion, it seemed, had been in storage for around thirty years: "I remembered it from a geology class. I remember the instructor saying the world had layers and layers, like an onion. I never forgot that image of the world."

The images and music are light; the case is not: at bottom, the civil rights struggle, says Yip, is about rights as fundamental and incontestable as gravity— about physical laws encoded, like genes in a DNA molecule, in Yip's ancient onion. Moreover, the lyrical "onion" line is set to the only blue melody line in the song; the effect of music and lyric together is electric. The bridge continues with associations appropriate to the eagle, but this time applied for the first time to the subject under discussion: now, it is natural for the spirit, not just the eagle, to soar and play. The music then returns to the song's initial A section, but the lyrics become personal, not associative; the mood imperative ("That's how it's gotta be"). "The Eagle" concludes openly as a civil rights anthem—without a trace of preachment.

It may be, though, that Arlen felt the burden of lightness too keenly in composing "The Eagle." It plays, but it does not quite soar; it is not only amiable, as Mordden wrote, it is perhaps too amiable. Its arrangement made it seem lighter still. It may ultimately be a gauge of how tenuous the idea of civil rights still was in 1944 that Yip and Harold decided upon so airy an anthem for so weighty a theme. Lena Horne's 1988 recording of "Eagle" (on *The Men in My Life*, Three Cherries Records TC 64411) rearranged the music and re-emphasized the lyrics in a way that made the song into the civil rights anthem Yip had initially intended.

Bloomer Girl's score is also unusual in that it contains just one love ballad. "Right as the Rain," which Jeff and Evelina sing to each other in the middle of the first act, seems in unexpected dialogue with "The Eagle and Me" in at least one particular: as Pompey justifies his freedom, so Jeff and Evelina justify their love with references to the inexorable laws of nature.

RIGHT AS THE RAIN

Right as the rain
That falls from above
So real, so right is our love

It came like the spring
That breaks through the snow
I can't say what it may bring
I only know
I only know
It's right to believe
Whatever gave your eyes this glow
Whatever gave my heart this song
Can't be wrong

It's right as the rain
That falls from above
And fills the world with the bloom
Of our love

As rain must fall
As day must dawn
This love, this love must go on.

For Yip and his peers, writing love-song lyrics was a tightrope walk, balancing the need for emotion against the fear of banality. "Ira wouldn't write any straight mushy love songs," Yip once said.

> Neither would I. Mine may be a bit more emotional than his but still avoid the clichéd metaphor. For instance, if I want to get real warm, I say, "You got a smile that makes the lilacs want to grow"—not "You are like the lilacs on my door."
>
> I needed a love song in *Bloomer Girl,* so I wrote "Right as the Rain." I didn't want to say, "Oh, I love you forever. You are the spring and the blossoms." I said it more poetically: "Right as the rain that falls from above. . . ." It's a good, mature evaluation of a love situation, not an attempt to compare feelings associated with love to a clichéd notion of romance. . . .
>
> It didn't say it's a miracle, sent by God, only something between us two. . . . It's a feeling on a plane of person to person, not riddled with myths or miracles.

Alec Wilder has observed that "Right as the Rain" flows, almost sectionless, in the manner of a Kern ballad. Arlen returns to the melody's front phrase at two other intervals in the course of the song, and for each of its three appearances, Yip sets "It's right" to the line's first notes. On the line's second appearance, Arlen follows it with a different passage. It's not quite different enough to be a bridge, though, so Yip begins the line with the same lyric, then varies it in quintessentially Harburgian fashion: "It's right *to believe.*" Arlen and Harburg bring the line back the third time, climactically, one octave higher and to a minor harmony.

The song ends with a three-line coda, against whose rising and falling notes Yip writes:

> As rain must fall
> As day must dawn
> This love, this love must go on.

Here, Jeff and Evelina's love is invested with a cosmic inexorability, which the music—suggesting regular, cyclical fallings and risings—reinforces. The mood also becomes imperative—as it did in the coda of "The Eagle and Me" and the verse of "When the Boys Come Home." Even in its sparing use of the imperative mood, *Bloomer Girl*'s lyrics pit the naturally ordained against the socially mandated.

Like Jeff and Evelina, Daisy, the maid, is eager for, if not exactly romantic involvement, then—well, sex. Her boyfriend is demanding she choose between him and her radical "bloomers," while her suffragist sisters are urging her to defer any such involvement for the moment. For all Yip's sympathy with the movement, there is no surer sin against nature, according to Harburg, than this deferral. It was a familiar theme for Yip: indeed, in his workbooks we come across the formulation,

> Mañana, mañana, mañana
> They don't wanna—

but that was too much like the song he had written for *Hold on to Your Hats.* This was *Bloomer Girl,* and the song became "T'Morra."

T'MORRA
(excerpt)

Verse.

T'morra is that better day
With rainbows in the sky
That's the picture people like to paint
But while I seek that better day

The years keep flyin' by
And lots of things that should be happenin'—ain't
'Til finally there comes this revelation
T'morra is the curse of civilization

First Chorus.

T'morra, t'morra,
Livin' for t'morra
Why is t'morra better than today?
T'morra, t'morra, lookin' for t'morra
My aunt became a spinster that way

The future, the future,
It's always in the future
What's the matter with now?
Postponin', postponin', a girl can bust postponin'
Take your t'morra and get
I'd rather, I'd rather have something to remember
Than nothin' to regret

Second Chorus. T'morra, t'morra,
It dawns on me with horra'
Love's gettin' far away and out of sight
T'morra, t'morra, why can't a lady borra'
A little of t'morra tonight?

The present, the present,
The present is so pleasant
What am I savin' it for?
Progressive, progressive, I'd rather be carressive
My heart is raisin' a row
Utopia, Utopia,
Don't be a dope, ya dope ya,
Get your Utopia now! . . .

Third Chorus. T'morra, t'morra
Oh isn't it deplore-a-
-ble the way a girl does fade?
Delayin', delayin' is drivin' me insayin'
My dialectics are clear
I'll hafta, I'll hafta
Give up my hereafta
For what I'm afta here.

The song is the comic expression of *Bloomer Girl*'s war between man and nature. "T'Morra"—that is, self-denial and repression—is the curse of civilization, of religion, of politics. The song connects deliberately overlong lines ("Lots of things that should be happenin'") to comically short ones ("Ain't"). It forces rhymes ("t'morra" with "horra"). The wordplay builds steadily through the choruses to the final rejection of both the political and religious abstractions—utopia and the hereafter—in whose name self-repression is justified. As philosophy *and* as wordplay, those two rejections climax the song. These two rejections, moreover, stamp "T'Morra" as a peculiarly personal song for Yip. With his brother's death, he had rejected the Hereafter; with the collapse of 1929, he had rejected the American promise of a worldly Utopia.

It is interesting to note that Yip's great comic wordplay song in his next show—"When I'm Not Near the Girl I Love" in *Finian's Rainbow*—also deals with the victory of sex over social restraint. Songwriting to Yip is wordplay, and Yip's wordplay was nowhere so antic, received no more bravura display, than in his songs about sex. The nearer the song subject to sex, the more Yip's libidinal energy comes plainly into view.

Bloomer Girl's first act ends with a fashion show at which the latest line of Applegate hoopskirts is displayed for the buyers. Evelina models the pièce de résistance, but just as she takes center stage, she drops her hoopskirt to reveal her bloomers underneath. The fashion show is ruined, her father is outraged, Jeff storms off, politics derails love—all in all, a great act 1 curtain.

The second act begins with a long expository number, "Sunday in Cicero Falls," only a portion of whose text is printed here. In the course of the number, the town's entire social order is alternately celebrated and satirized. The gentry go to church; the suffragists parade to announce their forthcoming production of *Uncle Tom's Cabin,* they are arrested, they fight back, they are hauled off; the gentry reemerge from church, dull order is restored. Reviewer John Chapman called the number "the finest combination of spectacle, movement, and music I have seen since . . . the 'Easter Parade' number" in Irving Berlin's 1933 revue, *As Thousands Cheer.*

SUNDAY IN CICERO FALLS
(excerpt)

Sunday in Cicero Falls
Sunday in Cicero Falls
In this lovely merry land
Main Street looks like a fairyland,
When the Angelus calls
Ginghams are bright
Collars are white
Sunday in Cicero Falls
Sunday in Cicero Falls
Hearts never blunder where
Girls wear such underwear
Sunday in Cicero Falls
Sunday in Cicero Falls

Sunday in Cicero Falls
Sunday in Cicero Falls
Shoes are brushed and shirts are starched
Hearts are pure and throats are parched
Sabbath has fallen on cobbles and walls
Thank merciful heaven just one day in seven
Is Sunday in Cicero Falls
Sunday in Cicero Falls
Boys may be quizzical
But not too physical
Sunday in Cicero Falls
Sunday in Cicero Falls . . .

The sinners join up with the virtuous fringe
They pass the saloon with that righteousness cringe
And Bartender Murphy remarks with a twinge
"Virtue is its own revinge" . . .

Old Banker Hodge with a nose for investment
Is making his weekly appeal to the test-ment
He's giving his conscience its weekly repairing
His morals are getting sabbatical airing
He's taking his soul out of camphor balls
Sunday in Cicero Falls
Sunday in Cicero Falls . . .

Even the rabbits inhibit their habits
On Sunday in Cicero Falls
Sunday in Cicero Falls.

In several aspects, "Sunday" is an unusual song. Arlen took advantage of the setting—a decorous ensemble number—to write three simultaneous vocal lines. Yip not only extracted every last ounce of repression out of Cicero Falls' fashions and morals, but he also took the opportunity to move beyond narration into something he seldom if ever attempted in other songs: slice-of-life poems concerning representative characters who do not appear elsewhere in the play. The quatrains on Banker Hodge and Bartender Murphy were throwbacks to the comic verse vignettes Yip had submitted to "The Conning Tower" in the twenties—but, here, the song afforded Yip the scope to range all over town.

The somnolence of Sunday was broken by a protest march that Dolly Bloomer organized announcing a production of *Uncle Tom's Cabin*. Mr. Applegate, long fed up with his sister-in-law's antics, has the group arrested for disturbing the peace. Evelina announces that if her aunt is being arrested, she wants to be arrested too. To her father's dismay, she joins Pompey and the women in jail.

There, Evelina, Dolly, and Cicero Falls' feminists encounter Pompey and two other apprehended runaway slaves, one of whom (played by the three-hundred-pound Richard Huey) sang the evening's showstopper: "I Got a Song." "That number could go on all night," noted the *Times*'s Lewis Nichols, "if management would permit."

Burton Rascoe, the one critic who panned *Bloomer Girl* (he was particularly unhappy with its politics), noted quite correctly that both the Huey character and "I Got a Song" had nothing directly to do with the rest of the show—yet on this one point, at least, he declined to complain. "It does not advance a plot or explain a character or clarify a situation," he noted. "It is just dropped in. Pretty good dropping, if you ask me."

The ceremonial "Sunday in Cicero Falls" is broken by a protest march organized by Dolly Bloomer, suffragette and freedom fighter, to publicize a local town production of the antislavery novel *Uncle Tom's Cabin* (by Harriet Beecher Stowe). Celeste Holm appears at center stage. (Theatre Collection, Museum of the City of New York.)

"I Got a Song" *was* just dropped in. It had been written initially for *Cabin in the Sky* and it went through twelve drafts before emerging triumphally in *Bloomer Girl*. (It was an intricate and difficult song to perform, and singer Huey was unable to get through it until, fortunately, the show's premiere performance.)

Rascoe was also right about the song's failure to advance the story or clarify a character; its point, rather, is thematic and political. With "I Got a Song," act 2 of *Bloomer Girl* shifts its primary focus to black rather than feminist concerns. The book runs dry on feminist story line and is concerned thenceforth chiefly with Pompey's fate, both for its own sake and for its impact on Jeff and Evelina's relationship. The remaining songs are chiefly those performed in the *Uncle Tom's Cabin* play-within-a-play. "I Got a Song" announces this shift and is, in its performance, something of a bridge between the struggles of women and blacks. Its setting, after all, is a jailhouse, and the chorus accompanying Huey is comprised solely of runaway slaves and incarcerated women.

I Got A Song
(excerpt)

I got a basket full of songs
Railroad song, a woman song, a sinner song, a bullfrog song
I got 'em! I got 'em!

I got a song
What kind of song?
I got a railroad song
He's got a railroad song

Railroad needs a hammer
Hammer gotta be
Railroad gits a hammer
And back of that hammer is little old me
Railroad needs the tracks
Little me lays the tracks
Now then come the facts
The big old train comes a-whistlin' by
It puff in your face and spit in your eye
Choo-choo-goodbye
That is the railroad song.

I got a song
What kind of song?
I got a woman song
He's got a woman song

Woman needs her lovin'
Lovin's gotta be
Woman gits her lovin'
And back of that lovin' is little old me

Woman needs her shoes
Little me gits the shoes
Now then comes the news
The shoes you bought ain't under her bed
Some big boy's shoes is there instead
Goo'bye you dead
That is a woman song
That is a woman song.

I got a song
What kind of song?
I got a bullfrog song
He's got a bullfrog song

Bullfrog needs a big swamp
Big swamp gotta be
Bullfrog gits a big swamp
And back of that swamp lives little old me
Bullfrog starts to croak
I yells "Don't you croak"
Then he up and spoke

"Oh the brown boy sing
And the bullfrog croak
But I got a greenback
You is broke
Uh-uh big joke"
That is the bullfrog song
That is the bullfrog song.

We got a freedom song
We got a freedom song
Freedom needs a sweet song
Sweet song's gotta be
Freedom gits a sweet song
And back of that song is little old me

Freedom needs a noise
Little me starts the noise
Now then comes the joys
The dawn comes up like a cinnamon bun
You sink your teeth in the rising sun
Amen! Some fun
That is a freedom song
That is a freedom song!

Got a railroad and woman and freedom song
Got to sing 'em while you're livin'
Cause you're dead so long
Makes it easy on the goin' and gettin' round
When you're travelin' on the upper
Or the underground
Railroad, woman, sinner, freedom got to be
And back of them all is little old me
Woo . . . Woo . . .
We got 'em, amen!

Again, the imperative mood: as Pompey and the eagle "gotta be free," so the freedom song has its own demands—"Gotta sing it while you're livin' / Cause you're dead so long"—and uses—"Makes it easy on the goin' and the gettin' round / When you're travelin' on the upper or the underground." Flashing by in a two-part chorus, it is Yip's raison d'être for his politics, for his art.

Bloomer Girl's action climaxes in the rather Pirandellian spectacle of the suffragists' production of *Uncle Tom's Cabin,* featuring, however improbably, Pompey as a runaway slave while his actual pursuers hover in the audience. The playlet proved curiously liberating for Harold and Yip (as it would later for Rodgers and Hammerstein in *The King and I*). The three short songs they wrote for *Cabin* (two of which are discussed here) are unconstrained by the normal standards of stage songwriting; they are removed from the boy-girl story line and the usual formal conventions. Above all, Arlen seems freed from the constraints of tone within which he had worked on the rest of the score.

"Liza Crossing the Ice" is a dramatic ensemble number until its solo passage in midsong radically shifts gears:

LIZA CROSSING THE ICE

Ensemble. Look out for the ice Eliza
Look out for the ice Eliza
Take care! Take care
The river is wide
Beware! Beware!
The turbulent tide.

Look out for the ice Eliza
Look out for the ice Eliza
Hold on

Solo. Oh Lord
This baby must be strong
So Lord
Please give him faith an' song!
But Lord
If the goin' is cruel
Then let him die like man
Not live like mule

Ensemble. Eliza, look out!
Look out! Eliza!
Look out for the ice!
Liza, Liza, Liza, Liza, Liza, Liza
Thank God!

With the sudden, soaring "Oh, Lord," we are transported into the tragic, bluesy terrain where Arlen was king, and which *Bloomer Girl* has to this point scrupulously avoided. Yip's lyric is strikingly different in style, too, from any that has come earlier in the show, relying in the solo portion almost exclusively on one-syllable words appropriate not only to the character but to the altered tone. There is one point of thematic continuity here, however: the Lord is called upon to provide not merely faith, but song. Unlike "The Eagle and Me," this is not a civil rights song. It is nearer the vein of the classic lament, and in it, Yip and Harold wail.

Cabin's climactic song, featuring Pompey playing a slave on the auction block, was, by the standards of the 1944 musical stage, virtually avant-garde. "Man for Sale" is not a conventional song, but a melodic, bluesy chant, set against harsh, shifting harmonies, now black, now Jewish. Yip emphasized its un-song-like character by eschewing all end-line rhymes, relying instead on the kind of internal rhymes and assonance of "Happiness Is a Thing Called Joe." It is the kind of number that began to appear in the musical theater in the sixties and thereafter: more operatic, less dependent on conventional melody and rhyme—although it is underpinned by the composer's and lyricist's craft in greater measure than most of its latter-day counterparts.

> MAN FOR SALE
>
> Man for sale
> Nice big man for sale
> Look at them hands look
> Look at them strong cotton pickin' hands
> Look at them rock-bustin' hands
> Log-rollin' steamboat-loadin' hands
> He good as forty mules
> Look at them shoulders
> Good shoulders
> They can hold up the sky
> He's yours for the price of a rabbit's foot
> And he don't eat much and he don't dream much.

"Man for Sale" ends abruptly with Pompey's arrest—a particularly Harburgian reminder of the turbulent world outside the theater. It is followed by the announcement of civil war, and by a ten-minute Agnes de Mille ballet that constituted an even more radical leap into the musical play of the future than "Man for Sale." It was conceived, de Mille was later to write, as "a serious ballet about women's emotions in war," and dramatically returned the show to the issues of war and peace with which it opened. But the dance brought to a head the crisis of tone that vexed what was to be nonetheless a successful show. In particular, it vexed *Bloomer Girl*'s director, E. Y. Harburg. In her autobiography, de Mille recalled its first performance in rehearsal:

> At the end of the showing there was not a sound. Harburg found his voice first, and stepping over the bodies of three prone, sweating girls, addressed me: "No. No. No. This is all wrong. Where is the wit? Where is the humor?"

De Mille revised the ballet three times with Arlen's strong support, but Harburg and the producers had resolved to remove it after their out-of-town opening, where, to their surprise, it proved to be a resounding success. Ever the realist, director Harburg and even producer Wilson were convinced: the ballet remained part of the show. "Goddammit!" Yip told de Mille after the Philadelphia opening, "I've begun to like the dreary thing."

In fact, the de Mille ballet culminated the increasing gravity of tone that characterizes *Bloomer Girl*'s second act and to which Yip and Harold contributed with Uncle Tom's Cabin. It was not Yip's accustomed tone, but it merged the issues of feminism and peace: Agnes de Mille's ballet was right as the rain for *Bloomer Girl*.

At the show's end, Jeff returns to cast his lot with the North and Evelina. Seeing the young couple reunited, the governor suggests to Dolly that she might like to become the governor's lady.

"Governor's Lady?" replies Dolly. "Hell, I'm going to be the Governor!"

As the troops march off to war, *Bloomer Girl* concludes with reprises of "When the Boys Come Home" and "The Eagle and Me" — the song of wartime and the song of the war's raison d'être. The juxtaposition of songs is Yip's attempt to define the egalitarian ideal for which the war is fought—deliberately if subtly fusing in the process both the Civil War and the Second World War. In this light, *Bloomer Girl* emerges as a personalized work of wartime popular front culture—but one that transcends that culture by its focus on the powerless and their arguments with America.

Arlen and Harburg wrote most of *Bloomer Girl*'s songs in Hollywood, only then coming east not only to work on the show but to participate (by performing the songs) in raising the funds. Ironically, one of their major investors was Yip's old nemesis, Louis B. Mayer, who was a close friend of producer John Wilson. (For that matter, the largest single outside investor in *Oklahoma!* had been Columbia's Harry Cohn. When it came to sensing the popularity of the new-style musical, the moguls were right on target—and it was a form to which their own studios began to turn in such movies as 1944's *Meet Me in St. Louis*.)

Bloomer Girl had its out-of-town tryout in Philadelphia in September. The presence of Celeste Holm (as Evelina) and Joan McCracken (as Daisy) out of the cast of *Oklahoma!* and of its choreographer, Agnes de Mille, ensured that the show would receive ample comparison to the Mamoulian-Rodgers-Hammerstein smash. (At the suggestion of composer Jule Styne, Dooley Wilson—*Casablanca*'s Sam—was cast in the role of Pompey.) Coming to Broadway, in fact, the word of mouth was all Yip could ask for: this was, the word had it, the first show since *Oklahoma!* that was a musical play of substantial merit, with lavish production values. Even before the show's October 5 Broadway opening, there was a run on tickets, and opening night marked Broadway's first wartime opening that was attended by theatergoers in formal dress. *Bloomer Girl* had become an event.

More important, it also became a smash hit. Critics praised the performances, the spectacle, the dancing, and (the *Times,* no less) Yip's direction. The score came in for particular praise—*Variety* typified the reviews in calling the score the best since *Oklahoma!*—though Louis Kronenberger in *P.M.* made a telling criticism: "If it has a weakness," he wrote, "that weakness is a rather paradoxical one: by maintaining so satisfactory a general level, *Bloomer Girl* lures you on to expect peak moments that it only occasionally achieves."

Strikingly *absent* from the contemporaneous critical response to *Bloomer Girl* is any discussion of the show's politics, its feminist politics in particular. In a 1965 letter, Yip would allude to the show's feminist dimensions:

> The soul and heart of the play and the main point of the plot is that it is Applegate's own daughter who changes his entire life, undermines his business, forces him to reconstruct it fundamentally, bringing about revolutionary changes in all of their lives. It is she who motivates the entire plot. . . .
>
> Another crucial point—Applegate picking a husband for Evelina, in the improbable and unlikely person of a Southern Slave-Owner. Any girl with a milligram of spirit would rebel against this, as indeed she does. But again, the fresh approach here is that though she does rebel, Jeff, despite being her father's choice, is a basically and unexpectedly decent person. He has growth in him; he can grasp new values. He is capable of *changing* his point of view and social outlook. This change in his character gives him distinction as a person, dimension as a human being. In the resolution of their deep personal conflict, based on disparate philosophies, he becomes a real man; and her part in his regeneration gives Evelina added stature as a woman.

But the kind of political discussion a *Bloomer Girl* should reasonably have engendered had been suspended for the duration of the war. Its feminism was a quarter century too early to find its properly appreciative audience—that was to come at its 1981 Goodspeed Opera House revival.

Above all, *Bloomer Girl* convinced critics that *Oklahoma!* had not been a one-shot, that the American musical was genuinely moving off in a new direction. Critic Arthur Pollock's comments on both shows faithfully caught the new conventional wisdom. "Both are so curious as musical comedies," he wrote, "that it becomes necessary to describe them as something more hightoned than that, so they are often spoken of as folk opera. Whatever the name by which you prefer to have them go, they are the best blend of comedy and music this country has ever seen."

In *Bloomer Girl,* Yip had the kind of show he long had sought to craft, and the public ratified his judgment. *Bloomer Girl* ran for 654 performances.

Wartime and Politics

The autumn of 1944 was surely one of the most high-powered and gratifying moments in Yip's career. No sooner had *Bloomer Girl* opened on Broadway than Yip turned his attention to producing the national election eve radio broadcast for the Roosevelt ticket. As one of the founders of the Hollywood Democratic Committee, Yip had been active in enlisting entertainment industry figures in Roosevelt's cause, and the election eve broadcast was to be the culmination of his efforts.

The broadcast featured songs by Harold Rome and Irving Caesar that Yip had commissioned for the event. It also featured three efforts of his own. One, with music by Arthur Schwartz, was an attack on the Republican candidate entitled "Don't Look Now, Mr. Dewey (But Your Record's Showing)."

But Yip's most notable contribution to the broadcast was a song of a somewhat different nature than any he had worked on before. It was called "Free and Equal Blues," and he had written it earlier that year with folk-song composer Earl Robinson. It was one of two songs he wrote that year with Robinson; the other was composed for a Democratic film entitled *Hell-Bent for Election,* which was funded by the United Auto Workers.

Yip's work with Robinson marked a turn to an overtly political kind of song. Robinson was a Seattle-born composer who upon graduating college in 1933 moved to New York, where he joined the Communist party and became music director of the Workers' Theater (which was absorbed into the Federal Theater Project in 1935). Earl's first songs were written for strikes in the tumultuous years of 1934–35. Later in the thirties, he wrote the classic union anthem, "The Ballad of Joe Hill" to Al Hayes's lyric, and the classic concert song, "Ballad for Americans" to the lyric by John Latouche (Vernon Duke's lyricist for *Cabin in the Sky*).

Earl Robinson composed the classic labor ballad "Joe Hill" and "Ballad for Americans" in the thirties. Yip and Earl wrote several politically oriented songs: "Free and Equal Blues" (1944); "The Same Boat, Brother" (1945); "Hurry Sundown" (1966), and "One Sweet Morning" (1969), a hymn to peace. (Courtesy Estate of Earl Robinson.)

In electing to work with Robinson, Yip signaled a desire to move toward a more political song than he could compose with Arlen—to see, in effect, if he could unite the worlds of Broadway and Woody Guthrie. Writing and directing *Bloomer Girl* was not enough: real political wars were blazing away, and Yip wanted to participate—not merely, like his peers, as a financial contributor, nor simply as the writer of political theater songs. He needed to enter politics as Yip Harburg, to write songs that had, as near as practicable, immediate political impact. Perhaps even more than his work in the theater, this was, as Yip conceived it, his freedom song.

The starting point for "Free and Equal Blues," as Earl recalled it, were army regulations under which

> a Southern white cracker could demand that he get blood only from a white-skinned person and this was backed up by the United States Army. They segregated the blood and the Red Cross supported that—way into the war. . . . I have a strong feeling that the song had some effect, because by the end of the war, the practice had been changed.

The song almost never got written, however, because Earl, by his own admission, "was pretty much a guy who needed lyrics first," and Yip just as badly needed the music before he wrote the words. Slowly, their creative impulses overcame deeply ingrained habits of work. "We both agreed," said Earl,

> we needed a refrain. He says, "Gimme a tune," and I was still not able to. So he turned out a lyric . . . and it was doggerel. The trouble with my turning out a tune to that is that it will also be doggerel. He says, "Gimme a *good* tune!" Finally, he gave me a dummy lyric: "That was news. That was news. And ever since that day, I got those free and equal blues."

The song begins with a quotation from W. C. Handy's "St. Louis Blues":

FREE AND EQUAL BLUES
(excerpt)

Spoken.   I went down to that St. James Infirmary
              And I saw some plasma there and I
              Ups and asks that doctor man—
              Was the donor dark or fair?
              The doctor laughed a great big laugh
              And puffed it right in my face!
              He said, "A molecule is a molecule
              And the darn thing has no race"

Sung.   And that was news,
              Yes that was news,
              That was very, very, very special news
              'Cause ever since that day I've got those
              Free and equal blues

              You mean you heard that doc declare
              The plasma in that test tube there

Spoken.   Could be white man, black man, yellow man, red?
              That's what he said!

              The doc put down his doctor book
              And gave me a very scientific look
              He spoke out plain and clear and rational
              "Metabolism is international!"

Sung.   And that was news,
Yes, that was news,
That was very, very, very special news
'Cause ever since that day I've got those
Free and equal blues

Spoken.   Yes, he rigged up his microscope
With some Berlin blue blood
And by gosh it was the same as Chung-King,
Kuibyshev, Chattanooga, Timbuctoo blood

Why, them Aryans who think they're noble
They don't even know the corpuscle is global
Tryin' to disunite us with their racial supremacy
Flyin' in the face of old man chemistry
Takin' all the facts and tryin' to twist 'em
But you can't overthrow the circulatory system!

Sung.   And that was news,
Yes, that was news
That was very, very, very special news
'Cause ever since that day I've got those
Free and equal blues. . . .

So listen you African and Indian and Mexican
Mongolian, Tyrolean and Tartar
The doctor's right behind
The Atlantic Charter

Makes no diff'rence if you're Kelly,
If you're Cohen, if you're Lopez
If you're Swenson, Jones or Litvinoff
Ev'ry man, ev'rywhere, is the same
When he's got his skin off

And that's the news
Yes, that's the news,
That's the free and equal blues.

The Democratic election eve broadcast, on which "Free and Equal" was performed by Robinson and Dooley Wilson, and which concluded with a ten-minute talk from Roosevelt himself, was clearly a high point in Yip's career as the bard of left liberalism.

Another was to come the following spring shortly after the San Francisco conference that established the United Nations. Radio producer Norman Corwin put together a live broadcast from San Francisco that CBS carried nationally. It was entitled "Unity Fair," and Yip provided the songs and some of the script as well. The broadcast was almost an anthology of Yip's popular front work: it included performances of "The Son of a Gun Who Picks on Uncle Sam," *Meet the People*'s "It's Smart to Be People," and a new Robinson-Harburg folk song, "The Same Boat, Brother." This new entry was directed against postwar isolationism and intended to promote a one-world perspective—indeed, it was given its inaugural performance by the One World Chorus.

THE SAME BOAT, BROTHER

Oh the Lord looked down from his holy place
Said, "Lordy me, what a sea of space
What a spot to launch the human race."
So he built him a boat for a mixed up crew
With eyes of black and brown and blue
And that's how come that you and I
Got just one world with just one sky

We're in the same boat, brother
We're in the same boat, brother
And if you shake one end
You're gonna rock the other
It's the same boat, brother

Oh the boat rolled on thru storm and grief
Past many a rock and many a reef
What kept 'em goin' was a great belief
That they had to learn to navigate
'Cause the human race was special freight
If we don't want to be in Jonah's shoes
We'd better be mates on this here cruise

'Cause it's the same boat, brother
We're in the same boat, brother
And if you shake one end
You're gonna rock the other
It's the same boat, brother

When the boilers blew somewhere in Spain
The keel was smashed in the far Ukraine
And the steam poured out from Oregon to Maine
Oh it took some time for the crew to learn
What's bad for the bow ain't good for the stern
If a hatch takes fire in China Bay
Pearl Harbor's decks gonna blaze away

For it's the same boat, brother
Yes it's the same boat, brother
And we must live with each other in the same boat,
The very same boat, brother.

"Unity Fair" was broadcast as the grand wartime alliance was publicly beginning to crumble, in the face of mounting criticism of Soviet control of Eastern Europe. The cold war was commencing, and "Unity Fair," though Yip could not have known it, was to be the last occasion on which a network allowed him to express his politics. The films never did. Only the theater allowed Yip that freedom.

Broadway's Resident Radical

"If I had been able to write tunes," Robinson says of what was to become Yip's next show, "I would have done the score for *Finian.*" Indeed, as originally conceived, *Finian* was to have been structured at least in part around Robinson-type songs. "Free and Equal Blues" was to have been the first act curtain number, and among the characters there still remains Woody, a union organizer-troubador modeled after Woody Guthrie but who has no Guthrie-esque songs.

With *Bloomer Girl,* Yip had found—and helped evolve—his ultimate medium of expression, the Broadway musical play. What he now sought was a far more *political* Broadway musical play than *Bloomer Girl.* The medium did not exist early in Yip's career; he was forty-seven when *Oklahoma!* came along to open up new possibilities. ("Gotta sing it while you're livin' / Cause you're dead so long.") It was time to politicize the musical play, to bring the standards and craft of theater song to political music. But Earl Robinson was unequal to the task and Harold Arlen was unwilling to attempt it.

"As a collaborator," Yip was to say of Arlen,

> Harold was the gentlest person I've ever worked with. He had such feeling for me as a writer in how he criticized the work—even when I stepped on his cerebral toes every now and then because he thought I was too involved in politics all the time and that it was polluting the stage. The stage was not a pulpit, not a place for "propaganda," which he called it. I called it education; he called it propaganda.
>
> Harold had a feeling for my striving to be poetic in everything I did and he forgave me the political exuberance which I exuded. [But] one of the reasons there was a little split when he started to work with Johnny Mercer was because he thought I was what Bert Lahr called "too fervent."
>
> [In time, Arlen came to see that my politics] was never destroying the entertainment value or the poetic value for the propaganda value. And besides, I never tried to propagandize. I tried to reason; I tried to educate. But he was very gentle with me. Most people were.

The "little split" began briefly in the early forties. It resumed after *Bloomer Girl* and was to last for ten years. "When you stop working with a composer," Yip once said, "it's like breaking up a marriage. Before Arlen, there was no composer I liked working with unequivocally."

So Yip turned again to Burton Lane—and for good reasons.

Finian's Rainbow is one of Broadway's vintage masterpieces. Opening in 1947, it ran 725 performances, and still plays in regional theaters and high schools today. Yip conceived and cowrote the book with Fred Saidy, wrote the lyrics with music by Burton Lane, and in general was the "auteur" and the "muscle" in the large collaboration required in a Broadway musical. Here the leprechaun, Og, played in the original version of *Finian's Rainbow* by David Wayne, is surrounded by children who are enchanted with his presence. Burton Lane said the only leprechaun he ever knew personally was Yip. (Collection of the Harburg Estate.)

Chapter 8

Finian's Rainbow

Look, look, look to the rainbow
Follow it over the hill and the stream
Look, look, look to the rainbow
Follow the fellow
Who follows a dream.

The success of *Oklahoma!* liberated Yip. In the seven years following *Oklahoma!*, Yip turned out three highly political musicals, each with a different composer: *Bloomer Girl* with Arlen (1944), *Finian's Rainbow* with Burton Lane (1947), and *Flahooley* with Sammy Fain (1951). Never before or again in his career would he be able to shape and control his shows as he would during this period. Besides writing the lyrics for all three shows, Yip conceived *Finian* and *Flahooley;* initiated and directed *Bloomer Girl;* coauthored the book for *Finian* (with Fred Saidy); and coauthored (with Fred Saidy), coproduced, and codirected *Flahooley.*

Of the three shows, it was *Finian* that allowed Yip the fullest and most successful expression of his talents and his politics. To the liberal egalitarianism of *Bloomer Girl, Finian* subtly but clearly appends in fable form an assault on capitalism. The show is that rarity of American popular culture, a social critique that goes beyond the standard populist assault on wealth and class inequities. *Finian* is a work of socialist analysis in the form of the American musical— something that no one else ever really attempted, let alone realized.

But *Finian*'s socialism is just one of the elements that gives the show its distinctly Harburgian character. In its humor and sentiment, its story and songs, all the complexities and contradictions that had suffused Yip's work as far back as "Paper Moon," receive their fullest development. All three of the main male characters—Finian, the scheming rainbow chaser; Woody, the union organizer-troubador; Og, the lustful leprechaun—are clearly refractions of Yip himself, an author-character identification all but unheard of on the classical musical stage. In the annals of what is essentially a collaborative medium, *Finian* stands out, at least until the heyday of Stephen Sondheim, as the most personal of the great musicals. In the Harburg canon, *Finian* stands out as Yip's most complex and fully realized achievement—his improbably triumphant masterpiece.

Finian grew from Yip's anger at the violent opposition to the fledgling black equality movement of the war years—specifically, his anger at the virulent racism expressed daily in Congress by Mississippi's Senator Theodore Bilbo and Representative John Rankin. "I remember more or less how *Finian* came to be," he told the Northwood Institute in a talk he gave during the seventies:

> It was written in Roosevelt's time. For the first time, the black man was being given some recognition. So it occurred to me to do a show about Bilbo and Rankin. The only way I could assuage my outrage against their bigotry was to have one of them turn black and live under his own [Jim Crow] laws and see how he felt about it. I was making a point to every white person: "Look—we use the word reincarnation. You might come back as a black, and here's how you'll be treated if you do. How do you like it?" I said to myself, "Gee, this is a great idea; how can I make it into a musical?" Well, it was a little grim. So I put it in my notebook for future reference and forgot about it.

It *was* grim—a mood that had no place in the Harburg esthetic or disposition. But the notion of attacking racism by transforming a white racist into a black man introduced an element with which Yip was more comfortable: fantasy. "I never like to write a play that's only about 'real' people," he once said. "I have to bring in a genie or a leprechaun or a rainbow."

The development of a suitably fantastical tale, however, required a remarkable leap both of association and imagination. "Two years later," Yip told the Northwood gathering, "I was reading James Stephen's *The Crock of Gold,* a beautiful book with all the lovely Irish names and the leprechaun. . . . I love Irish literature—James Stephen, Sean O'Casey. I felt easy working with Irish ideas." Yip continued:

> Of course, I was still fed up with our economic system and the whole idiocy of taking gold from California and planting it in Fort Knox. Suddenly, the three streams of thought about Bilbo and Rankin, the Irish stories, and about Fort Knox clicked in my mind. I said to myself, "Wouldn't it be wonderful if a pixie Irishman, Finian, poverty-stricken, working his hands to the bone year after year to feed his daughter, told himself, 'I'll never get anywhere diggin' this soil for spuds and potatoes. Every American is rich and you know why? Because they plant gold in Fort Knox. If I had a little gold I'd plant it there and get rich too.' Makes sense. Well, how can he get the gold? Only from the leprechauns, who have a crock of gold. So he'll have to lay a trap for a leprechaun."

Things began to work out in my mind. I next remembered an old Irish joke about an Irishman who manages to catch a leprechaun and borrow his crock of gold, to get the three wishes that come with it. He and his wife ride to Dublin to consider how to use the wishes wisely. They agree to sleep on the matter when Bridget, the wife, sees a beautiful waffle iron in a shop window. "Oh, Casey, I wish I had that waffle iron." And there it was beside her. Her husband, furious, shouts, "You used up one-third of our wishes! I wish the goddam waffle iron would get right up your ass and stay there!" And sure enough it does. Of course, it took the third wish to get it out. I never got over the implications of that story. You could relate it to the gold, for example: I wanted to show how gold turns to dross, and all that's left is the rainbow that leads to the crock of gold. That's all man has left: the rainbow.

So I thought, in my play, Bilbo or Rankin can be wished black. Then his transformation won't be through villainy but through whimsy. How do I build up to this, how does Rankin become the target? After the Irishman plants the crock of gold, two geologists find it and let the word out. Rankin hears and wants that ground. A greedy capitalist, he says, "I don't have to pay anything for it. Blacks live there and there's a covenant that it's for whites only, so we can throw the bunch of them out." Thus I show that racial prejudice is generated partly because of economic greed. . . .

Here's a show that was written in 1946. 1946. There had been no such song as "We Shall Overcome." There was no Martin Luther King. There was just a downright lack of civil rights for a minority of people whose skins were black. There were no movements and there were people who felt we should despair about life. Why should there be a thing like racism? It's so idiotic. Volumes and books and lectures and God knows what were written about it; nothing seemed to help. We thought of one way—how could we prick the bubble of this idiocy? How could we reduce all this thing to absurdity? Now you see how one thing usually leads to another— in order to show this folly, I used a dramatic form that will help us laugh this prejudice out of existence—the musical play.

So *Finian* begins as an attack on racism and capitalism. It ends, amid a flurry of plot turns and resolutions, as an attack on capitalism with a countervailing praise for cooperative human endeavor. *Finian* is surely the only American musical written in the shadow of Marx on the fetishism of commodities (but then, Yip was the only lyricist/librettist who included in his circle of friends the editors of the Marxist economics journal *Monthly Review*). The commodity of choice in *Finian* is, of course, gold. Early in act 1, Finian tells his daughter Sharon that they have come to America to get rich, as America has, through sheer proximity to gold.

Finian. (*Removes large envelope from his pocket and from that a small piece of note paper. Puts on pince-nez and reads*) I quote from myself. Quote. The peculiar nature of the soil in and about Fort Knox brings an additional quality of gold, hitherto unsuspected by either Karl Marx or the gold itself. This causes the gold to radiate a powerful influence on America.

(*Jumping on suitcase*) It fertilizes the oranges in Florida, activates assembly lines in Detroit, causes skyscrapers to sprout from the gutters of New York—and produces a bumper crop of millionaires.

(*Replaces paper and removes eyeglasses*) I rest me case.

Sharon. (*Astounded*) Father! You mean to say it's the gold in Fort Knox begets the riches of America?

Finian. Obviously. Else for why did they rush to dig it from the ground of California in 1849, only to bury it in the ground at Fort Knox a hundred years later?

By play's end, though, the gold has lost its magic: the three wishes have been wished: turning the senator black, then white again, and conferring the power of speech on Susan the Silent, the show's lead dancer (who therefore doesn't have to worry about singing or speaking). The pot of gold then turns to a chamber pot. "This little boom," says Finian of the wave of prosperity that has come to the black and white sharecroppers of Rainbow Valley, Missitucky, "This little boom is founded on an illusion."

Og the leprechaun brings forth the former pot of gold, now a chamber pot, and Finian speaks with Senator Billboard Rawkins (i.e., Bilbo and Rankin), who by now has been wished into liberalism as well as into several skins:

Finian. (*Giving Rawkins the pot*) May it throw some light on you. Keep it as a souvenir of a dyin' age.

(*A moment later a rainbow arches across the stage as Finian prepares to leave the valley. He bestows it on his daughter Sharon and her new husband Woody.*)

Finian. I turn it over to you as Ford the First turned over his factory to Ford the Third. Sure, there's no longer a pot o' gold at the end of it—but a beautiful new world under it.

So, "All man has left," Yip said in his Northwood talk, "is the rainbow"— Yip's personal talisman, his symbol of humankind's capacity to dream. The rainbow moves us from the dialectics of Marx to the contradictions of

Harburg. *Finian,* like so much of Yip's work ("Paper Moon," for instance, and the conclusion of *Oz,* but on a grander scale than either), is an act of demystification that celebrates belief. It is a clarion call for social change suffused with a kind of Arcadian utopianism; it is a paean to the freedom to roam and the impulse to settle down, to the blindness of love and the promptings of sex. It contrasts the laws of nature with the laws of man, which turn nature to property.

But *Finian* by no means romanticizes the state of nature, and, indeed, it celebrates the powers of science and technology, when put to democratic ends, to improve the human condition. The play begins as Rawkins seeks to stop the spread of rural electrification from a program that suspiciously resembles the Tennessee Valley Authority to the homes of Rainbow Valley's multiracial sharecroppers. Its ambiguous ending sees Finian leaving the valley for the magic kingdom of atomic power at Oak Ridge, Tennessee (lines usually cut from modern revivals as the immediate postwar infatuation with the peaceful uses of nuclear energy turned to trepidation).

Underlying the dialectics of *Finian* is Yip's belief in evolution, in the on-again, off-again march towards social improvement. There is no wild optimism here as to the outcome of the struggle, only the conviction that the struggle continues. "Ah, things are hopeless, hopeless," says Finian in the show's penultimate moment, as the magic and the gold vanish. But he recovers himself and roars, "But they're not serious!"—and he is off, chasing Finian's rainbow—Yip's rainbow—to the next pot of gold, the better dream.

For its creators, the show was something of a high-wire act, mixing Irish leprechauns and Southern sharecroppers, lampooning with humor America's most outrageous social conditions. This is assuredly heavy freight for a musical comedy to carry—yet carry it *Finian* does. Only once, in the assessment of composer Burton Lane, did Yip lose his footing. When he read the first draft of the book, Lane once said, he felt that, "Yip got angry in the second act and very heavy-handed, and I was able to get him out of it." Apparently, the excised material was nothing less than the original angry heart of the story. An early outline prepared by *Finian's* producers to solicit financial backing makes clear that the material in question concerned Rawkins's escapades as a black man— his inability to enter a restaurant, board a bus, and the like. Much of this material was apparently encased in a dream to soften its impact, but one crucial sequence was not—one in which Rawkins is almost lynched for having had sexual relations with a white woman: Mrs. Rawkins. In the context of a Harburgian fantasy, this was indeed, as Yip had said, "a little grim," and the scenes gave way to a verbal recounting from Rawkins to Og of the indignities he had suffered—sans any reference to lynchings and sex.

In the preparation of *Finian,* both book and score, "Yip was the one in control," Lane said. "He was the oldest and the most experienced, as among

Fred [Saidy] and me. There was no director before we went into rehearsal." Yip had first raised the subject of the *Finian* show with Saidy just three days after *Bloomer Girl*'s Broadway opening. Fred and he wrote the first outline of the book in Los Angeles in 1945 and Yip presented Lane with a first draft of the book in the spring of 1946. Before he went to Lane, though, he had taken it to Arlen, who viewed *Finian* as too political and declined the project. Yip thereupon approached Earl Robinson, and then both Robinson and Lane together, in the hope that Robinson would compose the show's more black and bluesy numbers and Lane would handle the Irish material, the ballads, and the more mainstream Broadway production numbers. Indeed, *Finian*'s first press release flatly announced that Robinson's "Free and Equal Blues" would be heard in the show. The same press release, from the spring of 1946, also announced that *Finian* was to be produced by Lee Sabinson and William Katzell. Sabinson and Katzell had just produced Arthur Laurents's *Home of the Brave* and were mulling over a dramatization of Howard Fast's *Freedom Road* when they elected, instead, to go with *Finian*. Sabinson and Katzell knew their politics, but *Finian* was their first musical—as, indeed, it was also to be for director Bretaigne Windust. But Robinson was not to do the score of *Finian,* nor did "Free and Equal Blues" appear in the production. Instead, *Finian*'s musical score was to be entirely the product of Burton Lane.

Yip had first met Lane at the outset of the depression, when the crash had forced Yip out of business and into songwriting. Lane at the time was still in his teens, a musical prodigy who had become something of a protégé of the Gershwin family. As Lane was to recall:

> I met Yip through Ira Gershwin. He brought us together. Yip was scrounging around in those days. . . . [W]hen I [next] met him, he was working with Vernon Duke and Jay Gorney and Johnny Green, before *Americana* (1932). Yip wanted to write with me right away. We wrote a few songs, but I didn't write with him professionally. We never did anything with those songs. There was always the hope that we'd do a show together or find a place to use the songs.

At age fifteen, Lane had been hired out of high school by J. J. Shubert and soon found himself working with Howard Dietz on some interpolated songs for the Broadway revue *Three's a Crowd*. At age twenty-one, in 1933, he moved to Los Angeles to write songs for the movies. Yip's and Burt's early professional collaboration came at MGM at the end of the thirties, when they were teamed on an Eleanor Powell musical; then *Hold on to Your Hats* followed shortly thereafter. Lane worked in Hollywood, with the admiration of his peers but otherwise in relative obscurity, until 1947. His distinguished career is marked by a cluster of popular classic songs but only a handful of Broadway shows—

1940's *Hold on to Your Hats, Finian* in 1947, and *On a Clear Day You Can See Forever* in 1965 with Alan Jay Lerner. Virtually every review of *On a Clear Day* commented on the excellence of Lane's score, remarked that he had composed another excellent score in *Finian*—and wondered where he had been in all the intervening years.

As Lane recalled, Yip felt himself very much the senior partner on *Finian*, at one point even introducing Lane as his pianist at a backers' try-out. The relationship between Lane and Harburg grew increasingly strained as *Finian* moved toward its opening.

And yet, Lane was to prove an ideal choice for *Finian*'s music, for reasons that Yip had identified a decade and a half earlier during their first meetings. As Lane recalled,

> I met Yip when I was sixteen years old . . . and when I was alone with Yip and we were going to write some songs together, I would play him tunes that reminded him of Romberg or Friml and then something that suddenly would come out and Yip said, "Gee, that's like George."

When Lane turned his attention to the *Finian* score seventeen years later, he was floundering no longer, but the style he had by then evolved encompassed both a European Friml sound and an American Gershwin sound in a unique mix of classic forms, European and American folk, and Broadway jazz. The mix was to prove exactly right for the highly cross-cultural *Finian*, whose songs are Irish, southern, black, and all Broadway. Og and Sharon bring Irish songs with them—"How Are Things in Glocca Morra?" "Look to the Rainbow," and the quasi-modernist gavotte, "Something Sort of Grandish." "Necessity" and "The Begat" are comic numbers in a show-biz-blues idiom. "When the Idle Poor Become the Idle Rich" closes with a mock-madrigal; "That Great Come and Get It Day" moves through black revival music, western hoedown music, and Broadway production number without missing a beat. "Old Devil Moon," for a popular song of its time, is daringly avant-garde in its melodic and harmonic jumps. The music must be as wildly diverse as the characters Yip created and assembled, and as tight and unified as the story Yip and Fred pulled together. It is both—Lane weaving all these strands into an exuberant score that is vintage Broadway at its best.

The heterogeneity of *Finian*'s score is evident from the start. As the curtain rises, the music makes the aural equivalent of a jump cut from an overture rich with strings and horns to the plaintive wail of Sonny Terry's harmonica in unaccompanied blues lament. The setting is Rainbow Valley in the state of Missitucky, and Terry is bewailing the foreclosure sale of land tilled by a biracial group of sharecroppers. "Rainbow Valley is as mythical as Glocca Morra," Yip once said; indeed, it seems a fantasy projection of such gallant and beleaguered experiments as the biracial Southern Tenant Farmers Union, which arose during the thirties. Within Rainbow Valley, relations between poor blacks and poor whites seem equable and harmonious; the Valley's racism is confined to Senator Rawkins, landlord and politician, and to his hired hands, who are busily tacking up auction signs as Terry continues his harmonica blues. As the sheriff attempts to begin the auction, his cries are lost in the song of the sharecroppers, who are anticipating the arrival of Woody Mahoney, the union organizer, with the funds to forestall the sale.

THIS TIME OF THE YEAR

All. Woody's comin'. Woody's comin'. Woody's comin'.

Sheriff. (spoken) Quiet, all of you, quiet! Tax sale gonna start now! *(Banging gavel loudly as chant of "Woody's comin'!" continues in background)* It's my duty to protect the people of Rainbow County!

First Sharecropper. (spoken) Who from?

Sheriff. (spoken)	The citizens! Hear ye! Hear ye!
All.	We can't be bothered with a mortgage man This time of the year
Sheriff. (spoken)	You'll be sorry, interferin' with the law!
All.	For Spring don't care about a mortgage plan This time of the year
Sheriff. (spoken)	I'm givin' you the last chance to get back your land.
All.	The dandelions in the dusky dell Don't give a hoot in hell They're gonna smell without collateral This time of the year This time of the year

Sweet merry buds and elderberry buds
Don't give a good ding ding dang
Corn's shootin' up
Fruit trees are fruitin' up
Go tell Rawkins to go hang, hang

Don't mess around here
This time of the year
You'll get it in the rear
This time of the year
Magnolias are sentimental
Persimmons are queer
Snapdragons won't pay no rental
This time of the year
Red cabbage and sweet potaters
Don't easily skeer
They'll sprout without real estaters
This time of the year

The choo-choo's comin' and it's mighty clear
Woody's here
He's up there ridin' with the engineer
Yes, Woody's here

Just look at that choo-choo puffin'
Let's give it a mighty cheer
Just look at that engine huffin'
Dang blast it all, Woody's here
Woody's here! Woody's here!

Get a load of that whistle blowin'
That whistle is good to hear
It's wantin' you to be knowin'
Dang blast it all, Woody's here
Woody's here! Woody's here!

Yip and Burton Lane, *left,* teamed up to create the memorable score of *Finian's Rainbow* (1947). Lane's musical ingenuity was a match for Yip's lyrics, and the score included a number of classics. But after the show, the team broke up, to the sorrow of each partner. (Courtesy Mr. and Mrs. Burton Lane.)

"This Time of the Year" is a quintessential opening number. It announces the arrival of one of the main characters, not only in lyrics but in heraldic music as well: the first line, "We can't be bothered with a mortgage man" suggests the army's reveille; the last lines are musical simulations of train whistles. But "This Time of the Year" is more than a curtain opener and arrival song. It is also an opening statement of some of Finian's concerns—most particularly, the juxtaposition between the laws of nature and those of men. The contrast is made clear not only by the lyric but also by the conflict between song and speech in which the song begins. The sheriff's laying down of man's law is spoken (or actually, shouted); the sharecropper's articulation of natural law is sung. The contrast is to run straight throughout the show: at no time do Rawkins and his henchmen sing (that is, in Rawkins's case, at no time until he is turned black). In this regard, *Finian* follows *Porgy and Bess,* in which the white representatives of the law are the only characters who do not sing. In the musical play à la Harburg, racists may speak but they may not sing: there is no music among the Rawkinses of this world.

Sharecroppers and sheriff leave the stage; Finian McLonergan and his daughter Sharon enter, all the way from Ireland. He brings with him a crock of gold, stolen from the leprechauns, which he will plant in Rainbow Valley's fertile soil. And Yip explains:

> The show has three or four different tracks. The lives of the following people are involved: Finian and Sharon, who are coming from Ireland to get their desires that they hope to create in Rainbow Valley. A man by the name of Woody and his sister Susan. Their lives are involved with the life of Finian because Sharon's going to fall in love with him and Susan, the sister of Woody, is going to fall in love with Og, a leprechaun. And of course, Billboard Rawkins, who is the antagonistic force.

> Now we have our *first scene*. We introduce the players. The father. A charming daughter and a funny charming little man who really has a human and interesting goal that we can identify with. Everybody identifies with the little man who has nothing and wants a little of life. And wants something for the person he loves. *Quick identification*. Quick interest. If you want to use Broadway terms, it's the hooker. Hook the audience. Especially that man with his humor and fun and crazy little notions when he makes fun. And they see this Rainbow Valley, which is nothing but shabby tobacco land that isn't half as green as Ireland or beautiful. And she doesn't know why she's come here. She asks, "What have we come all the way across a continent, across an ocean, in this sweet, green month of April, and for what?"

> At this point, no use arguing. Arguing will only be repetitious and the librettist finds he's stuck for further words. Who's the lyricist? Only the heightened emotion of song can supply the dramatic climax to the scene. So he calls upon the lyricist to help, and if the librettist and the lyricist are the same guy, then heaven and St. Patrick be with him.

> There are many ways of approaching a theme. In this case, it's Sharon's problem: how to handle this wily old man? . . . She will get him back to Ireland not by haranguing and frustration, but by something more subtle: nostalgia.

And it is an eminently nostalgic and universal ballad she proceeds to sing:

HOW ARE THINGS IN GLOCCA MORRA?

Verse.

I hear a bird
A Glocca Morra bird
It well may be
He's bringing me
A cheering word

I hear a breeze
A River Shannon breeze
It well may be
It's followed me
Across the seas
Then tell me please

Chorus.

How are things in Glocca Morra?
Is that little brook still leaping there?
Does it still run down to Donny Cove?
Through Killybegs, Kilkerry and Kildare?

How are things in Glocca Morra?
Is that willow tree still weeping there?
Does that laddie with the twinklin' eye
Come whistlin' by
And does he walk away
Sad and dreamy there?
Not to see me there?

So I ask each weepin' willow
And each brook along the way
And each lad that comes a whistlin'
Tooralay
How are things in Glocca Morra
This fine day?

"It was going to be the first song that the leading lady sang," Burt Lane remembered,

> and it was very important as the second song in the show to establish character, to establish a mood and a quality of what the rest of the score was going to be. I was struggling for a long time, while writing other things. You can't let one thing hold you up so you don't do anything.
>
> I had written "Grandish." I had written "Great Come and Get It Day" and was struggling to find an Irish melody that I thought was right for this

At the start of the cold war climate in the post-World War II years, many people were afraid to produce or invest in the "political musical" *Finian's Rainbow.* Yip lost his old composer Arlen but got Burton Lane. "How Are Things in Glocca Morra?" has become a classic, appealing to a universal nostalgia for lost happiness. (Collection of Harburg Estate.)

spot, and one of the great Irish melodies that I'm very moved by is "Oh Danny Boy." That has the kind of quality that can make you cry when it's sung properly. And I wanted to get something that was very touching and moving and I was having trouble. I said to Yip, "Give me a dummy title." So he gave me a dummy title, and the title was, "There's a Glen in Glocca Morra." Not a very inspiring title, but it was a meter, so it gave me something to fool around with.

And one night—this was after we had been working on the score for about three or four weeks—Yip came over to my house and said, "You know, we must get that song; it's Sharon's big song." So I said, "Yip, I'm so disgusted with myself" because I could not find anything to please myself. I said, "I must have a whole book of manuscript paper here and I must have fifty melodies." He said, "Let's hear something." I said, "All right, I'll start with the first one." And I started with the first one and this is what I played [plays the opening phrase of "How Are Things In Glocca Morra?"]. The look came over his face like I was crazy. I said to myself, "He looks as if he likes this thing." I got so close to it that I couldn't see it. He said, "Play it again." I played it again *and he started to sing the lyric.* The minute I heard, "How Are Things in Glocca Morra?" I began to like the tune. He made it a personal song instead of "There's a Glen in Glocca Morra." Then we went on from there.

Yip may have started to sing the lyric the moment he heard the music, but drafts of "Glocca Morra" range over more than fifty pages in his workbooks; "Glocca Morra" was not the product of automatic writing. Yip begins one draft of the verse in identical fashion to "April in Paris:" "April's in the air," he writes

> But where's that blackbird
> Where oh where?
> Over a wave around a vale
> Up a hill and down a dale—
> And me so many mile away

Irish place names by the dozens appear in "Glocca Morra"'s working drafts; Yip drew some of these from the play *Killycregs in Twilight* by Lennox Robinson. *Killycregs* is set in Connamara—a name Yip transmuted into the title of his song (with a little help from Stephens's *Crock of Gold*).

The lyric that eventually emerged from this process, like the lyrics for all of Sharon's songs, is rich in natural elements, in birds and brooks, rivers and willows. If the lyric for "April in Paris" works by association, the lyric for "Glocca Morra" works almost by incantation. The lyric is constructed around the repetition of sounds, beginning with the repetition in the first two lines of the verse, which introduces "Glocca Morra" as an adjective—"a Glocca Morra bird." The place names of the first stanza of the chorus function even less in a denotative vein, but the very repetition of these sounds, the singing of these names—"Killybegs, Kilkerry, and Kildare"—suggests an Old World ritual whose original meaning is lost, but that all the more therefore evokes nostalgia in the listener. The mood of pathos for a lost world is heightened then by the "weepin' willow" and the boy's "sad and dreamy" state. It is heightened as well by the added line in this stanza, "not to see me there," in which the melodic pattern is repeated on different notes. Yip said to Lane while writing "Glocca Morra," "You know the Irish always add a little bit."

The music and lyric of the song's release ("So I ask each weepin' willow" through "Tooralay") function to heighten the mood still further, unlike many releases that establish a contrast with the rest of the chorus. The willow, the brook, the lad all return, their distance from the singer underscored. With this last stanza, the nostalgia of the song becomes even more explicit: Glocca Morra is some lost Arcadian ideal, which the singer can ask after but not revisit. "Glocca Morra" is *Finian*'s major ballad, resung several times throughout the show, featured in the overture and at the final curtain. At the center of the only socialist American musical is a ballad not of worlds to come but of worlds that have been lost.

Finian and Sharon do not return to Ireland, of course. Sharon gives their money to Woody so he can forestall the foreclosure sale, in return for which Finian receives a plot of land in which to plant his gold. The Woody-Sharon boy-girl subplot then begins to unfold, as Sharon sings Woody a song about her father, his spirit and beliefs. "This pixilated little man had something she loved about him," Yip told Northwood:

> No matter how much trouble he put her through, he was always chasing rainbows, and she loved that about him. Somehow or other, he had infected her with that spirit. He was never sad, never down, never licked; he had the spirit of all mankind in him; he was the epitome of man's spirit. No matter how many times he's down, he picks himself up. So he can't get it one way—he'll get it another. That's the rainbow.

Finian, that is, sounds suspiciously like Yip, and his anthem encapsulates Yip's personal credo as fully and as well as any song Yip was ever to write.

LOOK TO THE RAINBOW

Verse.

On the day I was born
Said my father, said he
I've an elegant legacy
Waitin' for ye
Tis a rhyme for your lips
And a song for your heart
To sing it whenever
The world falls apart

Chorus.

Look, look, look to the rainbow
Follow it over the hill and stream
Look, look, look to the rainbow
Follow the fellow who follows a dream

Twas a sumptuous gift
To bequeath to a child
Oh, the lure of that song
Kept her feet runnin' wild
For you never grow old
And you never stand still
With whip-poor-wills singin'
Beyond the next hill

Look, look, look to the rainbow
Follow it over the hill and stream
Look, look, look to the rainbow
Follow the fellow who follows a dream

So I bundled me heart
And I roamed the world free
To the east with the lark
To the west with the sea
And I searched all the earth
And I scanned all the skies
But I found it at last
In my own true love's eyes

> Look, look, look to the rainbow
> Follow it over the hill and stream
> Look, look, look to the rainbow
> Follow the fellow who follows a dream
>
> Follow the fellow,
> Follow the fellow,
> Follow the fellow,
> Who follows a dream.

If some of these lyrics look familiar, they should. They are lifted, slightly altered, from a passage in a well-known song Yip had written eight years earlier:

> Follow, follow, follow, follow
> Follow the yellow brick road
> Follow the rainbow over the stream
> Follow the fellow who follows a dream.

He had dealt with it all eight years earlier, had he not? Not just following the dream, but the rainbow itself. But Yip was not done with the rainbow, apparently, and anyway, *Oz* hadn't gotten it exactly right. Yip ultimately did not wish to celebrate whatever it was that lay over the rainbow—much less affirm that there was no place like home. Look *to* the rainbow, this song proclaims, not over it; to the dreamer or the very act of dreaming, rather than the dream itself; to idealism and struggle and all that the rainbow signified for Yip.

The audience was prepared for "Look to the Rainbow" by a four-line poem that Sharon recited to Woody: "In Glocca Morra, where we come from, there's an old legend:

> You'll never grow old
> You'll never grow poor
> If you look to the rainbow
> Beyond the next moor.

The legend segues into the song's verse, the most "Irishized" passage in *Finian's* score. The lyric here is stylized Irish speech:

> Said my father, said he,
> I've an elegant legacy
> Waitin' for ye

set to a pentatonic melody underscored by the twanging of a harp: all in all, the best Broadway ballad equivalent of an Irish folk song.

There's more than a little autobiography in the last four lines of the verse: it was not until Yip's world had fallen apart in 1929 that he turned to, and was saved by, song and rhyme. By the same token, Finian's story—nurturing a pot of gold that turns to dross, then picking himself up and moving on—can be taken as a parable of Yip's career, pre- and post-1929, including the early painful loss of his older brother, his father's death in 1931, and the loss of his first wife in 1932. Small wonder, then, that the verse in "Rainbow" assumes as a matter of course that the world will fall apart: this is not just a Marxian belief in the cyclical nature of the economy, or even a chastened post-Holocaust view of the world. This is also existential certitude born of bitter personal history.

"Look to the Rainbow" may be a song about Finian and Yip, but it is sung by Sharon and, like "Glocca Morra," is suffused with natural imagery, as well as with the Irish language of epic legends and fairy tales—roaming from sky to sea to earth. The music for the chorus has a hymnlike quality, although the piece is actually a slow waltz. At its conclusion, the orchestra plays the piece without verbal accompaniment, first as a kind of court dance, next as a peasant dance: a gavotte followed by a jig.

The tension in "Rainbow" between a Finian song and a Sharon song is nowhere more evident than in the lyric's ambivalence on the question of roaming and settling down. The chorus and the second verse seem to come down on the side of the ongoing quest; the third verse, on the side of finding "it"—and there is no clear antecedent in the verse for exactly what "it" is—in "my own true love's eyes." The line rings true for Sharon and for the conventions of popular songwriting, but it hangs uneasily with the rest of the lyric. A lifetime of listening to popular song conditions us to accept "it" unquestioningly: it "works"—and it is surely not a viewpoint Yip dismisses out of hand. But as the rest of the lyric makes clear, the quest means at least as much to Yip as its object, real or imagined.

"Look to the Rainbow" remains one of the most neglected of Yip's and Burt's great songs. It may be that a songwriter is permitted only one rainbow masterpiece, and Yip already had his; it may be that it was one of the less commercially exploitable songs in a superb score. But there can be no question that Yip regarded it not merely as one of his best songs but even more as a summation of his credo. In his last years, he gave the song's title to a revue he had hammered together of his work, and when asked during an appearance on *The Dick Cavett Show* to sing a song, he obliged with a rendition of "Look to the Rainbow." The melody Lane had devised for the chorus gave the song a purity, almost a *gravitas,* that made it suitable to the large purpose for which Yip intended the song in 1947, and the larger purposes to which he was to set it in the years thereafter. (In 1987, Aretha Franklin's soul version further confirmed the song's spiritual qualities.)

The mysterious "it" that Sharon finds in her own true love's eyes is identified quite literally in *Finian*'s next song, and the attraction of settling down made quite clear—but in a way that subtly underscores Yip's ambivalence. Indeed, the skies/eyes rhyme of "Look to the Rainbow" is used anew:

> It's that old devil moon
> That you stole from the skies
> It's that old devil moon
> In your eyes.

With Sharon and Woody falling in love, Yip faced a dilemma he would have to confront throughout his career: "how to write a love song," as he told the Northwood Institute, "without getting clichéd about it." But *Finian* was a show of fantasy, magic, and spells, and that gave Yip his starting point. "There's a little bit of witchcraft in every love," he told Northwood.

> And I wanted a song here that would telegraph in the first act the quality of this girl, that really belongs to every girl, that is, the quality of bewitching a man. I wanted that witchcraft to be the specific thing I was emphasizing because I knew that in the second act she was going to be accused of witchcraft. And I want to telegram it to the audience so that I can reprise the song in the second act.

More than a little bewitching is required here, because Woody—clearly, Woody Guthrie's namesake and reflection—is eager to be traveling on. "I've got commitments," he tells Sharon. "This guitar and I got a big job to do all through this part of the country. . . ." However, he avers, he's "caught—trapped—by that old valley legend," which he proceeds to recite to Sharon. Like the poem that preceded "Rainbow," this poem too prepares the audience for a song of magic:

> They who meet on an April night
> Are forever lost in love.
> If there is moonlight all about
> And there's no moon above.

The two songs, really, are in dialogue with each other: "Rainbow" a testament to the freedom to roam; "Old Devil Moon" a magical ballad of entrapment.

OLD DEVIL MOON

I look at you and suddenly
Something in your eyes I see
Soon begins bewitching me
It's that old devil moon
That you stole from the skies
It's that old devil moon
In your eyes

You and your glance
Make this romance
Too hot to handle
Stars in the night
Blazing their light
Can't hold a candle
To your razzle dazzle

You've got me flying high and wide
On a magic carpet ride
Full of butterflies inside
Wanna cry, wanna croon
Wanna laugh like a loon
It's that old devil moon
In your eyes

Just when I think I'm
Free as a dove
Old devil moon
Deep in your eyes
Blinds me with love.

"Old Devil Moon," Yip told Max Wilk, was "strangely constructed. It doesn't have a verse and it isn't the ordinary 32-bar song at all." It certainly isn't, and the structure is just part of it. "Moon" falls neither among *Finian's* Old World songs, its blues songs, or its more conventional Broadway songs. It is, after all, a bewitching song, both seductive and disorienting—combining a sinuous melodic line with melodic leaps and harmonic shifts seldom found in popular music to that date. Indeed, "Moon" is that rare popular song that became a hit—and a jazz standard—despite the fact that it is all but unsingable by any but a trained singer.

The overall structure of the song is one of rising tension followed by exultant release. The first three lines are set to a tightly constructed back-and-forth musical line, the second and third lines paralleling the melody of the first, but each a little higher. On the word *old* in the fourth line, we come to the first midline long-held note in the song, and a reversal of the melody's hitherto upward movement: in place of the back-and-forth upward creep, the song now explodes in a downward cascade of notes. "Moon" now changes its character; it suddenly rocks out, lyrically as well as musically. Yip uses alliteration and assonance (with long vowels) on these crucial stressed notes in the downward spiral: old/moon/stole/skies/old/moon/eyes, and again: cry/croon/laugh/loon/old/moon/eyes. The release ("You and your glance" through "Razzle-dazzle"), like the opening part of the melody but with vertiginous musical complexity, reverts to the tension-heightening parallel rising lines. The second downward spiral is the song's lyrical payoff:

> Wanna cry, wanna croon
> Wanna laugh like a loon

is a lyric of romance at high tide—and Yip's insistence on "wanna" rather than "want to" renders it all the more seemingly spontaneous while giving greater aural impact to "cry" and "croon" by deemphasizing the lines' first two words.

"You give him a piece of music where there's explosiveness and he explodes with you, which helps the melody: with flat words . . . you don't hear the melody." Thus composer Jule Styne on his collaboration with Stephen Sondheim on *Gypsy*—but surely, it's an apt description of what happens in the explosive interval, lines four through seven, of "Old Devil Moon": music and lyrics explode together. The song's fourth line, moreover, is not just an explosive moment, but a pivotal one. "Moon"'s A section, the first three lines, is uncommonly different from its B section, the next four. It's in line four that "Old Devil Moon" moves from being a song of sexual desire to one of romantic exultation. There are many great songs that are either one or the other: Porter's "I've Got You under My Skin" and "Night and Day" are examples of the first, the

Gershwins' "'S Wonderful" an example of the second. "Old Devil Moon" is an example of a song that is both, a masterpiece of concision.

Interestingly, Yip and Burt had written the song that was to become "Old Devil Moon" some years earlier with an entirely different lyric. The original lyric of the A section dealt not with desire but repudiation, while the original lyric of the B section dealt not with the exuberance of love but the inability to break off the affair. What remains constant, though, is that the fourth line is where the shift in lyric occurs in both songs. Indeed, as the song was originally written, the shift in the lyric's story—between leaving and staying—is even greater than in "Moon." The weight of the transition was already manifest to the songwriters, even if the meaning of the music was still unclear.

In an interview with Deena Rosenberg, Lane recounted how the melody eventually became "Old Devil Moon":

> I had written a song, actually for Lena Horne, written for a film that was never made, so that the song was never used, and the lyric went:
>
> > I came to give you back that ring
> > Came to drop the whole darn thing
> > Had to take it on the wing
> > But now you're standing there
> > With that moon in your hair
> > And I swear this is where I came in. . . .
>
> Yip had written another love lyric for *Finian,* and it was a lovely song; it had a lovely lyric and a lovely idea. Actually, he had written it to a melody he liked that I also had had a long time. And although the song was very attractive, I didn't think it had enough excitement. . . . I can remember part of it:
>
> > Don't pass me by
> > What's your hurry, stranger?
> > Don't you know we only pass this way one time?
> > Moon shining high
> > But here's the danger
> > It may only shine this way for us one time
>
> It's that kind of a lovely folk idea. And I was trying to get Yip to use the melody of the other song, of "This Is Where I Came In," and I was not able to persuade him until one night Harold Arlen was over, and we had done a reading of the show for a group of people and Harold had attended it and stayed over after everybody had left, and then I played the other tune, and I said, "You know, I've been trying to get Yip to rewrite for this other melody because I think it would make a better song," and when he

heard it, he was the one who persuaded Yip to change his mind. Yip didn't want to rewrite a lyric! It meant a great deal to the show. It had a haunting and magical quality, you know. It dealt with witchcraft. It had more of the character of the show.

One idea was to remain constant in both of the lyrics that Yip wrote to Lane's music: the theme of romantic entrapment. "Moon" 's last stanza is neither tense nor exultant; it is, rather, deeply ambivalent in both music and lyrics about falling in love. The stanza is really a coda, like that which concludes *Bloomer Girl*'s "Right as the Rain," but the mood here is a much darker one, the tone more conflicted. It begins with another Harburg bird—

> Just when I think I'm
> Free as a dove

—like the lark in "Look to the Rainbow," like the Glocca Morra bird, like "Over the Rainbow" 's happy little bluebirds, a symbol for freedom to dream and explore. It concludes,

> Old devil moon
> Deep in your eyes
> Blinds me with love.

It is an uneasy resolution to an uneasy love song. No one, blinded with love, looks to the rainbow.

What Yip termed the fourth subplot in *Finian* concerns Og the leprechaun. If Finian is pixilated, Og is the pixie, the leprechaun who has followed Finian to America to reclaim the pot of gold. Without the gold buried in Irish soil, Og and his fellow leprechauns have begun to turn mortal—so much so that when Og meets Sharon, he is surprised by the feelings she arouses in him, attracted to a woman for the first time in his life. Half leprechaun, half mortal, he ventures a fledgling and most tentative and uncertain love song:

SOMETHING SORT OF GRANDISH

Og. Something sweet
Something sort of grandish
Sweeps my soul
When thou art near

My heart feels
So sugar candish
My head feels
So ginger beer

Something so dare-ish
So I don't-care-ish
Stirs me from limb to limb
It's so terrifish, magnifish, delish
To have such an amorish, glamorish dish

We could be
Oh, so bride and groomish
Skies could be
So blueish blue

Life could be
So love-in-bloomish
If my -ishes
Could come true

Sharon. Thou art sweet
Thou art sort of grandish
Thou outlandish cavalier
From now on
We're hand in handish
Romeo
Og. And Guenevere

Thou'rt so adore-ish
Toujour l'amourish
I'm so cherchez la femme
Sharon. Why should I vanquish, relinquish, resish
When I simply relish this hellish condish

Og.	I might be
	Manish-ish or mouse-ish
	I might be a fowl or fish
	But with thee
	I'm Eisenhowsish
	Please accept my proposish
Both.	You're under my skinnish
	So please be give-in-ish
	Or it's the beginish
	Of the finish of me.

As "Old Devil Moon" arose from an old Lane melody, so "Something Sort of Grandish" evolved from an old Harburg lyric, in this case, from a song he had written with Arlen in 1936 for the picture *Stage Struck*.

> You're Kinda Grandish
> (excerpt)
>
> You'd be kinda grandish
> If you weren't so darned offstandish
> When you ought to be hand-in-handish
> And a little give-in-ish with me

It's a cute lyric, but the later version improves upon it because the central conceit of the lyric, the running wild of the suffix *ish,* is integral to the hesitancy and uncertainty Og feels as he sings the song. The abundance of ish-es serves to qualify and distance all of Og's perceptions and emotions. Indeed, the very title is an expression of infatuation at three removes: "Something," "sort of," and "grandish" are all ways to beat about the bush. The lyric's associations, moreover, are those of a manchild: "sugar candish" and "ginger beer" are the images of preadolescence.

The music to which Yip reworked his lyric also suggests a great tentativeness, the notes of Lane's melody unfolding in delicate and unpredictable succession, like the musicalization of a child or a fawn learning to walk. Og, like Sharon, brings Old World music with him, and "Grandish" sounds a good deal like a minuet gone awry. At times, "Grandish" suggests a nonsardonic Kurt Weill.

"When I first got involved in the thing," Lane told Deena Rosenberg,

> I had to ask Yip, "What's a leprechaun?" And when I did a little research on it—of course, there's no music one could research—but you learn something about Irish folklore, and I had a feeling that his songs, that his

David Wayne, *top of ladder,* played the leprechaun in the original production of *Finian's Rainbow* in a classic performance that reflected Yip's own "grandish" spirit. Here the player and the author-lyricist share a pensive moment in the Columbia Studios during a playback of the cast album, 1947. The original cast album was re-issued as a CD by Columbia Records in 1992. (Billy Rose Theatre Collection, New York Public Library.)

first song, anyway, should have a kind of Old World feeling to it, a kind of classical gavotte or something of that kind, in that style, but be cockeyed.

> And the tune I came up with had a classic feeling but kind of an uneven meter so that it would be off-balance a little bit and Yip came up with a wonderful idea for a title. [The music] starts out and you think you're in the key of F and then you go into the key of C and so it's kind of a surprise.

With "Grandish" we have moved from witchcraft music to leprechaun music. The latter is more self-consciously whimsical: to create a deliberately forced rhyme for *cavalier,* Yip creates the historically and literarily improbable pairing of Romeo and Guenevere. As this is a duet, though, he has Sharon sing "Romeo," and Og chime in with "and Guenevere." The division of the line in this fashion not only suggests that Og and Sharon may not be an ideally mated team, but also amounts to a lyricist's wink at the audience: it's a joke lyric advertising itself as such.

Woody's sister Susan is a mute who speaks only through her dancing: the most convenient adjustment to an ailment that ever hit the Broadway stage. She dances her exuberance about Woody and Sharon's romance, which evolves into an ensemble production number:

Music starts

(Sharon *kisses* Woody, *then throws a rose to* Finian. Susan *goes into a joyous dance.*)

Henry. Susan's trying to tell you something.

Crowd. What's she sayin', Henry?

Henry. I can't tell—it's a secret! Woody, you tell them.

                           IF THIS ISN'T LOVE

Woody.	A secret, a secret
	She says she's got a secret
	A secret, a secret
	A secret kind of secret
	She's achin' for to shout it
	To every daffodil
	And tell the world about it
	In fact, she says she will
Chorus.	She says . . .
Woody.	She says . . .
	If this isn't love
	The whole world is crazy
	If this isn't love
	I'm daft as a daisy
	With moons all around
	And cows jumping over
	There's something amiss
	And I'll eat my hat if this isn't love
	I'm feelin' like the apple
	On top of William Tell
	With this I cannot grapple
	Because . . .
Chorus.	Because . . .
Woody.	You're so adora-bel!

If this isn't love
Then Winter is Summer
If this isn't love
My heart needs a plumber
I'm swingin' on stars
I'm ridin' on rainbows
I'm bustin' with bliss
And I'll kiss your hand if this isn't love

Sharon. If this isn't love
I'm Carmen Miranda
If this isn't love
It's red propaganda
If this is a dream
And if I should wake up
Will you hear a hiss
Will my face be red if this isn't love

Finian. I'm gettin' tired of waitin'
And stickin' to the rules
This feelin' calls for matin'
Like birds and bees and other animules

Chorus. If this isn't love
We're all seeing double
If this isn't love

Woody. I'm really in trouble
Sharon. If I'm not the girl
Woody. And I'm not the hero
Chorus. A kiss ain't a kiss
It's a crisis, man, if this isn't love
If this isn't love
If this isn't love
If this isn't love!

"If This Isn't Love" is the most conventional Broadway production number song in *Finian*'s score. It begins with an illustration of how folk singsong is transmuted into the Broadway idiom. "A secret, a secret / She says she's got a secret" is set to music that evokes a child's chanting while actually inaugurating a rather complicated melody.

Conventional or not, "If This Isn't Love" contains several characteristically Harburgian concerns and images. It has exultation of love, like "Old Devil Moon"; it has exasperation with the folkways of man as they impede nature, like "This Time of the Year"; it has "Devil Moon"'s stars and Finian's rainbows. It has as well the meshing of the composer's and lyricist's art. In the penultimate line of Woody's part of the song, the word "bustin'" comes on the song's highest note: the emotional high point of both the music and the lyric coincide.

Having been told of the discovery of gold on the sharecroppers' land, Rawkins schemes to get the land away from them, and the show turns its attention to the sharecroppers themselves. Six women are found working the tobacco fields—and discussing whether the tobacco will end up being puffed by Bogart into Lauren Bacall's eyes. We are a few light years removed from an unsullied peasantry, then—and suitably prepared for the first of *Finian*'s comic Broadway blues.

NECESSITY

Verse.
What is the curse
That makes the universe so all bewinderin'?
What is the hoax
That just provokes the folks they call God's childerin?
What is the jinx
That gives a body and his brother and ev'ry one
    aroun'
The run aroun'?

Chorus.
Necessity, necessity
That most unnecessary thing
Necessity
What throws a monkey wrench in
A fellow's good intention?
That nasty old invention
Necessity

My feet wanna dance in the sun
My head wants to rest in the shade
The Lord says, "Go out and have fun"
But the landlord says
"Your rent ain't paid."

Necessity, it's plain to see
What a lovely old world
This silly old world could be
But man, it's all in a mess
Account of necessity

Second Chorus.   Necessity, necessity
There ought to be a law against
Necessity
The jail would never been there
Except for folks who sin there
Well, how did I get in there?
Necessity

Oh, Satan's the father of sin,
And Cupid's the father of love,
Oh, hell is the father of gin
But no one knows the father of

Women.   You mean he's a—
(spoken)
First Woman.   Uh-huh

Necessity, necessity
That's the maximum that
A minimum thing could be
There's nothing lower than less
Unless it's necessity.

The first couplet announces "Necessity" as a Broadway comic blues. A black alto sings the first lines in the manner of black church music; the music itself is somewhat on the portentous side—all leading up to the deflation of the deliberate play-rhyme of "bewilderin'" with "childerin'." The deflation is compounded by the couplet that follows, with its first line stretched to the breaking point ("What is the jinx that gives a body and his brother and everyone aroun'"), as if an added wail is required to do justice to the problem. The second line, by comic contrast, is over in a flash: "The run aroun'." We are, in short, in Harburg lyric country.

As originally conceived, "Necessity" seems to have grown out of *Cabin in the Sky*'s "Life's Full of Consequence." At first, the song was entitled, "Circumstances," and Yip played with "You can't fool around with circumstances" as an opening. "Necessity," however, brought him nearer to a folk expression of alienation, and it was on that ground that he chose to build the song. One of his stanzas in his workbooks at Yale which did not make it into the final draft makes the point even more clearly:

> What is the big resistance
> Creates the biggest distance
> Twixt you and full existence?
> Necessity.

Musically, "Necessity"'s chorus features a bluesy melody sung over a comic vamp; lyrically, the song comprises Yip's clearest statement of the contrast between nature and human possibility with Yip's folk encapsulation of the social and economic order, necessity. The deck is more than a bit stacked here, particularly in the contrast of the Lord and the land. It's difficult to think of a religion whose Lord actually prompts his followers to "go out and have fun"— but this is Harburg's Lord, a Lord of begetting and abundance, all carrot, no stick. But the stick of capitalism is clear: "Your rent ain't paid."

Yip continues his account of the ending of act 1:

> Finian plants the gold in Rainbow Valley near Fort Knox. And when he plants that gold, he's planting a crop that has three wishes. After Finian leaves, two geologists come along, who are making a survey for the federal government and their meter shows a deposit of gold over the place where Finian just planted his gold crop.

> One geologist is white, the other black. They proceed to Billboard Rawkins's old plantation, where Rawkins ignores and insults the "nigra." Suddenly his antagonism is melted into the milk of human kindness when the black geologist says this little needle showed a great discovery of gold,

a great vein of gold on his property. A mint julep is brought out. He says, "The needle reacted so violently it broke." "Oh," Rawkins says, "that's too bad. Where exactly did this needle breaking occur?" He says on property so-and-so, which Finian had just bought. Then Buzz, Rawkins' stooge, says, "By God, we don't own it." "Well, who owns it?" "A foreigner by the name of Finian." "A foreigner?" Rawkins rages, "we've been having trouble with foreigners ever since we landed in this country." So by the use of words we explore one of the very things the play's about—we know there's nothing but foreigners in America; and yet there's this tradition of tribalism and race hatred and differences.

[Rawkins] wants to get the gold and he can't get the property. So now he asserts his power. And now we see how legislation works for power, even though the legislation is wrong. By invoking the law he also invokes the wrath of Sharon, this girl who doesn't understand our mores, doesn't understand the Civil War. She came here because there's this little Constitution that says everybody's free and equal. "Haven't you ever read it?" "No," he says, "I have no time to read it. I'm too busy defendin' it." She says, "You mean to chase these people off because their skins are black?" And she says something that isn't a curse, that isn't mean, that isn't vengeful at all, but is bewilderment. "Good God, I wish you'd know what it's like to be black in a country where it is wrong to be black. I wish you were black . . . so you would know what it would feel like to be in their skin." Unknowingly, she's standing over the crock of gold and this is the first wish. Before you know it there's big Senator Billboard turned into a black man and, fleeing, now has to come up against all the laws that he himself legislated.

The suddenly black Rawkins rushes off, stunned; as Woody rushes on to inform the sharecroppers that the Shears and Robust mail-order conglomerate has granted them unlimited credit as a result of the newfound gold. The sharecroppers ask when do they get all the things they have ever wished and hoped for. Woody responds in an exuberant song that *now* (not "t'morra") is "That Great Come-and-Get-It Day."

THAT GREAT COME-AND-GET-IT DAY

Woody.
On that great come and get it day
Won't it be fun when worry is done
And money is hay?
That's the time things'll come your way
On that great, great come and get it day

I'll get my gal that calico gown
I'll get my mule that acre of groun'
Cause word has come from Gabriel's horn
The earth beneath your plow
Is a buddin' and now it's your'n

Sharon.
Glory time's comin' for to stay
On that great, great come and get it day

All.
Come and get it

Preacher.
Sez here!
Sez it in the good book, it sez
A mighty mornin' is nigh

All.
Universal Fourth of July!

Woody.
Gonna get your freedom and pie

All.
Freedom, freedom, freedom, freedom pie
What a day for banjos ringin'
What a day for people in overalls
Can't you hear all the angels singin'?

Man.
Come and get your gravy and two meat balls!

Chorus.
Come and get it
Sez it in the good book
Hallelujah

Chorus.
Bells will ring in every steeple

Woman.
Come and get your test on the movie screen

All.
Come you free and you equal people

Man.
Come and get your beer and your benzedrine

All.
Sez here, come and get it, come!

Preacher.
There's gonna be a world shaken
Bread breakin' day!

Chorus.   Great day!

First Woman.   Does that mean I can get a washing machine?

Preacher.   Glory to you!

Second Woman.   Can I get a waffle iron?

Woody.   With your initials!

Boy.   Can I get a juke box?

Preacher.   Sez here

First Man.   How about a helicopter?

Preacher.   Helicopter?

All.   Hallelujah!
                     On that great come and get it day
                     Won't it be fun when worry is done
                     And money is hay
                     That's the time things'll come your way
                     On that great great come and get it day

Sharon.   My gown will be a calico gown
                     My feet will dance all over the town

Woody.   Cause word has come from Gabriel's horn
                     The earth beneath your plow is a buddin'
                     And now it's your'n

Chorus.   Yes now it's your'n

All.   Glory times
                     Comin' for to stay
                     On that great, great
                     Come and get it,
                     And keep it,
                     And share it,
                     Great, great
                     Come and get it day!

One of the distinguishing characteristics of *Finian's* score is that a number of the songs seem to be in a kind of dialogue with each other. "Old Devil Moon" is a response to "Look to the Rainbow," and in "Great Come and Get It Day" we find an answer to "Necessity," a movement, at first glance, from necessity to freedom. This is freedom, moreover, in its economic as well as political dimension, moving beyond, say, the liberal vision of *Bloomer Girl's* "The Eagle and Me" to a more openly socialist view of what freedom comprises: not just liberty but the sharing of abundance, "freedom and pie."

Initially, "Day" seems like a Broadway production number adaptation of such classic songs of black liberation as "Kingdom Coming," that sang not just of an end to slavery but of a promised jubilee year. Like the songs of the slaves and the songs of the civil rights movement still to come, "Day" sanctifies worldly revolution with Christian deliverance. "In the good book it sez," sings the preacher, "A mighty mornin' is nigh / Universal fourth of July." Sacred and secular intertwine as Gabriel's horn proclaims a message of expropriation to the sharecroppers: "Cause word has come / From Gabriel's horn / The earth beneath your plow / Is a-buddin' and now it's your'n."

But the revolution that was reshaping the America of 1946 was hardly a socialist one, and "Day" ultimately deals not just with the combining of the sacred and the secular but also with the collision between the sacred and the profane. The precipitating event for "Day," after all, is the sudden granting of an unlimited credit line: an explosion of purchasing power like that which transformed the United States at the close of the Second World War. The revolution only begins with freedom and land. In no time at all, the "people in overalls" are getting screen tests and benzedrine. While the music and lyrics of church tradition bracket each request, a succession of appliances is wished for, moving from the eminently practical (washing machine and waffle iron—Yip working in some of *Finian*'s source material here) to the extravagant (the juke box) to the ridiculous (the helicopter). And the church music, initially ennobling, becomes ironic as the requests grow more ludicrous.

While Lane's music for "Day" ranges from black spiritual to western cowpoke to Broadway bounce, these requests are not set to music at all. They are spoken or shouted, like the earlier pronouncements of Rawkins's henchmen. From the screen test through the helicopter, they are all without music. The Shears and Robust revolution was not one that Yip chose to invest with any poetry or music. "Is it necessary for the idle rich to manipulate our society," Yip said while introducing the show at Northwood, "so that consumption consumes the consumer?" The absence of music is a subtle critique in an otherwise stormily upbeat production number. The first act concludes, then, with a vision of the revolution as Yip would have it, of freedom and pie and the earth to those who work it, of a

> Come and get it
> And keep it
> And share it
> Great, great come and get it day.

Act 2 begins not with the day of deliverance, but of delivery: of the items ordered from the Shears and Robust catalog. Suitably reattired, the newly fashion-plated sharecroppers hold a fashion show song and dance. In Yip's words:

What happens in this country where money and gold are magical symbols to get power and comfort? The nouveau riche come on, and what happens? We want to satirize the folly of what happens to people who suddenly become affluent—from desperately needing things to desperately wanting them.

Now the sharecroppers of Rainbow Valley have got money [in the form of credit] to buy fur shorts. In this scene people came in dressed in all sorts of ridiculous, unnecessary things that we spend our money on. Hats that are unnecessary, clothes that didn't fit, high-life costumes, all absurdly unfitting to their lives, and they sing:

WHEN THE IDLE POOR BECOME THE IDLE RICH

Sharon.	When the idle poor become the idle rich You'll never know just who is who Or who is which Won't it be rich When ev'ryone's poor relative Becomes a "Rockefellative" And palms no longer itch What a switch!
Women.	When we all have ermine and plastic teeth How will we determine who's who underneath?
Men.	And when all your neighbors are upper class You won't know your Joneses from your As-tors
Sharon.	Let's toast the day The day we drink that drinkie up But with the little pinkie up The day on which The idle poor become the idle rich
Chorus.	Du du du doot de du, de du, de du du Du du du doot de du, de du, de doot
Sharon.	When a rich man doesn't want to work, He's a bon vivant Yes, he's a bon vivant But when a poor man doesn't want to work, He's a loafer, he's a lounger He's a lazy good for nothing He's a jerk

When a rich man loses on a horse
Isn't he the sport?
Oh, isn't he the sport?
But when a poor man loses on a horse
He's a gambler, he's a spender
He's a lowlife, he's a reason
For divorce

When a rich man chases after dames
He's a man about town
A man about town
But when a poor man chases after dames
He's a bounder, he's a rounder
He's a rotter, and a lot of
Dirty names

Chorus.   Du du du doot de du, de du, de du du
Du du du doot de du, de du, de doot
You'll never know just who is which
When the idle poor become the idle rich,

When the idle poor become the idle rich
You'll never know just who is who
Or who is which

Sharon.   No one can see the Irish or the Slav in you
For when you're on Park Avenue
Cornelius and Mike
Look alike

Women.   When poor Tweedle Dum is rich Tweedle Dee
This discrimination will no longer be

Men.   When we're in the dough and off of the nut
You won't know your banker from your but-ler

Sharon.   Let's make the switch
With just a few annuities
We'll hide those incongruities
In cloaks
From Abercrombie Fitch

Chorus.   When the idle poor become the idle rich
When the idle poor become the idle rich.

The cast of *Finian's Rainbow* in the dance preceding the song, "When the Idle Poor Become the Idle Rich"; poor Southern sharecroppers from Rainbow Valley exult over luxury clothes ordered on credit, which they never had before. Yip and Fred Saidy conceived a satiric scene where, said Yip, "consumption consumes the consumer." (Billy Rose Theatre Collection, New York Public Library.)

"Michael Kidd staged a ballet to precede 'Idle Poor,'" writes musical historian Ethan Mordden,

> in which penniless Southern sharecroppers exult in hifalutin' outfits ordered by mail on charge account: class now, pay later. It is one of the musical's most commentatively *immediate* images—the very picture of postwar America.

And Yip told the Northwood Institute audience:

People of the soil, bringing up tobacco as a crop, now suddenly go in for obvious baubles and funny things they don't need, so the audience must look at themselves a little bit and say, What are we doing to our values?

That is part of "Idle Poor"—the false consciousness part carried over from "Come-and-Get-It Day." The other part is what Yip termed its Pygmalion part—that the perception of behavior is a function of the class of the behaver. In a show intended to ridicule the double standards of race, "Idle Poor" is the one direct salvo against the double standards of class.

Like "Something Sort of Grandish," "Idle Poor" features music that juxtaposes an Old World, certainly upper-class formality, a slightly classical sound against a slightly screwy melody, and climaxes with the choral a cappella sung in the manner of a madrigal. The effect, as before, is of a somewhat sunnier Kurt Weill.

The plot now returns to Og, searching for the fairy crock of gold. Yip explains:

> He happens to meet the senator in the forest, hiding out. Two subplots and the main plot are now starting to come together. Og's loss of the crock of gold which has turned the senator black, all three plots hang on, around, and in a nucleus of one thing: the crock of gold. See how beautiful that is? It's mathematical. . . .
>
> We see Rawkins enter the glen. He's all disheveled, shabby from hiding out in the forest. He doesn't want people to see him in this terrible condition. He steals up behind our Og, peacefully singing on his crock of gold, grabs the apple out of his hand, "Gimme that!" and Og says, "You needn't grab; there's plenty of apples around."—"Well, I don't see 'em!"—"Well, naturally you don't. Mortals never can see *all* the apples they could have." We don't see all the products that we could produce if we do the right things. And he says, "An apple here, an apple there, little red apples everywhere," and he says "my, you must be hungry." Rawkins says, "Wouldn't you be hungry? I've been hiding out in this forest two weeks like a hunted 'possum.'"—What were you hidin' from?"—"I don't want my wife, my kids, my friends, to see me in this condition!"—"I see nothing wrong with you."—"Ya don't? Ya must be blind! Can't ya see I'm black?"—"Oh, yes. And I think it's very becoming."—Rawkins says, "I don't like bein' black. I'm a white man . . . at least I was a few weeks ago."—"Well, that's coincidence. I was green a few weeks ago. . . . Don't you find an occasional change of color interesting? Why don't you change your color again?"

Rawkins explains to Og, to whom the workings of a racist society are a total mystery, how he [Rawkins] is suddenly unable to board a bus or buy a beer—

because, he is compelled to explain to the uncomprehending Og, it's the law. He wrote it himself. Og concludes that Rawkins's skin-color transformation is still too superficial, and he uses his magic powers, in his best *Macbeth* manner, to wish Rawkins's soul into decency:

> Fiddle faddle foil and fiddle
> Cure this fuddled individdle
> Rise ye vapors and unwind
> This tangled medieval mind
> Breath of bee and bluebird wing
> Make this scowling spirit sing
> Palm of briar and sandalwood
> Season him with brotherhood
> Magic vapors, make this person
> A better person, not a worse'n.

The hitherto songless Rawkins rises up singing—a sure sign, in Harburg country, of his redemption. "I don't like villains in stories—out and out villains," Yip told Northwood. "I don't believe there are villains. I believe that people are products of their tradition, of their education, their environment and their upbringing. And let's be truthful about it: nobody's black and white. . . . People are paradox. The worst of people have some good in them. The best of people have some bad in them."

Rawkins is stumbled upon by a trio of black gospel singers whose baritone has run off with a woman. Rawkins volunteers to take his place and, a quartet once more, their song becomes a satire of man's population explosion:

THE BEGAT

Verse. The Lord made Adam, the Lord made Eve
He made 'em both a little bit naive
They lived as free as the Summer breeze
Without pajamas and without chemise
Until they stumbled on the apple trees
Then she looked at him, and he looked at her
And they knew immedjetly what the world was fer
He said give me my cane
He said give me my hat
The time has come
To begin the begat

Chorus.

The begat, the begat
So they begat Cain
And they begat Abel
Who begat the rabble
At the Tow'r of Babel

They begat the Cohens
And they begat O'Rourkes
And they begat the people
Who believed in storks

Lordy, Lordy,
How they did begat
How they be-be-begat
Even more than that
When the begat got to gettin' under par
They begat the daughters of the D. A. R.
They begat the Babbitts of the bourgeoisie
Who begat the misbegotten G. O. P.

It was pleasin' to Jezebel
Pleasin' to Ruth
It pleased the League Of Women shoppers in Duluth
Though the movie censors tried the facts to hide
The movie goers up and multiplied

Lordy, Lordy,
How they multiplied
How they multiplied
How they multiplied
Soon it swept the world, ev'ry land and lingo
It became the rage, it was bigger than Bingo

The whites begat
The reds begat
The folks who shoulda stood in bed begat
The Greeks begat
The Swedes begat
Why, even Britishers in tweeds begat
And Lordy, Lordy,
What their seeds begat

The Lapps and Lithuanians begat
Scranton, Pennsylvanians begat
Strict vegetarians begat
Honorary Aryans begat
Starting from Genesis they begat
Heroes and menaces begat
Fat filibusterers begat
Income tax adjusterers begat

'Twas natchaler and natchaler to begat
And sometimes a bachelor he begat
It didn't matter which-a-ways they begat
Sons of habitués begat

So bless them all who go to bat
And heed the call of the begat.

"The Begat" is surely one of those songs in *Finian* originally conceived as an Earl Robinson number, and again Lane turned out to have been thoroughly adept in this manner of song as well. It is a highly Broadwayized black number built around a comic lyric that features old jokes ("sons of habitués") and new, unlikely couplings ("Latts and Lithuanians / Scranton, Pennsylvanians").

"The Begat" is a curious song to put in the mouths of gospel singers—but then, the Harburg god is clearly, as Yip put it, pro-creation and pro-procreation. In this regard, "The Begat" helps to set up *Finian*'s final song, in which an ever-more-mortal Og must confront for the first time the promptings of sex. "I don't want to be human!" Og cries. "It's too inhuman!" As Yip told Northwood:

> He's hit by one of the most interesting things that ever happens to people, this little three-letter word called sex. This little leprechaun has never known an idiotic thing like sex before. He's never been troubled by it, and suddenly, now the delight of sex hits him, the joy of it. Nature says, go to it! And then his conscience, which has been conditioned by church, by American Puritanism, says, "Don't—sex is terrible." And now he's caught in between like every human being. The delight of sex; the guilt of it. And he feels that this thing, love, is eternal, that it will last forever. He's falling in love with Sharon. Suddenly he sees Susan, and he gets the same feeling. He falls in love with Susan and he's more conflicted. How can this eternal feeling be good for only two minutes?

Aroused, confused, Og bursts into what Stephen Sondheim has called the greatest eleven o'clock song in the annals of the American musical:

When I'm Not Near the Girl I Love

Oh my heart is beating wildly
And it's all because you're here
When I'm not near the girl I love
I love the girl I'm near

Ev'ry femme that flutters by me
Is a flame that must be fanned
When I can't fondle the hand that I'm fond of
I fondle the hand at hand

My heart's in a pickle
It's constantly fickle
And not too partickle, I fear
When I'm not near the girl I love
I love the girl I'm near

What if they're tall or tender
What if they're small or slender
Long as they've got that gender
I s'rrender
Always I can't refuse 'em
Always my feet pursues 'em
Long as they've got a "boo-som"
I woos 'em

I'm confessing a confession
And I hope I'm not verbose
When I'm not close to the kiss that I cling to
I cling to the kiss that's close

As I'm more and more a mortal
I am more and more a case
When I'm not facing the face that I fancy
I fancy the face I face

For Sharon I'm carin'
But Susan I'm choosin
I'm faithful to whos'n is here
When I'm not near the girl I love
I love the girl I'm near.

"After all," Yip once said, "lyric writing is word games. I just think language is the most playful thing there is, and if you can't play with language if you're a lyric writer, then what can you do?" If lyric writing is word games, "When I'm Not Near the Girl I Love" is word Olympics. Its central device is four nearly palindromic formulations, each one running a sentence forwards and backwards successively, to create the opposite meaning in the second half that is created in the first. If ever "Backwards ran sentences until reeled the mind," this is it (or, it is this).

And "When I'm Not Near" features games within games. The first release is built around rhymes with "pickle" culminating in the pleasant neologism, "not too partickle." The second release builds to another neologism, "whos'n" to rhyme with "Susan." These are words that *sound* funny—the first set of rhymes sounds like a hiccup; the second sounds as if it oozes out. The interlude is based on a string of two-syllable rhymes. The first three rhymes are set against an upwardly sliding musical tone (tennnnder/slennnder/gennnder), and together, the lines comprise one long "if clause." When the third slide has taken us musically as far as our ear tells us we can go, the "then clause" whizzes by in a flash: "I s'rrender." The effect is heightened in the rhymes of the second half of the interlude, which slide upward on the "Ooze" sound (refuuuuse 'em / purssssues'em / boooos-om).

It's a slippery song for a slippery subject—and the slipping and sliding begin with the topic sentence: each time the line "When I'm not near the girl I love" is sung, the three words that are about to be flung back in reverse order are slurred: neee-ar, giii-rl, looo-ove. On the other lines that use that melody, the slur is replaced by two distinct one-syllable words: "When I'm not *close to* the *kiss that* I *cling to,*" and so on. The line was originally composed for the slurred title phrase—although, then again, the musical line was originally composed in Burt Lane's sleep: "The title of the song," Lane recalled,

> was written in the script, in the first draft of the show that I read after Yip asked me to do it. And of course I was just tickled with that title. It was just wonderful coming out the way it did with the leprechauns beginning to turn mortal, and all I could think of was Yip. Yip was the only leprechaun I had ever met. But we were working on many songs. When you work on a show, you work on more than one thing at a time.

> Anyway, I had worked on other things, and then one night I woke up out of a sleep. A melody had occurred to me and I wrote it down. I wanted to get it, and I went back to sleep, and the next day, again, Yip, Freddy [Saidy], and I were meeting, talking, and I started to underscore their conversation [plays chord]. Yip picked up his ears and said, "What is that?" I said, "Oh, I don't know, just a . . ." He couldn't say, "That's

terrible." He'd ignore it if it was not something that was attractive to him. . . . But he stopped and said, "What is that?" I said, "Yip, I wrote it last night but I don't know where it would go." I had been subconsciously working with "When I'm Not Near the Girl I Love," but even then I did not associate that tune with that title. Yip said, "Play it again." I did and he started to sing these little slurs on "neee-ar the girrr-l"—and that made the title fit. But I hadn't thought of it, although subconsciously it must have been there all the time, because you don't write a tune that fits everything so right . . . without having it work subconsciously. He caught it and wrote one of his greatest lyrics.

Writing with Yip, Lane reflected, was often spontaneous combustion:

Yip would get very excited when he heard a tune. He'd bounce all over the room and he'd write. He was already clicking with lyrics. He'd go home and brush it up a little, but he would write while he was there, while he was all excited.

Lane described others of his collaborators as "agonizers," but not Yip. "Yip was all joy," he said. "He bounced."

Again, though, Yip's worksheets show "I'm Not Near" to have been anything but a completely spontaneous song. Indeed, the passage in the Yale worksheets which eventually was set to the verse began life as the words to the bridge of the chorus:

> I can't help but choose 'em
> My feet just pursues 'em
> If they've got a bosom
> Oh dear

and the words that eventually ended up in the bridge first emerged in a sentiment too callous for a leprechaun, no matter how mortal:

> For Sharon I'm carin'
> For Susan I'm choosin'
> No matter who whos'n she's dear.

The music Lane composed for "When I'm Not Near" is a somewhat rapid waltz. The melody is more "normal," the harmonies more regular than those for his other Og song, "Something Sort of Grandish." But at this point in the story, Og is more and more a mortal, his feelings more human, less tentative, and the music reflects that development.

"When I'm Not Near" is, as Sondheim put it, an eleven o'clock song, a song for that moment near the end of the show when composer and lyricist want to rouse an audience for the approaching curtain. Eleven o'clock numbers on Broadway today (with the decisive exception of Sondheim) are light shows that dazzle audiences with glitz. "When I'm Not Near" dazzles in a different manner, dazzles the brain rather than the eye.

Og's increasing humanness is actually integral to the resolution of *Finian's* story line. Sharon has been arrested for witchcraft for turning Rawkins black; she will be hanged at dawn unless Rawkins is turned white again. Finian goes to dig up the pot of gold to wish Rawkins white, but it is gone: unbeknownst to all, silent Susan has moved it. As Og searches for the crock, he tells Susan he wishes she could talk. Talk she does, and Og realizes he was standing over the crock when he made the wish. He digs up the crock, but just one wish remains, the wish he had reserved for his reversion to full leprechaunity. With the seconds ticking away for Sharon in best perils of Pauline fashion, Og remains torn between opting for fairyland or mortality—at which point, the Harburg life force decides the issue:

> Suddenly, he's undecided. He doesn't know what to do, he wants to go back to fairyland, and he says, "What shall I do? What shall I do? There's only one wish in the crock, and the only way I can get out of this dilemma is if I turn the senator white again. But if I turn the senator white, I lose the crock and I can't go back to fairyland. "I don't want to be human! I want to go back to fairyland!" But Susan embraces him and kisses him. And he's suddenly overwhelmed; and he says (in baritone), "Fairyland was never like this!" And he jumps up on the crock and says, "Rawkins, you scoundrel, I wish you white!" Thus love overcomes everything—the wish to go back to fairyland, the wish not to be a kid again, a Peter Pan, an ungrown person. He wants to grow up—he's ready to face all the discouragement, all the suffering, everything of life with that wonderful, overpowering thing called love. Fairyland is over. Childhood's over. Immaturity is over. The total man is coming into existence. The beauty of it!

> Now the senator is restored to his old skin color, white, but with a new friendly soul. Woody and Sharon have found each other and can live in Rainbow Valley.

> And the people become rich because the tractors they got *on credit* helped the tobacco leaves. Now, let's see what happens. For hundreds of years we have been living dedicated to the proposition that gold is the thing to make us happy. And now the little crock has brought all these people riches, the wealth, the tobacco, the idle poor have become the idle rich, and there's no

gold. The crock has turned to dross. The leprechaun is 100 percent mortal, and he's with Susan, in love with her, and Susan talks, and the farm is working, and Finian has found his rainbow for his daughter, and all the four plots have come together now in that one rainbow. A puzzle within a puzzle, all coming together. How glorious it is to solve that whole thing!

Finian has a desacralized happy ending: the magic is removed from its world. There are no more wishes, no more leprechauns, no more gold. We are left with worldly miracles only: boy gets girl, farmers get land, Missitucky gets a liberal senator—and one semiworldly miracle: Finian's rainbow shoots across the sky to guide him to his next dream. "Farewell, me friends," he shouts. "I'll see ye all some day in Glocca Morra." Woody asks Sharon where Glocca Morra is; she answers, "There's no such place, Woody—it's only in Father's head." As the curtain falls, the company sings:

> So to every weepin' willow
> To each brook along the way
> To each lad that
> Comes a-whistlin' Too-ra-lay
> May we meet in Glocca Morra
> One fine day.

No such place? No matter: nostalgia is best unsullied by reality, and nostalgic utopia is what the new musical play of the forties was in large measure about. The revolution in musical comedy may have been radical in form but it was nostalgic-utopian in its setting: for old Oklahoma (*Oklahoma!*) and old New England (*Carousel*), for old Scotland (*Brigadoon*), for old Ireland (*Finian*)— even for the Old West (*Annie, Get Your Gun*). Each of these celebrates a lost community, a vanishing small-town fraternity. The mood was by no means confined to musical theater; the Frank Capra masterpiece *It's a Wonderful Life*, which opened two weeks before *Finian* came to Broadway, is similarly drenched. The triumph of the cities, which in the twenties and thirties Broadway had both celebrated and exemplified, was continuing apace as indigenous regional cultures gave way to the national media; as the depression and the Second World War uprooted millions of people across the nation. In the forties, the winners of the cultural conflict waxed nostalgic over what had been lost: Broadway spoke for the vanishing old worlds.

Harburg, Saidy, and Lane try to have it both ways towards this nostalgia, nowhere more than at the final curtain. Glocca Morra does not exist, the book says; it is another myth exploded. But real or imaginary, the score celebrates it, pines for it, as the curtain descends. In its final moments, *Finian* both demystifies and keeps the dream intact: it is the quintessence of Harburgism.

Finian's closing moments also intensify the identification of the show's title character with the show's main author. Glocca Morra exists, Sharon tells us, "only in Father's head." But Finian then does something even more Harburgian than creating Glocca Morra: he moves on. Woody and Og have tried to leave, only to fall in love and settle down: it is a condition of Harburg men to look to the rainbow, though they may not always follow it over hill and stream. But Finian himself will not settle down. The rainbow draws him inexorably on.

As it did Yip. With *Finian*, Yip and Burt, who had worked together throughout the forties, had created with Fred Saidy a smash hit, their masterpiece—and then, against all logic, went their separate ways. As *Finian* moved toward its opening, Lane had felt demeaned by Harburg and did not wish to work with him again in theater. After a time, though, as Lane once told interviewers, "I was dying to be teamed with Yip, but Yip wanted to be like the eagle and me, wanted to be free, didn't want to be tied down." The old wanderlust persisted, though Yip was running out of first class composers equal to the demands of his lyrics and the Broadway musical play.

Yip moved on; Finian moved on; but the show settled down for a Broadway run of 725 performances. A good deal of its success was due to the success of its score. In the month between its out-of-town premiere in Philadelphia on December 10, 1946, and its New York opening on January 10, 1947, "How Are Things in Glocca Morra?" became a major radio hit, recorded by both Bing Crosby and Frank Sinatra and other singers. "Old Devil Moon," by contrast, achieved its prominence more slowly, though it did become an instant favorite of numerous jazz musicians intrigued by Lane's almost avant-garde writing. But *Finian*'s score was so rich it contained masterful songs largely overlooked to this day, "Look to the Rainbow" probably the most notable example. The reviews written of *Finian*'s opening tended to single out "Glocca Morra," and, as much for Michael Kidd's groundbreaking choreography as for the song itself, "That Great Come and Get It Day."

Finian received reviews that ranged from favorable with reservations to out-and-out raves, with special praise for the score, Kidd's choreography, and David Wayne's performance as Og. Black critics were particularly enthusiastic. "For the first time in this reviewer's memory," wrote Miles Jefferson in *Phylon*,

> intolerance in the Deep South has been subjected to light, but peppery, spoofing in a musical show, and this has been accomplished in the best of taste and with great style. . . . So completely a part of the show are the Negro performers, who compose more than one-third of the company, that it demonstrates an object lesson in race goodwill.

This mix of black and white performers dancing together for the first time in Broadway musical history was a breakthrough for which Yip fought long and hard. One critic praised Yip's satirical approach to the antiracist theme: "Prejudice is brought to trial at the bar of laughter. . . . In *Finian's Rainbow,* the fantasy is closer to the heart of reality than the allegedly realistic plays that create a fantastic distortion of life and its values."

The two deans of Broadway criticism saw *Finian* in another perspective. "Gilbert naturally aside," wrote George Jean Nathan, "it has in large part the most amusing musical fantasy book since the last really amusing one which I am too tired to dig that far back in my memory to identify." (As Nathan usually hated shows that wore their liberal hearts on their sleeve, he would have to have been particularly taken with the book to forgive it its politics.) And in the *New York Times,* Brooks Atkinson wrote: "It puts the American musical stage several steps forward for the imagination with which it is written and for the stunning virtuosity of the performance."

Yip's peers were particularly forthcoming in their praise. "This is a mere note to congratulate you," Cole Porter wrote Yip the morning after the opening, "and to thank you for allowing the public to appreciate your great talent." The man who had done the most to create the form in which Yip was now triumphant was even more effusive; his telegram of the same morning read: "Dear Yip, I love you. Will you marry me?" It was from Oscar Hammerstein.

In actuality, *Finian* stood at the intersection of two distinct cycles within forties popular culture: the nostalgic musical play and the postwar tolerance tract, the latter embodied in such contemporaneous works as *Home of the Brave, Gentlemen's Agreement,* and *Pinky.* Indeed, *Finian* prodded Hammerstein to the realization that this kind of crossover was possible. Two years later, he and Rodgers were to produce *South Pacific.* Ethan Mordden summarized the development of the musical art form in the forties: "Hammerstein and Harburg made Broadway dangerous for the routine."

Finally, it is impossible to subsume *Finian* under any category except the Harburg cycle, so radical are its politics and so personal its concerns. Though the spirit of the thirties Left hangs over *Finian,* there is no other comparable work that approaches its use and mixture of fable and fantasy, comedy and music. But while its racial liberalism was immediately obvious to any audience, its Marxism was apprehended at most on the level of parable only—the only level, that is, which would have been acceptable to a mainstream musical audience, most especially an audience of 1947. In the assessment of noted musical librettist Peter Stone,

> *Finian's Rainbow* was . . . extraordinarily political, [but] the audience had no idea of that. It was a socialist tract that made its point at a time when the entire country was in fear [of socialism]. If you ever want to reach people with a political tract, go study *Finian's Rainbow.*

It was doubtless an irony that Yip did not anticipate that this most radical of musicals became a Broadway smash just before the postwar reaction set in. (It was such a hit that the following year, 1948, it became the first American musical to be staged in postwar continental Europe.) Conceived near the end of the Roosevelt presidency and performed during the onset of the cold war and the blacklist, *Finian* proved to be more advanced relative to the politics of the time than Yip had initially intended.

By that measure, his next musical, *Flahooley,* another fantasy assault on capitalism, written and produced at the height of McCarthyism, was more than a little heroic, and more than a little quixotic—but only because it did not succeed.

Senator Joseph McCarthy (with pointer) instructs an agonized Boston lawyer, Joseph Welch (seated) on the alleged locations of the Communist Party apparatus during a Congressional hearing in 1954. When McCarthy slandered Welch's assistant (not present) he was stunned by Welch's query, "Have you no decency, sir?" The remark helped convert a new national television audience to oppose McCarthy, even though the House Un-American Activities Committee still survived. (AP)

Chapter 9

Flahooley, Jamaica, and the Blacklist

With more electronics
Facial tonics and perfume
With more high colonics
Than consumers can consume
The price will tumble
And the stocks will fall
And then what you gonna sell
When abundance freaks us all?

Flahooley

McCarthyism caught up with Yip in 1950. While working at MGM on a supremely "American" project, a Freed-unit musical version of *Huckleberry Finn,* he was blacklisted.

The blacklist had begun in 1947, when the studios announced that the ten "unfriendly" witnesses who had testified before the House Committee on Un-American Activities (HUAC) would not work again in the industry. It took a while, though, for the blacklist to spread beyond the original ten. Screenwriter and humorist Donald Ogden Stewart (who had scripted *The Philadelphia Story* at MGM in 1940) was one of nine additional unfriendly witnesses called before HUAC whom the committee never got around to interrogating, yet Stewart continued in MGM's employ for several years thereafter, and was working on the *Huck Finn* script when he also was severed from the project along with Yip.

When the axe fell, Yip had already completed three songs for the picture with Burton Lane. (While reluctant to work with Yip on a Broadway show, Lane later related, he had agreed to collaborate with Yip on a picture, since he would have coequal status with Yip as an employee of Arthur Freed.) "Yip had an arrangement with the studio [for] another show he wanted to do," Lane told Deena Rosenberg:

He could start *Huckleberry Finn,* give it four or five weeks, go off, and come back and finish it. The studio okayed that. When he went to New York, that's when the blacklist struck him. He never came back to finish the score.

271

"I got a call from Metro's lawyer, Mr. [J. Robert] Rubin," Yip recalled,

> and he said, "Look here, what are your politics?" and all that nonsense,
> and I said I had never joined the Communist party. I had just been one of
> those vociferous guys who was fighting injustice and joining all the move-
> ments at the time.

In his letter to Rubin, Yip sought to make clear his abhorrence of
totalitarianism:

> I am a Franklin Delano Roosevelt Democrat, believing firmly in everything
> he stood for. As a firm, almost fanatical believer in democracy, as a proud
> American, and as the writer of the lyric of the song "God's Country," I am
> outraged by the suggestion that somehow I am connected with, believe in,
> or am sympathetic with Communist or totalitarian philosophy.

He enclosed in the letter copies of the lyrics to "God's Country" and to "Brother,
Can You Spare a Dime?" and, a short time later, forwarded the lyrics to his
wartime anthems "Chin Up! Cheerio! Carry On!" and "The Son of a Gun Who
Picks on Uncle Sam." (Ironically, these songs of wartime patriotism were the
closest Yip ever came to the celebratory popular front Americanism he normally
eschewed.)

Beyond the anti-Stalin lyrics to "God's Country," there is evidence in Yip's
personal correspondence during the blacklist years of his loathing of Stalinism.
"In a new society which is setting its sights on greater humanitarianism in
economics, education, racial discrimination, and the greater brotherhood of all
people," he wrote Dr. Samuel Rosen in January 1953 (three years before
Khrushchev's denunciations of Stalin's crimes shook the true believers), "whole-
sale murder for political deviations destroys the faith of all good-hearted people
whose hopes were with them." In later years, Yip condemned the Soviet experiment even more explicitly for besmirching the socialist ideal.

Never a Party member and comfortable with denouncing the Stalinist system,
Yip was blacklisted for his associations with a host of organizations in which
Communists played major roles. These included, for instance, the Hollywood
Independent Citizens' Committee of the Arts, Sciences, and Professions
(HICCASP), an outgrowth of the wartime Hollywood Democratic Committee
and an organization which sympathetic historians Larry Ceplair and Steven
Englund called "the leading Popular Front alliance of liberals and radicals in
postwar Hollywood." Yip served as HICCASP's secretary, at the same time that
such mainstream liberals as playwright Marc Connelly and dancer Gene Kelly
were among its other officers, and Ira Gershwin was a board member. A more

costly association was one that Yip had with the 1948 Henry Wallace presidential campaign: Yip authored a campaign song with composer Milton Ager, and scripted Paul Robeson's remarks when Robeson chaired the campaign's Madison Square Garden rally a few weeks before the general election.

An avowed democratic socialist whose positions on issues moved in and out of alignment with those of the Communist party by a calculus that he alone professed to understand, Yip could and did claim that his professional work ranged from the relatively apolitical (in Hollywood) to the radically democratic (on Broadway). But such claims, it turned out, were totally beside the point to his inquisitors. "They didn't want anything," he later said. "They just wanted me off the picture. They paid me my contract and I got off."

What the inquisitors also wanted were the naming of names and a public ceremony of recantation, behavior that Yip considered totally outrageous. Later, he penned:

FOR THE BIRDS

The Eagle—fierce omniverous vulture—
Noble emblem of our culture,
Has been reduced to just a smidgen;
Who cooked his goose? The cool stool pigeon.

Yip's remonstrations with MGM's Rubin were just the first in a series of arguments he conducted with the blacklisters, always insisting on his own patriotism, trying to meet a zealous madness with an inadequate rationality. "A vivid example of one who worked to get off the list without breaching his own sense of propriety," Victor Navasky writes in *Naming Names,* his account of the blacklist, "may be found in the case of songwriter E. Y. Harburg. His series of letters and lunches as much as any show the thin line one had to walk to be true to oneself and still get by." But Yip did not get by. In November of 1950, Lane wrote Yip that Arthur Freed had told him, "I don't think Yip and Don Stewart will ever be able to work in a studio again—because they've been accused of being Communists." (In time, Yip predicted in a letter responding to Lane, "even Dore Schary [the liberal production chief at MGM] would be swallowed up.") Yip lived to thwart Freed's prediction, but his exile from pictures was to last twelve years. And it wasn't only pictures where the blacklist took effect. "I was also blacklisted from TV and radio," Yip later said.

> There was a book called . . . *Red Channels.* Just look in the book and see what kind of publicity I got. Norman Corwin, who was at that time probably the high caliph of radio, who's probably the best man radio ever had, and the most poetic—he and I got probably three pages each, which

is prime notice in *Red Channels,* and of course nobody would dare touch us or even mention our names.

But I was not barred from the theater. I was able to do *Flahooley* (1951) and later on, *Jamaica* (1957) and *The Happiest Girl* (1961), [though] it was harder to get backers. . . . I had to be checked out on everything, but . . . my plays made money and anything that makes money, they overlook. . . . They fine-combed my stuff a little, but . . . theater's the one place that had the guts to stand up and say things.

Indeed, no one criticized Yip's first blacklist-era Broadway show, *Flahooley* (1951) for its failure to say things. For all his troubles in Hollywood, Yip's standing on Broadway and his ability to control his shows was never higher than on *Flahooley. Bloomer Girl,* after all, had been a resounding hit in the new mode, and that was a project he had originated, directed, and lyricized. *Finian's Rainbow,* an entirely idiosyncratic project he had conceived, written lyrics for, and coscripted, was an even greater hit. If Yip and Fred Saidy, his *Finian* colibrettist who worked with him again on *Flahooley,* had another unconventional message for another unconventional show, they had the track record that could nonetheless engender support. By 1951, only Rodgers and Hammerstein, Irving Berlin, and Cole Porter had more clout on musical Broadway. "*Flahooley,*" wrote Ethan Mordden, "is the most Harburgian of musicals," because by the time of *Flahooley,* no one could impede Yip's designs. Yip and Saidy did not merely coauthor *Flahooley*'s book, they also line produced and codirected the show, with Yip, of course, providing the lyrics as well to Sammy Fain's music.

A number of *Flahooley*'s reviewers noted that it was the first Broadway musical of the season not to have been adapted from other material, but this barely scratches the surface of *Flahooley*'s originality. "The only adaptations that would ever tempt us," Yip told a *New York Herald Tribune* interviewer shortly before *Flahooley*'s premiere, "would be things like Shaw's *Man and Superman* or Barrie's *A Kiss for Cinderella.* But in the end we prefer our own crazy little notions." Only, there was nothing little about the notions behind *Flahooley.*

Set inside a toy manufacturing conglomerate, *Flahooley* employed puppets (the Bil Baird marionettes, who performed several of the numbers), dolls ("Flahooley" was the name of the manufacturer's new doll), and a genie (played by not-yet-Professor Irwin Corey), all in a musical send-up of corporate culture and the zeitgeist of witch-hunts and loyalty oaths. More fundamentally, *Flahooley* is a cautionary parable on atomic energy, and underpinning the entire piece, its raison d'être, is a comic contemplation of capitalism's systemic tendency towards overproduction and underconsumption. For better and worse, *Flahooley* is still our nearest approximation to a musical comedy version of *Das Kapital.*

Flahooley began with Yip's desire, he later said, to do a musical "showing how the economy works . . . that we cannot afford to lose the profit system if it means giving people everything they want." The specific illustration of this point, though, did not come to him until he was visited one day by his friend, Temple University philosophy professor Barrows Dunham, who was returning with his young son from a visit to a puppet factory.

That proved to be the inspiration for a story that unfolded with wild Harburgian leaps. *Flahooley* is set in the toy empire of B. G. Bigelow, where a fanciful toy designer, suitably named Sylvester Cloud, has just devised the company's Christmas season doll. In *Flahooley*'s first draft, which was substantially altered before the show reached Broadway, the doll's distinctive feature is to cry, "Dirty Red!" inducing terror and "loyalty jitters" throughout the Bigelow empire. Walls covered with ears close in on Sylvester, and a pumpkin-headed puppet (a reference to the "pumpkin papers" adduced by Whittaker Chambers as evidence against Alger Hiss) testifies against Sylvester. Like the first draft of *Finian,* Yip and Fred's first draft of *Flahooley* seethes with an anger that was excised long before the show reached the boards.

Indeed, in *Flahooley*'s revised version, the distinctive feature of the Flahooley doll is its infectious laugh. Bigelow authorizes its production for Christmastime—and is visited by a State Department official shepherding three emissaries from Saudi Arabia. They come bearing an ancient magic lamp that has lost its magic; since they are no longer capable of summoning forth its genie, they implore Bigelow to use his Disney-like wizardry to bringing the genie back. But Bigelow has more immediate worries: his rival, A.E.I.O.U. and Y. and Z. Schwartz, produces its own version of the Flahooley doll at a cheaper price. Loyalty tests of Bigelow employees are undertaken but to no avail; the factory must close down. At this point, Sylvester, getting hold of the magic lamp, unwittingly rubs it and brings forth the genie—portentously named Abou ben Atom. Abou protests to Sylvester that he does indeed exist: "Grow up, lad grow up!" Abou argues, "What is science, after all, but fairyland with an Oxford accent?" He then sets about his own magical chain reaction: he will produce for Bigelow all the Flahooleys the world will ever need, delighting all the world's children, free of charge. For a time, Bigelow believes he is saved, but as the dolls flood the world, he is alarmed. "Tell him to stop producing!" he shouts. "You're ruining my business!" "By building it up?" Abou asks. "A paradox—a most contradictory paradox. Is this logic peculiar to your century, old man? . . . I've come into a world of pure fantasy," Abou concludes,

> Where people magically beget
> All that on which their hearts are set,
> Then having got of that a lot,
> They cannot get what they've begot.
> What?

as projected images of Flahooley dolls cascade down on the audience at the conclusion of the first act.

Act 2 begins as the citizens of Capsulanti, Indiana, home to B. G. Bigelow, Inc., go on a rampage of destruction against the dolls, trying to track down the genie (who is hiding, it turns out, in the head of the Statue of Liberty). For a time, Sylvester becomes the object of their animus. "There's something cockeyed about all this," he says, "turning neighbors into snoopers—and spinsters into troopers." Abou is eventually apprehended by federal forces—CIA, FBI, HUAC (Arabia wants him back, too)—and suffers a nervous breakdown at the spectacle of mangled Flahooleys. In his hospital room, he complains to Flahooley herself (animated in this scene only) about humanity's inhumanity:

> *Abou.* If they use me badly, I will crack up their humpty-dumpty world—and turn them into dusty atoms twinkling in space.
>
> *Flahooley.* You wouldn't do that, would you?
>
> *Abou.* Can't help myself! I'm powerless before my own power!

Abou threatens to explode then and there—until Flahooley's tears cause him to reassess the situation.

> *Abou.* They're frightened! They don't hate us all. They're just not ready for us. I'm a premature genie—born ahead of my time. We must rectify the schedule. In the immortal words of Little Abner—let us scram.

In sum, this wasn't your usual Broadway musical. Both in its ambitions and daring, *Flahooley* was a breathtaking project. *Flahooley* came to the musical stage at a time when the nonmusical stage had yet to tackle the problem of atomic power (indeed, when the only popular work of any kind suggesting its terrors was John Hersey's *Hiroshima*). By the same token, no other work of fiction springs to mind that has as its central theme capitalism's limitations on abundance. As to its more immediate themes, *Flahooley* followed by only five months Arthur Miller's adaptation of Ibsen's *Enemy of the People* and preceded by three years *The Crucible*, Miller's more sustained assault on McCarthyism. But *Flahooley* was not intended for the more rarified realm of the dramatic stage, or the college circuit or the bohemia of Greenwich Village (off Broadway, in fact, did not yet exist). With *Flahooley,* the political avant-garde arrived nightly on the Broadway of Rodgers and Hammerstein and Irving Berlin.

The problem was Yip's leeway to infuse his shows with his politics had increased, but his politics had grown steadily more distant from the nation's. *Bloomer Girl* had been a liberal show produced at the apex of radical-liberal coalition. *Finian* had been a socialist show produced at the onset of the cold war. *Flahooley* was a Marxist show produced at the height of McCarthyism. "It came at a very bad time," Yip later noted. "I had already gotten in the doghouse with *Finian* and they thought this was a dangerous anticapitalist show, and anything that's anticapitalist is unpatriotic. I don't know what economics has to do with patriotism, but somehow these two funny ideas have been cemented in people's minds."

But *Flahooley*'s problem was not simply the daring and the scope of its political concerns: it was also the inadequacy of the plot that Yip and Fred had erected to express them. For dramaturgically, *Flahooley* wasn't much different from *Annie, Get Your Gun*—if not *Hellzapoppin'.* The boy-girl plot between Sylvester and his more practical girl friend, Sandy, plays out in thoroughly conventional fashion. B. G. Bigelow is the stock figure of a befuddled business-man, and much of the action concerns his seduction by an exotic Arabian dancer. The ending of the show created confusion during tryouts, on Broadway, and in all of Yip's subsequent revisions.

It was, however, a wildly eclectic evening in the theater: ranging from singing and dancing marionettes to the wordless vocal acrobatics of soprano-contralto Yma Sumac (she had a four-octave range), who played the Arabian dancer, to the only first act curtain number in American musical theater that deals with a crisis of overproduction. It was a bit much—*Finian* globalized and on fast-forward. "In the course of an evening," Brooks Atkinson noted in his review in the *Times,* "more plot crosses the stage than Macy's Thanksgiving Day Parade." Even in Ethan Mordden's defense of the show, written thirty years later, *Flahooley* comes in a little off the mark at which Yip and Fred had aimed. "His social prescriptions were so generalized and his satire so imaginative," Mordden wrote, "that he came over more as an absurdist than a social commentator." Disassembled, much of *Flahooley* is enchanting. Reassembled, it is one of the boldest, most fascinating and idiosyncratic failures of the American musical theater.

While Yip was working with Burton Lane on *Huck Finn,* he tried to interest Lane in collaborating on *Flahooley,* but Lane would have none of it. Yip's relegation of Lane to secondary rank on *Finian* still rankled. Moreover, col-laborating with Harburg the librettist appealed to Lane far less than with Harburg the lyricist. The lyricist, Lane said, was a supremely self-assured master of his craft, who would invariably change a lyric if the composer thought it needed alteration. Not so Harburg the librettist. Of the Harburg-Saidy team, Lane was to say, "Fred was always in the background. He would be insecure, too, but not as insecure [as Yip]. Yip was the one who would be aggressively antagonistic. Couldn't take any criticism at all [of the book]."

From Lane, Yip went to Arlen, but if *Finian* had proved too political to entice Harold, *Flahooley* was out of the question. The bridges to Vernon Duke had long since been burned. Yip had to find a new collaborator. He found an old one, Sammy Fain.

Fain was a veteran songwriter (like Arlen, the son of a cantor) who had known Yip virtually since the outset of Yip's career. He had been writing regularly in Hollywood since the early thirties, teamed with such lyricists as Irving Kahal and Ralph Freed (Arthur's brother). His most enduring hit was "I'll Be Seeing You." In recent years, he had contributed to a string of un-distinguished Broadway musicals as well: *Toplitzky of Notre Dame* (1946), *Alive and Kicking* (1950), and *Michael Todd's Peep Show '51.* There was no question that Fain could turn out a functional score for *Flahooley,* but Yip had long been accustomed to more than the merely functional. "I think I've been very lucky to work with men who were really original craftsmen, men like Arlen," he told Max Wilk. "Sammy Fain was, I would say, more on the common denominator, but he had a great sense of lovely melody which also seems to be part of me, too."

Unfortunately, *Flahooley's* music, save in a few places, is relatively routine, lacking the bite required for Yip's ideas. There was nothing routine, though, in *Flahooley's* first number, which was performed by the Bil Baird Marionettes, and addressed a mindless conformity that transcended the immediate context of the plot.

You Too Can Be a Puppet
(excerpt)

Tiddlee aie . . . Tiddlee aye
Tiddlee all your trouble away
You too can be a puppet
You too can be a puppet
Tiddlee swell . . . Tiddlee grand
Science has just discovered a gland
And now you too you too can be a puppet . . . A puppet . . .

You too can be a puppet
Unspoiled and uncorrupted
Far from Tammany and Standard Oil
And are you loy'l? Are you loy'l? . . .

You too can find your way to paradise
You too can find your way to paradise
Why be bothered with psychiatry?
Buy a tree and carve yourself a guy like me . . .

You too, you too can be a puppet
Be a puppet, be a puppet, be a puppet
Be a puppet
Be a puppet
Tiddlee aye, tiddlee dee, you can be just
As happy as we
Be a puppet not an also ran
Come out of the woodwork brother
And join the brotherwood of man
The brotherwood of man . . .

Sammy Fain, *right,* was the composer of such hits as "I'll Be Seeing You" before he and Yip became the songwriting team for *Flahooley* (1951), after Harold Arlen and Burton Lane turned down the option to work on the show. Yip and Fred Saidy also co-produced, co-directed, and co-authored this original musical fantasy. (Courtesy American Society of Composers, Authors, and Publishers [ASCAP].)

Faced with a genie who threatens to overproduce them into oblivion, the toymakers ponder their fate in a world of plenty.

> We're swamped, we're dead
> With more damn Flahooleys
> Than the kiddies can consume
> He may start on pianos and bananas and perfume
> He may flood the market for eternity
> And then how you gonna make an honest buck
> When things are free?

Flahooley's love song is the ballad Sandy sings to Sylvester, "Here's to Your Illusions" (an ultra-Harburgian title).

HERE'S TO YOUR ILLUSIONS
(excerpt)

Here's to all your dreams
Here's to your illusions
May they always lead you into my arms
Here's to all your hopes
And those sweet confusions
That charm you into seeing my charms

Here's to that trick of romance
That beguiles with a smile or a glance
And as long as you're in a trance
I stand a chance with you

So here's to love is blind
Here's to your illusions
Stay enchanted please
Put my heart at ease
For all the years to come.

"Here's to Your Illusions" is *Flahooley*'s "Old Devil Moon," the ballad of enchantment and blindness, but it lacks the disturbing intensity and shifts of mood that characterize Lane's effort. Musically, "Here's to Your Illusions" is an exceptionally graceful fox-trot, with none of the complexities that spurred Yip to his ambivalent tag in the earlier number. In this lyric, love is a trance, blindness, confusion, a trick, and yet Yip's characteristic distancing from romance is undercut here by the placidity of the music. Moreover, *Finian* counterposed idealism to monogamous settling down; "Here's to Your Illusions," in keeping with the unconflicted music, unites both impulses in more conventional fashion. But then, the conflict in *Flahooley* is located in historic forces extrinsic to the boy-girl relationship.

Sylvester's unveiling of his laughing doll was the occasion for the show's title song: a lively production number in which Yip took a number of swipes at authoritarianism and censorship in general, at the blacklisting of his own satiric talent in particular, and at the political difficulties he doubtless anticipated *Flahooley* itself would encounter. Again, excerpts:

Flahooley (1951) was the only Broadway musical ever to satirize the dire consequences of overproduction in a capitalist economy. Its major love ballad, aptly titled for both love and the economic system, "Here's to Your Illusions," was sung beautifully by Barbara Cook in her first Broadway star role. (Collection of Harburg Estate.)

FLAHOOLEY
(excerpt)

Get in the spirit of Flahooley
That laughing doll they call Flahooley
Flahooley's truly Yankee Dooley
Because it loves to laugh and let laugh . . .

Long as we can chuckle
Our knees will never buckle
We'll be free
As long as we
Can laugh with Flahooley . . .

Show me a land where a feller can't laugh
And I'll sell you that land for a buck and a half
Show me that land where they jail your wit
And I'll show you a land where no songs git writ

> Show me a land where they gag every gag
> And they choke every joke with chains
> And I'll show you a land without Donald Ducks
> And a land without Mark Twains . . .

Act 1 ends with a production number depicting a crisis of overproduction. The scene commences with exultant Bigelow employees reveling in the success of the Flahooley doll. Their images of paradise are every bit as materialistic as those of *Finian*'s sharecroppers. The number, "Jump Chillun Jump" concludes:

> Jump for that rainbow
> That silver lining
> That bluebird winging
> That sun a'shining
>
> That glory roadster
> Those yellow sweaters
> Those flashy neckties
> Those patent leathers
>
> We're on the cresta
> Of a fiesta
> Thanks to Sylvesta
> So jump little market, jump little dollar,
> Jump little taxes, jump little chillun
>
> Jump, jump, jump, jump, jump, jump little chillun, jump!

The music to the second stanza sounds a good deal like the chorus of "This Land Is Your Land," as the imagery of happiness turns from rainbows and bluebirds to sweaters and patent leathers (turns, in fact, on the glorious corruption, "glory road-ster"). As the scene progresses, though, Abou the genie won't stop the flood of Flahooleys until they glut the market and the stage. As Act 1 ends, Flahooleys shower over the audience as the chorus, to the same tune as "Jump Chillun Jump," sings:

> No more Flahooley
> No more Flahooley
> Please let's get rid of
> The whole snafu-ly
>
> One thing is sutton
> The market's gluttin'
> The price you're cuttin'
> Way down to nuttin'

> We're on the cresta
> Of a disesta
> A real catestra-
> phy
>
> Stop the Flahooley
> Stop the Flahooley
> Stop the Flahooley
> Stop the Flahooley
> Stop, stop, stop, stop, stop, stop
> Little genie
> Stop!

Act 2 begins with the citizens of Capsulanti witch-hunting Flahooleys, the genie, and Sylvester, cheering themselves on with the "Spirit of Capsulanti," to Fain's classic college fight song music:

> Break it up—cry the trumpets
> Break it up—say the drums
> Cut 'em down—shout the voices
> Sweep 'em out with the crumbs
> Send them back where they came from for an autopsy
> That's the spirit of Capsulanti!

Hospitalized with a nervous breakdown brought on by the witch-hunts and the spirit of Capsulanti, Abou is restored to health by a visit from a walking, talking, singing, dancing Flahooley. The genie's act 2 song to Flahooley is the show's equivalent to the leprechaun's act 2 song in *Finian*, "When I'm Not Near the Girl I Love." "The Springtime Cometh" is Yip's display of suffixes amok in *Flahooley*, his verbal dexterity reenlisted in the cause of sexual activity and entrusted, as usual, to his Puckish avatar:

> THE SPRINGTIME COMETH
>
> The Springtime cometh
> Humming-bird hummeth
> Little brook rusheth
> Merry maiden blusheth
> Ice man goeth
> For thy beauty bloweth
> Spring to me

The bright world shineth
Tender arm twineth
Starry eye gloweth
For they knoweth that without thee
Spring could never be

Daffodil . . . he can't stand still
Cap he flingeth
Cane he swingeth
Song he singeth
Ding dong day . . . Which is to say

The Springtime cometh
Humming-bird hummeth
Sugar plum plummeth
Heart, it humpty-dummeth
And to summeth up
The Springtime cometh for the love of thee.

Lad and lass
In tall green grass
Gaily skippeth
Nylon rippeth
Zipper zippeth
Ding dong day . . . which is to say

The Springtime cometh
Humming-bird hummeth
Geranee-yummeth
Chrysanthe-mummeth
Bubble gum gummeth
And the Springtime cometh for the love of thee.

Characteristically, Yip escalates the rhymes into steadily wilder neologisms, culminating in "geranee-ummeth" and "chrysanthe-mummeth." The number led into a comic dance and still more verses. Among them:

The Springtime cometh
Politics hummeth
They raise big rumpus
Candidates all stumpeth
Some sound dumbeth
And the Springtime cometh for the love of thee.

The Springtime cometh
Now we must runneth
Our task is done-eth
Our song is sung-eth
We're out of um-eths
And the Springtime cometh, that is plain to see.

Flahooley concludes at Christmastime, with Flahooleys for sale in an orderly fashion, and Abou returned to assure Sandy and Sylvester's marriage. The scene provides the setting for a song that is largely extrinsic to the action of the play, but that was at the time the most controversial. To Fain's Christmas carol/madrigal music, Yip set a choral ode to Christmas commercialism:

SING THE MERRY
(excerpt)

Sing the merry Christmas spirit
Sing the joys of brotherhood
In the ivy-covered walls of
Saks Fifth Ave. and Bergdorf Good.

Sing the Christmas holly climbing
Lord and Taylor's window pane
Bells rhyming, ding dong chiming
Sing the joys of cellophane
Tra-la-la-la-la—la-la-la
Tra-la-la-la-la-la-la-la-la

Sing the weary Christmas shopper
Sing the things for "her" and "him"
Sing the silver onion chopper
Sing the checkbook growing slim

Ring bells ring
From radio and mike
Sing the joy of Haig and Haig
And Lucky Strike . . .

Ring out the old, ring, Maestro, please
Ring in the new from Tiffany's
Ring in the bells that gaily peal
Dividends from Bethlehem and U.S. Steel . . .

Sing the pen and sing the pencil
Sing aluminum utensil
Sing the nylon—all together:
Sing the imitation leather . . .

Merry merry ding dong derry
Merry merry ding dong day/Ring!*
Ding dong day/Ring!*
Ding dong day/Ring!*

Sing the cashbox
Sing inflation
Sing the gadget overpriced
And for Christ's sake
May this nation
Soon give Christmas back to Christ

Sing ye merry, rest ye merry, spend ye merry,
Think ye merry men/Ring!*

*The "Ring!" is the sound of a cash register ringing up a sale.

This is far from brutally strong stuff—indeed, one could envision a lyric like this running, say, in *Mad* magazine at some point later in the fifties. But by the standards of 1951, a year of unsurpassed timidity, this was hackle-raising material. During the Philadelphia tryout, where the show was rapturously received, the decision was made to drop the song's last stanza ("Sing the cashbox," etc.) and when Capitol Records released the original cast album, the entire song was excised. The sticking point may have been Yip's linking of real stores and real companies with the suggestion of sacrilege and overpricing (hard to say which was thought the more inflammatory). "Sing the Merry" went unrecorded until Ben Bagley included it on an album of Yip's songs in 1980.

Flahooley opened in New Haven on April 9, 1951, to rave reviews and encountered similar success at its second stop in Philadelphia. Besides Yma Sumac, Irwin Corey, and the Bil Baird Marionettes, the cast also featured Ernest Truex as "toycoon" B. G. Bigelow and Barbara Cook in her Broadway debut as Sandy. The Philadelphia reviews stressed its suitability as family fare; it had, wrote one critic, "something of *Babes in Toyland* in its make up, a touch of *The Wizard of Oz*, a suggestion of *Finian's Rainbow.*" "*Flahooley,*" wrote another, "should become a stage institution to be revived again and again, to take the children to see . . . a beautiful fantasy."

Flahooley came to Broadway on May 14 to decidedly more mixed reviews. The spectacle, puppets, and overall level of production enchanted the critics

("Easily the most original musical of the season," wrote John Chapman in the *Daily News*). The score got mixed notices, generally positive for the lyrics, less so for the music. "Although Mr. Fain's music is not exactly inspired," wrote Brooks Atkinson, "it serves the purpose amiably enough." The politics got panned. George Jean Nathan praised *Flahooley's* originality, excoriated the score ("It is this over-all relative novelty that atones in my case for the inevitable mediocre tunes") and lamented, "It is a dreadful thought, however, that now that our social significance playwrights like Clifford Odets, Lillian Hellman and the like have abandoned social significance, it may be taken over by our music show writers." Bottom was reached in Robert Coleman's review with the "overheard quote":

> One first-nighter was overheard to say: "With the United States at war [in Korea], this is hardly the time to condemn a production system that has given us an amazingly high standard of living and, at the same time, managed to arm us and our allies." With employment at record peak, with this country facing its greatest crisis, we echo those sentiments.

More insightfully, a number of critics rightly noted the show's inability to haul all the thematic freight Yip and Fred had loaded upon it. Wrote Louis Sheaffer:

> E. Y. Harburg and Fred Saidy, who shun the routine and conventional as if it were the plague, have given another twirl to their free-wheeling imaginations and concocted, in "Flahooley," a new musical of striking originality and charm, one that goes farther than even their "Finian's Rainbow" in daring to be different.

> [But] Messrs. Harburg and Saidy have periodically yanked their story about so that they could have the opportunity to make some satiric points on the contemporary scene. Where the satire in "Finian's Rainbow" gave the impression of flowing spontaneously from the action, walked hand-in-hand with the other story elements, it appears sometimes in the new one to be interjected from the outside. The story doesn't get complete freedom to tell itself.

The columnists also took out after *Flahooley.* Dorothy Kilgallen and Ed Sullivan attacked its politics. *Flahooley* ran for forty-eight performances and closed at a loss. In her memoirs, coproducer Cheryl Crawford noted that the show was named after a laughing doll, and accurately assessed the show's problem: "*This* doll [i.e., Crawford] neither cried nor laughed, just was deeply disappointed that the writers had been unable to mix properly their delightful fancy with their serious intent."

Yip had not had a Broadway show go belly up on him since 1932, and he did not give up easily on *Flahooley.* It had a brief second life in San Francisco, with a few new songs with music from Burton Lane, under the name *Jollyanna;* and in 1952 the Los Angeles Civic Light Opera produced yet another version, also entitled *Jollyanna,* starring Bobby Clark and Mitzi Gaynor. But none of the revisions proved any more successful than the original, and for the same reasons.

Blacklist Years

For Yip, the blacklist did not take the form of unbroken exile. More frustratingly, he was invited on to a succession of projects, only eventually to be let go by producers who could not win his clearance. 1951 found Yip writing Paramount Board Chairman Y. Frank Freeman to assure him he had never been a Party member. (Burton Lane was trying to convince Freeman to film *Finian's Rainbow,* but Freeman would have none of it: Yip, he told Lane, was a "communist" and that was that.) Later that year, Yip began a picture at MGM with Arlen, but he was taken off the project after completing just one song. Yip did what he could to stay on the picture, assuring Freed that he had never supported the overthrow of the American government by force or violence. He would not recant or name names; he would play his inquisitors' game only to the extent of labeling his own work as valuable to the national security. Needless to say, that failed to suffice.

"After I was blacklisted," Yip later told one interviewer,

> a picture came up—this was about two or three years later—*Hans Christian Andersen,* and Goldwyn wanted me, and he sent his wife, Frances, to New York. She asked me to her hotel and I went to see her. She wanted me to do the lyrics for the picture and I said, "Fine." We had almost signed the contract and before a few weeks were up, bango, suddenly the verbal contract was dissolved and I didn't get the picture. She made it clear to me that they'd have trouble clearing me. I got it from the agent, Louie Shurr, that Goldwyn wanted me very badly, but he didn't want to have any trouble with the powers and the critics.

> Then the next thing that happened, I was in Martha's Vineyard, my summer home, and I got an emergency call. They wanted Harold Arlen and myself to do the Judy Garland picture, *A Star Is Born,* and Judy wanted us. [She] always has some feeling about how we're her good luck stars. Of course I was willing. And this time everything was set; Harold went on ahead of me and they talked about it, and I said, well I'm going to pack up and go, and I came back to New York and everything was set,

airplane and everything, and suddenly I got a telegram . . . from [Garland's husband, producer] Sid Luft: "Sorry, we can't clear you now. Judy heartbroken. We're certainly going to fight to get you cleared," and so on. But finally Harold had to get Ira Gershwin to do the thing for me. That kind of thing kept happening all the way through the fifties. This was about five or six years later, and so I lost one picture after another. In fact, I never got back to Hollywood for ten years.

It was one ignominious thing after another. It was not only frightening, but it just took all your dignity away and you realized what it is to live in a police state and understand the fear that people in such countries have of not knowing what's going to happen next. You keep thinking it's going to be over and then it's not.

It keeps hitting you. Some of the fellows, my friends, did commit suicide. A few did die. This was taking a toll on my friends, some of whom I was supporting at the time, like Henry Myers, who had done all these beautiful shows and couldn't make a living. He had just sold a pilot to one of the networks for $1,000 a week and the contract was abrogated and he went from $1,000 a week to penniless—couldn't work anywhere and you had to support him and you had to support ten others. And all around there was misery and heartbreak.

People borrowed from each other. Dalton Trumbo borrowed a lot of money [at the time of his imprisonment for contempt of HUAC]. If you read his book, I gave him some money and others gave him money, which he returned later on. I personally had royalties from shows and I had songs out that were making money and I had made a lot of money in Hollywood. I had made some investments [with the aid of his old friend, Harry Lifton]. I was a lucky guy.

In 1955 work was abruptly halted on production of John Hubley's animated feature-length version of *Finian's Rainbow* which was to feature the voices of Louis Armstrong, Ella Fitzgerald, Ella Logan, and Frank Sinatra, among others; it was killed, according to John Canemaker, by Roy Brewer, head of the International Alliance of Theatrical Stage Employees union (IATSE), after Hubley refused to appear and name names before the McCarthyite Hollywood Committee. After Hubley's refusal, Chemical Bank, the film's principal investor, withdrew all financial support.

In 1956, Arthur Freed had another project he wanted Yip and Harold to score. By then, the blacklist was five years old, and being kept alive chiefly by the tenacity of idiots, as Yip was to discover. "It was never only one thing," Yip later said.

Arthur Freed had a whole script written on Nellie Bly, the first woman journalist, who went around the world. They wanted Harold Arlen and myself to do the picture. Of course, Arthur Freed knew that would be a subject that interested me. And they sent for me, paid my fare, and we had started work on it. . . .

And Roy Brewer, who was head of the International Alliance of Theatrical Stage Employees unions and also a huge muckamuck in the legion of honor in the American Legion . . . now you notice how they worked it both ways . . . the head of the union, and the head of the legion, you see. So, with that kind of power, he held a sceptre and a club over the studios; they couldn't move. Now here was a man who was always in the ignominious position of having to fight for a two dollar raise for a man, you know, calling out strikes, being beaten the hell out of by the studio, and now he becomes head of all the studios. What a joyous, dramatic turn of events this was! The man who had to crawl, now was getting Louis B. Mayer and Jack Warner to crawl to him and say, "Please, can we use so-and-so, can we use Trumbo to write two scenes or a paragraph? Can we use Yip Harburg for just one lyric, please?" What a joyous position he had now. He was taking it all out on the studios. So when he found out I was on the picture *Nellie Bly*, he said, "Nothing doing. This picture will be boycotted." Arthur Freed got me in the office to apologize. "We can't help it, we're in a terrible spot. Will you please go see Roy Brewer and talk to him? We talked to him and he said you can clear things up if you just go over there."

So I went to see Roy Brewer one day. I wish I had a tape of that meeting. Number one, he called in a fellow by the name of, I think, Cardigan. Cardigan was an ex-Communist. He came in with a file of papers on me that was thicker than all my works. He had everything. I said, "What did I do in pictures that was subversive? Can you tell me?"

"We know all the tricks," he says.

"First of all," I said, "you say that I have ever been a Communist?"

He looked at me and he finally said, "Well, we must say this. We don't have anybody who has ever directly mentioned your name, who said you were in a cell or said you were a Communist."

I said, "All right. Number one, I am not a Communist. Now what the hell do you want of me?"

He said, "But you did things."

I said, "Like what?"

"Well, did you write a song called 'Happiness Is a Thing Called Joe'?"

I said, "Yes, for *Cabin in the Sky*. A big hit."

He said, "Which Joe were you talking about? Was it Joe Stalin?" Now, this is what I had to contend with. Either you bust out laughing or you throw the desk at him. I just broke into laughter. This got them mad.

"You gave money to China."—"Yes, I gave money to China."—"Did you give money to the Spanish Loyalists?"—"Yes, I gave money to the Spanish Loyalists."—"Why did you give money to the Spanish Loyalists?"—"They were fighting for my freedom. Did you want Nazi Germany to win?" Silly things like that. Finally they couldn't get anything on me, really, except in these idiotic things where I had given my money to. . . . "Are you a member of the Hollywood Democratic Committee?"—"Not only am I a member, I helped start it."

I said, "All right, why don't you want me to write *Nellie Bly*? I can get you a great score out of that; maybe we'll have some hit songs and it'll make you happy too. And then you wouldn't have to sit around here with all these grim faces. I could write some funny songs for you. You guys are very grim now." Well, this guy got madder and madder.

I said, "Now what do you want me to do?" He said, "Do you know the newspaper that the American Legion gets out?" They had a magazine, *The Legionnaire*. He said, "Well, three months ago," they opened up an issue, "here's an article by a good friend of yours, Edward G. Robinson." I took a look at the headline—"I Was a Dupe for the Communists." "He was in your position. He was not a member of the Communist party, but he was a dupe for it. You just write us one article along similar lines." I said, "No. I will not write one article. However, it's got nothing to do with politics. I've read your *Legionnaire* at times, and I think it's a fourth-rate magazine. And I will not write for anything that isn't a first-rate magazine. This is purely a literary idiosyncracy of mine." I refused to write the article and the show was called off. I never got to see *Nellie Bly*.

Throughout the blacklist decade, Yip reverted to light verse to jibe at the pervasive conformity, national security mania, and spiritual barrenness of the fifties.

ORGANIZATION MAN

The flannel suit,
The Dacron smile,
The drip-dry zest that sweeps him.
You can always tell
A man these days
By the Company that keeps him.

He took aim as well at one of the pioneer televangelists:

A SAINT . . . HE AIN'T

Good St. Paul and Vincent Peale
Are men of wholly different steel,
Yet both of holy calling.
St. Paul is most appealing
And Peale is most appalling.

Jamaica

As early as 1953, Yip had conceived a stage musical that would attack the emerging postwar American culture—money driven, hyperkinetic, conformist, synthetic, atomic—by contrasting it with a more natural, spiritual, bucolic civilization. The question was, where to situate (or perhaps, create from whole cloth) that countercivilization? In *Finian,* Missitucky sharecroppers eventually succumbed to the commercial culture. The new project, Yip felt, demanded an offshore setting. For a time, he referred to it as "the Haitian musical;" then he and Saidy relocated it to the fictitious Caribbean venue, "Pigeon Island," where they set the story of a "simple island boy whose girl longed for the complexities of an urban 'civilization.'" By 1956, *Pigeon Island* had acquired a star, the new singing sensation Harry Belafonte; a producer, David Merrick; a musical idiom, calypso; and a composer who was as fluent in that idiom as anyone could wish—Harold Arlen. Arlen's last show, the 1954 *House of Flowers,* had also been set in the Caribbean.

It had also acquired a first-rate book from Harburg and Saidy. It was no less political than *Finian* or *Flahooley,* mounting a rearguard action against colonialism and a frontal assault on commercial culture. Above all, it is the one musical of the brinkmanship fifties set in the shadow of the nuclear cloud that loomed over that decade. What distinguishes *Pigeon Island* from *Flahooley* is that *Pigeon Island*'s action fully sustains Yip and Fred's thematic aspirations. It marks a departure from their earlier work, too, in that the book is devoid of fantasy: there are no genies or leprechauns or spirits of any kind in *Pigeon Island,* and its magic is unfrocked early on.

The story centers around the courtship between Koli, the island's leading fisherman, and his girlfriend Savannah, who will not marry him until he agrees to take her to New York and demonstrate suitably careerist aspirations. The conflict between the natural and the civilized worlds also suffuses the island's two governments: that of the ineffectual British colonial administrator and that of Savannah's grandma, who guides the islanders by her presumably magical readings of the clouds. Early on, though, she tells her grandson: "I don't know nothin' about magic . . . . I'se only tryin' to help dem see wid dere eyes what dey feel in dere hearts."

The arrival of Joe Nashua from Harlem presents Koli with a rival for Savannah's affections and threatens to undermine Grandma's authority and Pigeon Island's precious insularity. Joe buys off the island's fishermen (all but Koli) for the more dangerous but highly paid activity of pearl diving. It marks the end of Eden: the island succumbs to commercialism, fights break out, and at the act 1 curtain, a huge mushroom-shaped cloud suddenly looms over the stage. In act 2, with an apparent nuclear holocaust having engulfed all the planet outside the island (their radio is down), Pigeon Island is reduced to the state of nature. Koli's fish become more precious than pearls, Savannah opts for Koli over Joe—at which point Grandma fixes the radio (the war was merely a storm, it turns out) and relinquishes her power to the governor (whom she was keeping doped up until she could straighten things out).

Pigeon Island was the most tightly and seamlessly integrated book on which Yip was ever to work. Yip and Harold's songs never intrude on the plot, but do double duty: advancing the story, and stepping back to comment upon it. "Push de Button" looks at the mechanization of civilization; "Hooray for de Yankee Dollar" at the effects of American tourism and investment; "Napoleon" at the transience of human glory; "Monkey in the Mango Tree" at the downward spiral of evolution toward civilization; "Incompatibility" at the roadblocks to relationships; "Ain' It de Truth?" at the need to seize the day. "Leave de Atom Alone" is self-explanatory.

Pigeon Island was rich in commentary songs and satirical list songs—perhaps overrich. "You can't have a show full of ballads," Arlen told his biographer, Edward Jablonski, in discussing the project, but in fact, *Pigeon Island*'s problem is the absence of first-rate ballads. Too many of the songs are witty commentary; the score lacks variety. The blues are not part of the Caribbean musical idiom, but for Arlen to do a score for a largely black company (especially after Belafonte had to drop out and the show was restructured as a vehicle for Lena Horne) and not include a blues ballad suggests that part of *Pigeon Island*'s potential was never realized. For all its showcasing of Yip's wit and ideas, the

Lena Horne's first starring role on Broadway was *Jamaica* (1957); it also starred Ricardo Montalban. The show's score satirized American automated urban life, tourism, and the transience of powerful figures. (Billy Rose Theatre Collection, New York Public Library.)

music is second-drawer Arlen. He himself told Jablonski that it fell short of his mark and lacked the musical unity of *Bloomer Girl, St. Louis Woman,* and *House of Flowers.* Arlen was reluctant to do another calypso musical. It is a score that Alex Wilder, Arlen's most strident defender, declines to discuss in his essay on Arlen in *American Popular Song, 1900–1950.*

 Pigeon Island's other problem was even more basic: it ceased to be *Pigeon Island.* In mid-1956, Belafonte underwent surgery on his vocal chords; his voice would not be fully restored for an entire year thereafter. Merrick thereupon engaged Lena Horne for the role of Savannah, and in place of a tightly integrated book show, *Pigeon Island* became *Jamaica,* a largely plotless evening of theater that was a triumphal revue for Lena Horne. Songs written for other characters were rewritten and reassigned. What was potentially a notable musical play became instead an evening of terrific entertainment. But *Jamaica*'s songs were written as the score for the tightly plotted *Pigeon Island,* and it is in that context that we shall look at several of them.

Jamaica begins with Koli's attempts to court Savannah, which she rebuffs in a song that presents her vision of a gloriously mechanized Manhattan. The lyric, like all the lyrics in *Jamaica,* is set in a pidgen English, and some, though not all, of the images are those that would occur to Savannah. As is the case with most of *Jamaica*'s commentary songs, no further attempt is made to mediate or refract Yip's sensibility through that of the character. Like the Japanese in *The Mikado,* the islanders of Jamaica provide an exotic voice through which the concerns and idiosyncracies of their creator come through all the louder and clearer.

PUSH DE BUTTON
(excerpt)

Verse.   There's a little island on de Hudson
              Mythical, magic and fair
              Shining like a diamon' on de Hudson
              Far away from worriment and care
              What an isle
              What an isle
              All the natives relax there in style
              What a life
              What a life
              All de money controlled by de wife

              On this little island on de Hudson
              Ev'ryone big millionaire
              With his own cooperative castle
              Rising in de air conditioned air
              Life is easy
              Livin's lazy
              On this isle where crazy dreams come true
              All you do is

Chorus.   Push de button
              Up de elevator
              Push de button
              Out de orange juice
              Push de button
              From refrigerator
              Come banana short cake and
              Frozen goose

Push de button
Wipe de window wiper
Push de button
Rinse de baby diaper
Push de button
Wanna fry de fish
Push de button
Wash de dish
Push de button, pooosh
De button

What an isle
What an isle
Where de automat feed ev'ry chile
Where de brave
And de free
Live and love electronically

Push de button
Don't be small potatah
Be a tycoon
Big manipulatah
Pooosh
Apply de little finger and
Pooosh
De button . . .

Push de button
Don't be antiquated
Get de baby
All prefabricated
Pooosh,
Apply de little finger and
Pooosh
De button!

In "Cocoanut Sweet," Koli's love song to Savannah, Yip's lyric relies scrupulously on natural imagery. As "Cocoanut Sweet" makes clear, the tension between enchantment and freedom, which has characteristically afflicted romantic relations in Harburg librettos, is absent from *Jamaica*. Here, the conflict is between the natural and social worlds, and the ballad, like *Bloomer Girl*'s "Right as the Rain," links the protagonists' romance to the natural order.

COCOANUT SWEET

Cocoanut sweet
Honey-dew new
Jasmine an' cherry an' juniper berry
That's you

Cocoanut sweet
Buttercup true
Face that I see in the blue Caribbean,
That's you

Catch me the smile you smile
And I'll make this big world my tiny island
Shining with spice and sugar plum
Cage me the laugh you laugh
And I will make this tiny, shiny island
My little slice of kingdom come

The wind may blow
The hurricane whip up the sky
The vine go bare
The leaf go dry

But when you smile for me
Spring tumble out of the tree
The peach is ripe, the lime is green
The air is touched with tangerine

And cocoanut sweet
Honey-dew new
Ev'rything dear that wants to cheer
The nearness of you
How it all come true
Wherever we meet
The magic of cherry and berry
And cocoanut sweet . . .

"Cocoanut Sweet"'s release ("The wind may blow / The hurricane whip up the sky," etc.) suggests both musically and lyrically, if only for a moment, Arlen's "Stormy Weather" (particularly since the number was reassigned by the director from Koli's character to Savannah's to enable Lena Horne to sing it). It points up what is missing from *Jamaica*'s score: a serious song in the blues idiom.

In contrast to the precision of Yip's satirical lyrics, the rhyme scheme of "Little Biscuit" is playful. As in "Cocoanut Sweet," the images are drawn from nature, and the song has become a small jazz classic.

> LITTLE BISCUIT
> (excerpt)
>
> Little biscuit, I'm your oven
> Little apple I'm your tree
> Little woman, I'm your lovin'
> Most emphatically
> You can't get along without me . . .
>
> Little strawberry, I'm your basket
> Sweet little sweet potato I'm your pie
> Little question, I'm your answer
> If you ask it . . .
>
> Little moonstone, little diamon'
> I won't stop this crazy rhymin'
> Till you and me are community property
>
> Like it read in the book
> Like it sing in the song
> You can't get along
> You can't get along without me.

An equally indigenous voice, but one that Yip deplores, is heard in "Hooray for de Yankee Dollar," a lyric in which Yip depicts not only the corruption of the native culture but the rendering of the natural world into a money-driven one:

> HOORAY FOR DE YANKEE DOLLAR
> (excerpt)
>
> Big boat in de bay
> Small boat give salute
> De tourist arrive
> In grey flannel suit

Big car on de deck
Big trunk in de hold
De Yankees arrive
Wid money dat fold . . .

Banana won't fall
Papaya won't stir
Till Yankee arrive
Wid legal tender . . .

Hooray for de Yankee dollar
Beautiful Yankee dollar
Jackson, Lincoln, George Washington
Sons of liberty
Brought de Yankee dollar 'round
To make us free.

Koli's argument with Joe as to the merits of civilization concludes with "Monkey in the Mango Tree," in which the monkey of the title contemplates Yip's midcentury *Homo Manhattanus* and denies any Darwinian link to same. No mean phrasemaker, in the last stanza the monkey runs the phrase "monkey's uncle" into the Gilbertian "and his cousins and his aunts."

Monkey in the Mango Tree

Three monkeys in the mango tree
Were indulging in philosophy
And as I walked by the mango tree
One of them addressed himself to me

Hey man, is it true what they say?
Hey man, is it true that today
They claim that my brothers and me
Are the predecessors of humanity?

Hey man, why you give us bad name?
Hey man, it's a blight and a shame
To claim this uncivilized cuss
Could have been descended from the likes of us

How can you have de brazen face
To scandalize our noble race?
Don't identify yourself with me,
Said de monkey in de mango tree

Would a monkey do what silly man will do?
Live in de jungle of Madison Avenue
Fight his neighbors with a gun and knife
Love his horses and divorce his wife?

Would de monkey love a girl in zipper pants
Mud packs, girdles and deodorants?
Falsies fillin' out de vital spot
How de hell de feller know just what he got?

Hey man, why you give us bad name?
Hey man, it's a blight and a shame
To claim most unbiblically
That this chump could once have been a chimpanzee

Dat de monkey language
De monkey very clever
Which is to say in his own way
Would a monkey ever

Analyze his psyche, amortize his soul,
Tranquilize his frontal lobes with alcohol?
Televise his follies and the life he lives
Eulogize his gargles and his laxatives?
Simonize his teeth, lanolize his hands
Hormonize his chromosomes with monkey glands?
Mechanize de Greeks, modernize de Turks
And then with one little atom (poof!)
Atomize de works?

Hey man, do you call it fair play?
Hey man, is it cricket to say
Dat de monkey and his uncles and his cousins
And his aunts
Are de parents of such foolishment and decadence?
Don't identify yourself with me,
Said de monkey in de mango tree.

The conversion of *Jamaica* into a vehicle for Lena Horne enabled Yip and Harold to resurrect a number they had written for her in the 1943 film, *Cabin in the Sky,* but which never was filmed. The song, though, was too good not to be revived, however great its distance from the calypso idiom. The music is more accessible, direct, swinging, than any other number in the *Jamaica* score. Yip's lyric here directly expresses his philosophy of the real—the solid, the mellow, the dignified—and its adversaries: guilt, sin, being uncouth. It also provides some clues as to why the number was never filmed: the third and fourth lines are a direct and casual denial of an afterlife, rather unlikely material for an MGM musical.

AIN' IT DE TRUTH?
(excerpt)

Life is short, short, brother!
Ain' it de truth?
An' dere is no other
Ain' it de truth?
You gotta rock that rainbow
While you still got your youth
Oh! Ain' it de solid truth?

Was a guy called Adam
Ain' it de truth?
Said: "Now look here, Madam"
Ain' it de truth?
"You got to bite dat apple
While you still got dat tooth"
Oh! Ain' it de mellow truth?

Long as there's wine and gin
To drown your troubles in
What's all dis talk o' sin
Rise 'n' shine and fall in line

Get dat new religion
Ain' it de truth?
Fo' you is dead pigeon
Ain' it de truth?
'Cause when you're laid horizontal
In dat telephone booth
Dere'll be no breathin' spell
It's only natural
Ain' it de gossipel truth?

Life is short, short, brother!
Ain' it de truth?
An' dere is no other
Ain' it de truth?
So if you don't love livin'
You is slightly uncouth
Oh! Ain' it de dignified truth?

Said dat gal Dubarry
Ain' it de truth?
Love is cash and carry
Ain' it de truth
You got to shake it down
Or stir it up with vermouth
Oh! Ain' it de visible truth? . . .

It's de truth, de truth
It's de solid, mellow truth.

Jamaica's next, and most directly political song, may have been more germane in the eighties than it was in 1957. Indeed, much of the lyric to "Leave de Atom Alone" anticipates more latter-day comic assaults on nuclear energy: "You most exasperated / When radioactivated / And cannot be located / On telephone" certainly prefigures the spirit of "One Nuclear Bomb Can Ruin Your Whole Day."

LEAVE DE ATOM ALONE

Verse. Ever since de apple
In de garden wid Eve
Man always fooling wid things
That cause him to grieve
He fool wid de woman
De rum and hot blood
And he almost wash out
Wid de forty day flood

But not since de doom day
In old Babylon
Did he fool wid anything so diabolical
As de cyclotron

So if you wish to avoid
De most uncomfortable trip to paradise
You will be scientific
And take my advice

Chorus.   Leave de atom alone
Leave de atom alone
Don't get smart alecksy
With de galaxy
Leave de atom alone

If you want to keep riding in Cadillac car
If you don't want to surely
Go to heaven prematurely on a shooting star
If it pleasure your heart
To keep smoking that big fat cigar
Let me drive de point home
Leave de atom alone

If you want Mississippi to stay where it is
If you want to see Wall Street
And General Motors continue in biz
If you want Uncle Sam to keep holding
What's yours and what's his
If you're fond of kith and kin
In their skin and bone
Don't fool around with hydrogen
Leave de atom alone

Bad for de teeth
Bad for de bone
Don't fool with it
Leave it alone

If you like Paris in the Springtime
London in de Fall
Manhattan in de Summer
With music on de mall
Stop fooling with de fallout
Above de cosmic ball
Or you will soon be fissionable material

Bad for de teeth
Bad for de bone
Don't fool with it
Leave it alone

Don't mess around you dopes
Lay off the isotopes
Don't you fuss with the nucleus
Don't go too far with de nuclear
Don't get gay with de cosmic ray
You'll burn your fingers
And you'll lose your hair
And you leave big smog
In de atmosphere

You most exasperated
When radioactivated
And cannot be located
On telephone
Go back to rock'n'roll-a
Rum and Coca-Cola
Go back to Eve
But leave de atom alone

Bad for de teeth
Bad for de bone
Spoil your complexion
Tie up de traffic
Jam up de plumbing
Lose your sweet disposition
Don't fool with it
Leave it alone!

"Leave de Atom Alone" stands out among Yip's lyrics in that it could have been addressed directly to a new audience whose existence Yip might not yet have even discerned. It is a song for the late fifties nonrock rebellion—that fledgling, half-counter, half-straight culture that was flourishing not only in Greenwich Village but also on college campuses. Its troubadors were Tom Lehrer, the Kingston Trio, the Limelighters, and to a certain extent, Harry Belafonte: entertainers for a generation that rejected the old politics without having yet invented a new one, a generation that still had an affinity for the old culture, both its folk songs and its more urbane theater music. Fifteen years later, Yip made some rather self-conscious and fleeting attempts to reach the rock generation, but those efforts were clearly doomed from the start. To be sure, the fifties rebellion was waged by a transitional, short-lived generation: by 1962, the model antinuclear war song was already Bob Dylan's "A Hard Rain's A'Gonna Fall." For a few short years, though, there was a new audience for such songs as "Leave de Atom Alone," but it was an audience with which Yip failed to connect.

In act 2 of *Jamaica*, the governor is incapacitated and his assistant Cicero vests himself with the majestic office of governor pro tem. He is unceremoniously put back in his place by his girlfriend, Ginger, and her girlfriend, Savannah, who remind him that "Napoleon's a pastry."

NAPOLEON

Napoleon's a pastry
Bismark is a herring
Alexander's a creme de coco mixed with rum
And Herbie Hoover is a vacu-um

Columbus is a circle
And a day off
Pershing is a square
What a pay-off
Julius Caesar is just a salad on the shelf
So little brother get wise to yourself

Life's a bowl and it's
Full of cherry pits
Play it big and it throws you for a loop
That's the way with fate
Come today we're great
Comes tomorrow we're tomato soup

Napoleon's a pastry
Get this under your brow
What once usta be a roosta'
Is just a dusta' now

Dubarry is a lipstick
Pompadour's a hair-do
Good Queen Mary just floats along from pier to pier
Venus De Milo's just a pink brassiere

Sir Gladstone is a bag
Ain't it shocking?
And the mighty Kaiser
Just a stocking
The Tzar of Russia
Is now a jar of caviar
And Cleopatra is a black cigar

Yes, my honey lamb
Swift is just a ham
Lincoln's a tunnel
Coolidge is a dam
Yes, my noble lads
Comes today, we're fads
Comes tomorrow, we're all subway ads

Homer is just a swat
King John, a you-know-what
Get this under your brow
All these big-wheel controversials
Are just commercials now

Better get your jug of wine and loaf of love
Before that final vow.

Yip and Harold had first written "Napoleon's a Pastry," with different words to a different tune, for the 1937 show *Hooray for What?* from which it was excised during the tryouts.

"Napoleon's A Pastry" (1937)   "Napoleon" (1957)

"Napoleon's A Pastry" (1937)	"Napoleon" (1957)
Napoleon's a pastry	Napoleon's a pastry
Louis Fourteenth is only a chair	Bismark is a herring
Here's the moral in black and white	Alexander's a creme de coco mixed with rum
We may be spongecake overnight	And Herbie Hoover is a vacu-um
Bismark's a herring—it's funny somehow	Columbus is a circle
Herbie Hoover's a vacuum now	And a day off
Here is the moral—you make your scoop	Pershing is a square
And wind up tomato soup	What a pay-off
	Julius Caesar is just a salad on the shelf
	So little brother get wise to yourself
Every big tycoon goes the same way soon	Life's a bowl and it's
Julius Caesar is a bust on the shelf	Full of cherry pits
Fellah get wise to yourself	Play it big and it throws you for a loop
Here's the moral—the moral is clear	That's the way with fate
After love there's no more	Comes today we're great
So what in the world are we waiting for?	Comes tomorrow we're tomato soup

For the second go-round, Arlen composed a slow, rocking comic blues, with shorter melody lines more attuned to a "list" song. The music, that is, follows the shift in thematic emphasis upon which Yip and Harold had agreed: the new version would largely drop the love-now message of the old and focus more exclusively on the transience of human glory. Both of the songs that Yip and Harold revived and updated for *Jamaica,* "Napoleon's a Pastry" and "Ain' It de Truth?" were mortality songs, comic blues meditations on the fleetingness of life, power, and fame. Clearly, the concern was not new to Yip—these were, after all, revivals—but their joint resurfacing suggested that the subject was taking on a new relevance.

Indeed, Yip's involvement with *Jamaica* itself provided him with a painful lesson on the transience of power. With the failure of *Flahooley,* Yip's control over his Broadway projects waned considerably. It was David Merrick, not Yip, who was calling the shots on *Jamaica,* and the show began to slip from Yip's grasp when Merrick and director Robert Lewis took the signing of Lena Horne as a chance to reconstruct the show. Arlen biographer Jablonski has chronicled the changes that overtook the project:

> The work of librettists Harburg and Saidy was reshaped to fit the handsome form of the star. Staging was planned so that Miss Horne could stand and sing as she had done so successfully at the Waldorf. Songs that had been planned for others were given to her, and by the time *Jamaica* opened Miss Horne was literally singing half the show. This was, of course, fine for Arlen and Harburg, song writers, but not so good for Harburg and Saidy, librettists.

The commercial logic behind the changes was unassailable. Horne had long been one of the nation's leading night club and cafe society entertainers, but she had yet to have a Broadway vehicle. When she had announced her upcoming role in *Jamaica* during a guest appearance on the Ed Sullivan show, advance ticket sales soared to nearly a million dollars. The more Horne, Merrick concluded, the bigger the box office. The out-of-town previews made clear the show needed cutting. For Merrick, the obvious target was the book. For a time, Yip still thought an artistically suitable compromise could be reached. On the road with the show, he wrote an ailing Arlen back in New York:

> The show, like every creation in rehearsal, is a hodge-podge of whirly-gig and raw nerve tissue. Out of it somehow will come discipline and tempo, light and color, words and music, harmony and laughter. The ego will be nourished, the scars healed, and I will be off on my white charger toward greener fields and sweeter challenges.

By the time the show had moved from Philadelphia to Boston, though, the battle was lost. Again, Jablonski:

> Harburg, serving as spokesman for the authors, found himself and Fred Saidy locked out of the theater. Arlen, who had come up to Boston despite his illness, found it simplest to keep out of the melée, though he faithfully sided with the writers against the management and director, who Harburg felt were distorting the book to make it only a Lena Horne vehicle and a palpable Broadway hit. By the Boston opening on October 8 the die was cast, for any further libretto changes would have only added to the confusion. But it assured Harburg and Saidy the role of sitting ducks for the critics.

By the end of the fifties, Yip had to keep in good shape while trying to fight off the effects of the blacklist, being locked out of the theatre during *Jamaica* by producer David Merrick, and in general suffering the "slings of fortune." (Collection of Harburg Estate.)

In fact, critical reception for *Jamaica* was fairly rapturous, though it tended to treat the show less as a musical than as a Lena Horne revue. "*Jamaica*," wrote Brooks Atkinson, "is a beautiful, jovial, old-fashioned musical comedy that has been produced and staged with taste and style." *New York Herald Tribune* critic Walter Kerr enjoyed the evening but wondered where the book had gone: "Can you make a whole show," he asked, "out of sheet music?" There could be no clearer index of Yip's fall from power than the critics' faulting him, of all people, for a too-skimpy libretto. Kerr also blew hot and cold on the lyrics. He tallied

no fewer than four E. Y. Harburg lyrics dedicated to preserving the social significance that was so stimulating in the Thirties and is so uncomfortable now. Mr. Harburg is, as everyone knows, an absolutely dandy lyricist when he is being lyrical; the "crickets doin' nip-ups around the columbine" is in his vein. But there are an enormous number of rhymes involving barbituates, cyclotrons, Anna Lucasta, and the fact that we may all soon be "fissionable material," and I suspect that the title of one of these forays—"Leave de Atom Alone"—might well have been taken more seriously by the authors.

Years later Lena Horne recalled that "when Josephine Premice sang 'Leave the Atom Alone' on the road, it was a blockbuster, [but] opening in New York, nothing happened." Walter Kerr was right to react against the imbalance in the score, but his reading of Yip's relation to its zeitgeist was off. Politically, *Jamaica* was not a thirties museum piece, but a harbinger of the sixties. (In the composition of cast and crew, too: backstage, Charlie Blackwell was Broadway's first black stage manager, and Yip and Lena ensured an integrated chorus; but it was years before the changes of the sixties helped move white Broadway toward equal opportunity.)

The Merrick-Horne *Jamaica* was a roaring success, running over 550 performances on Broadway before it closed in April of 1959. Success came with a price, however: the show had been tailored so exactly to Lena Horne's dimensions that it was effectively unrevivable without her. The original *Jamaica,* by contrast, was presented with its book restored at Cleveland's Karamu Theater in December, 1959. The production was scheduled to run for a few weeks only, but the run was extended for several months.

Yip viewed *Jamaica*'s success with a professional's ironic detachment. As he wrote a friend:

> I did not come in for the opening of *Jamaica* because I did not feel spiritually attached to it. It ended up as a good sock entertainment completely overhauled and commercialized for Lena Horne with the soul of creative intention raped and debauched. However, this is what the American critics and the major part of the audience evidently want and it is off to a smash hit. I will therefore follow Omar Khayyam's advice and take the cash and let the credit go.

But the times were changing again. In the autumn of 1960, with the Eisenhower presidency drawing to a close and John Kennedy campaigning for the White House, two movies were released that credited Dalton Trumbo as their screenwriter. The blacklist years were finally over.

The following year, Yip returned to Hollywood to write what would be his last full score with Arlen. The project was no Freed-unit musical, though, but rather a full-length animated UPA/Warner Bros. cartoon. Nonetheless, *Gay Purr-ee* featured stellar singing talents, most notably, Judy Garland as the voice of the heroine and Robert Goulet as that of the hero, and today still has a cult following and strong video cassette and CD sales.

The animated film *Gay Purr-ee* (1962) first became a cult film, then a family video that survives in the nineties. (Collection of Harburg Estate.)

The blacklist was gone, but it had outlasted the classical Hollywood musical that Yip had helped to shape. For after 1960, there were to be no more Arthur Freed musicals. Yip was now free to pursue his livelihood in other media besides the theater—but with whom? His contemporaries were working sporadically, if at all, and Yip considered their successors, with a few exceptions, a distinctly less talented lot than his old-time, now sometime collaborators. And outside the realm of theater song, a revolution in musical taste was building that threatened to marginalize Yip's kind of song at the very moment that his kind of politics were beginning to inch back into favor.

Chapter 10

The Sixties and the Sunset Years

Time you old gypsy man
Thief on the wing
Drugged me with rhapsodies
Tricked me with Spring . . .

Time you old vagabond
Riddle me this
What did you do with forever and ever
That sealed every kiss?

By the midsixties, Yip was the last member of the class of 1895–96 still plying the lyricist's trade. Larry Hart had died in 1943, Oscar Hammerstein in 1960. Ira Gershwin had retired in the midfifties; Howard Dietz's last show came to Broadway in 1963. Writing a musical (which is to say, writing and rewriting and going on the road with the show and rewriting some more) is an arduous task, and with the passage of time and changes in musical taste, many within the generation of classic Broadway songwriters had effectively ended their careers: both Irving Berlin and Cole Porter, for instance, did their last shows in the midfifties. Writing Arthur Freed for MGM's permission to use "Ain' It de Truth?" in *Jamaica,* Yip uncharacteristically acknowledged that the show's travails had taken its toll on the team of Arlen and Harburg. "Even though we are the same age as thirty years ago," he wrote, "for some reason it feels different."

Harold Arlen and Burton Lane, to be sure, were both very much around in the early sixties, but after *Gay Purr-ee,* Yip would not again write more than an occasional song with either one. The mental illness of Arlen's wife, Anya, left Harold both withdrawn and depressed; her death in 1970 only worsened Arlen's condition. Attractive projects materialized on which Yip and Harold had to pass: Arthur Laurents, foremost of the new librettists (*West Side Story* and *Gypsy* are two of his late-fifties shows), wanted to do a book for the duo in 1963, but they did not take him up on his offer.

The situation between Yip and Burt Lane was, if anything, even more troubled. For a number of years, each brought project ideas to the other, only to have the other decline to work on them. In the fifties, Lane proposed a musical on the founding of the state of Israel, which Yip rejected. Yip tried to interest Burt in *Flahooley,* in a musical based on Aesop's fables, and in a project they referred to as "the Village Blacksmith idea," all of which Lane turned down. Yip's fourth suggestion, the "Angelina" story, intrigued Lane, only to have Yip lose interest. Yip accused Burt of unwillingness and inability to work on *any* show. In his defense, Burt sent an agonizing letter to Yip in the spring of 1956. "I can't think of a composer who wouldn't give his right so-and-so to work with you," Burt wrote. "You are a tremendous lyric writer."

But Burt then zeroed in on Yip's librettos, calling them unwieldy and gratuitously political ("The story lost all direction," he writes of the Aesop project, "and again it became a story with too many themes that didn't belong together"). "Every idea you worked on had to have social significance," Burt wrote. "I thought this was wrong especially when the social significance was being brought in whether or not it belonged." Lane's letter also makes clear that their relationship was badly strained.

> In spite of the deep affection I know we have for one another, it's unfortunate that resentments have been built up in the past which, inadvertently, have caused us to misunderstand and misinterpret each other's actions and words. . . . But one cannot undo the past. One can only try to understand it.

There was, of course, a younger generation of Broadway composers who had emerged during the fifties—whose talents, however, Yip did not rate very highly. Around 1961, Yip authored a piece for Gerald Gardner entitled, "The Young Composers." In it, he expressed admiration for some of the younger lyricists, Stephen Sondheim and Sheldon Harnick in particular, but complained that

> these youngsters are not producing the great songs that a Hart or a pair of Gershwins produced when they—and the century—were in their thirties. . . . I suspect that much of the difference springs from the way in which shows are written today, much from the lack of great composers to challenge the lyricists to write greatly, and much from the climate of our times. . . .
>
> [A] cross that the Sondheims and Harnicks must bear is that they are not writing with a Richard Rodgers, a Jerome Kern or a Harold Arlen. For a great song requires a great composer.

Yip never published "The Young Composers." It may be that he realized if he wished to stay active in the theater, he might himself have to collaborate with one of the objects of his criticism.

And yet, throughout the sixties and seventies, Yip continued to work on projects and songs, and saw two of his shows come to Broadway. Despite the retrospective recognition he was finally beginning to receive, though, it was a frustrating period. The last dozen years of Yip's life were spent trying to write for shows or films that were never produced. When he died of a heart attack in 1981, he was en route to a story conference about a film for which he hoped to do the lyrics: Robert Louis Stevenson's *Treasure Island.*

Yip, Aristophanes, and Offenbach

In 1961, Yip brought a show to Broadway that was an acknowledgment of—or end run around—his composer problem. The show was *The Happiest Girl in the World,* and all its songs were by the team of E. Y. Harburg and Jacques Offenbach (1819–80).

Yip's original plan was to do a musical version of *Orpheus* set to Offenbach's music. As he had always preferred to set lyrics to music rather than write the lyrics first, a collaboration with Offenbach would not alter his normal work patterns. (Besides, like Arlen and Sammy Fain, Offenbach was the son of a cantor.) In an odd sort of way, the idea seemed a natural. Yip commissioned Jay Gorney to research the Offenbach *oeuvre.* In time, Jay pored over 113 operas and operettas to assemble the score. "We wanted to use tunes that were not too well known, yet had a classic strain," Yip said, "ones that would be vaguely familiar to most people."

One problem, as usual, was the book. Yip had first asked blacklisted screenwriter Dalton Trumbo to have a go at adapting *Orpheus* into a musical libretto. But Trumbo had had no experience at musicals, and Yip reluctantly (and ironically) rejected his draft as "too political"! Yip turned next to Ben Hecht, veteran playwright and screenwriter, but Hecht's outline also failed to satisfy Yip and Fred.

By 1958, Yip had revised the tale from that of *Orpheus* to that of *Lysistrata,* Aristophanes' classic comedy in which the women of Athens refuse sexual relations with their husband-soldiers until they agree to bring the endless war against Sparta to a halt. Aristophanes was augmented by Yip's own adaptations of Bullfinch's tales of the gods. The libretto was entrusted to Fred Saidy and Henry Myers, and with Gorney as music adaptor and Yip doing the lyrics and story, the writing end of the project was entrusted entirely to blacklistees.

Constrained, perhaps, by Aristophanes and Bullfinch, *Happiest Girl* features one of Yip's least complex plots. He and Fred Saidy made a major change in Aristophanes by bringing the gods into Lysistrata's strike—and that because the endless war is threatening the gods' legitimacy. "Unless you give us peace," Lysistrata implores the Olympians, "we can no longer give you faith." The scene then shifts to Olympus, where Zeus warns his fellow gods that they are likely to go the way of their Babylonian and Sumerian predecessors unless they can bring the war to the close. It is Diana, the goddess of chastity, who conceives the idea of withholding sex from the warriors; she proceeds to earth to inspire Lysistrata and the other Athenian women, but is tempted to involve herself in much the same manner as Og in *Finian* (though Yip respects Greek mythology and Diana does not succumb). In all this, the gods are opposed by Pluto, who takes on any number of guises, including that of an Athenian head of state, in order to break the strike and keep the war going. At the play's end, though, even Pluto has become a peace advocate, since he foresees that war will destroy the planet and thereby all those who serve *him*.

The most striking thing about *Happiest Girl* is that it manages to be at once about eight years ahead of its time thematically and eighty years behind it in style and music. The book, and more particularly the lyrics, are really addressed to American, not Athenian, military interventionism, to the justifications that the United States was to use in a few years to destroy much of Vietnam. Athens, one lyric instructs us, is "the only great democracy"; and "woe / to the foe / who refuses to be free." Yip entered the sixties a vehement critic of American militarism. One of Yip's poems of the period, frequently recited during concert performances by the Chad Mitchell Trio, is characteristic of his concerns:

AN ATOM A DAY KEEPS THE DOCTOR AWAY

> We've licked pneumonia and T.B.
> And plagues that used to mock us,
> We've got the virus on the run,
> The small pox cannot pock us;
> We've found the antibodies for
> The staphylo-strepto-coccus.
>
> But, oh, the universal curse
> From Cuba to Korea,
> The bug of bugs that bugs us still
> And begs for panacea!
> Oh, who will find the antidote
> For Pentagonorrhea?

This antiwar spirit pervades the Lysistrata story and lyrics. Its message could have connected with at least some of the late fifties rebellion audience: indeed, some of the lyrics read like a more pointed and polished Tom Lehrer send-up of U.S. foreign policy. And yet, this was not the only spirit in evidence in *Happiest Girl*.

The Broadway show *The Happiest Girl in the World* (1961), adapted from Aristophanes's *Lysistrata* by Yip and Fred Saidy, spoke out against American imperialism and for the power of women. Here, the (male) executives: *From left,* Lee Guber, producer; Yip, lyricist-conceiver; Cyril Ritchard, director and actor who played Pluto, the champion of war; Fred Saidy, coauthor, with Henry Meyers. The music consisted of Jay Gorney's selections from Jacques Offenbach. Every one of the creators except Guber (and Offenbach and Aristophanes) had been blacklisted in the fifties. (Billy Rose Theatre Collection, New York Public Library.)

Happiest Girl, to be sure, had relatively little of the Minsky-burlesque side of Aristophanes, which runs a distant second to Offenbach's more elegant and genteel raciness. Indeed, most of *Happiest Girl*'s reviewers (not a wildly Dionysian crew) noted with some relief the degree to which the evening's other dominant "elder" was more Offenbach than Aristophanes. The assertion, although accurate, tended to miss the point, inasmuch as the evening's real dominant elders, the ones whose spirits most pervaded *Happiest Girl,* were Gilbert and Sullivan.

In Offenbach, Yip had found a collaborator in many ways Sullivan's counterpart. Offenbach and Sullivan overlapped in musical period (much of their greatest writing comes from the 1870s), in their chosen genre (light opera), and in the musical conventions to which they adhered. Since the day Ira Gershwin had first played recordings of *Pinafore* and *The Mikado* for Yip, Gilbert had been Yip's model lyricist—as he was Ira's and Larry Hart's—the one whose work Yip and his cohorts strove to emulate within a modern American context. But by 1960 that context was becoming increasingly alien to Yip, and here was a composer whose music lent itself to Gilbertian lyrics.

There are two distinct kinds of reflections on romance in the score of *Happiest Girl*. Love-song lyrics are less conflicted here than in earlier works, and the threats to love more purely external—the war, in particular. Balancing them off are the comic lyrics for Pluto, for whom Yip has reserved his best lines, as Milton did for Satan—though the parallel should probably not be pursued any further. Even Pluto is not really a Harburgian foe of romantic illusion, but of moralistic hypocrisy. In *Happiest Girl* the complexities of Yip's views on romance and conviction are not so much resolved as simply bypassed. But then, the Offenbach music with which Yip worked was somewhat more lush and premodern, less conflicted and ambivalent, than that of Yip's contemporary collaborators.

Happiest Girl's opening number, from which we excerpt, mixes some of the score's rather few 1960 zeitgeist jokes ("Oedipus for future wrecks") with a sustained send-up of American interventionist rhetoric:

THE GLORY THAT IS GREECE
(excerpt)

Pluto.   Strike up the cymbals for the glory that is Greece
The land of pottery and poetry and peace
Where children speak
In classic Greek
Where everything we make is pure antique

We're here to celebrate with music and with mirth
The one and only great democracy on Earth
So make it known
With baritone

Kinesias.   That we're the only, only great democ-

Pluto.   -Racy to give to history
The sandal and the smock,
The vase and Odyssey,
And slaves with Ph.D.,
And all because we're free.

Chorus.	We're free.
	We're free.
Kinesias.	Nobody tells us what to eat or what to drink,
	Nobody tells us what to read or what to think,
	The one who does
	Is made to blush.
	Yes, the Greeks have a word for that bird,
	And that word is—TUSH!
Three Vestal Virgins.	Sing glory to his name,
	It belongs to history now,
	Solidify his fame,
	With this laurel on his brow
	We place this laurel wreath upon
	The brow that saved the Parthenon,
	Classic work so nobly made.
Senator.	Good for future tourist trade.
Kinesias.	Each backward nation is our protege and ward,
	We bring them culture with our cultivated sword.
	We set them free
	From tyranny
Pluto.	And woe
	To the foe
	Who refuses to be free. . . .
	Strike up the cymbals for the glory that is Greece,
	The land of lute and lyre and the Golden Fleece.
	We give you sex
	That's ambi-dex
	We give you Oedipus for future wrecks
All.	This is the Grecian age, the Grecian century,
	With Grecian gold and Grecian gods to keep us free
	On every isle,
	On every sea
	Gold . . . Grecian,
	Gods . . . Grecian,
	For all time to be . . .
	There's joy and peace in Greece,
	And Golden Fleece in Greece
Pluto.	We're up to here in Greece . . .
All.	In Greece, in Greece, in Greece, in Greece,
	The glory that is Greece.

In a poignant farewell song that Lysistrata sings to her husband Kinesias, who is returning to battle, Yip conflates images of freedom with those of romance, a confluence that works perfectly well within the score, though it goes against the grain of many earlier Harburg ballads. But here the threat to love comes less from individual ambivalence than from the dictates of a senseless war.

SHALL WE SAY FAREWELL?

Shall we say farewell,
Farewell to Spring,
Farewell to love and to loveliness?

Shall we mute the songs we used to sing
And drink to the end of friendliness,
Shall the free wind never blow again?
Shall the free heart never know again
The smile, the kiss
The song
The whispering hope of a brighter tomorrow?

Shall we say farewell to laughter,
Knowing well
That Spring has lost its spell
The sorry, sorry day we say farewell.

Lysistrata leads the women of Athens in taking an oath that manages to anticipate by several years the "Make love, not war" slogan of the sixties antiwar movement, while also harkening back to a Gilbertian vocabulary. The choral repetition of the last half of Lysistrata's final lines places us squarely within Gilbert country.

LYSISTRATA'S OATH
(excerpt)

Lys.   And now on this girdle of Diana
      We take this sacred oath of chastity:
      Till there's peace in the air
      We'll abandon Aphrodite
      Not a bed will we share
      Not a bed and not a nightie
      Not a man does there live

	Whom we do not vow to scare off Not an inch will we give For we firmly swear to swear off! . . .
Women.	Not an inch, not a hair, Not a bone . . . will we share; When he raves with despair We'll send him packing.
A Woman.	If he plead or attack He'll be sacked from the sack—
Second Woman.	And he's not crawling back Until he starts cracking.
Several Women.	Not for king or for crown Will a Zeus's son seduce us. Not for king or for crown Shall we girls lay . . . down our arms.
All the Women.	So by Venus and by Jove And by all the gods above us War is hate . . . Love is love And a hater cannot love us. We must turn the fighting leopard Back into a gentle shepherd. Love is love . . . hate is hate And the two won't tete a tete . . .
Lys.	Strike out with fist in velvet glove Make way for "Operation Dove."
Echo.	'Ration Dove . . .
All.	It's war on war through love Not either-or, But love or war, No less no more. Just love or war!

Happiest Girl's ballad is set to Offenbach's "Barcarolle." In "Adrift on a Star," wandering is no longer a metaphor for questing and idealism but a rather confusing given in a meaningless, arbitrary world. Yip later remarked that this lyric tried to bring "Paper Moon" into the space age, both songs suggesting that a connection to one other person can help make sense of a drifting universe.

ADRIFT ON A STAR

Here we are
Adrift on a star
Alone in a silent sky

Lost in space
Together we face
The wonder of where and why

Why a sky without an end
A sea without a chart?

Why the rain and why the rose
And why the trembling heart?

The moon, the tide, the years
They go rolling along
Oh music of the spheres
Are there words to your song?
Is there a bright gleaming goal
Ending this brief barcarole?

Here we are
Adrift on a star
And what is the journey for?

Can it be
The heart is the sea
And love is the golden shore?

That wherever you are
In this star-sprinkled dome
If there's love in your star
You're home
You're home.

Despite the old Broadway "girlee" slant of the illustration on the song's cover and of the show's title, this was an antiwar and profeminist show in 1961—before the Vietnam War and before the rise of the women's movement in the late sixties. *Happiest Girl,* however, did not succeed on Broadway. (Collection of Harburg Estate.)

Happiest Girl, starring Cyril Ritchard (who also directed) as Pluto and Janice Rule as Diana, opened on Broadway in April 1961, to mixed notices: a few raves, a number of reservations, no out-and-out pans. Most of the criticism was directed at the show's hybrid conception. Yip's lyrics were generally though not universally well received; the production was acclaimed; Janice Rule was the subject of unanimous praise. For all that, the show lasted just ninety-seven performances. It probably *was* too much of a hybrid, in particular, its combination of prematurely sixties politics and 1880 music was far too idiosyncratic a refraction of Yip's roots and sensibilities. The book, whose holes were filled in by Ritchard's ill-fitting glitzy direction, didn't help.

The Sixties

As the smog of fifties politics lifted, Yip threw himself into a wide range of left-wing movements and activities that flourished in the sixties. There were benefits, advertisements, rallies, publications, and appearances by candidates championing civil rights, the environment, the antiwar movement. Yip wrote for a stunningly broad array of them, from campaign songs for routinely mainstream Democratic candidates (like New York governor Hugh Carey) to occasional light verse in the Marxist journal *Monthly Review.* In the middle sixties, he took a shot at Soviet and artistic censorship (and indirectly at the cold war) in his book of light verse entitled *Rhymes for the Irreverent:*

YEVTUSHENKO?

"I'm not afraid of atom bombs,"
Said Khrushchev, "And they know it;
I'm not afraid of anything,
Except, perhaps, a poet."

A best selling book by Rachel Carson, *Silent Spring,* about the destruction of the environment, inspired Yip to one more great political song, with music from a composer he had never before been able to interest in this kind of project. Yip and Harold Arlen wrote "The Silent Spring" in 1963 (the year of the John Kennedy and Medgar Evers murders), but its imagery and music are so disturbing, and its sense of the betrayal of the American promise so acute, that it seems a song that could have been written in that seminal year of American disasters, 1968.

THE SILENT SPRING

Not a leaf is heard to murmur,
Not a bird is there to sing
And bewild'ring eyes
Scan the fearful skies
Asking why this strange and silent Spring?

Children hide and roses tremble
Doors are dark and shades are down
And the rains of hate
Rust the garden gate
As the ghost of Spring stalks the town

Is this the land where flags were flown
To bring this hopeful world a dream
Of Spring unknown?
Is this the dream?
Is this the Spring?
The silent Spring that silent men
Have reaped and sown?

Silent men, take heart, take wing,
And sing away this silent Spring.

Arlen's music begins with quiet, short phrases, culminating in a downward and disturbingly dissonant phrase in the last line of the first stanza. As with "April in Paris," another song with short suggestive opening phrases, Yip begins the lyric imagistically, and with deliberate mystery. Something—a sickness, a malaise, an unnameable disaster?—is being described. The images of the second stanza are even more disturbing, as Yip depicts symptoms of terror: something new, not just for theater song lyrics (or concert song lyrics), but new for Yip as well. Indeed, the strength of the lyric lies in the precision of the imagery—a leafless, birdless hard rain, "the rains of hate," children and adults hiding indoors—and the deliberate ambiguity of the catastrophic cause. Is it ecological? nuclear? spiritual? or all three?

Arlen shifts in the release ("Is this the land," etc.) to longer phrases and greater intervals between notes. This is music in his "yearning" vein. What is yearned for, we learn, is the lost promise of the nation, lost through silence and timidity, racial conflict, and assassinations of leaders.

In the two-line coda (the song's pattern is AA'BC), Arlen composes two short upward phrases, then soars upward in the final line (on "a-*way*") to subside to the tonic at the conclusion. The soaring music also illustrates the sense of the lyric: song, as a metaphor for conviction and political action, is the remedy for this national/global malady. It is not a perfect lyric—some of the formulations (e.g., line two's "is there") appear stilted—but its movement from imagery to analysis (the "failed promise" release) to exhortation is brilliantly concise. "Silent Spring" has an immediacy and urgency that its ambiguities only enhance. It could well have been a song for Martin Luther King's assassination—or a ballad for the antinuclear movement, or, a quarter-century ahead of its time, an anthem for the Greens.

Yip was aroused by the politics of the sixties but was deeply alarmed by the new sixties music:

> The songs I'm hearing today . . . make me fearful because I know that when the language of songs begins to decay, watch out. . . . Songs are the fever chart of the nation, the thing that tells you what's wrong, whether we're beautiful, whether we're ugly, whether we're violent, whether we're lost.

In Yip's cosmology, the nation's songs were the measure of the state of the Union. Yip's new concern, genuine in itself, also masked (though not always) his rage at the marginalization of his own kind of music. In an interview with author Studs Terkel, Yip let his anger come through, first poetically, then directly:

> Here's my little tirade [he told Terkel] against the songs I hear today, called:

> MUSIC ON THE ROCKS

> Hail the songs—the latest rages
>   Dripping from guitar and pen,
> All are destined for the ages—
>   Like, I mean, from five to ten.

> The new songs are antigrammatical and antipoetical. They're tasteless, violent, and unmelodic.

For all his aversion to the newer music, Yip did on occasion lend his talents to folk songs, to songs for the brave new audience he often despaired of reaching. One such occasion arose when Earl Robinson arrived on his doorstep in the midsixties with a title song he was working on for the Otto Preminger film, *Hurry Sundown.* Yip was uninterested in the kind of contractual arrangement Preminger had offered, but when Earl started to play, Yip couldn't help himself. "Yip said, 'It needs more,'" Robinson recalled, "and he practically improvised the next musical phrases. It [the music] almost sounds like Yip. It's the way he talked." (Perhaps Yip *could* make up folk music on the spur of the moment, as he had once demonstrated to Terkel.)

Hurry Sundown

My seed is sown now
My field is plowed
My flesh is bone now
My back is bowed

So hurry sundown
Be on your way
And hurry me a sun up
From this beat-up sundown day

Hurry down sundown
Be on your way
Weave me tomorrow
Out of today

Hurry down sundown
Get thee begone
Get lost in the sunrise
Of the new dawn

Hurry down sundown
Take this old day
Wrap it in new dreams
Send it my way
Send it my way
Send it my way

Preminger, it turned out, didn't want the song, but Milt Okun, arranger for Peter, Paul, and Mary, did. It was Yip's only song to make the charts during the sixties.

As the industry grew harder and harder to crack, Yip's more characteristic response was to revert to verse. In 1965, he published a collection of his poetry under the title *Rhymes for the Irreverent;* in 1976 he followed it with another light verse anthology, *At This Point in Rhyme.* The market in light verse had long since vanished, but it cost far less money and agony to publish a volume of verse than it did to mount a Broadway show.

Topically, the volumes covered the waterfront; here was Yip on politics, Yip on music, and around this time in an unpublished verse, Yip—harking back to classical form—on the decline of lyrics and song:

After he turned sixty-five, Yip took up golfing as his major sport; he took his aging with humor and maintained his high level of energy in artistic and political efforts. (Collection of Harburg Estate.)

Where are the bards that pleasured me,
Guiterman, Hoffenstein, F.P.A.,
Dorothy Parker—B.L.T.,
Gilbert and Edna St. Vincent Millay?
Where are the triolets, rondeaus, pray,
Where are the ballad and balladeer?
Shades of Nineveh and Pompeii,
Where are the rhymes of yesteryear?

Where are the minstrels, gimmick free?
Glocca Morra? Greece? Cathay?
Alas, in Nashville, Tennessee,
Twanging their cliché hearts away,
Whining out ditties with nasal spray,
Hash for the soundtrack engineer.
Oh, Hart, oh Porter, oh Gershwin, say,
Where are the rhymes of yesteryear?

Where is the lyrical *joie d'esprit*?
Where "thou witty, thou swell, thou gay?"
Woe to the culture that woos TV
Where sponsors flourish and songs decay,
Where clay is hailed as cloisonné
And catch-penny poet is sage and seer.
Then hail McKuen—Farewell Benet!
Where are the rhymes of yesteryear?

L'envoi

Babe! Let the juke box bang and play.
Here's to the music. Here's to the beer!
Both have been canned—and lackaday . . .
Where are the rhymes of yesteryear?

The poem underscores again the great divide of 1921–22: there is not a single modernist in Yip's pantheon. With the class of 1895–96, Yip had begun writing light verse before there was a music to which it could be set. As far as Yip was concerned, that music had gloriously come and sadly gone, leaving him where he had begun: writing light verse.

Not all Yip's struggles during this period were confined to songs and shows. He had, after all, had a hand in some of the most successful and seminal musicals in Broadway history, but for years, none of them was brought to the screen. Their politics were too radical, it was said, or the characters were black and the

AT THIS POINT IN RHYME

E.Y. HARBURG'S POEMS

E.Y. Harburg
Rhymes for the Irreverent
Illustrated by Seymour Chwast

During the sixties and seventies, Yip published two books of light political verse and posed for the great caricaturist Al Hirschfeld and at the statue of *Alice in Wonderland*'s White Rabbit in Central Park, New York City. (Top left: © Al Hirschfeld. Drawing reproduced by special arrangement with Hirschfeld's exclusive representative, The Margo Feiden Galleries Ltd. New York; Top right: Crown Publishers; bottom: Collection of the Harburg Estate.)

moviegoers white; whatever the reason, these were not vehicles to bring before the great audience during the fifties. But by the sixties, Hollywood was showing some interest in *Bloomer Girl* and *Finian*. Twentieth Century-Fox took an option on *Bloomer Girl,* and by 1966 had a screenplay in hand that Yip loathed—not that it mattered: the film was never made. A television version survives—also loathsome.

Yip and Burt had been promoting *Finian* for the movies since 1949, and by the midsixties, it finally seemed as if it would be made. Warners hired Yip and Fred to do the screenplay, but a young musical neophyte, Francis Ford Coppola, was engaged to direct (it was his second film) and Yip and Fred had little to do with it. The most surprising part of the package was the casting of Fred Astaire as Finian. Lane, for all his great admiration for Astaire, couldn't see it, and cautioned Yip against going ahead with the project. As Lane recalls, "Yip said, 'I want to see the picture made before I die.' They made it, and it was a disaster." Yip ended up agreeing with Burt that the musical had been badly mangled. (Yet a video cassette of the film *Finian* remains highly popular in the nineties.)

Darling of the Day

Yip's last musical to reach Broadway was *Darling of the Day* in 1968, when Yip was seventy-two. It was the only one of his book shows, stretching clear back to 1937's *Hooray for What?*, for which Yip did not write or cowrite either the story or the libretto, and the only one, other than *Bloomer Girl*, for which he did not originate the project. *Darling of the Day* was conceived by the Theater Guild in 1964 as a musical adaptation of the Arnold Bennett novel *Buried Alive* and, more immediately, its 1943 Nunnally Johnson film adaptation, *Holy Matrimony,* one of the classic if more obscure Hollywood studio-era comedies. Nor was Yip originally part of the package. It was only at the insistence of *Darling*'s composer, Jule Styne, that Yip was given the assignment.

By the time of the Guild's 1964 announcement, Jule Styne had emerged as perhaps the most talented of the second generation of Broadway composers, the generation toward which Yip had expressed such ambivalence in his un-published essay just a few years earlier. Placing Styne neatly within one or another generation, however, is no easy matter. He was born in 1905, the same year as Harold Arlen, and was seven years *older* than Burt Lane. But Styne came to songwriting and shows relatively late. He had first been a child prodigy classical pianist, then an early leader of a celebrated jazz group in Chicago, then a vocal coach for Hollywood studios. Not until the late thirties did he begin writing songs for films. His hits included such standards as "Time after Time" and "Just in Time." His first Broadway show was *High Button Shoes* (1947), which inaugurated a string of hits including *Gentlemen Prefer Blondes, Bells Are Ringing, Gypsy,* and *Funny Girl.*

Styne's more recent lyricists had all been second generation, too: Comden and Green, Bob Merrill, Stephen Sondheim. But for the *Darling* project, Styne hoped to come in with his own *My Fair Lady,* and over the initial objections of the Guild, demanded Harburg as lyricist. Yip, the Guild told him, would be difficult, and too socially conscious. Styne would have none of this. "Yipper was the right man for it," he later said, "and Armina [Marshall, a Guild executive] finally bought him. I'd been dying to work with him for years."

Yip had loved the 1943 film, but had no such reaction to *Darling*'s initial book, which was reassigned to veteran playwright S. N. Behrman, then to Fred Saidy, and finally to the screenwriter who had initially transferred it to the screen, Nunnally Johnson. In time, Johnson turned out a libretto nearly as witty and sympathetic as his 1943 picture. Set in the first decade of the century, the story centers around Priam Farll, a reclusive painter of genius who returns to his native Britain after a Gaugin-like, self-imposed twenty-year exile in the South Seas. Dreading the pretensions and acclaim of the society and art worlds that are about to be showered upon him, Farll is suddenly presented with an opportunity to escape them all. On the evening of his return, his manservant, Henry Leek, dies of a sudden heart attack, and the attending physician assumes that it is Farll, not Leek, who has succumbed. Farll does not correct his misimpression, with the result that Leek is interred as Farll in Westminster Abbey, and Farll takes up a new fictitious life as Leek.

The plot thickens. From the South Seas, Leek had been corresponding through a matrimonial agency with a working-class spinster back home in Britain, and, sight unseen, they had agreed to marry. When Farll (qua Leek) meets her—she is named Alice Chalice—he is at first charmed, then enchanted: she is homey, honest, down-to-earth, the antithesis of everything he hates about the art world. The two soon marry and settle down in the working-class village of Putney-on-the-Thames. But Farll is utterly unable to resist the temptation to paint, and when money gets tight, Alice secretly sells some of his works to a local pub. Genius will out, of course: Britain's leading art dealer comes across the paintings and realizes Farll is still alive; and thus ends act 1.

In act 2 a lawsuit ensues between the dealer and his leading patron, who had thought she had the Farll market safely cornered; Farll is exposed and Alice chagrined at the prospect of becoming Lady Farll and having to abandon her working-class friends. The story concludes in a Gilbert and Sullivan trial scene in which Farll persuades the court to rule he is Leek, lest the court have to acknowledge that a butler has been interred in Westminster Abbey and "dark will be England's course."

As *Darling* developed, it turned largely into a domestic musical; relatively few of the songs were set amid the show's art world/upper-class settings and characters. Yip had hoped the show would offer him a number of Gilbert and Sullivan

Yip, *seated right*, singing along with the composers, *seated*, Burton Lane (*Finian's Rainbow*), *standing, left to right*, Jule Styne (*Darling of the Day*), Jay Gorney ("Brother, Can You Spare a Dime?"), and his book publisher, Nat Wartels, at an ASCAP party in 1976 celebrating the publication of Harburg's new book *At This Point in Rhyme*. (Courtesy American Society of Composers, Authors, and Publishers [ASCAP].)

tableaux, but in fact, *Darling*'s Gilbertian potential is realized only in its climactic trial scene. Other numbers refract some of Yip's own characteristic concerns, but on the whole, the songs of *Darling of the Day* are less a personal revelation than a testament to his thoroughgoing professionalism.

Darling begins in an art gallery that is featuring a Farll retrospective. Farll and Leek, just off the boat and unrecognized, attend the show—one day before Farll's scheduled official welcome—and Farll is reminded of why he left Britain in the first place. "He's a Genius" is an excellent expository number, introducing the audience to the British art world and to the protagonist who cannot bear its hypocrisies. Oxford, the art dealer, begins the song:

HE'S A GENIUS

Oxford. He's a most peculiar artist with a most peculiar mind
And I wouldn't call his attitude
Especially refined

He's an upper class eccentric
Who refuses to conform
To the proper, the respected,
The established and the norm

He just won't be nice to people
Who are most precisely nice
I precisely mean the people
Who can pay the nicest price

He's derisive of the kingdom,
Disrespectful to the crown
If his brushes were artillery,
They would blow the empire down!

But . . . He's a genius, a smashing genius
Though we loathe him we unhappily must say
He sells better than Murillo
Or El Greco and Utrillo
Priam Farrl, Priam Farrl
He's the darling, darling of the day

Farll. When I see these silly flunkies
What I'd give to live at ease
Back in Java with the monkeys
And the wholesome chimpanzees
What's a knighthood to this victor
If I have to live with these
Give me back the boa constrictor
'Neath the tropic jungle trees

Leek. But you're a genius
A knighted genius
And that is what a genius has to pay

Farll. Something tells me that my cue is
To be somewhere east of Suez
Priam Farll, Priam Farll
Kipling calls me back to Mandalay!

All.	But . . .
	. . . He's a genius, a blooming genius
Oxford.	Though he's obviously made of baser clay
	We must smile as if delighted
	That the blighter will be knighted
All.	For a knighthood makes a painting distingué
	He's a genius, a smashing genius
	He sells better than Da Vinci or Monet
	He's a rebel, he's a wrecker
	But a boon to the exchequer
	Priam Farll, Priam Farll
	He's the darling, darling of the day.

A great deal of *Darling*'s action is carried in song—for instance, Farll's sudden inspiration and decision to let the doctor's mistake go uncorrected and thereby switch places with his dead manservant. Here's an excerpt:

TO GET OUT OF THIS WORLD ALIVE

Oh the pity, pity, pity
To be gone when the committee
Comes to welcome you with speeches and bouquets
Oh the sorrow, sorrow, sorrow
To be sleeping late tomorrow
While the bishop is propounding his clichés

Oh the sadness to be missing
All the hand and buttock kissing
At the Earl of Piffles teas from four to five
I say wouldn't it be ducky
If a man could be that lucky
And get out of this world alive . . .

And the song's conclusion:

If this culture has the feature
Of a vulture, should a creature
Be indicted for attempting to contrive
To do a little switching
With his butler if he's itching
To get out of this world alive.

Similarly, the scene in which Farll meets Alice and is charmed by her spunk is also carried in song. Farll has secretly confided his true identity to his cousin Duncan, who, thinking Farll is Leek gone mad, summons the police. Alice arrives to save the day:

A Gentleman's Gentleman
(excerpt)

Alice.

Oh, where would Britain be without a gentleman's
gentleman?
And how would old Brittania rule a wave?
And generals would die without their boots on
The admirals would sink without their suits on
We wouldn't be superior
Without a paid inferior
To teach us how superiors behave

Oh, what would Britain do without a gentleman's
gentleman?
How could we tell the lowest from the best?
Back of their lordshipses and their worshipses
Upon whose brows our glories rest
Back of their highnesses
With crowns upon their sinuses
Is the man who keeps their trousers pressed . . .
By his virility, the frail nobility
In every stately home survives

Don't be so uppity
The man who serves your cup-a-tea
Is the gentleman's gentleman
The man on whom Britainnia thrives.

The courtship of Alice and Farll culminates in a waltz. "I knew this was a simple little lady," Styne said, "and I wanted a simple tiny little chord. I don't have to prove anything melodically. It's got to be tinkle-tinkle; it's in Putney and they don't know sophisticated things." The lyric is similarly tailored to the couple's tentativeness about getting involved—enabling the audience to sense how the love affair between Alice and Priam begins to take shape in this duet:

LET'S SEE WHAT HAPPENS

Let's give the waltz a chance,
Let's dance and let's see what happens
Let us carouse while Strauss
Caresses the strings
Even the shy may fly on musical wings
They say music can do
The most unusual things

Let's take a step or two or three
And let's see what happens
Let us pretend, my friend,
It's only a spree
And if a great adventure happens to happen
Won't we be happy it happened
To you and me?

The lines, "Let us pretend, my friend, it's only a spree" express, again, Yip's sense of the fun and adventure with which one should approach the delicate and often dark prospect of loving another soul.

While working on the *Darling* score, Yip did something completely against his normal patterns of work. He brought in a poem to Styne and asked Styne to set it to music: "I wrote music first for Yip," Styne said,

> except for one thing—a poem called "Sunset Tree," which he gave me. He had written this poem. He thought it would fit, and he said, "See what you can do with it." The greatest joy he got was when I brought him back the thing. He loved it. Yip was amazed at "Sunset Tree."

And Alice and Priam, two middle-aged lovers, sang:

SUNSET TREE

When April's dreams are over
And all her songs are sung,
When the years are old and the hills are old
And only our hearts are young,
Then ev'ry sweet small wonder
Will still more wondrous be
In the brave new light of a world grown bright
Under the sunset tree
Under the sunset tree

Let youth have its apple blossoms,
Fair on the bough above,
But not so fair as the fruit we share
In the harvest time of love
Spring is a young man's fancy
In a world that is fancy free,
But to know the grace of a warm embrace
When the heart is folly free
Is to know why the bold leaf turns to gold
Under the sunset tree
Under the sunset tree.

The fact that Yip authored the lyric first reflects, no doubt, the personal nature of "Sunset Tree." It is all the more striking in that "Sunset Tree" is *Darling*'s eleven o'clock song, the song near the end of the show, the slot Yip characteristically reserved for his Puckish anthems of verbal dexterity and sexual wanderings: "When I'm Not Near the Girl I Love" and "The Springtime Cometh." "Sunset Tree" may stand as Yip's idealization of what a long and unpretending love can be.

The climax of *Darling of the Day* comes with "Butler in the Abbey," the trial scene where Farll delivers a summary on the dire consequences of his being declared alive, while his adversaries interpose objections and the judge and spectators offer their comments. The pattern of assertion and reaction comes directly from Gilbert and Sullivan's *Trial by Jury,* but the escalation of comic content and rhyme is pure Yip: the first chorus culminates in the Shakespeare-Bacon reference, the second in the spectacle of "Gladstone and Disraeli . . . singing 'Eli Eli.'" This was to be Yip's last song on Broadway, and he went out near the top of his form.

BUTLER IN THE ABBEY
(excerpt)

Farll.   When word gets out there's a butler in the abbey
Dark will be England's course
The pound will drop
And Parliament will swap
Its kingdom for a horse
Our colonies across the seven seas
Will laugh with a great guffaw
They'll up and cheer
That socialism's here

Lady Vale and   And so will Bernard Shaw!
Pennington.

Farll.   Lord Nelson on his colonade
Will tear his marble hair
And dive into that plebian fountain
In Trafalgar Square
Big Ben will ring with a small ding ding
In its Anglo-Saxon shame
When word gets out there's a butler in the abbey
Mud . . . Mud will be Britain's name.

Picture ev'ry hero in Westminster
Laid out grandly on his sacred pad
Wailing there is something shabby
Going on in this here abbey

Farll.   Bli'me we've been blighted, we've been had!

Browning will report it to Ten Downing
Johnson shout, "Why isn't Boswell here?"
Shakespeare will be shaken
And awaken Francis Bacon,
And then each deny the other wrote King Lear

Dickens will be definitely stricken
Pitt will cry the empire is dissolved
Gladstone and Disraeli will be singing "Eli, Eli"
And Darwin wish he never had evolved . . .

All.   The marble arch and London Bridge
Will sag with a sagging fame
When word gets out there's a butler in the abbey
Mud mud mud mud

Farll. (speaks) May it please your lordship, if I am not Henry Leek, then . . .

All.   Mud will be Britain's name!

Darling was a troubled show right from the start. The only aspect of production that proceeded smoothly was the collaboration between Jule and Yip. As Styne recalled:

> He's a very easy fellow to work with because when two people are working, if they both have a mutual respect, then you're secure and you can say, "Yip, I don't like that word. . . ." He says, "We'll get another," with his big pencil and that big sheet of paper. He'll give you another word. Want another note? I'll give you another note. Want a pick-up? I'll give you a pick-up. That's when you know where you are.

They appeared to be the only two participants in *Darling*, however, with any such assurance. Even as the librettists went through a revolving door, the announced director, Peter Wood, left to be replaced by Albert Marre, himself to be replaced by twenty-four-year-old novice Stephen Vinaver, who had one off-Broadway revue to his credit. But the hunt for the proper librettist and director paled beside that for the proper Priam Farll. Laurence Olivier, Peter Finch, and Rex Harrison turned down the offer; Robert Shaw found the lyrics insufficiently British; John Gielgud loved the lyrics and the part but couldn't sing a note; Alfred Drake, Christopher Plummer, Richard Harris, Victor Borge (!) all said no. In the end, the part fell to Vincent Price—who, for all his experience in films, was a newcomer to the musical stage. "He was an art collector," said Styne. "He knew paintings. Some people thought he was British."

Under the title *Married Alive!* the show opened in Toronto, and was immediately in serious trouble. In a role that called for the kind of spirit Rex Harrison had brought to the part of Henry Higgins, Vincent Price was performing as if embalmed, and director Vinaver was doing little if anything to bring more life to the enterprise.

When *Married Alive!* reached Boston on December 20, it was thoroughly panned. Critic Elliot Norton wrote, "The strange thing about *Married Alive!* is the uninspired performance of Vincent Price. What a pity for him and for *Married Alive!*, too." But could a leading man—the only "name" in the cast—be replaced one month before the Broadway opening? As events had it, it was Vinaver who went (to be replaced by Noel Willman); it was Nunnally Johnson who went (he took his name off the credits in the final week before the Broadway opening), and it was the title *Married Alive!* that went, to be replaced by *Darling of the Day.* But Vincent Price remained.

Darling opened on Broadway on January 27, 1968, to mixed-to-favorable reviews, with one fatal exception. Styne's music drew everything from raves to pans, but Yip's lyrics received almost universal praise. Richard Watts and George Oppenheimer loved the lyrics, and critics proved as positive toward Patricia Routledge's Alice as they were negative to Vincent Price's Farll.

Perhaps the most balanced appraisal was that from Walter Kerr, which ran in the Sunday *Times*. Kerr loved Routledge and loathed Price ("his self-congratulatory chuckles could be sold as candy in the lobby"). By the standards of 1968, he found the score and the lyrics utterly wonderful. "It's an enormous relief," he wrote, "to sit in a theater and feel that somewhere, some time, a literate mind's been at work." (Indeed, it is evident from *Darling*'s reviews that by 1968, many reviewers had belatedly realized that the kind of lyrics Yip and his peers had provided Broadway were an endangered species, a realization from which *Darling* almost benefited, betokening the renewed attention accorded Rodgers and Hart, Gershwin, et al. a few years later.) Kerr very much liked Johnson's book as well: "All I can say is that when the *plot* draws applause in a musical—it did at one point on opening night—an odd and gratifying state of affairs may be said to exist."

The *Times*'s daily critic, Clive Barnes, also liked *Darling,* except that he was not the critic who had covered it on opening night. The *Times* review had been filed by the paper's back-up critic, Dan Sullivan, who found the proceedings far too bland. The power of the *Times* (or Kerr and Barnes) was unable to overcome the power of the *Times* and the mixed notices. *Darling* closed on February 23, after its thirty-second performance, losing what was then a record of over $700,000 (long since far surpassed). Yip and Jule tried to revive the project in later years but never got it off the ground.

"The ones that hurt the most," Styne later said, "are the ones that might have been."

What a Day for a Miracle

In 1968, Yip began work on another new musical. It was an adaptation of Henry Myers's 1939 novel *Our Lives Have Just Begun* and told the story of the thirteenth century Childrens' Crusade, in which fifty thousand French, Belgian, and German children voyaged to the Holy Land of Jerusalem to free it from "the infidels"—after the adults' crusades had repeatedly failed. Yip saw the work as an allegorical rendering of the quest of the younger generation of the sixties for a new promised land in America. This crusade never got to Broadway. But it did have a tryout production at the University of Vermont, and some of Yip's lyrics, to music by Larry Orenstein and Jeff Alexander, spoke to the times on his own terms and in his own idiom.

One of the lyrics expressed Yip's tongue-in-cheek appreciation of romance, a view he now attributed, not uncritically, to much of the sixties generation. It was to be sung by a traveling troubador, who served the war effort by entertaining the wives whom the dukes and barons had left alone in their castles:

WHEN YOU HAVE FORGOTTEN MY KISSES

This brief little flutter of passion
This gay little fly-by-night fling
Will live in the songs that I fashion
And throb in the rhymes that I sing

'Twill live, 'twill live on
The lips of all lovers
Who'll swear they are sharing our flame
When you have forgotten my kisses
And I have forgotten your name

The minstrel whose love is his lyre
Must play on the heart strings of France
And make every sinful desire
A ballad of deathless romance

So fondle me dearly
Let's sin more sincerely
That others may bask in our flame
When you have forgotten my kisses
And I have forgotten your name

So what if on waking tomorrow
We look at each other once more
And whisper "Your face is familiar"
And "Where have I met you before?"

Hi-ho, not to know
When an old is a new love
Will always keep true love aflame
So please keep forgetting my kisses
And I'll keep forgetting your name

(*spoken*)
And I, uh . . . have forgotten your name . . .

Yip's critical support of the New Left was never to reach an audience. His last attack on the "Old Right" was confined almost entirely to poetry. *At This Point in Rhyme,* his 1976 volume of light verse, dealt at some length and with considerable relish with the Watergate scandal, which Richard Nixon, the old Left's great nemesis, had brought upon himself. The scandal was the immediate subject of at least one short meditation:

HISTORY LESSON

This we learn from Watergate:
That almost any creep'll
Be glad to help the government
Overthrow the people.

THE ENEMY LIST

Socrates and Galileo
   John Brown, Thoreau, Christ, and Debs
Heard the night cry "Down with traitors!"
   And the dawn shout "Up the rebs!"

Lives of great men all remind us
   We can write our names on high,
And departing leave behind us
   Thumbprints in the FBI.

The Endgame Songs

Above all, Yip never stopped writing songs or working on shows. During the seventies he produced an occasional song with old collaborators like Arlen and Sammy Fain. He tried repeatedly to find some material that would interest and energize Arlen to return to composing. Yip developed a musical outline of the Liam O'Flaherty/John Ford classic, *The Informer,* but Arlen could not bring himself to be involved. In 1976, Yip succeeded in turning out two songs with Harold. They were Arlen's last compositions (he died in 1983).

The first is a wrenching ballad that Harold and Yip wrote for Harold and Anya, Arlen's wife, who had died in 1970, only in her midfifties.

PROMISE ME NOT TO LOVE ME

Promise me not to love me
Or adore me for a lifetime
Promise me not to waste a single sigh
On one good-bye

Love is by far too bitter sweet
For hearts that beat too truly
Promise me not to waste a tear
On hearts that cannot hear

Better to make this moment
A moonbeam affair
Than to wake each night
With the nightmare fright
That one of us won't be there

Promise me that you'll never know
The pain of so much wanting
Promise me that you'll never know
What love can do
Promise me not to love me
As I love you.

It is a poignant song and a well-crafted lyric, with the kind of final-line kicker that Yip had learned from O. Henry and in the light verse mines sixty years earlier. It is in the third stanza, the release, where both music and lyric soar. Arlen's music is not merely melancholy here, as it is throughout the song, but first suspenseful, then urgent. Yip's lyric, in turn, moves from the general to a palpably concrete experience. This is one of the very few passages—perhaps the only one—in American theater song (it was inserted in the 1981 revival of *Bloomer Girl* at the Goodspeed Opera House) where the imagery of loss is conveyed by elderly talents, who bring to the subject an intimacy with death and aging. It is an altogether riveting moment.

Ostensibly dealing with relationships, Yip and Harold's final song actually afforded Yip one last opportunity to write a testament to the dreamer who outlasts the dream:

END OF A BEAUTIFUL FRIENDSHIP

Looks like the end of a beautiful friendship
Looks like I'm back in circulation again
Sounds like love's old refrain is waning
Sounds like the end of a grand amen

Looks like the fairy tale season is over
Gone is the palace and the pumpkin and all
Gone is the true prince
With the blue prints
Gone is the Cinderella and the magic ball

Ring bells
Ring out the merry, but temporary, bride
Ring out the weddin' march that's headin'
Straight for the great divide
Hallelujah!

Here's to the end of a beautiful friendship
Here's to the star-dust that we promised to share
Here's to our beautiful illusions
May they still be there . . .
For my next affair.

It is the lyric of a songwriter who has been in and out of innumerable creative partnerships, two marriages, numerous ideological passions, the lyric of an utterly serious but irreverent romantic. The song, said Yip, was about "the feeling that life is a series of trials and errors, and that there was still a next time. . . . But also, if you die when the dream dies, then you're not really a civilized person." A tough idea for neophyte idealists.

While Yip's emotions during these years were surely mixed with anger and sadness, his tone remained witty and whimsical. Now, he quipped, the kids were "pulling his legacy." In the early seventies, Yip wrote another song with his old collaborator, Sammy Fain, that dealt with the sixties generation. Later Yip explained:

A songwriter is really a journalist of the time with music. I mean, I've got to be au courant, or there'd be no hit songs, would there? Anyhow, yes, I thought very much about the younger generation and their conflict about themselves, about love—this is an age of conflict. Nobody knows what love is. Who they are. Or where they are. In my time we were cocky. We knew where we were going—and we went straight to hell.

I, WHOEVER I AM

I, whoever I am
Love, whatever that is
You, whoever you are
If I could let my heart commit me

Bells would probably ring
Birds would possibly sing
Stars would fall from the sky
But I wouldn't know what hit me

My little world isn't ready for Aquarius
Bang-ups and hang-ups can split a guy in two
But if ever my heart
Dares to make up its mind
I won't be just a blind
Stray little, frail little lamb

I'll love you so
If ever I know
Whoever I am.

In the early seventies Yip and Fain also wrote the nostalgic "Where Has the Rainbow Gone?" and Yip wanted to use this also in a retrospective revue for which his songs would provide the libretto. Yip almost got the show off the ground with producer Claire Nichtern in the midseventies: "The show is a chronicle of the past half century," Yip said,

> my life and times in rhyme. It shows that everything changes and everything stays the same. It is nostalgic because the songs are familiar, but it is also timely. The show is about hustling rainbows, selling skies of blue. The songs become the libretto.

While this particular effort broke up in the "Buffalo shootout" (the director was fired before the opening and the choreographer and actors quit the show), Yip continued work on the concept and new songs for "the revue" for the rest of his life. In his appearances at New York's Ninety-second Street Y (whose "Lyrics and Lyricists" series he helped conceive with Maurice Levine and inaugurated in 1970), on the *Dick Cavett Show,* on CBS's *60 Minutes,* Yip was able to bring his work—in piecemeal fashion, to be sure—before new audiences.

In 1978, Yip teamed up with Phil Springer, a much younger, rock-and-pop-oriented composer. Over the last three years of Yip's life, the team produced fifteen songs. Springer recalls,

Yip, about age eighty, still kept his sense of hard-edged wonder and puckish humor; he became mentor to many younger writers. In 1980 he and other Broadway writers helped found the Musical Theatre Program at New York University's Tisch School of the Arts, which in the early nineties is still the only university-based writing program in which authors and composers collaborate to create musical plays. (Collection of Harburg Estate.)

Yip always wanted these songs for a revue. He was really planning a revue; we didn't think of [these songs] as pop. But Yip, depending on the song we wrote, was hoping we could have a couple of popular hits, real, real hard.

Some of Yip's work with Springer represented his attempt to come to terms with a new music and a new world from which he felt profoundly estranged. Yip introduced one of these songs at his 1980 concert at the Ninety-second Street Y:

I decided to come out of the dark rock of ages into the luminous age of rock with a song by Phil Springer at the piano, which I hope will hit the Top 40 while I'm still in the low eighties. It will be played in all the disco shelters where the bombs can still fall on you, but you won't be able to hear them.

The prices go up and the dollar goes down
The heavenly smog hangs over the town
But the crazy old world goes spinnin' along
And I keep singin' my crazy song
They say it's all gonna end in a bang
But somehow I know I'll go hangin' on

The fish can't swim, the birds can't fly
The mushroom cloud floats merrily by
But the crazy old world goes spinnin' around
And I keep makin' my crazy sound
And echoes of my simple song
Will linger when the whole thing's long, long gone

Old Billy Graham is hawkin' the hereafter
The Rev'rend Moon keeps selling me the sky
But the ancient breeze still rocks the trees
With laughter, ever livin' laughter
While they cry

They've given up on the human race
The only hope is up in space
When the eagle crows and Wall Street cracks
And they all go to heaven in Cadillacs
I'll still be finger pickin' on my guitar
Pickin' out notes where the sweet dreams are
In song
While the crazy old world goes spinnin' spinnin' along
Spinnin', spinnin' ever spinnin' with me hangin' on

When Moscow missiles whistle, "Hello Frisco"
And crazy shooting stars go zooming by
The test tube babes will rave
"Hey, dig that disco"
Psychedelic disco in the sky

They'll boogie on down to kingdom come
With Gabriel's horn and Lucifer's drum
And the heavens will rock and the firmament roll
And the oil come a-gushing out of Hollywood Bowl

I'll still be finger pickin' on my guitar
Pickin' out notes where the sweet dreams are
In song
While the crazy old world goes spinnin' spinnin' along
Spinnin', spinnin' ever spinnin' with me hangin' on.

"Yip was searching for a contemporary way of expression," Phil Springer said, but:

> We didn't have any time. That's the problem. Yip was tired. He had pneumonia the year that we were working. If we had had the time we would have searched for a contemporary mode of expression. I would have forced us into it and he would have gone along with it. The only problem with Yip was that he couldn't find a guy that he was comfortable with, not that he didn't want to write contemporary.

In the seventies, Yip wrote several songs with Sammy Fain; one is a tribute to a great comedian. Yip talked about it with an interviewer in 1980:

> Not to have known Jimmy Durante is not to have known my favorite comedian. He was married to a lovely lady who died long before Jimmy did. It was a dear and darling marriage, and he had cute and endearing terms for her. He always called her Mrs. Calabash. And every time he was through with a program on television, he walked downstage and a spotlight hit him, and in the shadow of that spotlight he'd always say his parting words, "Goodnight Mrs. Calabash, wherever you are."

GOODNIGHT MRS. CALABASH, WHEREVER YOU ARE

Goodnight Mrs. Calabash
Wherever you are
Are you waving at me
From your favorite star?

The star that you wished on
When once we were young
For dreams to be dreamed
And songs to be sung

Goodnight Mrs. Calabash
I blow you a kiss
'Til we meet and we laugh
And perhaps reminisce

Then finally I'm sure that we
Will know the myst'ry of
The unfinished song that will go on
As long as there's love.

"The aim of a song," Yip once said, "is to make a specific thing general, to give a thing a universal quality rather than a specific quality"—and his intent here was to "touch everybody, whether you knew Jimmy Durante or not. [Mrs. Calabash] came to finally symbolize, I suppose, that rare thing called a good marriage."

Yip kept returning to write with his old comrades. In 1980, when Yip handed Burt Lane the title of this next song, Lane created a tune within the great Broadway musical tradition, and Yip responded with a lyric that returned to some of the themes (and one of the lines) of his 1932 Vernon Duke collaboration, "Where Have We Met Before?" This was Yip and Burt's last song together, and Burt and Maxine Sullivan first recorded it in 1990.

Where Have I Seen Your Face Before?

Where have I seen your face before?
Where did your eyes meet mine?
Was it in time or space before
Or on some Valentine?

Where did we greet the dawn before
Once when the world was fair?
Was it in Glocca Morra or
Perhaps in Berkeley Square?

Maybe in a thousand years
Someday in some garden
I will look at you this way and say
"Beg your pardon"

Where have I seen your face before
Lighting my way to grace?
How did I face the world before,
Before I saw your face?

Yip was adjusting inwardly and physically to older age and the Great Disappearance. He reflected on it with his characteristic humor—as Noel Langley once said of him, taking "the world seriously, but himself lightly."

Gerontology or Springtime for Senility

At forty I lost my illusions,
At fifty I lost my hair,
At sixty my hope and teeth were gone
And my feet were beyond repair.

At eighty, life has clipped my claws,
I'm bent and bowed and cracked—
But I can't give up the ghost because
My follies are all intact.

Although not his final lyric, "Time, You Old Gypsy Man," written in 1979 with Phil Springer, can easily be read as Yip's final summing up. When Phil played him the music, he was inspired to compose a lyric about the lyricist's symbols and the lyricist's craft, about youth and romance—and about time's theft of them all.

TIME, YOU OLD GYPSY MAN

Time, you old gypsy man
Thief on the wing
Drugged me with rhapsodies
Tricked me with Spring

Fiddled me off my feet
Danced me on air
Sprinkled my daydreams with golddust
Then silvered my hair

Silvered my hair you rogue
Crinkled my eyes
Whistled the bird of youth
Out of my skies

Time, you old vagabond
Riddle me this
What did you do with forever and ever
That sealed every kiss?

You packed up your tambourines
Stilled your guitars
Slipped off into the night
Turned off the stars

Stripped me song and spring
Robbed me of rhyme
Fled in your carnival caravan
But you old gypsy man—
Thanks for a glorious time.

The withdrawal of song and spring and rhyme in the final stanza clearly means nothing less than the taking away of life itself.

And Death

On March 5, 1981, Yip, one month shy of eighty-five, was driving alone on Sunset Boulevard in Brentwood, California, near his old home on Bentley Drive when he was instantly struck dead due to a massive heart convulsion whose features were foreshadowed several years before. His car drifted across the lane at slow speed after a stoplight, and ran into an oncoming car head on. No one in the other car was injured, and that driver reported that he saw no one at the wheel of Yip's car. The media reported inaccurately that Yip's death was due to the car accident. He was on his way to a story conference for a film version of Robert Louis Stevenson's *Treasure Island.*

Afterword

Without a final cadence, there is no song. And at the end of the great ballads, there is a lingering warm, sweet, and joyous sorrow. All these feelings will remain in the hearts of those of us who loved Yip's great lyrics, the great songs and the man himself.

> So, good night, Yipper, wherever you are.
> We blow you a kiss
> To your favorite star . . .
>
> And finally, we know
> The mystery of
> That unfinished song
> That will go on
> As long as there's love.

Epilogue: Yip On Cosmic Mysteries

Life is short, short, brother!
Ain' it de truth?
And there is no other
Ain' it de truth?

So if you don't love living
You is slightly uncouth,

Oh! Ain' it de dignified truth?

If you want to be a writer, an actor, an artist, you've got to ask what you're living for, what life is about. We're here on this planet, a very small earth in a big galaxy within a bigger firmament, and everything is a question of birth and growth and life and death and mystery and the beautiful thing of trying to find out why we're here. Maybe we never will. But the process of discovery . . . is basic.

The ability to use our imagination is, I think, the reason for being alive, and the reason for man's existence. Whatever it was that created this mystery called life, that we're all looking for, that we're paying gurus to tell us about, and trying to find a reason for in the stars—it's clear that our ability to imagine is limitless. The world which starts with a blob of protoplasm has developed, as we know from Darwinian theories, from an amoeba to a man. And man has an imagination which is greater than the "hard" reality of life.

WE IS MARCHIN'

Nature is a copiously
Hopeful cornucopia
Of protoplasmic organisms
Groping for utopia.

Before you start anything, however, whether it's a song or a poem or a building, you've got to have a plan. Before you have a plan, though, you have the dream; and it's there you find your inspiration. Where that inspiration comes from is a mystery, but every human being is blessed with a computer up here, a brain, where lies the marvelous ability to imagine, the ability to dream. This is what separates animal from man. Animals cannot dream. . . . Nor can they laugh, or understand a joke and this is what makes man really the superior animal. So we must use laughter as a means for educating, teaching.

FOR THE MAN OF EXTINCTION

Hammacher Schlemmer is selling a shelter,
A push button palace, fluorescent repose;
Electric devices
For facing a crisis
With frozen fruit ices and cinema shows.

Hammacher Schlemmer is selling a shelter,
All chromium kitchens and rubber tile dorms;
With water-proof portals
To echo the chortles
Of weatherproof mortals in hydrogen storms.

What a great come-to-glory emporium,
To enjoy a deluxe moratorium,
Where nuclear heat
Can beguile the elite
In a crème-de-la-crème crematorium!

One of the things that bothered me about my society was that there were so many problems in the world. My approach to solving these problems was to make people see the folly of them, the foibles of them, or the mythology of them. If you look at them from an Olympian point of view, like Puck in *Midsummer Night's Dream,* and say, "What fools these mortals be," then you can make people laugh. And if you can make them laugh, you can make them see their follies. And if they see their follies, they will analyze their problems, and then maybe get the solutions. So laughter and humor play an important part in my approach to the theatre. . . . When you lose humor, you're in a disaster area.

FAIL SAFE

It's a hundred billion dollars
Every year at your expense,
For the Pentagon to gadget up
Our national defense.

But it's comforting to know that
In the up and coming war,
We'll be dying far more safely
Than we ever died before.

That doesn't say humor is the only approach. Everybody approaches his art through his own psyche and methods. I am giving you mine. My approach is through satire because humor is the greatest solvent that I know of. It takes the arrogance out of people. We all hear many different political views. People disagree so strongly they even want to kill each other.

History

We learn this after every war,
That life is not worth dying for.

Fission Fashion

When nuclear dust has extinguished their betters,
Will the turtles surviving wear people-neck sweaters?

We've Come a Long Way, Buddy

An ape, who from the zoo broke free,
  Was cornered in the library
With Darwin tucked beneath one arm,
  The Bible 'neath the other.

"I can't make up my mind," said he,
  "Just who on earth I seem to be—
Am I my brother's keeper
  Or am I my keeper's brother?"

I'm a fellow who's watched the human situation over the years with a satiric eye. I'm always asking people, are you going to live your lives in a Greek tragedy, or take a chance and buy a ticket on a ship, to who-knows-where, and try to give people a little fun along the way. . . .

Seated One Day at the Organ

When our organs have been transplanted
And the new ones made happy to lodge in us,
Let us pray one wish be granted—
We retain our zones erogenous.

The gags in a farce make you laugh, but the people are not real and what they say has little human or emotional content. What is important in dramatic theatre is the conflict. Loving each other and fighting each other. The intolerant, and the intolerant being antagonized . . . the paradox of life; this is the paradox of human relationships and the basis of true art.

Repent in Pleasure

A little secret sinning now and then,
Should not disturb the saintliest of men;
For when your life is spent, and sun has set,
'Tis easier to repent than to regret.

Do unto Others?

"Love thy neighbors as thyself?"
Hide that motto on the shelf!
Let it lie there, keep it idle
Especially if you're suicidal.

I think that the world is an experiment. A man in a laboratory experiments with a test tube, so the world is nature's experiment. Nature is to survive. Nature is to have birth, creation, growth and it is constantly trying to find a species that will live in harmony with its laws and all its elements. And so far she has tried many species. She's tried the albatross and the albatross went out of business. She's tried the dinosaur; the dinosaur went out of business. As soon as they get too big for themselves, and too powerful, something happens to the species. In fact, nature has tried hundreds and hundreds of species. Man is nothing more than another species which so far has shown the greatest acumen for survival, but he is not any greater than any of these other species, and nature has no use for a guest that is not a good guest. . . . If we can't be decent human beings and have respect for one another and know the laws of nature and the laws of mankind, nature's got no use for us and will wipe us out as easily as she did any of the smaller species.

Columbus is a circle
And a day off
Pershing is a square
What a pay-off
Julius Caesar is just a salad on the shelf
So little brother get wise to yourself

Life's a bowl and it's
Full of cherry pits
Play it big and it throws you for a loop
That's the way with fate
Comes today we're great
Comes tomorrow we're tomato soup

Napoleon's a pastry
Get this under your brow
All those big wig controversials
Are all commercials now.

Reality in life is digging, planting seeds, pulling wheat out of the ground, selling it to somebody, he resells it, you make a profit, you eat, you pay rent. We all can do that, but you don't progress that way. The way you progress is by dreaming of a society so much superior to the one that's passed—one step at a time—that man will finally evolve into the kind of human being that at present we do not dream of.

ON A CLEAR DAY FROM MOUNT WILSON

With magic gear through stratosphere
    Beyond the stars we grope,
But there's more to be found
    In the drop of a tear
Than there is in a telescope.

How do we make the society work, and still not let our temperaments or our egos stand in the way? How do we get a better man? We've had all the fine miracle revolutions the world could possibly dream of. We've learned to fly, we've learned to use atomic energy, in medicine we've made terrific strides, but we have not yet learned how to curb our egos, how to think honestly, without the primitive emotions of greed, power or hostility getting in the way.

OH SOLAR MIO

The world would be a safer place,
    If someone had a plan,
Before exploring Outer Space,
    To find the Inner man.

It'll take a long time for man to evolve. That's why we need a different system right from the beginning, a different goal for what man is about on this earth, and different training from kindergarten up. We've got to make a new man. We've got to make a social man rather than an individual conqueror. This is the toughest thing that we have to deal with. The brain . . . is capable of devising some day a social system that will be more in tune with man's basic instincts to love and to survive.

But before you can use your imagination, you must have something to imagine with, a basis for imagining on, and the basis is your literature, poetry and the values of which I've been talking. And now you are ready to go ahead and start planning.

SIMPLE ANSWERS TO COSMIC MYSTERIES

To the Puzzle of Space and Spheres:
Cheers!

To the riddle of life's dim goal:
Skoal!

To the wherefore of cosmic ray:
Santé!

To the reaper and all his brood:
Salud!

To the heaven or hell above ya:
Naz Darovya!

To the transience of human beauty:
Saluté!

To the folly of man's grim tale:
Wassail!

To the furious fates that defy him:
L'Chaim!

"And the feeling that life is a series of trials and errors, and that there is still a next time . . . but also, if you die when the dream dies, then you're not really a civilized person." E. Y. (Yip) Harburg. (Photo by Barbara Bordnick.)

Appendixes

Musical Theater: Plays and Songs of E. Y. Harburg

Earl Carroll's Sketch Book (revue)

Produced by Earl Carroll at the Earl Carroll Theater. Opened July 1, 1929. 400 performances. Directed by Earl Carroll. Dialogue staged by Edgar MacGregor. Choreographed by LeRoy Prinz. *Lyrics* by E. Y. Harburg, Irving Kahal, Benee Russell, Charles Tobias, Harry Tobias, Benny Davis, Abner Silver, Jean Herbert, Billy Rose. *Music* by Jay Gorney, Phil Cohen, Arnold Johnson, Benee Russell, Vincent Rose, Charles Tobias, Ted Snyder, Abner Silver, Irving Actman. Sketches by Eddie Cantor; additional dialogue by Eddie Welch. Sets by Bernard Lohmuller. Lights by Max Teuber. Costumes by Florence Weber.

Cast included William Demarest and Patsy Kelly.

Songs: "Legs, Legs, Legs," "Kinda Cute," "Like Me Less, Love Me More," "Papa Likes a Hot Papoose" (Gorney); "Crashing the Golden Gates" (Gorney, Cohen).

The Garrick Gaieties (revue)

Produced by the Theatre Guild at the Guild Theater. Opened June 4, 1930; 158 performances. Reopened October 16, 1930, for 12 performances. Directed by Philip Loeb. Choreographed by Olin Howland. *Lyrics* by E. Y. Harburg, Ira Gershwin, Allen Boretz, Edward Eliscu, Henry Myers, Newman Levy, Paul James, Thomas McKnight, Willard Robison, Johnny Mercer, Josiah Titzell, Harold Goldman, Ronald Jeans. *Music* by Vernon Duke, Marc Blitzstein, Richard Myers, Ned Lehac, Charles M. Schwab, Kay Swift, Thomas McKnight, Willard Robison, Everett Miller, Peter Nolan. Sketches by Carroll Carroll, Leo Poldine (Leopoldine Damrosch), Sally Humason, Gretchen Damrosch Finletter, Landon Herrick, Sterling Holloway, Benjamin M. Kaye, Newman Levy, Louis M. Simon. Sets by Kate Drain Lawson. Costumes by Kate Drain Lawson, Louis M. Simon.

Cast included Philip Loeb, Sterling Holloway, Nan Blackstone, Ruth Chorpenning, Imogene Coca, Ray Heatherton.

Songs: "I Am Only Human After All," "Too, Too Divine" (Duke/lyrics cowritten by Gershwin); "Shavian Shivers" (Duke).

Earl Carroll Vanities (Eighth edition) (revue)

Produced by Earl Carroll at the New Amsterdam Theater. Opened July 1, 1930. 215 performances. Directed by Earl Carroll. Dialogue staged by Priestly Morrison. Choreographed by LeRoy Prinz. *Lyrics* by E. Y. Harburg, Ted Kohler, Reg Connelly, James Campbell, Stella Unger. *Music* by Jay Gorney, Harold Arlen, Ray Noble, James P. Johnson. Sketches by Eddie Welch, Eugene Conrad. Sets by Hugh Willoughby. Costumes by Charles LeMaire, Florence Weber, Vincente Minnelli.

Cast included Jimmy Savo, Jack Benny, Patsy Kelly.

Songs: "Kneedeep in June," "Love Boats," "I Came to Life," "Going Up" (Gorney). The following songs are listed on card in archive file but do not appear in program: "Ring Out the Blues," "Ah, Jus' Like You," "Troubadours" (Gorney); "Old Devil Sea," "Baby, Be Yourself," "Hold Your Man," "Laugh It Down" (Duke); "Glory," "Can't Get Along," "Foolish Baby" (Johnny Green/lyrics cowritten by Robert Tours and E. Heyman); "Oh My, What a Wonderful World" (Gorney/lyrics cowritten by Robert Tours). ASCAP list also includes "Ring Out the Blues."

The Vanderbilt Revue

Produced by Lew Fields, Lyle D. Andrews at the Vanderbilt Theater. Opened November 5, 1930. 13 performances. Directed by Lew Fields, Theodore J. Hammerstein. Choreographed by John E. Lonergan, Jack Haskell. *Lyrics* by E. Y. Harburg, Dorothy Fields, Ben Black, David Sidney, Edward Eliscu. *Music* by Mario Braggiotti, Jimmy McHugh, Jacques Fray, Edward Horan, Ben Black. Sketches by Kenyon Nicholson, Ellis O. Jones, Sig Herzig, Edwin Gilbert, Arthur Burns, James Coghlan, E. North. Sets by Ward & Harvey. Costumes by Robert Stevenson.

Cast included Joe Penner, Evelyn Hoey, M. Dalsky's Russian Choir, Lulu McConnell.

Song: "Ex-Gigolo" (Braggiotti).

Billy Rose's Crazy Quilt (revue) (also known as Crazy Quilt)

Produced by Billy Rose at the Forty-fourth Street Theatre. Opened May 19, 1931. 79 performances. Directed by Billy Rose. *Lyrics* by E. Y. Harburg, Billy Rose, Ira Gershwin, Bud Green, Mort Dixon, Edward Eliscu, Ned Wever, James Dyrenforth, Lorenz Hart, Edgar Leslie. *Music* by Lou Alter, Milton Ager, Richard Rodgers, Ned Lehac, Rowland Wilson, Carroll Gibbons, James V. Monaco, Manning Sherwin. Sketches by David Freedman; additional dialogue by Herman Timberg. Choreographed by Sammy Lee. Lights by Clark Robinson. Costumes by Fanny Brice.

Cast included Fanny Brice, Phil Baker, Tamara.

Songs: "The Crazy Quilt Sextette" (composer unknown/lyrics cowritten by Rose). Chicago program (Shubert Apollo Theater, October 4, 1931): "Ladies of the Evening" (composer unknown), "It's in the Air" (Alter/lyrics cowritten by Rose); "Oh, It Looks Like Rain" (Ager).

Ziegfeld Follies (1931) (revue)

Produced by Florenz Ziegfeld, assisted by Gene Buck at the Ziegfeld Theatre. Opened July 1, 1931. 165 performances. Directed by Edward Clarke Lilley. Choreographed by Bobby Connolly. *Lyrics* by E. Y. Harburg, Gene Buck, Barry Trivers, J. P. Murray, Mack Gordon, Noel Coward, Charles Farrell. *Music* by Jay Gorney, Hugo Riesenfeld, Dave Stamper, Ben Oakland, Harry Revel, Dimitri Tiomkin, Noel Coward. Sketches by J. P. Murray, Mark Hellinger, Gene Buck. Sets by Joseph Urban. Costumes by John W. Harkrider.

Cast included Harry Richman, Ford Buck and John Bubbles, Ruth Etting, Helen Morgan.

Song: "Mailu" (Gorney, Riesenfeld).

Shoot the Works! (revue)

Produced by Heywood Broun, in association with Milton Raison at the George M. Cohan Theater. Opened July 21, 1931. 87 performances. Directed by Ted Hammerstein. Choreographed by Johnny Boyle. *Lyrics* by E. Y. Harburg, Irving Berlin, Ira Gershwin, Leo Robin, Dorothy Fields, Ann Ronell, Alexander Williams, Herbert Goode, Max and Nathaniel Lief, Walter Reisch. *Music* by Jay Gorney, Vernon Duke, Irving Berlin, Joseph Meyer, Philip Charig, Robert Stolz, Jimmy McHugh, Ann Ronell, Alexander Williams, Michael H. Cleary. Sketches by Nunnally Johnson, H. I. Phillips, Dorothy Parker, Heywood Broun, E. B. White, Peter Arno, Sig Herzig, Milton Lazarus, Jack Hazzard, Edward J. MacNamara, Muriel Pollock, Herbert Goode. Sets and lights by Henry Dreyfuss. Costumes by Charles LeMaire, Kiviette.

Cast included Heywood Broun, Imogene Coca, George Murphy.

Songs: "Muchacha" (Gorney, Duke), "Hot Moonlight" (Gorney).

Ballyhoo of 1932

Produced by Norman Anthony, Lewis Gensler, Bobby Connolly and Russell Patterson. Opened at the 44th Street Theatre on September 6, 1932. 95 performances. Directed by Messrs. Anthony, Connolly, Gensler, Patterson and Gus Shy. Choreographed by Bobby Connolly. *Lyrics* by E. Y. Harburg. *Music* by Lewis Gensler. Sketches by Norman Anthony; additional dialogue by Sig Herzig. Sets and costumes by Russell Patterson.

Cast included Willie and Eugene Howard, Jeanne Albert, Lulu McConnell, Bob Hope, Vera Marshe, Hugh Cameron, Gloria Gilbert, Tom Harty, Donald Stewart, Albertina Rasch Dancers (headed by Dorissa Nelova).

Songs: "Falling Off the Wagon," "Thrill Me," "Old-Fashioned Wedding," "How Do You Do It?" "Man About Yonkers," "Ballyhujah," "Love and Nuts and Noodles (Bring 'Em Back Alive)," "Riddle Me This," "What Have You Got to Have."

Additional songs which do not appear in program but were listed by Yip Harburg in Yale University's archive materials: "I'm Off of You," "Ballyhooey Lassies (Opening Act II)," "I'm Tired of Love," "I Lerve You," "Baby, We're Through," "You Didn't Do Right by

Me" (earlier version of "Buds Won't Bud"), "How About a Little Date for Breakfast?" "She'll Be Coming 'Round the Catskill Mountains," "As Long as We Have Bromo Seltzer in Our Love Nest."

Per ASCAP List: "You Satisfy," "Thank My Stars," "I'm One of God's Children" (all published 1958).

(J. P. McEvoy's New) Americana (revue)

Produced by Lee Shubert at the Shubert Theatre. Opened October 5, 1932. 77 performances. Directed by Harold Johnsrud. Choreographed by John Boyle, Charles Weidman. *Lyrics* by E. Y. Harburg, Johnny Mercer. *Music* by Jay Gorney, Richard Myers, Harold Arlen, Burton Lane, Henry Souvaine. Sketches by J. P. McEvoy. Sets and lights by Albert R. Johnson. Costumes by Constance Ripley.

Cast included Charles Weidman and Dancers (including Jose Limon), Doris Humphrey Dance Group.

Songs: "Uncle Sam Needs a Man Who Can Take It" (composer unknown); "Get That Sun into You" (Myers); "Whistling for a Kiss" (Myers/lyrics cowritten by Mercer); "Satan's Li'l Lamb" (Arlen/lyrics cowritten by Mercer); "You're Not Pretty but You're Mine" (Lane); "Brother, Can You Spare a Dime?" "Five Minutes of Spring" (Gorney); "Let Me Match My Private Life with Yours" (Duke).

The Great Magoo (play with music)

Produced by Billy Rose at the Selwyn Theater. Opened on December 2, 1932. 11 performances. *Lyrics* by E. Y. Harburg, Billy Rose. *Music* by Harold Arlen. Book by Ben Hecht, Gene Fowler. Sets by Herman Rosse. Costumes by Constance Ripley.

Cast included Charlotte Granville, Victor Kilian, Dennie Moore, Jack Hazzard.

Song: "It's Only a Paper Moon" ("If You Believed in Me") (lyrics "cowritten" by Rose)

Walk a Little Faster (revue)

Produced by Courtney Burr at the St. James Theatre. Opened December 7, 1932. 119 performances. Directed by Monty Woolley. Choreographed by Albertina Rasch. *Lyrics* by E. Y. Harburg. *Music* by Vernon Duke. Sketches by S. J. Perelman, Robert McGunigle. Sets by Boris Aronson. Costumes by Kiviette.

Cast included Bobby Clark, Paul McCullough, John Hundley, Donald Burr, Dave and Dorothy Fitzgibbon, Evelyn Hoey.

Songs: "That's Life," "Unaccustomed As I Am," "Off Again, On Again," "April in Paris," "Where Have We Met Before?" "A Penny for Your Thoughts," "So Nonchalant (lyrics cowritten by C. Tobias)," "Time and Tide," "Speaking of Love," "End of a Perfect Night," "Manhattan's the Loneliest Isle" (cut).

Ziegfeld Follies (1933–34 edition)

Produced by Mrs. Florenz Ziegfeld (Billie Burke), Shuberts (uncredited) at the Winter Garden Theater. Opened January 4, 1934. 182 performances. Directed by Bobby Connolly, John Murray Anderson, Edward Clarke Lilley, E. Hartman. Choreographed by Robert Alton. *Lyrics* by E. Y. Harburg, Ballard MacDonald, Billy Rose, Billy Hill, Edward Heyman. *Music* by Vernon Duke, Samuel Pokrass, Joseph Meyer, Richard Myers, Dana Suesse, Peter DeRose, Billy Hill, James F. Hanley. Sketches by H. I. Phillips, Fred Allen, Harry Tugend, David Freedman. Sets by Watson Barratt, Albert R. Johnson. Lights by John Murray Anderson. Costumes by Russell Patterson, Raoul Pene du Bois, Charles LeMaire, Kiviette.

Cast included Fanny Brice, Jane Froman, Willie and Eugene Howard, Vilma and Buddy Ebsen, Eve Arden, Everett Marshall, Brice Hutchins (Robert Cummings), Ina Ray (Hutton).

Songs: "That's Where We Come In," "The Follies Choral Ensemble," "Fifth Avenue—A Sidewalk in Paris," "To the Beat of My Heart," "Careful with My Heart" (Pokrass); "Moon about Town" (Suesse); "Suddenly" (Duke/lyrics cowritten by Rose); "This Is Not a Song" (Duke/lyrics cowritten by Hartman); "Time Is a Gypsy" (Myers); "Water under the Bridge," "I Like the Likes of You," "What Is There to Say," "(It's) Smart to Be Smart" (cut), "Stop That Clock" (cut) (Duke).

New Faces (of 1934) (revue)

Produced by Charles Dillingham at the Fulton Theater. Opened March 15, 1934. 149 performances. Conceived and directed by Leonard Sillman. Production supervised by Elsie Janis. *Lyrics* by E. Y. Harburg, Viola Brothers Shore, Nancy Hamilton, June Sillman, Everett Marcy, J. J. Robbins, Robert Sour, Harold Goldman, James Shelton, Haven Johnson, George Hickman. *Music* by Morgan Lewis, Warburton Guilbert, Donald Honrath, George Grande, Martha Caples, James Shelton, Walter Feldkamp, Cliff Allen, Haven Johnson, George Hickman, Charles Schwab, Sandro Corona. Sketches by Viola Brothers Shore, Nancy Hamilton, Newman Levy, John Goodwin, William Griffith, Mindret Lord, Beth Wendall. Sets and costumes by Sergei Soudeikine.

Cast included Leonard Sillman, Imogene Coca, Henry Fonda.

Song: "'Cause You Won't Play House" (Lewis/lyrics cowritten by Hamilton).

Life Begins at 8:40 (revue)

Produced by Messrs. Shubert at the Winter Garden Theater. Opened August 27, 1934. 237 Performances. Directed by John Murray Anderson, Philip Loeb. Choreographed by Robert Alton and Charles Weidman. *Lyrics* by E. Y. Harburg and Ira Gershwin. *Music* by Harold Arlen. Sketches by Ira Gershwin and E. Y. Harburg, David Freedman, H. I. Phillips, Alan Baxter, Henry Clapp Smith, Frank Gabrielson. Sets by Albert Johnson. Costumes by Kiviette, James Reynolds, Raoul Pene du Bois, Billy Livingston, Wynn, Pauline Lawrence, Irene Scharaff.

Cast included Bert Lahr, Ray Bolger, Brian Donlevy, Luella Gear, Frances Williams, Dixie Dunbar, Charles Weidman Dancers.

Songs: "Life Begins," "Spring Fever," "You're a Builder Upper," "My Paramount-Publix-Roxy Rose," "Shoein' the Mare," "Quartet Erotica (We're Not What We Used To Be)," "Fun to Be Fooled," "C'est la Vie," "What Can You Say in a Love Song," "Let's Take a Walk around the Block," "Things," "(All) The Elks and Masons," "It Was Long Ago," "I Couldn't Hold My Man," "Weekend Cruise (Will You Love Me Monday Morning as You Did on Friday Night?)," "Beautifying the City," "I Knew Him When" (cut), "I'm A Collector of Moonbeams" (cut).

Continental Varieties (vaudeville revue)

Produced by Arch Selwyn, Harold B. Franklin at the Little Theatre. Opened October 3, 1934. 77 performances. No director listed. *Lyrics* by E. Y. Harburg. *Music* by Jean Delettre, Manuel de Falla. Book—Mr. Balieff's discourses by Irving Caesar. Costumes by Jeanne Lanvin, Marcel Rochas.

Cast included Vicente Escudero, with his Sacre Mont Gypsies and Carmita, Deslys and Clark.

Song: "I Need New Words" (Delettre).

Stop Press (revue)

Produced by Hassard Short at the Adelphi Theater (London). Opened February 21, 1935. Directed by Clifford Wheatley. *Lyrics* by E. Y. Harburg, Edward Heyman. *Music* by Johnny Green.

Cast included Dorothy Dickson, Edwin Styles, Charles Collins, Eve Becke, Margaret Sande.

Song: "How Can I Hold You Close Enough?"

The Show Is On (revue)

Produced by Messrs. Shubert at the Winter Garden Theater. 237 performances. Opened December 25, 1936; reopened September 18, 1937 for 17 performances. Directed by Vincente Minnelli, Edward Clarke Lilley. Choreographed by Robert Alton. *Lyrics* by E. Y. Harburg, Howard Dietz, Lorenz Hart, Ira Gershwin, Norman Zeno, Ted Fetter, Stanley Adams, Herman Hupfeld. *Music* by Harold Arlen, Vernon Duke, Will Irwin, Arthur Schwartz, Hoagy Carmichael, Richard Rodgers, George Gershwin, Herman Hupfeld. Sketches by David Freedman, Moss Hart.

Cast included Beatrice Lillie, Bert Lahr, Reginald Gardiner, Mitzi Mayfair, Paul Haakon, Gracie Barrie.

Songs: "Song of the Woodman" (Arlen), "Long As You've Got Your Health" (Irwin/lyrics cowritten by Zeno).

Hooray for What?

Produced by Messrs. Shubert at the Winter Garden Theater. Opened December 1, 1937. 200 performances. Directed by Howard Lindsay. Choreographed by Robert Alton. Ballets by Agnes de Mille. *Lyrics* by E. Y. Harburg. *Music* by Harold Arlen. Book conceived by E. Y. Harburg, written by Howard Lindsay and Russel Crouse, from an idea by E. Y. Harburg. Sets by Vincente Minnelli. Costumes by Raoul Pene du Bois.

Cast included Ed Wynn, Paul Haakon, June Clyde, Vivian Vance, Jack Whiting, Leo Chalzel, Hugh Martin, Ralph Blane, Five Reillys, Sue Hastings Marionettes, Al Gordon's Dogs.

Songs: "Hooray for What?" "God's Country," "I've Gone Romantic on You," "Moanin' in the Mornin'," "Viva for Geneva," "Life's a Dance," "Napoleon's a Pastry" (cut after opening), "Down with Love," "A Fashion Girl," "That Night at the Embassy Ball," "In the Shade of the New Apple Tree," "Buds Won't Bud" (cut), "I Click Ze Heel and Keez Ze Hand" (cut).

Hold on to Your Hats

Produced by Al Jolson and George Hale at the Shubert Theater. Opened September 11, 1940. 158 performances. Directed by Egdar MacGregor. Choreographed by Catherine Littlefield. *Lyrics* by E. Y. Harburg. *Music* by Burton Lane. Book by Guy Bolton, Matt Brooks, Eddie Davis. Sets and costumes by Raoul Pene du Bois. Lights by Feder.

Cast included Al Jolson, Martha Raye, Jack Whiting, Bert Gordon, Gil Lamb, Jinx Falkenburg, Joyce Matthews.

Songs: "Way Out West Where the East Begins," "Hold on to Your Hats," "Walkin' Along Mindin' My Business," "The World Is in My Arms," "Would You Be So Kindly," "Life Was Pie for the Pioneer," "Don't Let It Get You Down," "There's a Great Day Coming Mañana," "Then You Were Never in Love," "Down on the Dude Ranch," "She Came, She Saw, She Can Canned," "Old-Timer," "Swing Your Calico" (cut), "Looks Like I'm Off'o Ya (Now That I'm on to Ya')" (cut), "Bedtime on the Prairie" (cut), "Crispy, Crunchy Crackers" (unused).

Sticks and Stones (political revue)

Produced by Motion Picture Artists' Committee. Opened in Los Angeles in 1941. *Lyrics* by E. Y. Harburg, Ira Gershwin. *Music* by Johnny Green.

Song: "Baby, You're News."

Bloomer Girl

Produced by John C. Wilson in association with Nat Goldstone. Opened October 5, 1944 at the Shubert Theatre. 654 performances. Directed by E. Y. Harburg, William Schorr. Choreographed by Agnes de Mille. *Lyrics* by E. Y. Harburg. *Music* by Harold Arlen. Book by Sig Herzig, Fred Saidy, based on the play by Lilith and Dan James. Sets and Lights by Lemuel Ayers. Costumes by Miles White.

Cast included Celeste Holm, Margaret Douglass, Joan McCracken, David Brooks, Dooley Wilson, Mabel Taliaferro, Richard Huey, John Byrd, Butler Hixon.

Songs: "When the Boys Come Home," "Evelina," "Welcome Hinges," "Farmer's Daughter," "It Was Good Enough for Grandma," "The Eagle and Me," "Right as the Rain,"

"T'Morra, T'Morra," "The Rakish Young Man with the Whiskers," "Pretty as a Picture," "Sunday in Cicero Falls," "I Got a Song," "Lullaby (Satin Gown and Silver Shoe)," "Simon Legree," "Liza Crossing the Ice," "I Never Was Born," "Man for Sale." Added in 1976: "Promise Me Not to Love Me," "Little Big Man," " 'Till We All Belong."

Blue Holiday (variety show)

Produced by Irvin Shapiro and Doris Cole at the Belasco Theater. Opened May 21, 1945. 8 performances. Directed by Monroe B. Hack. Choreographed by Katherine Dunham. *Lyrics* by Al Moritz, E. Y. Harburg, Lewis Allen, Warren Cuney, Morey Amsterdam. *Music* by Al Moritz, Earl Robinson, Herbert Kingsley, Josh White, Morey Amsterdam, Duke Ellington. Sets by Perry Watkins. Costumes by Kasia.

Cast included Ethel Waters, Mary Lou Williams, Josh White, Willie Bryant, Timmie Rogers, Katherine Dunham Dancers, The Hall Johnson Choir, Lillian Fitzgerald, Evelyn Ellis, Muriel Gaines, The Chocolateers, The Three Poms.

Song: "Free and Equal Blues" (Robinson).

Finian's Rainbow

Produced by Lee Sabinson and William R. Katzell at the 46th Street Theatre. Opened January 10, 1947. 725 performances. Directed by Bretaigne Windust. Choreographed by Michael Kidd. *Lyrics* by E. Y. Harburg. *Music* by Burton Lane. Book by E. Y. Harburg and Fred Saidy. Sets and lights by Jo Mielziner. Costumes by Eleanor Goldsmith.

Cast included Ella Logan, Albert Sharpe, Donald Richards, David Wayne, Anita Alvarez, Lyn Murray Singers, Eddie Bruce, Tom McElhany, Alan Gilbert, Robert Pitkin, Royal Dano, Lorenzo Fuller, Augustus Smith, Jr., Ralph Waldo Cummings, William Greaves, Lucas Aco, Nathaniel Dickerson, Diane Woods, Jane Earle, Roland Skinner, Maude Simmons, Arthur Tell, Jerry Laws, Louis Sharp, Michael Ellis, Harry Day, Norma Jane Marlowe, Elayne Richards.

Songs: "This Time of the Year," "How Are Things in Glocca Morra?" "Look to the Rainbow," "Old Devil Moon," "Something Sort of Grandish," "If This Isn't Love," "Necessity," "That Great Come-and-Get-It Day," "When the Idle Poor Become the Idle Rich," "The Begat," "When I'm Not Near the Girl I Love."

Flahooley

Produced by Cheryl Crawford in association with E. Y. Harburg and Fred Saidy at the Broadhurst Theatre. Opened May 14, 1951. 40 performances. Directed by E. Y. Harburg and Fred Saidy. Choreographed by Helen Tamiris. *Lyrics* by E. Y. Harburg. *Music* by Sammy Fain. Book by E. Y. Harburg and Fred Saidy. Sets and lights by Howard Bay. Costumes by David Ffolkes.

Cast included Ernest Truex, Jerome Courtland, Edith Atwater, Irwin Corey, Barbara Cook, The Bil Baird Marionettes, Yma Sumac, Stanley Carlson, Bil Baird, Cora Baird, Fay De Witt, Nehemiah Persoff and Louis Nye.

Songs: "You Too Can Be a Puppet," "Here's to Your Illusions," "B. G. Bigelow, Inc.," "Who Says There Ain't No Santa Claus?" "Flahooley," "The World Is Your Balloon,"

"He's Only Wonderful," "Jump, Little Chillun (Jump, Chillun, Jump)," "Spirit of Capsulanti," "Happy Hunting," "Enchantment," "Scheherezade," "Come Back, Little Genie," "The Springtime Cometh," "Sing the Merry," "Lament" (cut), "Scheherezade's Interlude" (cut), "Song of the Enchanted Rope" (cut), "Christmas Song" (cut), "You Need a Little Magic" (Lane; published 1984), "A Day Late and a Dollar Short" (added 1973), "That Mysterious Lady Called Love" (Fred Coots; added 1958), "Where Has the Rainbow Gone?" (added 1978).

Jollyanna

Produced by Edwin Lester at the Los Angeles Philharmonic Auditorium. Opened August 11, 1952. Number of performances unknown. Directed by Jack Donahue. Choreographed by Lew Christensen. *Book and lyrics* by E. Y. Harburg, Fred Saidy (adapted from their original musical *Flahooley*). *Music* by Sammy Fain, with additional numbers by William Friml and Burton Lane. Sets by Howard Bay. Lights by Peggy Clark. Costumes by Jay Morley.

Cast included Bobby Clark, Mitzi Gaynor, John Beal, Biff McGuire, Marthe Errolle, Beverly Tyler, Bil Baird's Marionettes.

Songs (from the original *Flahooley*): "B. G. Bigelow, Inc.," "The World Is Your Balloon," "You Too Can Be a Puppet," "Jump, Chillun, Jump," "Come Back, Little Genie," "Scheherezade," "The Springtime Cometh." Songs added: "A Gal Named Cinderella," "Leave a Message" (Friml), "Jollyanna" (Friml), "Fabulous" (Friml), "You Need a Little Magic" (Lane), "What's Gonna Happen (If We Don't Find the Genie)?" (Lane), "How Lucky Can You Get?"

Jamaica

Produced by David Merrick at the Imperial Theater. Opened October 31, 1957. 555 performances. Directed by Robert Lewis. Choreographed by Jack Cole. *Lyrics* by E. Y. Harburg. *Music* by Harold Arlen. Book by E. Y. Harburg, Fred Saidy. Sets by Oliver Smith. Lights by Jean Rosenthal. Costumes by Miles White.

Cast included Lena Horne, Ricardo Montalban, Josephine Premice, Joe Adams, Ossie Davis, Erik Rhodes, Adelaide Hall, Augustine Rios, Roy Thompson, Hugh Dilworth.

Songs: "Savannah," "Savannah's Wedding Day," "Pretty to Walk With (That's How a Man Gets Got)," "Push de Button," "Incompatibility," "Little Biscuit," "Cocoanut Sweet," "Pity de Sunset," "Hooray for de Yankee Dollar," "What Good Does It Do?" "Monkey in the Mango Tree," "Take It Slow, Joe," "Ain't It de Truth," "Leave de Atom Alone," "For Every Fish (There's a Little Bigger Fish)," "I Don't Think I'll End It All Today," "Napoleon," "Noah" (cut), "Whipporwill" (cut), "There's a Sweet Wind Blowin' My Way" (added 1980; cut prior to opening).

The Happiest Girl in the World

Produced by Lee Guber at the Martin Beck Theater. Opened April 3, 1961. 96 performances. Directed by Cyril Ritchard. Choreographed by Dania Krupska. *Lyrics* by E. Y. Harburg. *Music* by Jacques Offenbach. Book by Fred Saidy, Henry Myers, based on

Aristophanes' *Lysistrata* and Bullfinch's stories. Musical research by Jay Gorney. Sets and lights by William and Jean Eckart. Costumes by Robert Fletcher.

Cast included Cyril Ritchard, Janice Rule, Dran Seitz, Bruce Yarnell, Lainie Kazan, David Canary.

Songs: "Cheers for the Hero," "The Glory That Is Greece," "The Happiest Girl in the World," "The Greek Marine Hymn," "Shall We Say Farewell?" "Never Bedevil the Devil," "Whatever That May Be," "Eureka," "Lysistrata's Oath," "Vive la Virtue," "Adrift on a Star" (Barcarolle), "That'll Be the Day," "How Soon, Oh Moon?" "Lovesick Serenade," "Five Minutes of Spring," "Never Trust a Virgin."

Notes: Songs created for later versions: "Excuse My Laughter," "Strategy," "Honestly," "The Magic Falute," "Persian Women," "Hup-Two-Three," "Politics," "When the Heart Is Too Young," "Little Old Gehenna."

ASCAP lists the following titles, which do not appear anywhere else: "Sick, Sick, Sick," "The Old Pied Piper."

Additional songs listed as unused by Yip Harburg in the E. Y. Harburg Collection at Yale University: "Sabre Song," "My Mind Says Don't," "Scratch a Wife and Find a Doll," "We're Off to the Races," "When Your Heart Is Too Young," "Where Have I Heard That Song Before?" "Who Needs a Woman?" "Chic, Chic, Chic Are We," "The Lonesomest Girl in the World," "Rhodope's Tavern."

Darling of the Day (pre-Broadway title Married Alive!)

Produced by Theatre Guild and Joel Schenker at the George Abbott Theater. Opened January 27, 1968. 33 performances. Directed by Noel Willman. Choreographed by Lee Theodore. *Lyrics* by E. Y. Harburg. *Music* by Jule Styne. Book based on Arnold Bennett's *Buried Alive*. Sets by Oliver Smith. Lights by Peggy Clark. Costumes by Raoul Pene du Bois.

Cast included Vincent Price, Patricia Routledge, Brenda Forbes, Peter Woodthorpe, Beth Howland.

Songs: "Mad for Art," "He's a Genius," "To Get Out of This World Alive," "It's Enough to Make a Lady Fall in Love," "A Gentleman's Gentleman (Where Would Britain Be Without a Butler)," "Double Soliloquy," "Let's See What Happens," "Panache," "I've Got a Rainbow Working for Me," "Money, Money, Money," "That Something Extra Special," "What Makes a Marriage Merry," "Not on Your Nellie," "Sunset Tree," "Butler in the Abbey."

Additional songs listed by Yip Harburg in the Harburg Archive materials at New York Public Library: "Come Back to God/Me" (not used), "A Blushing Bride" (cut), "That Stranger in Your Eyes" (cut), "I'm Simpally Mad for Bones" (cut), "Putney on the Thames" (cut), "Henry Leek," "Lying in State," "Don't Pour the Thames into the Rhine" (not used), "Westminster Funeral," "Priam Farll," "When I Marry Alice," "The Darling of the Day." Vocal selections: "Isn't This a Day" (not used). Per O'Keefe Centre (Toronto) program: "Lady Alice" (montage).

What a Day for a Miracle

Never opened in New York. Produced by the University of Vermont, Burlington at the University of Vermont Arena Theatre. Opened April 29, 1971. 6 performances. Directed by Anthony Wiles. *Lyrics* by E. Y. Harburg. *Music* by Henry Myers, Larry Orenstein, Jeff Alexander. Book by Henry Myers, based on his novel, *Our Lives Have Just Begun.*

Cast included Scott Jacoby, Wayne Grace.

Songs: "Demon in the Compass," "Grown Ups," "He Will Walk with Thee," "Jerusalem," "La Tra Ma La," "Little Ships," "Little World, Good Morning," "Lost Sheep," "The Sermon, the Sword, and the Song," "The Song of Assisi," "Wake Up," "What a Day for a Miracle," "When You Have Forgotten My Kisses," "Who Will Walk with Me?" "The Wolf of Gubbio," "The Word is Love."

Film Songs

Applause

Produced by Jesse L. Lasky, Walter Wanger for Paramount. Released October 9, 1929 (New York premiere). 82 minutes. Directed by Rouben Mamoulian. *Lyrics* by E. Y. Harburg, Joe Young, Dolly Morse, Billy Rose, Art Fitch, Kay Fitch, Bert Lowe, Raymond Klages, Lindsay McPhail, Walter Michels. *Music* by Jay Gorney, E. Ray Goetz, Pete Wendling, Joseph Burke, Harry Linke, Fats Waller, Lindsay McPhail, Walter Michels, J. Fred Coots, Art Fitch, Kay Fitch, Bert Lowe. Dialogue and scenario by Garrett Fort, based on the novel by Beth Brown. Photographed by George Folsey. Edited by John Bassler.

Cast included Helen Morgan, Joan Peers, Fuller Mellish, Jr., Henry Wadsworth, Jack Cameron, Dorothy Cumming.

Songs: "What Wouldn't I Do for That Man" (Gorney).

The Battle of Paris

Produced by Paramount Famous Lasky Corporation. Released November 30, 1929. 80 minutes. Directed by Robert Florey. *Lyrics* by Cole Porter, Howard Dietz. *Music* by Cole Porter, Jay Gorney. Screenplay by Gene Markey. Photographed by Bill Steiner.

Cast included Gertrude Lawrence, Charles Ruggles, Walter Petrie, Gladys Du Bois, Arthur Treacher, Joe King.

Song: "Battle of Paris" (composer unknown). Typed lyrics listed by Yip Harburg in Yale University Archive materials.

Glorifying the American Girl

Produced by Paramount Famous Lasky Corporation; Florenz Ziegfeld, supervisor. Released December 7, 1929. 87 minutes. Directed by Millard Webb. Revue director, John Harkrider. Ballets by Ted Shawn. *Lyrics* by E. Y. Harburg, Irving Berlin, Leon Zimmerman, Rudy Vallee, Walter Donaldson, Benny Davis, Harry Akst. *Music* by Jay Gorney, Irving Berlin, Leon Zimmerman, Rudy Vallee, Walter Donaldson, Benny Davis, Harry Akst. Screenplay by J. P. McEvoy, Millard Webb. Photographed by George Folsey.

Cast included Mary Eaton, Dan Healy, Helen Morgan, Eddie Cantor, Rudy Vallee, Edward Crandall, Mr. and Mrs. Florenz Ziegfeld, Otto Kahn, Texas Guinan, Mayor and

Mrs. Jimmy Walker, Ring Lardner, Noah Beery, Norman Brokenshire, Johnny Weissmuller, Adolph Zukor.

Songs: "What Wouldn't I Do for That Man" (Gorney).

Roadhouse Nights

Produced by Paramount Famous Lasky Corporation. Released February 21, 1930. 68 minutes. Directed by Hobart Henley. *Lyrics* by E. Y. Harburg and Irving Kahal. *Music* by Jay Gorney and Sammy Fain. Screenplay by Garrett Fort, based on a story by Ben Hecht. Photographed by William Steiner. Edited by Helene Turner.

Cast included Helen Morgan, Charles Ruggles, Fred Kohler, Jimmy Durante, Fuller Mellish, Jr., Leo Donnelly, Tammany Young, Joe King, Lou Clayton, Eddie Jackson.

Songs: "It Can't Go on Like This" (Gorney), "Just a Melody for a Memory" (Gorney, Fain/lyrics cowritten by Kahal)

Leave It to Lester

Produced by Paramount-Publix Corporation. Released June 11, 1930 (per AFI Catalog). Directed by Frank Cambria, Ray Cozine. *Lyrics* by E. Y. Harburg. *Music* by Johnny Green.

Cast included Lester Allen, Evelyn Hoey, Hal Thompson.

Song: "I'm Yours."

The Sap from Syracuse

Produced by Paramount-Publix Corporation. Released July 25, 1930. 70 minutes. Directed by A. Edward Sutherland. *Lyrics* by E. Y. Harburg. *Music* by Vernon Duke, Johnny Green. Screenplay by Gertrude Purcell, from *A Sap from Syracuse* by John Wray, Jack O'Donnell, and John Hayden. Photographed by Larry Williams. Edited by Helene Turner. Art direction by William Saulter.

Cast included Jack Oakie, Ginger Rogers, Granville Bates, George Barbier, Sidney Riggs, Betty Starbuck, Vera Teasdale, J. Malcolm Dunn, Bernard Jukes, Walter Fenner, Jack Daly.

Songs: "How I Wish I Could Sing a Love Song," "Ah, What's the Use?" (Green); "Capitalize That Thing Called It" (Duke, Green).

Queen High

Produced by Frank Mandel, Laurence Schwab for Paramount-Publix Corporation. Released August 8, 1930. 75 minutes. Directed by Fred Newmeyer. *Lyrics* by E. Y. Harburg, Dick Howard (Howard Dietz), Edward Eliscu, B. G. DeSylva. *Music* by Arthur Schwartz, Henry Souvain, Ralph Rainger, Lewis Gensler. Screenplay by Frank Mandel, based on the play *A Pair of Sixes* by Edward H. Peple, adapted from the musical comedy by Laurence

Schwab, B. G. DeSylva, Lewis Gensler. Photographed by William Steiner. Edited by Barney Rogan.

Cast included Stanley Smith, Ginger Rogers, Charles Ruggles, Frank Morgan, Helen Carrington, Theresa Maxwell Conover, Tom Brown, Betty Garde, Nina Olivette, Rudy Cameron.

Songs: "I Love the Girls in My Own Peculiar Way" (Souvain), "Brother, Just Laugh It Off" (Schwartz, Rainger).

Heads Up

Produced by Paramount-Publix Corporation. Released October 12, 1930. 76 minutes. Directed by Victor Schertzinger. Dance directed by George Hale. *Lyrics* by E. Y. Harburg, Lorenz Hart, Don Hartman. *Music* by Vernon Duke, Richard Rodgers, Victor Schertzinger. Screenplay by John McGowan, Jack Kirkland, adapted from the musical of the same name by Richard Rodgers, Lorenz Hart, John McGowan, and Paul Gerard Smith. Photographed by William Steiner.

Cast included Charles Rogers, Victor Moore, Helen Kane, Margaret Breen, Helen Carrington, Gene Gowing, Billy Taylor, Harry Shannon, C. Anthony Hughes, John Hamilton, Stanley Jessup, Preston Foster.

Songs: "Heads Up," "Until Today I Had No Tomorrow," "I May Fall in Love Again" (Duke)

Song Service

Produced by Paramount-Publix Corporation. Released October 24, 1930. Directed by Norman Taurog. *Lyrics* by E. Y. Harburg. *Music* by Peter DeRose.

Song: "Just Another Dream Gone Wrong."

Office Blues

Produced by Paramount Publix Corporation. Released November 21, 1930 (copyright date). One reel. Directed by Mort Blumenstock. *Lyrics* by E. Y. Harburg. *Music* by Peter DeRose.

Cast included Clairborne Bryson, Ginger Rogers.

Song: "Office Blues."

Follow the Leader

Produced by Paramount-Publix Corporation. Released December 5, 1930. 76 minutes. Directed by Norman Taurog. *Lyrics* by E. Y. Harburg, B. G. DeSylva, Lew Brown, Irving Kahal. *Music* by Arthur Schwartz, Ray Henderson, Sammy Fain, Ralph Rainger. Screenplay by Gertrude Purcell, Sid Silvers, from the musical comedy *Manhattan Mary* by

William K. Wells, George White, B. G. DeSylva, Lew Brown, Ray Henderson. Photographed by Larry Williams. Edited by Barney Rogan. Art direction by William Saulter. Costumes by Caroline Putnam.

Cast included Ed Wynn, Ginger Rogers, Stanley Smith, Lou Holtz, Lida Kane, Ethel Merman, Bobby Watson, Donald Kirke, William Halligan, Holly Hall, Preston Foster, James C. Morton.

Songs: "Brother, Just Laugh It Off" (Rainger, Schwartz).

Ihre Hoheit Befiehlt (Her Highness Commands) (German film)

Produced by UFA Films. Copyrighted March 4, 1930. A 1931 release. 92 minutes. Directed by Hanns Schwartz. *Lyrics* by Robert Gilbert. English version, E. Y. Harburg. *Music* by Werner R. Heymann. Screenplay by Paul Frank, Billie Wilder.

Cast included Willy Fritsch, Kaethe von Nagy, Reinhold Schuenzel, Paul Heidemann, Kenneth Rive, Carl Platen, Erich Kestin.

Song: "I'll Make a Home for Your Love (in This Heart of Mine)."

Sein Liebeslied (His Love Song) (German film)

Produced by Superfilm-Tobis; associated Cinema release. Released November 18, 1931. 95 minutes. Directed by Geza von Bolvary. *Lyrics* by Walter Reisch; English lyrics by E. Y. Harburg. *Music* by Robert Stolz. Screenplay by Walter Reisch, Fritz Schulz. Photographed by Willy Goldberger, Max Brink. Architecture by Robert Neppach.

Cast included Willi Forst, Paul Otto, Fee Malten, Oskar Karlweiss, Anne Goerling.

Song: "My Fortune Is Love."

Ronny (German film)

Produced by UFA Films. Released April 13, 1932. 72 minutes. Directed by Reinhold Schunzel. *Lyrics* by Ernst Welisch and Rudolph Schanzer. English lyrics by E. Y. Harburg. *Music* by Emmerich Kalman. Screenplay by Emmerich Pressburger, Reinhold Schunzel. Photographed by Fritz Arno. Scenarists: Emmerich Pressburger, Reinhold Schunzel.

Cast included Kaethe von Nagy, Otto Wallburg, Willy Grill, Willy Fritsch.

Song: "You Are My First Love."

Oh, Fräulein Grete

Released in 1932. *Lyrics* by E. Y. Harburg. *Music* by Juan Llossas.

Song: "You'll Never Lose Me."

Moonlight and Pretzels

Produced by Rowland-Brice for Universal. Released August 22, 1933. 72 minutes. Directed by Karl Freund. Dialogue directed by Monte Brice. Dances staged by Bobby Connolly. *Lyrics* by E. Y. Harburg, Herman Hupfeld, Al Siegel. *Music* by Jay Gorney, Herman Hupfeld, Al Siegel, Sammy Fain. Screenplay by Monte Brice, Arthur Jarrett. Continuity, Sig Herzig. Photographed by William Miller. Costumes by Brymer.

Cast included Leo Carrillo, Mary Brian, Roger Pryor, Lillian Miles, William Frawley, Herbert Rawlinson, Bobby Watson, Jack Denny and His Orchestra.

Songs: "Ah, But Is It Love?" "Moonlight and Pretzels," "Dusty Shoes," "Let's Make Love Like the Crocodiles" (Gorney); "There's a Little Bit of You (in Every Love Song)" (Fain).

Take a Chance

Produced by Rowland-Brice for Paramount. Released November 26, 1933. 80 minutes. Directed by Laurence Schwab, Monte Brice. *Lyrics* by E. Y. Harburg, Billy Rose, Arthur Swanstrom, B. G. DeSylva, Herman Hupfeld. *Music* by Harold Arlen, Herman Hupfeld, Jay Gorney, Lou Alter, Billy Rose, Richard Whiting, Nacio Herb Brown, Vincent Youmans, Roger Edens. Screenplay adapted by Laurence Schwab, B. G. DeSylva, Monte Brice, from the musical comedy by Sid Silvers, Nacio Herb Brown, Laurence Schwab, Richard Whiting, Vincent Youmans. Photographed by William Steiner.

Cast included James Dunn, Cliff Edwards, June Knight, Lillian Roth, Charles ("Buddy") Rogers, Lilian Bond, Marjorie Main.

Song: "It's Only a Paper Moon (If You Believed in Me)" (Arlen/lyrics cowritten by Rose), "New Deal Rhythm" (Edens/lyrics cowritten by Rose).

Shoot the Works!

Produced by Albert Lewis, associate producer for Paramount. Released July 6, 1934. 82 minutes. Directed by Wesley Ruggles. *Lyrics* by E. Y. Harburg, Ben Bernie, Ralph Rainger, Walter Bullock, Leo Robin. *Music* by Jay Gorney, Leo Robin, Mack Gordon, Harry Revel, Al Goering. Screenplay by Howard J. Green; dialogue by Claude Binyon, from *The Great Magoo* by Ben Hecht, Gene Fowler. Photographed by Leo Tover. Art direction by Hans Dreier, Robert Usher.

Cast included Jack Oakie, Ben Bernie and Band, Dorothy Dell, Rosco Karnes, William Frawley.

Song: "Hot Moonlight" (Gorney).

The Count of Monte Cristo

Produced by Reliance Production for United Artists. Released September 26, 1934. 113 minutes. Directed by Rowland V. Lee. *Lyrics* by E. Y. Harburg. *Music* by Johnny Green. Screenplay by Philip Dunne, Dan Totheroh, Rowland V. Lee, from Alexandre Dumas's work. Photographed by Peverell J. Marley. Edited by Grant Whytock. Art direction by John Ducasse Schulze. Costumes by Gwen Wakeling.

Cast included Robert Donat, Elissa Landi, Louis Calhern, O. P. Heggie, Sidney Blackmer, Raymond Walburn, William Farnum.

Song: "The World Is Mine."

Broadway Gondolier

Produced by Warner Bros. Released July 17, 1935. 100 minutes. Directed by Lloyd Bacon. *Lyrics* by Al Dubin. *Music* by Harry Warren. Screenplay by Warren Duff, Sig Herzig, from a story by Herzig, E. Y. Harburg, and Hans Kraly. Photographed by George Barnes. Edited by George Amy. Art direction by Anton Grot. Gowns by Orry-Kelly.

Cast included Dick Powell, Joan Blondell, Adolphe Menjou, Louise Fazenda, William Gargan, George Barbier, Grant Mitchell, Joseph Sauers, The Mills Brothers, Judy Canova Family.

Song: "Careful with My Heart" (Senia Pokrass).

Manhattan Moon

Produced by Stanley Bergerman for Universal. Released August 19, 1935. 62 minutes. Directed by Stuart Walker. *Lyrics* by E. Y. Harburg. *Music* by Karl Hajos. Screenplay by Robert Harris, adapted by Robert Presnell and Barry Trivers, Ben Grauman Kohn, Aben Kandel, based on a story by Robert Harris. Photographed by Charles Stumar. Edited by Phil Cahn.

Cast included Ricardo Cortez, Dorothy Page, Henry Mollison, Hugh O'Connell, Luis Alberni, Henry Armetta, Regis Toomey.

Songs: "My Other Me."

The Singing Kid

Produced by Warner Bros.; a First National Strand release. Released April 3, 1936. 85 minutes. Directed by William Keighley. Dances staged by Bobby Connolly. *Lyrics* by E. Y. Harburg, Irving Mills, Cab Calloway. *Music* by Harold Arlen, Irving Mills, Cab Calloway. Screenplay by Robert Lord, adapted by Warren Duff, Pat C. Flick. Based on a story by Robert Lord. Photographed by George Barnes. Edited by Tom Richards. Art direction by Carl Weyl. Costumes by Orry-Kelly.

Cast included Al Jolson, Allen Jenkins, Lyle Talbot, Frank Mitchell, Edward Everett Horton, Yacht Club Boys, Cab Calloway and His Band.

Songs: "I Love to Sing-a," "Save Me, Sister," "You're the Cure for What Ails Me," "My How This Country Has Changed," "Here's Looking at You" (Arlen).

Stage Struck

Produced by Robert Lord for Warner Bros. Released September 27, 1936. 90 minutes. Directed by Busby Berkeley. *Lyrics* by E. Y. Harburg. *Music* by Harold Arlen. Screenplay by Tom Buckingham, Pat C. Flick, based on a story by Robert Lord, Warren Duff. Photographed by Byron Haskin. Edited by Tom Richards. Costumes by Orry-Kelly.

Cast included Dick Powell, Joan Blondell, Warren William, Frank McHugh, Jeanne Madden, Spring Byington, Lulu McConnell, Yacht Club Boys.

Songs: "In Your Own Quiet Way," "Fancy Meeting You," "You're Kinda Grandish," "The New Parade."

Gold Diggers of 1937

Produced by Hal Wallis; Warner Bros.-First National release. Released December 24, 1936. 100 minutes. Directed by Lloyd Bacon. Musical numbers created and directed by Busby Berkeley. *Lyrics* by E. Y. Harburg, Al Dubin. *Music* by Harold Arlen, Harry Warren. Screenplay by Warren Duff, adapted from the play *Sweet Mystery of Life* by Richard Maibaum, Michael Wallace, George Haight. Photographed by Arthur Edeson. Edited by Thomas Richards.

Cast included Dick Powell, Joan Blondell, Victor Moore, Glenda Farrell, Osgood Perkins.

Songs: "Speaking of the Weather," "Let's Put Our Heads Together," "Life Insurance Song," "Hush Ma Mouth" (Arlen).

Merry Go Round of 1938

Produced by B. G. DeSylva for Universal. Released November 25, 1937. 90 minutes. Directed by Irving Randall. Dances staged by Carl Randall. *Lyrics* by E. Y. Harburg, Harold Adamson, Mort Dixon. *Music* by Harold Arlen, Jimmy McHugh, Harry Woods. Screenplay by Monte Brice, A. Dorian Otvos, based on a story by Monte Brice, Henry Myers. Photographed by Joseph Valentine. Edited by Ted Kent, Charles Maynard.

Cast included Bert Lahr, Jimmy Savo, Billy House, Alice Brady, Mischa Auer, Joy Hodges, Louise Fazenda, John King, Barbara Read, Dave Appolon.

Song: "Song of the Woodman" (Arlen).

The Wizard of Oz

Produced by Mervyn LeRoy for Metro-Goldwyn-Mayer. Released August 17, 1939. 100 minutes. Directed by Victor Fleming. Musical numbers staged by Bobby Connolly. *Lyrics* by E. Y. Harburg. *Music* by Harold Arlen. Musical adaptation by Herbert Stothart. Screenplay by Noel Langley, Florence Ryerson, Edgar Allan Woolf, adapted from L. Frank Baum's book. Photographed by Harold Rosson, Allen Davey. Edited by Blanche Sewell. Art direction by Cedric Gibbons. Set decoration by Edwin B. Willis. Costumes by Adrian. Special effects by Arnold Gillespie.

Cast included Judy Garland, Frank Morgan, Ray Bolger, Bert Lahr, Jack Haley, Billie Burke, Margaret Hamilton, Charley Grapewin, Pat Walshe, Clara Blandick, The Singer Midgets, Mitchell Lewis, Toto.

Songs: "Over the Rainbow," "Ding Dong! the Witch Is Dead," "We're Off to See the Wizard," "If I Only Had a Brain," "If I Only Had a Heart," "If I Only Had the Nerve," "The Merry Old Land of Oz," "If I Were King of the Forest," "The Jitterbug" (cut), "Munchkinland," "Lullaby League," "Lollipop Guild," "Renovation Sequence" (Arlen); "Optimistic Voices" (Arlen, Stothart).

Babes in Arms

Produced by Arthur Freed for Metro-Goldwyn-Mayer. Released October 19, 1939. 96 minutes. Directed by Busby Berkeley. *Lyrics* by E. Y. Harburg, Lorenz Hart, Arthur Freed, Edward Madden, Eubie Blake, Noble Sissle, Roger Edens, Stephen Foster. *Music* by Harold Arlen, Richard Rodgers, Nacio Herb Brown, Gus Arnheim, Abe Lyman, Eubie Blake, Noble Sissle, Percy Wenrich, Roger Edens, Stephen Foster. Screenplay by Jack McGowan, Kay Van Riper, from the musical by Richard Rodgers and Lorenz Hart. Photographed by Ray June. Edited by Frank Sullivan. Art direction by Merrill Pye; Costumes by Dolly Tree.

Cast included Mickey Rooney, Judy Garland, Charles Winninger, Guy Kibbee, June Preisser, Margaret Hamilton.

Song: "God's Country," (Arlen), "Let's Take a Walk around the Block" (Arlen/lyrics cowritten by Ira Gershwin) (unused)

[A Day] At the Circus

Produced by Mervyn LeRoy for Metro-Goldwyn-Mayer. Released November 16, 1939. 87 minutes. Directed by Edward Buzzell. Choreographed by Bobby Connolly. *Lyrics* by E. Y. Harburg. *Music* by Harold Arlen. Screenplay by Irving Brecher. Photographed by Leonard Smith. Edited by William H. Terhune. Art direction by Cedric Gibbons, Stan Rogers. Set decoration by Edwin B. Willis.

Cast included Groucho, Harpo, and Chico Marx, Margaret Dumont, Florence Rice, Kenny Baker, Eve Arden, Nat Pendleton, James Burke, Jerry Marenghi, Fritz Feld, Barnett Parker.

Songs: "Lydia the Tattooed Lady," "Two Blind Loves," "Step Up and Take a Bow," "Swingali."

Andy Hardy Meets Debutante

Produced by Metro-Goldwyn-Mayer. Released August 1, 1940. 85 minutes. Directed by George B. Seitz. *Lyrics* by E. Y. Harburg, Lester Santly, Benny Davis, Milton Ager, Arthur Freed, Nacio Herb Brown. *Music* by Harold Arlen, Lester Santly, Benny Davis, Milton Ager, Arthur Freed, Nacio Herb Brown. Screenplay by Annalee Whitmore, Thomas Seller, based on characters created by Aurania Rouvenol. Photographed by Sidney Wagner, Charles Lawton. Edited by Harold F. Kress.

Cast included Lewis Stone, Mickey Rooney, Cecilia Parker, Fay Holden, Judy Garland, Ann Rutherford, Diana Lewis.

Song: "Buds Won't Bud" (Arlen).

Babes on Broadway

Produced by Arthur Freed for Metro-Goldwyn-Mayer. Released December 31, 1941. 118 minutes. Directed by Busby Berkeley. *Lyrics* by E. Y. Harburg, Ralph Freed, Harold Rome, Al Stillman, Vincente Paiva, Jararaca. *Music* by Burton Lane, Roger Edens, Harold Rome, Vincente Paiva, Jararaca. Screenplay by Fred Finklehoffe, Elaine Ryan, based on a story by Burton Lane. Photographed by Lester White. Edited by Frederick Y. Smith. Costumes by (Robert) Kalloch.

Cast included Mickey Rooney, Judy Garland, Virginia Weidler, Ray McDonald, Richard Quine, Fay Bainter, Donald Meek, James Gleason, Alexander Woollcott.

Songs: "Anything Can Happen In New York," "Chin Up, Cheerio, Carry On" (Lane).

Rio Rita

Produced by Pandro S. Berman for Metro-Goldwyn-Mayer. Released May 7, 1942. 91 minutes. Directed by S. Sylvan Simon. *Lyrics* by E. Y. Harburg, Joseph McCarthy, Nilo Barnet, Lacerdo. *Music* by Harold Arlen, Harry Tierney, Meyerbeer, Nilo Barnet, Lacerdo. Screenplay by Richard Connell, Gladys Lehman; special material John Grant; a remake of the 1929 film, based on the musical by Joseph McCarthy, Harry Tierney, Guy Bolton, Fred Thompson. Photographed by George Folsey. Edited by Ben Lewis. Costumes by Robert Kalloch, Gile Steele. Special effects by Warren Newcombe.

Cast included Bud Abbott, Lou Costello, Kathryn Grayson, John Carroll.

Songs: "Long Before You Came Along," "A Couple of Caballeros," "Poor Whippoor-will," "It's Such Unusual Weather" (unused) (Arlen).

Ship Ahoy

Produced by Jack Cummings for Metro-Goldwyn-Mayer. Released June 25, 1942. 95 minutes. Directed by Edward N. Buzzell. Dances staged by Bobby Connolly. *Lyrics* by E. Y. Harburg, Walter Ruick, Edward Madden, Allan Roberts, Doris Fisher. *Music* by Burton Lane, Margery Cummings, Walter Ruick, Percy Wenrich, Allan Roberts, Doris Fisher. Screenplay by Harry Clark, based on a story by Matt Brooks, Bradford Ropes, Bert Kalmar. Photographed by Leonard Smith, Robert Planck. Edited by Blanche Sewell. Art direction by Cedric Gibbons, Harry McAfee. Set decoration by Edwin B. Willis. Costumes by Robert Kalloch.

Cast included Eleanor Powell, Red Skelton, Bert Lahr, Virginia O'Brien, Tommy Dorsey and His Orchestra, Frank Sinatra, Connie Haynes, The Pied Pipers.

Songs: "The Last Call for Love" (Cummings, Lane); "Poor You," "I'll Take Tallulah" (Lane).

Panama Hattie

Produced by Arthur Freed for Metro-Goldwyn-Mayer. Released October 1, 1942. 80 minutes. Directed by Norman Z. McLeod. Dances staged by Vincente Minnelli, Danny Dare. *Lyrics* by Cole Porter. Additional lyrics by E. Y. Harburg, Phil Moore, Theodore F. Morse. *Music* by Cole Porter. Additional music by Burton Lane, Walter Donaldson, Roger Edens, J. LeGon, Sir Arthur Sullivan. Screenplay by Jack McGowan, Wilkie Mahoney, based on the musical by B. G. DeSylva, Herbert Fields, Cole Porter. Photographed by George Folsey. Edited by Blanche Sewell. Art direction by Cedric Gibbons. Set decoration by Edwin B. Willia, Hugh Hunt. Costumes by (Robert) Kalloch.

Cast included Red Skelton, Ann Sothern, "Rags" Ragland, Ben Blue, Marsha Hunt, Virginia O'Brien, Alan Mowbray, Dan Dailey, Jr., Jackie Horner, Carl Esmond, Lena Horne, The Berry Brothers.

Song: "The Son of a Gun Who Picks on Uncle Sam" (Lane).

Cairo

Produced by Metro-Goldwyn-Mayer. Released November 5, 1942. 101 minutes. Directed by W. S. Van Dyke II. *Lyrics* by E. Y. Harburg, Howard Dietz. *Music* by Harold Arlen, Arthur Schwartz. Screenplay by John McClain, based on an idea by Ladislas Fodor. Photographed by Ray June. Edited by James E. Newcombe. Art direction by Cedric Gibbons. Set decoration by Edwin S. Willis. Costumes by (Robert) Kalloch.

Cast included Jeannette MacDonald, Robert Young, Ethel Waters, Reginald Owen, Grant Mitchell, Lionel Atwill, Edward Ciannelli, Mitchell Lewis, Dooley Wilson.

Songs: "The Waltz Is Over," "Cairo," "Keep the Light Burning Bright (in the Harbor)," "Buds Won't Bud" (Arlen).

Presenting Lily Mars

Produced by Joseph Pasternak for Metro-Goldwyn-Mayer. Released April 29, 1943. 106 minutes. Directed by Norman Taurog. *Lyrics* by E. Y. Harburg, Paul Francis Webster, Ralph Freed, Lew Brown, Dorothy Terris (Theodora Morse). *Music* by Burton Lane, Walter Jurmann, Roger Edens, Sammy Fain, Julian Robledo. Screenplay by Richard Connell, Gladys Lehman, based on Booth Tarkington's novel. Photographed by Joseph Ruttenberg. Edited by Albert Akst. Art direction by Cedric Gibbons. Special effects by Warren Newcombe.

Cast included Judy Garland, Van Heflin, Fay Bainter, Richard Carlson, Spring Byington, Marta Eggerth, Tommy Dorsey and His Orchestra, Bob Crosby and His Orchestra.

Song: "Tom, Tom, the Piper's Son" (Lane), "Paging Mr. Greenback" (Brown, Fain, Edens) (unused).

Cabin in the Sky

Produced by Arthur Freed for Metro-Goldwyn-Mayer. Released May 27, 1943. 98 minutes. Directed by Vincente Minnelli. *Lyrics* by John Latouche; additional lyrics by

E. Y. Harburg, Ted Fetter, Cecil Mack, Lew Brown, Ted Persons. *Music* by Vernon Duke; additional music by Harold Arlen, Duke Ellington, Ford Dabney, Mercer Ellington. Screenplay by Joseph Schrank, based on the musical by Lynn Root, Vernon Duke, John Latouche. Photographed by Sidney Wagner. Edited by Harold F. Kress.

Cast included Ethel Waters, Eddie "Rochester" Anderson, Lena Horne, Louis Armstrong, Rex Ingram, Kenneth Spencer, "Bubbles" (John W. Sublett), Oscar Polk, Mantan More-land, Willie Best, Fletcher Rivers, Leon James, Bill Bailey, "Buck" (Ford L. Washington), Butterfly McQueen, Ruby Dandridge, Nicodemus, Ernest Whitman, Duke Ellington and His Orchestra, Hall Johnson Choir.

Songs: "Happiness Is a Thing Called Joe," "Life's Full of Consequence," "Li'l Black Sheep," "Ain't It De Truth" (cut), "Some Folk Work," "Jezebel Jones" (unused), "Petunia's Prayer" (Arlen).

Du Barry Was a Lady

Produced by Arthur Freed for Metro-Goldwyn-Mayer. Released August 19, 1943. 101 minutes. Directed by Roy Del Ruth. Dances staged by Charles Walters. *Lyrics* by Cole Porter; additional lyrics by E. Y. Harburg, Ralph Freed. *Music* by Cole Porter; additional music by Burton Lane, Lew Brown, Roger Edens. Screenplay by Irving Brecher, adapted by Nancy Hamilton from the musical by Herbert Fields, B. G. DeSylva, Cole Porter. Photographed by Karl Freund. Edited by Blanche Sewell. Art direction by Cedric Gibbons. Set decoration by Edwin B. Willis, Henry Grace. Costumes by Irene, Shoup, Gile Steele.

Cast included Red Skelton, Lucille Ball, Gene Kelly, Virginia O'Brien, "Rags" Ragland, Zero Mostel, Donald Meek, Douglas Dumbrille, George Givot, Louise Beavers, Tommy Dorsey and His Orchestra.

Song: "Salome" (Edens).

Thousands Cheer

Produced by Joseph Pasternak for Metro-Goldwyn-Mayer. Released September 13, 1943. 126 minutes. Directed by George Sidney. *Lyrics* by E. Y. Harburg, Ralph Freed, Harold Adamson, Andy Razaf, Ralph Blane, Walter Ruick, Roger Edens, Sam M. Lewis, Joe Young, Paul Francis Webster, Harold Rome, Lew Brown. *Music* by Burton Lane, Earl Brent, Dmitri Shostakovich, Harold Rome, Ferde Groffe, Fats Waller, Herbert Stothart, Hugh Martin, Roger Edens, Lew Brown, Walter Ruick, Walter Jurmann, Mabel Wayne. Screenplay by Paul Jarrico, Richard Collins. Photographed by George Folsey. Edited by George Boemler. Art direction by Cedric Gibbons, Daniel B. Cathcart. Set decoration by Edwin B. Willis, Jacques Mesereau. Costumes by Irene.

Cast included Kathryn Grayson, Gene Kelly, Mary Astor, John Boles, Ben Blue, Mickey Rooney, Judy Garland, Red Skelton, Eleanor Powell, Ann Sothern, Lucille Ball, Virginia O'Brien, Frank Morgan, Lena Horne, Marsha Hunt, Marilyn Maxwell, Donna Reed, Margaret O'Brien, June Allyson, Gloria DeHaven, Kay Kyser, Bob Crosby and Benny Carter Bands, Jose Iturbi, Frances Rafferty, Don Loper.

Songs: "Let There Be Music" (Brent), "United Nations on the March" (Shostakovich/ lyrics cowritten by Rome), "Private Miss Jones" (Stothart/lyrics cowritten by Brent) (unused).

Princess O'Rourke

Produced by Hal B. Wallis for Warner Bros. Released November 5, 1943. 93 minutes. Directed by Norman Krasna. *Lyrics* by E. Y. Harburg, Ira Gershwin. *Music* by Arthur Schwartz. Screenplay by Norman Krasna. Photographed by Ernest Haller. Edited by Warren Low. Art direction by Max Parker. Set decoration by George James Hopkins.

Cast included Olivia de Havilland, Robert Cummings, Charles Coburn, Jack Carson, Jane Wyman, Gladys Cooper, Ruth Ford.

Song: "Honorable Moon."

Song of Russia

Produced by Joseph Pasternak for Metro-Goldwyn-Mayer. Released February 10, 1944. 107 minutes. Directed by Gregory Ratoff. Dances staged by David Lichine. *Lyrics* by E. Y. Harburg. *Music* by Jerome Kern. Screenplay by Paul Jarrico, Richard Collins, based on a story by Leo Mittler, Victor Trivas, Guy Endore. Photographed by Harry Stradling. Edited by George Hively. Art direction by Cedric Gibbons. Special effects by Arnold Gillespie.

Cast included Robert Taylor, Susan Peters, John Hodiak, Robert Benchley, Michael Chekhov, Darryl Hickman, Feodor Chaliapin.

Song: "And Russia Is Her Name."

Cover Girl

Produced by Arthur Schwartz for Columbia. Released March 30, 1944. 105 minutes. Directed by Charles Vidor. Dances staged by Val Rasset, Seymour Felix, Gene Kelly, Stanley Donen. *Lyrics* by Ira Gershwin, E. Y. Harburg. *Music* by Jerome Kern. Screenplay by Virginia Van Upp; adaptation by Marion Parsonnet, Paul Gangelin; story by Erwin Gelsey. Photographed by Rudolph Mate, Allen M. Davey. Edited by Viola Lawrence. Art direction by Lionel Banks, Cary Odell. Set decoration by Fay Babcock.

Cast included Rita Hayworth, Gene Kelly, Lee Bowman, Phil Silvers, Jinx Falkenburg, Leslie Brooks, Eve Arden, Otto Kruger, Jess Barker, Anita Colby, Curt Bois, Ed Brophy, Thurston Hall.

Song: "Make Way for Tomorrow."

Kismet

Produced by Everett Riskin for Metro-Goldwyn-Mayer. Released August 22, 1944. 100 minutes. Directed by William Dieterle. *Lyrics* by E. Y. Harburg. *Music* by Harold Arlen; musical score by Herbert Stothart. Screenplay by John Meehan, adapted from the play by Edward Knoblock. Photographed by Charles Rosher. Edited by Ben Lewis. Art direction by Cedric Gibbons, Daniel B. Cathcart. Costumes by Irene. Set decoration by Edwin B. Willis, Richard Pefferle. Special effects by A. Arnold Gillespie, Warren Newcombe.

Cast included Marlene Dietrich, Ronald Colman, James Craig, Edward Arnold, Hugh Herbert, Joy Ann Page, Florence Bates.

Songs: "Willow in the Wind," "Tell Me, Tell Me Evening Star," "I See a Morning Star" (unused) (Arlen).

Meet the People

Produced by E. Y. Harburg for Metro-Goldwyn-Mayer. Released September 7, 1944. 90 minutes. Directed by Charles Reisner. *Lyrics* by E. Y. Harburg, Lorenz Hart. *Music* by Burton Lane, Richard Rodgers, Sammy Fain. Screenplay by S. M. Herzig, Fred Saidy, suggested by a story by Sol and Ben Barzman, Louis Lantz. Photographed by Robert Surtes. Edited by Alexander Troffey.

Cast included Lucille Ball, Dick Powell, Virginia O'Brien, Bert Lahr, "Rags" Ragland, June Allyson, Vaughn Monroe Orchestra, Spike Jones City Slickers.

Songs: "In Times Like These," "Schicklegruber" (Fain); "It's Smart to Be People" (Lane); "Heave-Ho, Let the Wind Blow" (Arlen) (unused).

Hollywood Canteen

Produced by Alex Gottlieb for Warner Bros. Released December 15, 1944. 124 minutes. Directed by Delmer Daves; musical numbers directed by LeRoy Prinz. *Lyrics* by E. Y. Harburg, Cole Porter, Ted Koehler, Harold Adamson, Larry Neal, Jean Barry, Bob Nolan. *Music* by Burton Lane, Cole Porter, Vernon Duke, M. K. Jerome, Jimmy Mundy, Bob Nolan, Ray Heindorf. Screenplay by Delmer Daves. Photographed by Bert Glennon. Edited by Christian Nyby. Set direction by Leo Kuter. Set decoration by Casey Roberts. Costumes by Milo Anderson.

Cast included Robert Hutton, Joan Leslie, Dane Clark, Joan McCracken, The Andrews Sisters, Jack Benny, Julie Bishop, Betty Brodel, Barbara Brown, Joe. E. Brown, Eddie Cantor, Kitty Carlisle, Jack Carson, Joan Crawford, Helmut Dantine, Bette Davis, Faye Emerson, Victor Francen, John Garfield, Sydney Greenstreet, Alan Hale, Paul Henreid, Ida Lupino, Dennis Morgan, Janis Paige, Eleanor Parker, Roy Rogers and Trigger, Zachary Scott, Alexis Smith, Sons of the Pioneers, Barbara Stanwyck, Craig Stevens, Joseph Szigeti, Jane Wyman, Jimmy Dorsey and His Band, Carmen Cavallaro and His Orchestra.

Song: "You Can Always Tell a Yank" (Lane).

Can't Help Singing

Produced by Felix Jackson for Universal. Released December 25, 1944. 89 minutes. Directed by Frank Ryan. *Lyrics* by E. Y. Harburg. *Music* by Jerome Kern. Screenplay by Lewis R. Foster, Frank Ryan, from a story by John Klorer, Leo Townsend, based on the novel *Girl of the Overland Trail* by Samuel J. and Curtis J. Warshawsky. Photographed by Woody Bredell, W. Howard Greene. Edited by Ted J. Kent.

Cast included Deanna Durbin, Robert Paige, Akim Tamiroff, David Bruce, Leonid Kinskey, Clara Blandick.

Songs: "Can't Help Singing," "Elbow Room," "More and More," "Any Moment Now," "Californ-i-ay," "Swing Your Sweetheart 'Round the Fire," "I'll Follow Your Smile," "Once in a Million Moons" (unused), "There'll Come a Day" (unused).

Hell-Bent for Election (animated short subject)

Produced by United Auto Workers. Released in 1944. 14 minutes. Directed by Charles M. Jones. *Lyrics* by E. Y. Harburg. *Music* by Earl Robinson. Screenplay by Robert Lees.

Song: "You Gotta Get Out and Vote."

The Affairs of Susan

Produced by Hal Wallis for Paramount. Released March 28, 1945. 110 minutes. Directed by William A. Seiter. *Lyrics* by E. Y. Harburg. *Music* by Franz Waxman. Screenplay by Thomas Monroe, Laszlo Gorog, Richard Flourney, based on a story by Thomas Monroe and Laszlo Gorog. Photographed by David Abel. Edited by Edna Warren.

Cast included Joan Fontaine, George Brent, Dennis O'Keefe, Don DeFore, Rita Johnson, Walter Abel, Byron Barr, Mary Field, Frances Pierlot, Lewis Russell, Vera Marshe, Frank Faylen, James Millican, Robert Sully, John Whitney, Jerry James, Crane Whitney.

Song: "Something in My Heart."

Centennial Summer

Produced by Otto Preminger for Twentieth Century-Fox. Released July 17, 1946. 104 minutes. Directed by Otto Preminger. Dances by Dorothy Fox. *Lyrics* by E. Y. Harburg, Oscar Hammerstein II, Leo Robin. *Music* by Jerome Kern. Screenplay by Michael Kanin, based on the novel by Albert E. Idell. Photographed by Ernest Palmer; special photographic effects by Fred Sersen. Edited by Harry Reynolds. Art direction by Lyle Wheeler, Lee Fuller. Set decoration by Thomas Little. Special effects by Fred Sersen.

Cast included Jeanne Crain, Cornel Wilde, Linda Darnell, William Eythe, Walter Brennan, Constance Bennett, Dorothy Gish, Barbara Whiting, Larry Stevens, Kathleen Howard, Buddy Swan, Charles Dingle.

Song: "Cinderella Sue" (Kern).

California

Produced by Seton I. Miller for Paramount. Released January 14, 1947. 97 minutes. Directed by John Farrow. *Lyrics* by E. Y. Harburg. *Music* by Earl Robinson. Screenplay by Frank Butler, Theodore Strauss, based on a story by Boris Ingster. Photographed by Ray Rennahan, Gordon Jennings. Edited by Eda Warren. Art direction by Hans Dreier, Roland Anderson. Set decoration by Sam Comer, Ray Moyer. Costumes by Edith Head, Gile Steele. Special effects by Gordon Jennings.

Cast included Ray Milland, Barbara Stanwyck, Barry Fitzgerald, George Coulouris, Albert Dekker, Anthony Quinn, Frank Faylen.

Songs: "Said I to My Heart Said I," "California or Bust," "California," "I Should'a Stood in Massachusetts," "Lily-I-Lay-De-O."

Additional songs listed by Yip Harburg in the Harburg Archive at New York Public Library: "The Man with the Initials," "The Gold Rush."

Huckleberry Finn (unproduced film)

Produced by Arthur Freed for Metro-Goldwyn-Mayer in 1951. Directed by Vincente Minnelli. *Lyrics* by E. Y. Harburg. *Music* by Burton Lane. New first draft screenplay by Donald Ogden Stewart.

Cast included Gene Kelly, Danny Kaye (proposed).

Songs: "Don't Run Mirandy," "That Fine Sunday Feeling," "Jumpin' Jubilee."

Notes: Yip was blacklisted starting with this unfinished film.

The Adventures of Huckleberry Finn was produced in 1960 by Samuel Goldwyn, Jr.

A previous attempt at a musical score had been made by Hugh Martin and Ralph Blane; subsequently, Burton Lane and Alan Jay Lerner also wrote a score, part of which was used in the 1960 film.

April in Paris

Produced by William Jacobs for Warner Bros. Released December 24, 1952. 101 minutes. Directed by David Butler. Dances staged by LeRoy Prinz. *Lyrics* by E. Y. Harburg. *Music* by Vernon Duke, Sammy Cahn. Screenplay by Jack Rose, Melville Shavelson. Photographed by Wilfred M. Cline. Edited by Irene Morra.

Cast included Doris Day, Ray Bolger, Claude Dauphin, Eve Miller, Georeg Givot, Paul Harvey, Herbert Farjeon.

Song: "April in Paris" (Duke).

Gay Purr-ee (animated film)

Produced by Henry G. Saperstein; Warner Bros. release of UPA Productions. Released December 5, 1962. 86 minutes. Directed by Abe Levitow. *Lyrics* by E. Y. Harburg. *Music* by Harold Arlen. Screenplay by Dorothy and Chuck Jones; additional dialogue by Ralph Wright. Photographed by Roy Hutchcroft, Dan Miller, Jack Stevens, Diane Keegan. Edited by Sam Horta, Earl Bennett; supervising editor, Ted Baker. Art direction by Victor Haboush. Production design by Robert Singer, Richard Ung, "Corny" Cole Ray Aragon, Edward Levitt, Ernest Nordli. Color Stylists: Don Peters, Gloria Wood, Robert Inman, Phil Norman, Richard Kelsey. Animation by Ben Washam, Phil Duncan, Hal Ambro, Ray Patterson, Grant Simmons, Irv Spence, Don Lusk, Hank Smith, Harvey Toombs, Volus Jones, Ken Harris, Fred Madison.

Voices included Judy Garland, Robert Goulet, Red Buttons, Hermione Gingold, Paul Frees, Morey Amsterdam, Mel Blanc, Julie Bennett, Joan Gardner.

Songs: "Paris Is a Lonely Town," "Mewsette," "Roses Red-Violets Blue," "Take My Hand, Paree," "The Horse Won't Talk," "The Money Cat," "Little Drops of Rain," "Bubbles," "Free at Last" (unused).

I Could Go on Singing (British film)

Produced by Stuart Millar and Laurence Turman for Barbican Films. A United Artists release. Released May 15, 1963. 99 minutes. Directed by Ronald Neame. *Lyrics* by E. Y. Harburg, Howard Dietz, Maxwell Anderson, Cliff Friend, Sir Arthur Sullivan. *Music* by Harold Arlen, Arthur Schwartz, Kurt Weill, Cliff Friend. Screenplay by Mayo Simon, from a story by Robert Dozier. Photographed by Arthur Ibbetson. Edited by John Shirley. Art direction by Wilfred Singleton. Sets designed by John Hoesli. Costumes by Edith Head.

Cast included Judy Garland, Dirk Bogarde, Jack Klugman, Aline MacMahon, Gregory Phillips, Pauline Jameson, Jeremy Burnham, Russell Waters, Gerald Sim, Leon Cortez.

Song: "I Could Go on Singing (Till the Cows Come Home)" (Arlen).

Finian's Rainbow

Produced by Joseph Landon for Warner Bros.-Seven Arts. Released October 9, 1968. 145 minutes. Directed by Francis Ford Coppola. Dances staged by Hermes Pan. *Lyrics* by E. Y. Harburg. *Music* by Burton Lane. Photographed by Philip Lathrop. Edited by Melvin Shapiro. Production designed by Hilyard M. Brown. Costumes by Dorothy Jeakins. Set decoration by William L. Kuehl.

Cast included Fred Astaire, Petula Clark, Tommy Steele, Don Francks, Keenan Wynn, Barbara Hancock.

Songs: "(That) Old Devil Moon," "How Are Things in Glocca Morra?" "Look to the Rainbow," "If This Isn't Love," "When I'm Not Near the Girl I Love," "Something Sort of Grandish," "That Great Come-and-Get-It-Day," "This Time of the Year," "When the Idle Poor Become the Idle Rich," "The Begat."

Appendix 3

Radio and Television Shows and Songs

Ever Ready Radio Hour

"The Mayor of Hogan's Alley" (one-act musical play). Broadcast February 19, 1929; CBS radio. *Script* by E. Y. Harburg (uncredited). *Music* by Jay Gorney, Henry Souvaine.

Cast: Don Barclay.

"How's the Judge" (one-act musical play). Broadcast May 14, 1929; CBS radio. *Script* by E. Y. Harburg (uncredited). *Music* by Jay Gorney, Henry Souvaine.

"For Dear Old Delta" (two-act musical play). Broadcast in 1929; CBS radio. *Script* by E. Y. Harburg (uncredited). *Music* probably by Jay Gorney, Henry Souvaine, but authorship not specified on script.

Franklin D. Roosevelt Election Eve Broadcast (radio)

Produced by the Democratic National Committee. Broadcast November 6, 1944; NBC and CBS radio.

Performers included Humphrey Bogart, James Cagney, Jimmy Durante, Judy Garland, Dooley Wilson, Earl Robinson.

Songs with lyrics by E. Y. Harburg included "Don't Look Now Mr. Dewey (But Your Record's Showing)" (Schwartz); "Free and Equal Blues," "You Gotta Get Out and Vote" (Robinson).

Unity Fair

(Radio Broadcast at the Opening of the United Nations in San Francisco; under title of *Columbia Presents Corwin*.)

Presented by Norman Corwin. Broadcast June 17, 1945; CBS radio. *Lyrics* by E. Y. Harburg. *Music* by Burton Lane, Earl Robinson.

Cast: Alfred Drake.

Songs: "It's Smart to Be People," "The Son of a Gun Who Picks on Uncle Sam" (Lane); "The Same Boat, Brother" (Robinson).

The Great Mans Whiskus (television motion picture)
(Alternate title: The Great Man's Whiskers.)

Produced by Universal City Studios. Telecast February 13, 1973; NBC. 96 minutes, color, 16 mm. Directed by Philip Leacock. *Lyrics* by E. Y. Harburg. *Music* by Earl Robinson. Teleplay by John Paxton, from a one-act play by Adrian Scott. Photographed by John F. Warren. Edited by John Elias.

Cast: Dean Jones, Ann Sothern, John McGiver, Harve Presnell, Beth Brickell, Dennis Weaver, Isabel Sanford.

Song: "Wilderness Man," "Things Go Bump in the Night."

Appendix 4

Alphabetical List of Yip Harburg's Song Titles (537)

"Adrift on a Star," 1961, *The Happiest Girl in the World,* Offenbach

"An African Song (on That Great Civilized Morning)," 1964, Okun, Kobluk, Frazier, Mitchell

"Ah, But Is It Love," 1933, *Moonlight and Pretzels,* Gorney

"Ah, Jus' Like You," 1930, *Earl Carroll Vanities,* Gorney

"Ah, What's the Use," 1939, *The Sap from Syracuse,* Green

"Ain't It de Truth," 1943, *Cabin in the Sky* (cut); 1957, *Jamaica,* Arlen

"(All) The Elks and Masons," 1934, *Life Begins at 8:40* (lyrics cowritten by Gershwin), Arlen

"And Russia Is Her Name," 1943, *Song of Russia* (first performed at Russian War Relief Benefit, Hollywood Bowl), Kern

"And Yet the World Rolls On," J. Meyer, H. Mayer

"Angelina," 1977, Lane

"Ankle Up the Altar with Me," 1930, *The Garrick Gaieties,* Meyers

"Any Moment Now," 1944, *Can't Help Singing,* Kern

"Anything Can Happen in New York," 1941, *Babes on Broadway,* Lane

"April in Paris," 1932, *Walk a Little Faster,* Duke

"Arabian for Get Happy," 1951, *Flahooley,* Fain

"As Long As We Have Bromo Seltzer in Our Love Nest," 1932, see note under *Ballyhoo of 1932* entry (app. 1)

"B. G. Bigelow, Inc.," 1951, *Flahooley; Jollyanna,* Fain

"Baby, Be Yourself," 1930, *Earl Carroll Vanities,* Duke

"Baby, We're Through," 1932, see note under *Ballyhoo of 1932* entry (app. 1)

"Baby, You're News," 1939, *Sticks and Stones* (lyrics cowritten by Gershwin), Green

"Ballyhooey Lassies," 1932, see note under *Ballyhoo of 1932* entry (app. 1)

"Ballyhujah," 1932, *Ballyhoo of 1932,* Gensler

"Battle of Paris," 1929, *Battle of Paris,* composer unknown

"Beautifying the City," 1934, *Life Begins at 8:40* (lyrics cowritten by Gershwin), Arlen

"Bedtime on the Prairie," 1940, *Hold on to Your Hats* (cut), Lane

"The Begat," 1947, *Finian's Rainbow;* 1968 film, Lane

"A Blushing Bride," 1968, see note under *Darling of the Day* entry (app. 1), Styne

"Brother, Can You Spare a Dime?" 1932, *Americana,* Gorney

"Brother, Just Laugh It Off," 1930, *Queen High; Follow the Leader,* Rainger, Schwartz

"Bubbles," 1962, *Gay Purr-ee,* Arlen

"Buddy, Can You Spare a Buck?" 1976, Gorney

"Buds Won't Bud," 1938, *Andy Hardy Meets Debutante; Hooray for What?* (cut); *Cairo,* Arlen

"Bunny Song," 1969, Sternberg

"Butler in the Abbey," 1968, *Darling of the Day,* Styne

"Cairo," 1942, *Cairo,* Schwartz

"California," 1947, *California,* Robinson

"California or Bust," 1947, *California,* Robinson

"Californ-i-ay," 1944, *Can't Help Singing,* Kern

"Calypso Kitty," 1941, Sigman, Meyer, Harburg

"Can't Get Along," 1930, *Earl Carroll Vanities,* Green

"Can't Help Singing," 1944, *Can't Help Singing,* Kern

"Capitalize That Thing Called It," 1930, *The Sap from Syracuse,* Duke, Green

"Careful with My Heart," 1934, *Ziegfeld Follies, 1933–34; 1935, Broadway Gondolier,* Pokrass

"'Cause You Won't Play House," 1934 *New Faces* (lyrics cowritten by Hamilton), Lewis

"C'est la Vie," 1934, *Life Begins at 8:40* (lyrics cowritten by Gershwin), Arlen

"Change of Sky," 1980, Springer

"Chant," 1957, *Jamaica,* Arlen

"Cheers for the Hero," 1961, *The Happiest Girl in the World,* Offenbach

"Chic, Chic, Chic Are We," 1961, see note under *The Happiest Girl in the World* entry (app. 1)

"Chin Up, Cheerio, Carry On" 1941, *Babes on Broadway,* Lane

"Christmas Song," 1951, *Flahooley* (cut), Fain

"Cinderella Sue," 1946, *Centennial Summer,* Kern

"Cocoanut Sweet," 1957, *Jamaica,* Arlen

"Come Back, Little Genie," 1951, *Flahooley, Jollyanna,* Fain

"Come Back to God/Me," 1968, see note under *Darling of the Day* entry (app. 1)

"A Couple of Caballeros," 1942, *Rio Rita,* Arlen

"Crashing the Golden Gates," 1929, *Earl Carroll's Sketch Book,* Gorney, Cohen

"Crazy Old World," 1979, Springer

"The Crazy Quilt Sextette," 1931, *Crazy Quilt* (composer unknown/lyrics cowritten by Rose).

"Crispy Crunchy Crackers," 1940, *Hold on to Your Hats* (unused), Lane

"Daisy and Rainbows," 1969, Previn, Arlen

"The Darling of the Day" 1968, see note under *Darling of the Day* entry (app. 1)

"A Day Late and a Dollar Short," added 1973 to *Flahooley,* Fain

"Demon in the Compass," 1971, *What a Day for a Miracle,* Orenstein, Alexander

"Ding Dong! The Witch Is Dead," 1939, *The Wizard of Oz,* Arlen

"Do I Need You?" n.d. Green

"Don't Let It Get You Down," 1940, *Hold on to Your Hats,* Lane

"Don't Look Now, Mr. Dewey (But Your Record's Showing)," 1944, election eve broadcast for Franklin D. Roosevelt, Schwartz

"Don't Pour the Thames into the Rhine," 1968, see note under *Darling of the Day* entry (app. 1)

"Don't Run Mirandy," 1951, *Huckleberry Finn,* Lane

"Dorine," 1931, Gorney

"Double Soliloquy," 1968, *Darling of the Day,* Styne

"Down on the Dude Ranch," 1940, *Hold on to Your Hats,* Lane

"Down with Love," 1937, *Hooray for What?* Arlen

"Drivin' and Dreamin'," 1979, Springer

"Duet," 1931, Gorney

"Dusty Shoes," 1933, *Moonlight and Pretzels,* Gorney

"The Eagle and Me," 1944, *Bloomer Girl,* Arlen

"Edelaine," 1979, Springer

"Elbow Room," 1944, *Can't Help Singing,* Kern

"The Elks and Masons," see "(All) The Elks and Masons"

"The Enchanted Clock," 1979, Springer

"Enchantment," 1951, *Flahooley,* Fain

"End of a Beautiful Friendship," 1976, Arlen

"End of a Perfect Night, 1932, *Walk a Little Faster,* Duke

"Eureka," 1961, *The Happiest Girl in the World,* Offenbach

"Evelina," 1944, *Bloomer Girl,* Arlen

"Excuse My Laughter," 1961, see note under *The Happiest Girl in the World* entry (app. 1)

"Ex-Gigolo," 1930, *The Vanderbilt Revue,* Braggiotti

"An Extra Little Shilling," see "That Something Extra Special"

"Fabulous," 1952, *Jollyanna,* Friml

"Falling Off the Wagon," 1932, *Ballyhoo of 1932,* Gensler

"Fancy Meeting You," 1936, *Stage Struck,* Arlen

"Farmer's Daughter," 1944, *Bloomer Girl,* Arlen

"A Fashion Girl," 1937, *Hooray for What?* Arlen

"Fifth Avenue—A Sidewalk in Paris," 1934, *Ziegfeld Follies,* 1933–34, Pokrass

"Five Minutes of Spring," 1932, *Americana,* Gorney

"Five Minutes of Spring," 1961, *The Happiest Girl in the World,* Offenbach

"Flahooley," 1951, *Flahooley,* Fain

"The Follies Choral Ensemble," 1934, *Ziegfeld Follies,* 1933–34, Pokrass

"Foolish Baby," 1930, *Earl Carroll Vanities* (lyrics cowritten by Tours, Heyman), Green

"For Every Fish (There's a Little Bigger Fish)," 1957, *Jamaica,* Arlen

"Free and Equal Blues," 1944, election eve broadcast for Franklin D. Roosevelt; 1945, *Blue Holiday,* Robinson

"Free at Last," 1962, *Gay Purr-ee* (unused), Arlen

"Freedom Is the Word," 1964, Lane

"Friendly Henry Wallace," 1948, Ager

"Fun to Be Fooled," 1934, *Life Begins at 8:40* (lyrics cowritten by Gershwin), Arlen

"A Gal Named Cinderella," 1952, *Jollyanna,* Fain

"A Gentleman's Gentleman (Where Would Britain Be without a Butler)," 1968, *Darling of the Day,* Styne

"Get That Sun into You," 1932, *Americana,* Myers

"The Girl That Was," 1969, Sternberg

"Glory," 1930, *Earl Carroll Vanities,* Green

"The Glory That Is Greece," 1961, *The Happiest Girl in the World,* Offenbach

"God's Country," 1937, *Hooray for What?;* 1939 *Babes in Arms,* Arlen

"Going Up," 1930, *Earl Carroll Vanities,* Gorney

"The Gold Rush," 1947, see note under *California* entry (app. 2).

"Goodnight, Mrs. Calabash," 1972 (ASCAP 1982), Fain

"Gotta Get Out and Vote," see "You Gotta Get Out and Vote"

"Great Guns, How the Money Rolls In," 1943, Fain

"The Greek Marine Hymn," 1961, *The Happiest Girl in the World,* Offenbach

"Grown Ups," 1971, *What a Day for a Miracle,* Orenstein, Alexander

"Hanging Out a Rainbow (over the U.S.A.)," 1943, (Ralph Freed), Fain

"The Happiest Girl in the World," 1961, *The Happiest Girl in the World,* Offenbach

"Happiness Is a Thing Called Joe," 1943, *Cabin in the Sky,* Arlen

"Happy Hunting," 1951, *Flahooley,* Fain

"Have You Heard About the Meeting?" 1945, Robinson

"He Has Such Charm (Il Est Charmant)," 1932, Moretti

"He Will Walk with Thee," 1971, *What a Day for a Miracle,* Orenstein, Alexander

"Heads Up," 1930, *Heads Up,* Duke

"Heave-Ho, Let the Wind Blow," 1944, *Meet the People* (unused), Arlen

"Henry Leek," 1968, see note under *Darling of the Day* entry (app. 1)

"Here's Looking at You," 1936, *The Singing Kid,* Arlen

"Here's to Your Illusions," 1951, *Flahooley,* Fain

"He's a Genius," 1968, *Darling of the Day,* Styne

"He's Only Wonderful," 1951, *Flahooley,* Fain

"Hitchhikers (on That Highway Called Life)," 1973, Springer

"Hold on to Your Hats," 1940, *Hold on to Your Hats,* Lane

"Hold Your Man," 1930, *Earl Carroll Vanities,* Duke

"Honestly," 1961, see note under *The Happiest Girl in the World* entry (app. 1)

"Honorable Moon," 1943, *Princess O'Rourke* (lyrics cowritten by Gershwin), Schwartz

"Hooray for de Yankee Dollar," 1957, *Jamaica,* Arlen

"Hooray for What?" 1937, *Hooray for What?* Arlen

"The Horse Won't Talk," 1962, *Gay Purr-ee,* Arlen

"Hot Moonlight," 1931, *Shoot the Works!;* 1934 film, Gorney

"How About a Little Date for Breakfast," 1932, see note under *Ballyhoo of 1932* entry (app. 1)

"How Are Things in Glocca Morra?" 1947, *Finian's Rainbow;* 1968 film, Lane

"How Can I Hold You Close Enough?" 1935, *Stop Press* (lyrics cowritten by Heyman), Green

"How Do You Do It?" 1932, *Ballyhoo of 1932,* Gensler

"How I Wish I Could Sing a Love Song," 1930, *The Sap from Syracuse,"* Green

"How Lucky Can You Get," 1952, *Jollyanna,* Fain

"How Soon, Oh Moon?" 1961, *The Happiest Girl in the World,* Offenbach

"How's by You," 1936, Arlen

"Hup-Two-Three," 1961, see note under *The Happiest Girl in the World* entry (app. 1)

"Hurry Sundown," 1966, Robinson

"Hush Ma Mouth," 1936, *Gold Diggers of 1937,* Arlen

"I Am Only Human After All," 1930, *The Garrick Gaieties* (lyrics cowritten by Gershwin), Duke

"I Came to Life," 1930, *Earl Carroll Vanities,* Gorney

"I Click Ze Heel and Keez Ze Hand," 1937, *Hooray for What?* (cut), Arlen

"I Could Go on Singing ('Till the Cows Come Home)," 1963, *I Could Go on Singing,* Arlen

"I Couldn't Hold My Man," 1934, *Life Begins at 8:40* (lyrics cowritten by Gershwin), Arlen

"I Don't Think I'll End It All Today," 1957, *Jamaica,* Arlen

"I Got a Song," 1944, *Bloomer Girl,* Arlen

"I Knew Him When," 1934 (ASCAP 1964), *Life Begins at 8:40* (cut) (lyrics cowritten by Gershwin), Arlen

"I Lerve You," 1932 (published 1958), see note under *Ballyhoo of 1932* entry (app. 1)

"I Like the Likes of You," 1934, *Ziegfeld Follies, 1933–34*, Duke

"I Love the Girls in My Own Peculiar Way," 1930, *Queen High*, Souvain

"I Love to Sing-a," 1936, *The Singing Kid*, Arlen

"I May Fall in Love Again," 1930, *Heads Up*, Duke

"I Need a Change of Sky," 1973, Ellington

"I Need New Words," 1934, *Continental Varieties*, Delettre

"I Never Was Born," 1944, *Bloomer Girl*, Arlen

"I See a Morning Star," 1944, *Kismet* (unused), Arlen

"I Should'a Stood in Massachusetts," 1947, *California*, Robinson

"I, Whoever I Am," 1973 (ASCAP 1982), Fain

"If Every Day Were Valentine's Day," 1977, Fain

"If I Didn't Have You," 1931, Ager

"If I Only Had a Brain," 1939, *The Wizard of Oz*, Arlen

"If I Only Had a Heart," 1939, *The Wizard of Oz*, Arlen

"If I Only Had the Nerve," 1939, *The Wizard of Oz*, Arlen

"If I Were King of the Forest," 1939, *The Wizard of Oz*, Arlen

"If This Isn't Love," 1947, *Finian's Rainbow*; 1968 film, Lane

"If You Believed in Me," see "It's Only a Paper Moon"

"Igual Que Tu," 1931, Gorney

"Il Est Charmant," see "He Has Such Charm"

"I'll Follow Your Smile," 1944, *Can't Help Singing*, Kern

"I'll Make a Home for Your Love (in This Heart of Mine)," 1931, *Her Highness Commands*, Heyman

"I'll Take Manila," 1941, *I'll Take Manila* (became *Ship Ahoy*) (unused), Lane

"I'll Take Tallulah," 1942, *Ship Ahoy*, Lane

"I'll Thank You to Stay Out of My Dreams," 1936, Arlen

"I'm a Collector of Moonbeams," 1934, *Life Begins at 8:40* (cut) (lyrics cowritten by Gershwin), Arlen

"I'm Not Myself," 1934, Arlen

"I'm Off of You," see note under *Ballyhoo of 1932* entry (app. 1)

"I'm One of God's Children," see note under *Ballyhoo of 1932* entry (app. 1)

"I'm Simpally Mad for Bones," 1968, see note under *Darling of the Day* entry (app. 1)

"I'm Tired of Love," see note under *Ballyhoo of 1932* entry (app. 1)

"I'm Yours," 1930, *Leave It to Lester*, Green

"In a Jocular Vein," 1982, Hellerman

"In the Back of a Hack," 1930 (ASCAP 1956), Gorney

"In the Shade of the New Apple Tree," 1937, *Hooray for What?* Arlen

"In Times Like These," 1944, *Meet the People*, Fain

"In Your Own Quiet Way," 1936, *Stage Struck*, Arlen

"Incompatibility," 1957, *Jamaica*, Arlen

"Isn't It Heavenly," 1933, Myer

"Isn't This a Day," 1968, see note under *Darling of the Day* entry (app. 1)

"It Can't Go on Like This," 1930, *Roadhouse Nights* (lyrics cowritten by Kahal), Gorney

"It Was Good Enough for Grandma," 1944, *Bloomer Girl*, Arlen

"It Was Long Ago," 1934, *Life Begins at 8:40* (lyrics cowritten by Gershwin), Arlen

"It's a Happy World," 1931, Levant

"It's a Short, Short Walk to a Long Sleep," 1974, Sternberg

"It's Enough to Make a Lady Fall in Love," 1968, *Darling of the Day,* Styne

"It's in the Air," 1931, *Crazy Quilt* (lyrics cowritten by Rose), Alter

"It's Only a Paper Moon (If You Believed in Me)," 1932, *The Great Magoo;* 1933, *Take a Chance,* (lyrics cowritten by Rose), Arlen

"It's Smart to Be People," 1944, *Meet the People;* 1945, *Unity Fair* (radio), Lane

"It's Smart to Be Smart," see "Smart to Be Smart"

"It's Such Unusual Weather," 1942, *Rio Rita* (unused), Arlen

"I've a Rendezvous with Spring," 1933, Duke

"I've Gone Romantic on You," 1937, *Hooray for What?* Arlen

"I've Got a Rainbow Working for Me," 1968, *Darling of the Day,* Styne

"Jerusalem," 1971, *What a Day for a Miracle,* Orenstein, Alexander

"Jezebel Jones," 1943, *Cabin in the Sky* (unused), Arlen

"The Jitterbug," 1939, *The Wizard of Oz* (cut), Arlen

"Jollyanna," 1952, *Jollyanna,* Friml

"Jump Little Chillun" ("Jump, Chillun, Jump"), 1951, *Flahooley; Jollyanna,* Fain

"Jumpin' Jubilee," 1950, *Huckleberry Finn,* Lane

"Just a Melody for a Memory," 1930, *Roadhouse Nights* (lyrics cowritten by Kahal), Fain, Gorney

"Just Another Dream Gone Wrong," 1930, *Song Service,* DeRose

"Keep the Light Burning Bright (in the Harbor)," 1942, *Cairo,* Harburg

"Kinda Cute," 1929, *Earl Carroll's Sketch Book,* Gorney

"Kneedeep in June," 1930, *Earl Carroll Vanities,* Gorney

"La Tra Ma La," 1971, *What a Day for a Miracle,* Orenstein, Alexander

"La Vieja Luna," 1979, Lane

"Ladies of the Evening," 1931, *Crazy Quilt* (lyrics cowritten by Rose) (composer unknown)

"Lady Alice," 1968, see note under *Darling of the Day* entry (app. 1)

"Lament," 1951, *Flahooley* (cut), Fain

"The Last Call for Love," 1942, *Ship Ahoy,* Cummings, Lane

"Last Night When We Were Young," 1935, Arlen

"Laugh It Down," 1930, *Earl Carroll Vanities,* Duke

"Leave a Message," 1952, *Jollyanna,* Friml

"Leave de Atom Alone," 1957, *Jamaica,* Arlen

"The Legend of Niagara," 1930, Gorney

"Legs, Legs, Legs," 1929, *Earl Carroll's Sketch Book,* Gorney

"Let Me Match My Private Life with Yours," 1932, *Americana,* Duke

"Let There Be Music," 1943, *Thousands Cheer,* Brent

"Let's Forget Tomorrow Tonight," 1934, Grover

"Let's Make Love Like the Crocodiles," 1933, *Moonlight and Pretzels,* Gorney

"Let's Put Our Heads Together," 1936, *Gold Diggers of 1937,* Arlen

"Let's See What Happens," 1968, *Darling of the Day,* Styne

"Let's Take a Walk around the Block," 1934, *Life Begins at 8:40* (lyrics cowritten by Gershwin), Arlen

"Life Begins," 1934, *Life Begins at 8:40* (lyrics cowritten by Gershwin), Arlen

"Life Insurance Song," 1936, *Gold Diggers of 1937,* Arlen

"Life Was Pie for the Pioneer," 1940, *Hold on to Your Hats,* Arlen

"Life's a Dance," 1937, *Hooray for What?* Arlen

"Life's Full of Consequence," 1943, *Cabin in the Sky,* Arlen

"Like Me Less, Love Me More," 1929, *Earl Carroll's Sketch Book,* Gorney

"Li'l Black Sheep," 1943, *Cabin in the Sky,* Arlen

"Lily-I-Lay-De-O," 1947, *California,* Robinson

"Little Big Man," added in 1976 to *Bloomer Girl,* Arlen

"Little Biscuit," 1957, *Jamaica,* Arlen

"Little Drops of Rain," 1962, *Gay Purr-ee,* Arlen

"Little Old Gehenna," 1961, see note under *The Happiest Girl in the World* entry (app. 1)

"Little Ships," 1971, *What a Day for a Miracle,* Orenstein, Alexander

"Little World, Good Morning," 1971, *What a Day for a Miracle,* Orenstein, Alexander

"Liza Crossing the Ice," 1944, *Bloomer Girl,* Arlen

"Lollipop Guild," 1939, *The Wizard of Oz,* Arlen

"The Loneliest Isle," see "Manhattan's the Loneliest Isle"

"The Lonesomest Girl in the World," 1961, see note under *The Happiest Girl in the World* entry (app. 1)

"Long As You've Got Your Health," 1936, *The Show Is On* (lyrics cowritten by Zeno), Irwin

"Long Before You Came Along," 1942, *Rio Rita,* Arlen

"Look to the Rainbow," 1947, *Finian's Rainbow;* 1968 film, Lane

"Looks Like I'm off'o Ya (Now That I'm on to Ya)," 1940, *Hold on to Your Hats* (cut), Lane

"Looks Like the End of a Beautiful Friendship, 1978, Arlen

"Losing You," 1933, Pokrass

"Lost Sheep," 1971, *What a Day for a Miracle,* Orenstein, Alexander

"Love and Nuts and Noodles (Bring 'Em Back Alive)," 1932, *Ballyhoo of 1932,* Gensler

"Love Being What It Is," 1978, Van Heusen

"Love Boats," 1930, *Earl Carroll Vanities,* Gorney

"Love Comes in Many Different Colors," 1979, Springer

"Lovesick Serenade," 1961, *The Happiest Girl in the World,* Offenbach

"Lullaby (Satin Gown and Silver Shoe)," 1944, *Bloomer Girl,* Arlen

"Lullaby League," 1939, *The Wizard of Oz,* Arlen

"Lydia, the Tattooed Lady," 1939, *[A Day] At the Circus,* Arlen

"Lying in State," 1968, see note under *Darling of the Day* entry (app. 1)

"Lysistrata's Oath," 1961, *The Happiest Girl in the World,* Offenbach

"Mad for Art," 1968, *Darling of the Day,* Styne

"The Magic Falute," 1961, see note under *The Happiest Girl in the World* entry (app. 1)

"Mailu," 1931, *Ziegfeld Follies,* Gorney, Riesenfeld

"Make Way for Tomorrow," 1944, *Cover Girl* (lyrics cowritten by Gershwin), Kern

"Man About Yonkers," 1932 (published 1958), *Ballyhoo of 1932,* Gensler

"Man for Sale," 1944, *Bloomer Girl,* Arlen

"The Man on the Money-Go-Round," 1979, Springer

"The Man with the Initials," 1947, see note under *California* entry (app. 2)

"Manhattan's the Loneliest Isle," 1932, *Walk a Little Faster* (cut), Duke

"Meeting Song," 1945, Robinson

"Mewsette," 1962, *Gay Purr-ee,* Arlen

"The Merry Old Land of Oz," 1939, *The Wizard of Oz,* Arlen

"Missouri Misery," 1934, Suesse

"Moanin' in the Mornin'," 1937, *Hooray for What?* Arlen

"The Money Cat," 1962, *Gay Purr-ee,* Arlen

"Money, Money, Money," 1968, *Darling of the Day,* Styne

"Monkey in the Mango Tree," 1957, *Jamaica,* Arlen

"Moon about Town," 1934, *Ziegfeld Follies,* 1933–34, Suesse

"Moonlight and Pretzels," 1933, *Moonlight and Pretzels,* Gorney

"More and More," 1944, *Can't Help Singing,* Kern

"The More We See of People, the Better We Like Horses," 1936, Arlen

"The Movies Gonna Get Ya If You Don't Watch Out," 1940, Lane

"Muchacha," 1931, *Shoot the Works!* (stage and film), Gorney, Duke

"Munchkinland," 1939, *The Wizard of Oz,* Arlen

"My Fortune is Love," 1931, *Sein Liebeslied (His Love Song),* Stolz

"My Heart Is Like the Willow," 1969, Alexander and Orenstein

"My, How This Country Has Changed," 1936, *The Singing Kid,* Arlen

"My Little Prayer," 1931, Gorney

"My Mind Says Don't," 1961, see note under *The Happiest Girl in the World* entry (app. 1)

"My Other Me," 1935, *Manhattan Moon,* Hajos

"My Paramount-Publix-Roxy Rose," 1934, *Life Begins at 8:40* (lyrics cowritten by Gershwin), Arlen

"Napoleon," 1957, *Jamaica,* Arlen

"Napoleon's a Pastry," 1937, *Hooray for What?* (cut), Arlen

"Necessity," 1947, *Finian's Rainbow,* Lane

"Never Bedevil the Devil," 1961, *The Happiest Girl in the World,* Offenbach

"Never Trust a Virgin," 1961, *The Happiest Girl in the World,* Offenbach

"New Deal Rhythm," 1933, *Take a Chance* (lyrics cowritten by Rose), Edens

"The New Parade," 1936, *Stage Struck,* Arlen

"New York Is Full of Aliens," 1929, "The Mayor of Hogan's Alley" ("Ever Ready Radio Hour"), Gorney

"Night," 1932, Ager

"No Me Creas," 1931, Gorney

"Noah," 1957, *Jamaica* (cut), Arlen

"Not on Your Nellie," 1968, *Darling of the Day,* Styne

"The Oath," see "Lysistrata's Oath"

"Off Again, On Again," 1932, *Walk a Little Faster,* Duke

"Office Blues," 1930, *Office Blues,* DeRose

"Oh, It Looks Like Rain," 1931, *Crazy Quilt,* Ager

"Oh My, What a Wonderful World," 1930, *Earl Carroll Vanities* (lyrics cowritten by Tours), Gorney

"Old Devil Moon," 1947, *Finian's Rainbow,* 1968 film, Lane

"Old Devil Sea," 1930, *Earl Carroll Vanities,* Duke

"The Old Pied Piper," 1961, see note under *The Happiest Girl in the World* entry (app. 1)

"Old Timer," 1940, *Hold on to Your Hats,* Lane

"Old-Fashioned Wedding," 1932, *Ballyhoo of 1932,* Gensler

"Once in a Million Moons," 1944, *Can't Help Singing* (unused), Kern

"One Sweet Morning," 1971, Robinson

"Optimistic Voices," 1939, *The Wizard of Oz,* Arlen, Stothart

"Over the Rainbow," 1939, *The Wizard of Oz*, Arlen

"Paging Mr. Greenback," 1943, *Presenting Lily Mars* (unused) (lyrics cowritten by Brown), Fain, Edens

"Panache," 1968, *Darling of the Day*, Styne

"Papa Likes a Hot Papoose," 1929, *Earl Carroll's Sketch Book*, Gorney

"Paper Moon," see "It's Only a Paper Moon"

"Paris Is a Lonely Town," 1962, *Gay Purr-ee*, Arlen

"A Penny for Your Thoughts," 1932, *Walk a Little Faster*, Duke

"Persian Women," 1961, see note under *The Happiest Girl in the World* entry (app. 1)

"Petunia's Prayer," 1943, *Cabin in the Sky*, Arlen

"Philadelphia (America's Home Town)," 1979, Springer

"Pity de Sunset," 1957, *Jamaica*, Arlen

"Politics," 1961, see note under *The Happiest Girl in the World* entry (app. 1)

"Poor Whippoorwill," 1942, *Rio Rita*, Arlen

"Poor You," 1942, *Ship Ahoy*, Lane

"Pretty as a Picture," 1944, *Bloomer Girl*, Arlen

"Pretty Little Words," 1932, Levant

"Pretty to Walk With (That's How a Man Gets Got)," 1957, *Jamaica*, Arlen

"Priam Farll" 1968, see note under *Darling of the Day* entry (app. 1)

"Private Miss Jones," 1943, *Thousands Cheer* (unused) (lyrics cowritten by Brent), Stothart

"Promise Me Not to Love Me," added in 1976 to *Bloomer Girl*, Arlen

"Push de Button," 1957, *Jamaica*, Arlen

"Putney on the Thames," 1968, see note under *Darling of the Day* entry (app. 1)

"Quartet Erotica (We're Not What We Used To Be)," 1934, *Life Begins at 8:40* (lyrics cowritten by Gershwin), Arlen

"The Rakish Young Man with the Whiskers," 1944, *Bloomer Girl*, Arlen

"Rendezvous with Spring," 1942, Duke

"Renovation Sequence," 1939, *The Wizard of Oz*, Arlen

"Rhodope's Tavern," 1961, see note under *The Happiest Girl in the World* entry (app. 1)

"Riddle Me This," 1932, *Ballyhoo of 1932*, Gensler

"Right as the Rain," 1944, *Bloomer Girl*, Arlen

"Ring Out the Blues," 1930, *Earl Carroll Vanities*, Gorney

"Roses Red-Violets Blue," 1962, *Gay Purr-ee*, Arlen

"Sabre Song," 1961, see note under *The Happiest Girl in the World* entry (app. 1)

"Said I to My Heart, Said I," 1947, *California*, Robinson

"St. Francis Prayer," 1971, *What a Day for a Miracle*, Orenstein, Alexander

"Salome," 1943, *DuBarry Was a Lady*, Edens, Brent

"The Same Boat, Brother," 1945, *Unity Fair* (radio), Robinson

"Saroyan," 1979, Springer

"Satan's Li'l Lamb," 1932, *Americana* (lyrics cowritten by Mercer), Arlen

"Savannah," 1957, *Jamaica*, Arlen

"Savannah's Wedding Day," 1957, *Jamaica*, Arlen

"Save Me, Sister," 1936, *The Singing Kid*, Arlen

"Say It!" 1931, Levant

"Scheherezade," 1951, *Flahooley; Jollyanna*, Fain

"Scheherezade's Interlude," 1951, *Flahooley* (cut), Fain

"Schicklegruber," 1944, *Meet the People,* Fain

"Scratch a Wife and Find a Doll," 1961, see note under *The Happiest Girl in the World* entry (app. 1)

"The Sermon, the Sword and the Song," 1971, *What a Day for a Miracle,* Orenstein, Alexander

"Shall We Say Farewell," 1961, *The Happiest Girl in the World,* Offenbach

"Share a Little," 1941, Lane

"Shavian Shivers," 1930, *The Garrick Gaieties,* Duke

"She Came, She Saw, She Can Canned," 1940, *Hold on to Your Hats,* Lane

"She'll Be Coming 'Round the Catskill Mountains," 1932. See note under *Ballyhoo of 1932* entry (app. 1)

"Shoein' the Mare," 1934, *Life Begins at 8:40* (lyrics cowritten by Gershwin), Arlen

"Sick, Sick, Sick," 1961, see note under *The Happiest Girl in the World* entry (app. 1)

"The Silent Spring," 1963, Arlen

"Simon Legree," 1944, *Bloomer Girl,* Arlen

"Sing the Merry," 1951, *Flahooley,* Fain

"Smart to Be Smart, 1934, *Ziegfeld Follies,* 1933–34 (cut), Duke

"So Nonchalant," 1932, *Walk a Little Faster* (lyrics cowritten by Tobias), Duke

"Some Folk Work," 1943, *Cabin in the Sky,* Arlen

"Something in My Heart, 1945, *The Affairs of Susan,* Waxman

"Something Sort of Grandish," 1947, *Finian's Rainbow;* 1968 film, Lane

"The Son of a Gun Who Picks on Uncle Sam," 1942, *Panama Hattie;* 1945, *Unity Fair* (radio), Lane

"The Song of Assisi," 1971, *What a Day for a Miracle,* Orenstein, Alexander

"Song of the Enchanted Rope," 1951, *Flahooley* (cut), Fain

"Song of the Woodman," 1936, *The Show Is On; Merry Go Round of 1938,* Arlen

"Speaking of Love," 1932, *Walk a Little Faster,* Duke

"Speaking of the Weather," 1937, *Gold Diggers of 1937,* Arlen

"Spirit of Capsulanti," 1951, *Flahooley,* Fain

"Spring Fever," 1934, *Life Begins at 8:40* (lyrics cowritten by Gershwin), Arlen

"The Springtime Cometh," 1951, *Flahooley; Jollyanna,* Fain

"Stay Out of My Dreams," 1955, from unproduced film, *The Amazing Nellie Bly,* Arlen

"Step Lightly, Lady," 1959, Acquaviva

"Step up and Take a Bow," 1939, *[A Day] At the Circus,* Arlen

"Stop That Clock," 1934, *Ziegfeld Follies,* 1933–34 (cut), Duke

"Strange As It Seems," 1931, Duke

"Strategy," 1961, see note under *The Happiest Girl in the World* entry (app. 1)

"Suddenly," 1934, *Ziegfeld Follies,* 1933–34 (lyrics cowritten by Rose), Duke

"Sunday in Cicero Falls," 1944, *Bloomer Girl,* Arlen

"Sunset Tree," 1968, *Darling of the Day,* Styne

"Swing Your Calico," 1940, *Hold on to Your Hats* (cut), Lane

"Swing Your Sweetheart 'Round the Fire," 1944, *Can't Help Singing,* Kern

"Swingali," 1939, *[A Day] At the Circus,* Arlen

"Take It Slow, Joe," 1957, *Jamaica,* Arlen

"Take My Hand, Paree," 1962, *Gay Purr-ee,* Arlen

"Take My Song," 1932, Borganoff

"Tell Me, Tell Me, Evening Star," 1944, *Kismet,* Arlen

"Thank My Stars," 1932 (published 1958), see note under *Ballyhoo of 1932* entry (app. 1)

"Thank You, Columbus," 1941, *Ship Ahoy* (unused), Lane

"Thanks for the Use of Your Heart," 1977 (ASCAP 1982), Fain

"That Fine Sunday Feeling," 1951, *Huckleberry Finn*, Lane

"That Great Come-and-Get-It Day," 1947, *Finian's Rainbow*; 1968 film, Lane

"That Mysterious Lady Called Love," added 1958 to *Flahooley*, Coots

"That Night at the Embassy Ball," 1937, *Hooray for What?*, Arlen

"That Old Devil Moon," see "Old Devil Moon"

"That Something Extra Special," 1968, *Darling of the Day*, Styne

"That Stranger in Your Eyes," 1968, see note under *Darling of the Day* entry (app. 1)

"That'll Be the Day," 1961, *The Happiest Girl in the World*, Offenbach

"That's Life," 1932, *Walk a Little Faster*, Duke

"That's Where We Come In," 1934, *Ziegfeld Follies*, 1933–34, Pokrass

"Then I'll Be Tired of You," 1934, Schwartz

"Then You Were Never in Love," 1940, *Hold on to Your Hats*, Lane

"There'll Come a Day," 1944, *Can't Help Singing* (unused), Kern

"There's a Great Day Coming Mañana," 1940, *Hold on to Your Hats*, Lane

"There's a Little Bit of You (in Every Love Song)," 1933 *Moonlight and Pretzels*, Fain

"There's a Sweet Wind Blowin' My Way," added 1980 to *Jamaica* (cut prior to opening), Arlen

"Things," 1934, *Life Begins at 8:40* (lyrics cowritten by Gershwin), Arlen

"Things Go Bump in the Night," 1973, *The Grate Mans Wiskurs* (television), Robinson

"This Is Not a Song," 1934 *Ziegfeld Follies*, 1933–34 (lyrics cowritten by Hartman), Duke

"This Time of the Year," 1947, *Finian's Rainbow*; 1968 film, Lane

"Thrill Me," 1932, *Ballyhoo of 1932*, Gensler

"'Till We All Belong," 1976, added to *Bloomer Girl*, Arlen

"Time and Tide," 1932, *Walk a Little Faster*, Duke

"Time Is a Gypsy," 1934, *Ziegfeld Follies*, 1933–34, Meyers

"Time, You Old Gypsy Man," 1979, Springer

"To Get Out of This World Alive," 1968, *Darling of the Day*, Styne

"To the Beat of My Heart," 1934, *Ziegfeld Follies*, 1933–34, Pokrass

"Tom, Tom the Piper's Son," 1943, *Presenting Lily Mars*, Lane

"T'Morra, T'Morra," 1944, *Bloomer Girl*, Arlen

"Too, Too Divine," 1930, *The Garrick Gaieties* (lyrics cowritten by Gershwin), Duke

"Troubadours," 1930, *Earl Carroll Vanities*, Gorney

"Two Blind Loves," 1939, *[A Day] At the Circus*, Arlen

"Unaccustomed As I Am," 1932, *Walk a Little Faster*, Duke

"Uncle Sam Needs a Man Who Can Take It," 1932, *Americana*, composer unknown

"Under the Sunset Tree," see "Sunset Tree"

"United Nations on the March," 1943, *Thousands Cheer*, Shostakovich/Harburg, Rome

"Until Today I Had No Tomorrow," 1930, *Heads Up*, Duke

"Unusual Weather," 1962 (ASCAP 1980), Arlen

"Viva for Geneva," 1937, *Hooray for What?* Arlen

"Vive La Virtue," 1961, *The Happiest Girl in the World*, Offenbach

"Wake Up!" 1971, *What a Day for a Miracle*, Orenstein

"Walkin' Along Mindin' My Business," 1940, *Hold on to Your Hats*, Lane

"The Waltz Is Over," 1942, *Cairo*, Schwartz

"Water under the Bridge," 1934, *Ziegfeld Follies, 1933–34*, Duke

"Way Out West Where the East Begins," 1940, *Hold on to Your Hats*, Lane

"Weekend Cruise (Will You Love Me Monday Morning as You Did on Friday Night),"
  1934, *Life Begins at 8:40* (lyrics cowritten by Gershwin), Arlen

"Welcome Hinges," 1944, *Bloomer Girl*, Arlen

"We're Not What We Used To Be," see "Quartet Erotica"

"We're Off to See the Wizard," 1939, *The Wizard of Oz*, Arlen

"We're Off to the Races," 1961, see note under *The Happiest Girl in the World* entry
  (app. 1)

"Westminster Funeral," 1968, see note under *Darling of the Day* entry (app. 1)

"We've Got a Lot of Catching Up to Do," 1979, Springer

"What a Day for a Miracle," 1971, *What a Day for a Miracle*, Orenstein, Alexander

"What Can You Say in a Love Song?" 1934, *Life Begins at 8:40* (lyrics cowritten by
  Gershwin), Arlen

"What Good Does It Do?" 1957, *Jamaica*, Arlen

"What Have You Got to Have," 1932, *Ballyhoo of 1932*, Gensler

"What Is There to Say," 1934, *Ziegfeld Follies, 1933–34*, Duke

"What Makes a Marriage Merry," 1968, *Darling of the Day*, Styne

"What Wouldn't I Do for That Man," 1929, *Applause; Glorifying the American Girl*,
  Gorney

"Whatever That May Be," 1961, *The Happiest Girl in the World*, Offenbach

"What's Gonna Happen (If We Don't Find the Genie?)," 1952, *Jollyanna*, Lane

"When I Marry Alice," 1968, see note under *Darling of the Day* entry (app. 1)

"When I'm Not Near the Girl I Love," 1947, *Finian's Rainbow;* 1968 film, Lane

"When the Boys Come Home," 1944, *Bloomer Girl*, Arlen

"When the Heart Is Too Young," 1961, see note under *The Happiest Girl in the World*
  entry (app. 1)

"When the Idle Poor Become the Idle Rich," 1947, *Finian's Rainbow;* 1968 film, Lane

"When the Wind Blows South," 1937, Arlen

"When You Have Forgotten My Kisses," 1971, *What a Day for a Miracle*, Orenstein,
  Alexander

"When Your Heart Is Too Young," 1961, see note under *The Happiest Girl in the World*
  entry (app. 1)

"Where Are You?" 1932, Gorney

"Where Has the Rainbow Gone?" added 1978 to *Flahooley*, Fain

"Where Have I Heard That Song Before?" 1961, see note under *The Happiest Girl in the
  World* entry (app. 1)

"Where Have I Seen Your Face Before?" 1981, Lane

"Where Have We Met Before?" 1932, *Walk a Little Faster*, Duke

"Whipporwill," 1957, *Jamaica* (cut), Arlen

"Whistling for a Kiss," 1932, *Americana* (lyrics cowritten by Mercer), Myers

"Whistling in the Dark," 1929, Souvaine

"Who Needs a Woman," 1961, see note under *The Happiest Girl in the World* entry
  (app. 1)

"Who Says There Ain't No Santa Claus?" 1951, *Flahooley*, Fain (revised 1973)

"Who Will Walk with Me," 1971, *What a Day for a Miracle*, Orenstein, Alexander

"Why Do You Roll Those Eyes?" 1932, Robinson

"Wild Red Cherry River," 1979, Springer

"Wilderness Man," 1973, *The Grate Mans Whiskurs* (television), Robinson

"Willow in the Wind," 1944, *Kismet*, Arlen

"The Wolf of Gubbio," 1971, *What a Day for a Miracle*, Orenstein, Alexander

"A Woman without a Man," 1942, Schwartz

"The Word Is Love," 1971, *What a Day for a Miracle*, Orenstein, Alexander

"The World Is in My Arms," 1940, *Hold on to Your Hats*, Lane

"The World Is Mine," 1934, *The Count of Monte Cristo*, Green

"The World Is Your Balloon," 1951, *Flahooley; Jollyanna*, Fain

"Would You Be So Kindly," 1940, *Hold on to Your Hats*, Lane

"You Are My First Love," 1932, *Ronny* (lyrics cowritten by Welisch, Schanzer), Kalman

"You Can Always Tell a Yank," 1944, *Hollywood Canteen*, Lane

"You Didn't Do Right by Me" (earlier version of "Buds Won't Bud"), 1932, Suesse

"You Gotta Get Out and Vote," 1944, *Hell-Bent for Election*; 1944, election eve broadcast for Franklin D. Roosevelt, Robinson

"You Gotta Live Today," 1931, Gorney

"You Need a Little Magic," 1951 (published 1984), *Flahooley; Jollyanna*, Lane

"You Satisfy," see note under *Ballyhoo of 1932* entry (app. 1)

"You Started Something," 1931, Gorney

"You Too Can Be a Puppet," 1951, *Flahooley; Jollyanna*, Fain

"You'll Never Lose Me," 1932, *Oh, Fräulein Grete*, Llossas

"You're a Builder Upper," 1934, *Life Begins at 8:40* (lyrics cowritten by Gershwin), Arlen

"You're Kinda Grandish," 1936, *Stage Struck*, Arlen

"You're Not Pretty but You're Mine," 1932, *Americana*, Lane

"You're the Cure for What Ails Me," 1936, *The Singing Kid*, Arlen

Selected Discography

Compiled by Fred Carl

Musicals and Film

Life Begins at 8:40 (1934)

Harold Arlen and Vernon Duke Revisited, Vol. II
Painted Smiles PS 1373

This Ben Bagley-produced 1980 release includes a medley of numbers from *Life Begins at 8:40*.

The Wizard of Oz (1939)

The Wizard of Oz—Original movie soundtrack
CBS Special Products AK 45356

Hold on to Your Hats (1940)

E. Y. Harburg Revisited
Painted Smiles PS 1372

A 1980 recreation produced by Ben Bagley.

Bloomer Girl (1944)

Selections from Bloomer Girl, featuring Members of the Original New York Production
Decca DL 8015
reissue—MCA 1436E

With Celeste Holm and David Brooks.

Finian's Rainbow (1947)

Finian's Rainbow
Columbia CK 4062

Original cast recording, with Ella Logan and David Wayne.

Hits from Finian's Rainbow
Columbia/Harmony Records HS 11286

With Rosemary Clooney, Ella Logan, Frank Sinatra, Dean Martin, Sammy Davis, Jr., Bing Crosby, Debbie Reynolds, and The McGuire Sisters.

Flahooley (1951)

Flahooley
Broadway Angel ZDM 7-64764-2-1

Original cast recording, with Barbara Cook and Jerome Courtland.

Jamaica (1957)

Jamaica
RCA LSO 1103

Original cast recording, with Lena Horne, Ricardo Montalban, and Josephine Premice.

The Happiest Girl in the World (1961)

The Happiest Girl in the World
Columbia KOS 2050

Original cast recording, with Cyril Ritchard and Janice Rule.

Darling of the Day (1968)

Darling of the Day
RCA LSO 1149

Original cast recording, with Vincent Price and Patricia Rutledge.

Harold Arlen Collections

Harold Arlen Sings, 1930–1937
JJA Records JJA 1975-9

Includes "God's Country," "In the Shade of the New Apple Tree," "You're a Builder-Upper," "Fun To Be Fooled," "Shoen' the Mare," and "What Can You Say in a Love Song?"

Harold Arlen and His Songs
Capitol Records T635

Includes "It's Only a Paper Moon" and "Over the Rainbow."

Harold Arlen Sings
Mark56 Records 683

Includes "Moanin' in the Mornin'," "Buds Won't Bud," "Evelina," "Last Night When We Were Young," "T'Morra, T'morra," "Hooray for Love," and a *Jamaica* demonstration disc with Arlen singing "Little Biscuit," "What Good Does It Do?" "Take It Slow, Joe," "Push de Button," "Savannah," "Cocoanut Sweet," and "Napoleon."

Harold sings Arlen (with a friend)
Columbia AOS 2920

Includes "Little Buscuit," "Ding-Dong! The Witch Is Dead," and "In the Shade of the New Apple Tree."

Harold Arlen Songbook Recordings

Harold Arlen in Hollywood, 1934–1954
JJA Records JJA 19763

Soundtrack recordings, including, among others, "Happiness Is Just a Thing Called Joe" and "Buds Won't Bud" by Ethel Waters; "Ain't It de Truth" by Lena Horne; "Lydia, The Tatooed Lady" by Groucho Marx; and "Fancy Meeting You" by Dick Powell and Jeanne Madden.

The Harold Arlen Songbook
BMG 9936-2-R

Includes Lena Horne, Julie Andrews, and Marilyn Maye singing "It's Only a Paper Moon," "Over the Rainbow," "Happiness Is Just a Thing Called Joe," and "Cocoanut Sweet," among other songs.

The Great American Composers—Harold Arlen
Music Collection 2C2 8015 C21 8015/C22 8015

Includes among its thirteen Arlen/Harburg songs "Over the Rainbow" by Rosemary Clooney, "Last Night When We Were Young" by Vic Damone, and "Let's Take a Walk around the Block" by Doris Day.

Smithsonian Collection of Recordings—American Songbook Series: Harold Arlen
Sony Music Special Products RD 048-5 A 22407

Includes 7 Arlen/Harburg songs: "Over the Rainbow" by Judy Garland, "You're a Builder-Upper" by Ethel Merman, "It's Only a Paper Moon" by Nat "King" Cole, "Happiness Is Just a Thing Called Joe" by Frances Wayne, "Lydia, the Tattooed Lady" by Bobby Short, "Last Night When We Were Young" by Tony Bennett, and "Right as the Rain" by Maureen McGovern.

Burton Lane Songbook Recordings

Michael Feinstein Sings the Burton Lane Songbook, Vol. 1
Elektra Nonesuch 9-79243-2

Includes "Anything Can Happen," "How Are Things in Glocca Morra," "Old Devil Moon," "When I'm Not Near the Girl I Love," "Look to the Rainbow," and "If This Isn't Love."

Michael Feinstein Sings the Burton Lane Songbook, Vol. 2
Elektra Nonesuch 9-79285-2

Includes "The World Is in My Arms," "Poor You," "Where Have I Seen Your Face Before," and "Don't Let It Get You Down."

The Lady's in Love with You: Maxine Sullivan Sings the Music of Burton Llane
Harbinger Records MGCD 773

Includes "Poor You," "How Are Things in Glocca Morra," and the first recording of "Where Have I Seen Your Face Before."

Forthcoming Recordings

In addition to the above, three recordings are forthcoming as of publication time; all titles are for descriptive purposes only.

Yip Harburg at the Ninety-second Street YM-YWHA's inaugural "Lyrics and Lyricists" presentation, December 20, 1970
DRG Records

Includes the entire 1971 YM-YWHA presentation, which features Yip Harburg singing "Brother, Can You Spare a Dime?" "Over the Rainbow," "Paper Moon," "Lydia, the Tatooed Lady," "If I Only Had a Brain," "The Sprigtime Cometh," "April in Paris," and many more sung by Yip and Broadway performers.

The E. Y. Harburg Songbook
Smithsonian Collection of Recordings

Includes performances of twenty-three songs by various singers, including "Lydia, the Tatooed Lady" by Groucho Marx, "Then I'll Be Tired of You" by Lena Horne, "I'm Yours" by Billie Holiday, "He's Only Wonderful" by Sarah Vaughn, "April in Paris" by Doris Day, "Fun to Be Fooled" by Tony Bennett, "I Like the Likes of You" by Bobby Short, "Old Devil Moon" by Margaret Whiting, "Brother, Can You Spare a Dime?" by Bing Crosby, "Look to the Rainbow" by Dinah Washington, "It's Only a Paper Moon" and "Over the Rainbow" by Yip Harburg, and others.

Fancy Meeting You—Phillip Officer

Phillip Officer sings twenty-one songs, among them "Look to the Rainbow," "If This Isn't Love," "Let's Take a Walk around the Block," "April in Paris," "Over the Rainbow," "Where Have I Seen Your Face Before," "Stranger in Your Eyes," "Poor You," "Would You Be So Kindly," "Then I'll Be Tired of You," "Where Has the Rainbow Gone," and "Right as the Rain."

Selected Recordings of Songs

Many of the above collections contain other versions of the following songs.

"April in Paris"

Ella Fitzgerald & Louis Armstrong	*Ella & Louis* Verve 825 373-2
Cleo Laine	*Cleo's Choice* Quintessence Jazz QJ-25401 Mono
Frank Sinatra	*Come Fly with Me* Capitol CDP 7 48469

Sarah Vaughn   *Sarah Vaughn with Clifford Brown*
                                Emarcy 814 641-2

"Brother, Can You Spare a Dime?"
Al Jolson   *Al Jolson on the Air*
                                Sandy Hook Records 2003
Abbey Lincoln   *You Gotta Pay the Band*
                                Verve 314 511 110-2
The Weavers   *The Weavers' Almanac*
                                Vanguard VMD 79100

"Down with Love"
Judy Garland   *Judy! That's Entertainment*
                                Capitol SM-11876
Barbara Streisand   *The Second Barbra Streisand Album*
                                Columbia CS 8854

"The Eagle and Me"
Lena Horne   *Here's Lena*
                                20th Century-Fox Records TFM-3115 Mono

                                The Men in My Life
                                Three Cherries Records TC 6441

"Happiness Is Just a Thing Called Joe"
Ella Fitzgerald   *The Harold Arlen Songbook, Vol. 1*
                                Verve 817 527
Ethel Waters   *The Favorite Songs of Ethel Waters*
                                Mercury MG-20051

                                *Miss Ethel Waters Performing in Person Highlights
                                   from Illustrious Career*
                                Monmouth-Evergreen Records MES/6812 Stereo

"I'm Yours"
Ruth Etting   *Ten Cents a Dance*
                                Amx-Living Era CD AJA 5008
Billie Holiday   *Strange Fruit*
                                Atlantic SD 1614

"It's Only a Paper Moon"
Natalie Cole   *Unforgettable, with Love*
                                Elektra 9 61049-2
Ella Fitzgerald   *The Best of Ella*
                                MCA MCA2-4047

                                The Harold Arlen Songbook, Vol. 1
                                Verve 817 527
Frank Sinatra   *Adventures of the Heart*
                                Columbia CL 953
James Taylor   *A League of Their Own—Music From the Motion
                                   Picture*
                                Columbia CK 52919

"Last Night When We Were Young"

Carmen McRae	*Leonard Feather Series: The Greatest of Carmen McRae*
	MCA Records MCA-2-4111
Frank Sinatra	*The Frank Sinatra Story, Vol. 3: In the Wee Small Hours*
	Capitol SC 052-81 177
Mel Torme and George Shearing	*An Elegant Evening*
	Concord Records CJ-294
Julie Wilson	*The Harold Arlen Songbook*
	DRG 5211

"Look to the Rainbow"

Dinah Washington	*Dinah!*
	Emarcy 842 139-2

"Old Devil Moon"

Carmen McRae	*The Finest of Carmen McRae: The Bethlehem Years— "You'd Be So Easy to Love"*
	Bethlehem BCP-6004
Frank Sinatra	*Songs for Swingin' Lovers!*
	Capitol CDP 7 46570 2
Mel Torme	*Mel Torme Swings Shubert Alley*
	Verve UMV 2521
Margaret Whiting	*Then and Now*
	DRG 91403

"Over the Rainbow"

Ella Fitzgerald	*The Harold Arlen Songbook, Vol. 2*
	Verve 817-528-2
Frank Sinatra	*Romantic Songs from the Early Years*
	Harmony/Columbia HS11205
Barbra Streisand	*One Voice*
	Columbia CK 40788
Sarah Vaughn	*Sarah Vaughn in the Land of Hi-Fi*
	Emarcy 826 454-2

"Right as the Rain"

Mildred Bailey	*"Love to Singa!": The Other Side of Harold Arlen*
	Jass Records 7
Barbra Streisand	*The Second Barbra Streisand Album*
	Columbia LP-CS 8854
Maureen McGovern	*Another Woman in Love*
	CBS MK 42314

Notes

All interviews, tapes, and other materials for which no location is noted can be found in the E. Y. Harburg Collection, New York Public Library for the Performing Arts, Lincoln Center. In the following section "E. Y. Harburg Collection" refers to the collection held at Yale University's Historical Sound Archive.

Preface

p. x "Harold Arlen's *Bloomer Girl,* full . . ."
Brooks Atkinson, *Broadway* (New York: Macmillan, 1970), 347.

"Harold Arlen's 'Over the Rainbow'"
Promotional brochure for *American Songbook Series,* Smithsonian Collection of Recordings.

p. xi The craft of collaboratively created . . .
See Deena Rosenberg, *Fascinating Rhythm: The Collaboration of George and Ira Gershwin* (New York: Dutton, 1991).

p. xii "chameleon"
E. Y. Harburg, in Bernard Rosenberg and Ernest Goldstein, *Creators and Disturbers: Reminiscences by Jewish Intellectuals of New York* (New York: Columbia University Press, 1982), 146.

"Yip was all joy"
Burton Lane, interview with Ernest Harburg, Brad Ross, and Arthur Perlman, July 10, 1984.

Prologue

p. 1 The question . . . is
Yip Harburg, "Lyrics and Lyricists" series, Ninety-second Street YM-YWHA, February 2, 1972.

Chapter 1

p. 5 Unless you know your roots . . .
Yip Harburg, UCLA lecture, February 3, 1977.

p. 6 "Year of birth has more . . ."
Malcolm Cowley, *Exile's Return: A Narrative of Ideas* (New York: Viking Press, 1951), 315.

p. 8 I'm a New Yorker . . .
Yip Harburg, in Rosenberg and Goldstein, *Creators,* 137–38.

A 1908 census of 250 . . .
Irving Howe, *World of Our Fathers: The Journey of the East European Jews to America and the Life They Found and Made* (New York: Simon and Schuster, 1976), 148.

p. 9   "Jewish socialism"
Howe, *World of Our Fathers*, 323.

"The drama of life"
Yip Harburg, in Rosenberg and Goldstein, *Creators*, 138.

p. 10   The nickname Yip . . .
Yip Harburg, undated interview with Studs Terkel.

My parents were Orthodox Jews . . .
Yip Harburg, in Rosenberg and Goldstein, *Creators*, 138–39.

"Atheist" (poem)
In Yip Harburg, *Rhymes for the Irreverent* (New York: Grossman Publishers, 1965), 2.

p. 11   Anyhow, I found a substitute temple . . .
Yip Harburg, in Rosenberg and Goldstein, *Creators*, 139.

This was a theatre of vivid . . .
Howe, *World of Our Fathers*, 460.

The Yiddish theatre was my first . . .
Yip Harburg, in Rosenberg and Goldstein, *Creators*, 139.

p. 12   I was always a kid . . .
Yip Harburg, undated interview with Deena Rosenberg.

My passion to be an actor . . .
Yip Harburg, in Rosenberg and Goldstein, *Creators*, 140.

The next great big impact . . .
Yip Harburg, undated interview with Deena Rosenberg.

p. 13   I liked school because . . .
Yip Harburg, in Rosenberg and Goldstein, *Creators*, 140.

"Those of us who were . . ."
Yip Harburg, in Max Wilk, *They're Playing Our Song* (New York: Atheneum, 1973), 218.

p. 14   At public school . . .
Yip Harburg, interview with Deena Rosenberg, June 1978.

There was no place . . .
Yip Harburg, in Rosenberg and Goldstein, *Creators*, 140.

Every immigrant family . . .
Yip Harburg, interview with Deena Rosenberg, June 1978.

"I am a rebel by birth . . ."
Yip Harburg, in Wilk, *They're Playing*, 227.

[I attended] Townsend Harris Hall . . .
Yip Harburg, in Rosenberg and Goldstein, *Creators*, 140.

p. 15   My passion for humorous verse . . .
Yip Harburg, in Rosenberg and Goldstein, *Creators*, 141.

Perhaps my first great literary idol . . .
Yip Harburg, in Rosenberg and Goldstein, *Creators*, 141.

p. 17   "It was the age of light verse"
Yip Harburg, undated interview with Deena Rosenberg.

"forum for metropolitan urbanity"
F. Scott Fitzgerald, "My Lost City," *The Crack Up* (New York: New Directions Paperback, 1956), 26.

"When Adams accepted things . . ."
Yip Harburg, in Wilk, *They're Playing*, 219.

p. 18   "We were well-versed . . ."
Yip Harburg, undated radio interview with Studs Terkel.

"My roots are Shakespeare"
Yip Harburg, interview with Deena Rosenberg, June 1978.

In fact, the black songwriters . . .
See Philip Furia, *The Poets of Tin Pan Alley: A History of America's Great Lyricists* (New York: Oxford University Press, 1990), chap. 2.

"As early as 1921"
Sally Ashley, *FPA: The Life and Times of Franklin Pierce Adams* (New York: Beaufort Books, 1986).

"lyric conscious"
Ira Gershwin, "Words and Music," *New York Times*, November 9, 1930.

p. 19   "He [Ira] didn't have the fears . . ."
Yip Harburg, interview with Deena Rosenberg, June 1978.

p. 20   "His theories . . ."
Richard Rodgers, *Musical Stages: An Autobiography* (New York: Random House, 1975), 27.

Some big alumnus came along . . .
Yip Harburg, interview with Deena Rosenberg, June 1978.

p. 23   "French Forms for Collection Departments" (poem)
Yip Harburg, "Conning Tower," *New York World*, ca. 1920s. E. Y. Harburg Collection, Historical Sound Archives, Yale University Library.

p. 24   "Cupid's Boomerang" (poem)
Yip Harburg, "Conning Tower," *New York World*, ca. 1920s. E. Y. Harburg Collection.

"Definition" (poem)
Yip Harburg, "Conning Tower," *New York World*, ca. 1920s. E. Y. Harburg Collection.

"The Eternal Urge" (poem)
Yip Harburg, "Conning Tower," *New York World,* ca. 1920s. E. Y. Harburg Collection.

p. 25   I'd see Ira every week . . .
Yip Harburg, interview with Deena Rosenberg, June 1978.

"We made a lot of money . . ."
Yip Harburg, in Wilk, *They're Playing,* 220.

"I was relieved when the Crash . . ."
Yip Harburg, in Louis (Studs) Terkel, *Hard Times: An Oral History of the Great Depression* (New York: Pantheon, 1970), 20.

p. 26   "I'd signed a contract . . ."
Yip Harburg, in Wilk, *They're Playing,* 220.

I immediately got hold of Ira . . .
Yip Harburg, interview with Deena Rosenberg, November 1980.

p. 27   "I was released . . ."
Yip Harburg, in Terkel, *Hard Times,* 20.

"I met Yip through Ira . . ."
Burton Lane, interview with Ernest Harburg and Bernard Rosenberg, April 11, 1983.

p. 28   "I had my fill . . ."
Yip Harburg, in Terkel, *Hard Times,* 20.

Chapter 2

p. 29   They each have something different . . .
Yip Harburg, undated radio interview with Michael Jackson, KABC.

"The musical theater scene was quite . . ."
Yip Harburg, undated interview with Deena Rosenberg.

p. 30   "lyric-conscious audience"
Gershwin, "Words and Music."

"It was your music . . ."
Yip Harburg, letter to Richard Rodgers, November 29, 1961. E. Y. Harburg Collection.

"Larry Hart was a brilliant . . ."
Yip Harburg, undated interview with Deena Rosenberg.

"To make the transition . . ."
Yip Harburg, undated radio interview with Studs Terkel.

p. 31   Given a fondness for music . . .
Ira Gershwin, *Lyrics on Several Occasions,* 120.

p. 32   The evolution of a lyricist's craft . . .
Sarah Schlesinger, unpublished article, 1991.

p. 33   "We met"
Yip Harburg, undated letter to Jay Gorney. E. Y. Harburg Collection.

"Now that I read these scripts"
Yip Harburg, annotations written for the E. Y. Harburg Collection.

"We wrote a dozen or so . . ."
Yip Harburg, interview with Deena Rosenberg, November 11, 1980.

p. 36 "I had never heard . . ."
Yip Harburg, interview with Deena Rosenberg, November 11, 1980.

"A great song requires . . ."
Yip Harburg, interview with Deena Rosenberg, November 11, 1980.

p. 37 "When you're doing musical comedy"
Yip Harburg, interview with Deena Rosenberg, November 11, 1980.

"Early songs used in pictures . . ."
Yip Harburg, annotations written for the E. Y. Harburg Collection.

p. 38 "When I'm not near the composer . . ."
Yip Harburg, "Words by E. Y. Harburg," *60 Minutes,* CBS television, March 5, 1978.

Being a very eclectic guy . . .
Yip Harburg, in Rosenberg and Goldstein, *Creators,* 146.

p. 40 "A good lyric writer"
Yip Harburg, interview with Deena Rosenberg, June 1978.

"Yip bedazzled me . . ."
Johnny Green, interview with Ernest Harburg, Arthur Perlman, and Brad Ross, July 17, 1985.

p. 43 "infallible ear"
Phil Springer, interview with Ernest Harburg, Arthur Perlman, and Brad Ross, May 9, 1985.

p. 44 "very basic lyrics of Yip Harburg"
Lena Horne, spoken introduction to "Thrill Me," *Lena at the Sands,* RCA Victor LPM-2364.

"The revues were built around . . ."
Yip Harburg, interview with Deena Rosenberg and Mel Gordon, November 15, 1980.

"They don't make them like . . ."
Yip Harburg, interview with Deena Rosenberg and Mel Gordon, November 15, 1980.

Americana had a theme . . .
Yip Harburg, interview with Deena Rosenberg and Mel Gordon, November 15, 1980.

p. 45 "It was the first such show . . ."
Yip Harburg, in Rosenberg and Goldstein, *Creators,* 144.

Yip Harburg taught me . . .
Johnny Mercer, in Wilk, *They're Playing,* 142.

"I was walking along the street"
Yip Harburg, in Terkel, *Hard Times,* 20.

p. 47 Once you drilled an oil well . . .
Yip Harburg, "Brother, Can You Spare a Dime?" worksheets. E. Y. Harburg Collection.

p. 48 I grew up when America . . .
Yip Harburg, "Lyrics and Lyricists" series, Ninety-second Street YM-YWHA, December 20, 1970.

p. 50 "In the song"
Yip Harburg, in Terkel, *Hard Times,* 21.

"[I was] well aware . . ."
Yip Harburg, "Lyrics and Lyricists" series, December 20, 1970.

Deryck Cooke has written . . .
See Deryck Cooke, *The Language of Music* (Oxford: Oxford University Press, 1959), 122.

"baffling plaint"
Yip Harburg, "Lyrics and Lyricists" series, Ninety-second Street YM-YWHA, February 2, 1972.

p. 52 The Shubert brothers . . .
Yip Harburg, radio interview with Paul Lazarus, WBAI, March 2, 1980.

p. 54 "The Messrs. Gorney and Harburg . . ."
Gilbert Gabriel, *New York American,* October 6, 1932.

"plaintive and thundering"
Brooks Atkinson, *New York Times,* October 6, 1932.

"deflates the rolling bombast . . ."
Unknown author, *Theatre Arts Monthly* 16 (July-December 1932): 961.

"Everyone picked up the song"
Yip Harburg, in Terkel, *Hard Times,* 21.

p. 55 "I met Vernon Duke . . ."
Yip Harburg, in Wilk, *They're Playing,* 222.

p. 57 "It was at Ira's"
Vernon Duke, *Passport to Paris* (Boston: Little, Brown, 1955), 223.

no two people were less alike . . .
Duke, *Passport,* 414.

Vernon brought with him . . .
Yip Harburg, in Wilk, *They're Playing,* 223.

p. 58 "the sophisticate" and "the liberator"
Lena Horne, interview with Deena Rosenberg and Ernest Harburg, November 20, 1992.

"His absorption of American . . ."
Alec Wilder, *American Popular Song* (New York: Oxford University Press, 1972), 357.

"the greatest of the running clowns"
Brooks Atkinson, *Broadway* (New York: Macmillan, 1970), 316.

"honey-haired and honey-voiced"
Duke, *Passport,* 267.

"That's when I discovered . . ."
Yip Harburg, in Wilk, *They're Playing,* 221.

"I recall Bobby running . . ."
Duke, *Passport,* 273.

p. 60   "I liked Vernon's facility"
Yip Harburg, in Wilk, *They're Playing,* 223.

was in love with Paris.
Yip Harburg, "Lyrics and Lyricists" series, December 20, 1970.

p. 61   was written . . . in New York . . .
Duke, *Passport,* 267–68.

So I went down to Cook's Tours . . .
Yip Harburg, "Lyrics and Lyricists" series, December 20, 1970.

p. 63   "It is immediately clear"
Wilder, *American Popular Song,* 358.

p. 64   "a member of the newer school . . ."
New York Times, January 8, 1933, sec. 9.

"Heard some of your lyrics . . ."
Larry Hart, telegram to Yip Harburg, November 18, 1932. E. Y. Harburg Collection.

Chapter 3

p. 65   "Harold and I met through Earl . . ."
Yip Harburg, "Harburg on Arlen," series of interviews with Deena Rosenberg, February 1977.

p. 66   "Billy Rose was a producer . . ."
Yip Harburg, "Lyrics and Lyricists" series, December 20, 1970.

p. 68   "a very innocent lyric"
Wilder, *American Popular Song,* 261.

Eugene O'Neill took five hours . . .
Yip Harburg, interview with Deena Rosenberg, June 1978.

"There's a saving grace called love"
Yip Harburg, in Wilk, *They're Playing,* 222.

p. 69   I think everybody . . .
Yip Harburg, "Lyrics and Lyricists" series, December 20, 1970.

"Larry Hart had few . . ."
Yip Harburg, as told to Gerald C. Gardner, "The Young Composers," unpublished piece, 1961. E. Y. Harburg Collection.

p. 70   "Harburg and I were summoned . . ."
Duke, *Passport*, 284.

p. 75   "The release . . ."
Wilder, *American Popular Song*, 359.

"Master of Hearts" (poem)
Yip Harburg, "Conning Tower," *New York World*, ca. 1928. E. Y. Harburg
Collection.

"I write for my peers"
Yip Harburg, "Harburg on Arlen."

p. 76   "with wonderful charm . . ."
Yip Harburg, interview with Deena Rosenberg and Mel Gordon, November 15,
1980.

p. 77   "This show really meant something"
Harold Arlen, in John Lahr, *Notes on a Cowardly Lion: The Biography of Bert
Lahr* (New York: Alfred A. Knopf, 1969), 138.

"We got together every night . . ."
Yip Harburg, interview with Deena Rosenberg, November 1980.

"Ira had a Wodehousian lightness . . ."
Yip Harburg, undated interview with Deena Rosenberg.

"Yipper is a Gilbert and Sullivan . . ."
Harold Arlen, in Edward Jablonski, *Harold Arlen: Happy with the Blues*
(Garden City, N.Y.: Doubleday, 1961), 110.

"Harold was the most fastidious . . ."
Yip Harburg, "Harburg on Arlen."

p. 78   "Even though he's known as the pope . . ."
Yip Harburg, undated radio interview with Jonathan Schwartz, WNEW.

"It was a completely perfect score . . ."
Ray Bolger, in Jablonski, *Harold Arlen*, 91.

"Ira and I had a point of view"
Yip Harburg, interview with Deena Rosenberg and Mel Gordon, November 15,
1980.

"We had this big Munich clock . . "
Yip Harburg, in Wilk, *They're Playing*, 154.

p. 81   "Harold is a very, very . . ."
Yip Harburg, in Wilk, *They're Playing*, 153.

"an extension of the same idea"
Yip Harburg, interview with Deena Rosenberg, June 1978.

I was saying life is . . .
Yip Harburg, "Lyrics and Lyricists" series, December 20, 1970.

p. 83   "Two very interesting guys"
Harold Arlen, in Wilk, *They're Playing*, 162.

p. 85   "His aim is at once . . ."
Isaac Goldberg, in Jablonski, *Harold Arlen*, 93.

"Bert Lahr . . . starts in burlesque"
Yip Harburg, interview with Deena Rosenberg and Mel Gordon, December 14, 1980.

"When DeSylva, Henderson and Brown . . ."
Yip Harburg, in Lahr, *Notes*, 138.

p. 86   "I said to Yip . . ."
Burt Lahr, in Lahr, *Notes*, 136.

p. 87   Lahr came onstage in a tuxedo . . .
Lahr, *Notes*, 139.

p. 88   His wig rebels again . . .
Lahr, *Notes*, 140.

p. 89   "He fussed and fumed . . ."
Harold Arlen, in Lahr, *Notes*, 139.

"No one could write for [Bert] . . ."
Harold Arlen, in Lahr, *Notes*, 141.

"Many outstanding writers . . ."
Lahr, in Lahr, *Notes*, 141.

p. 90   "It was a real people's country"
Yip Harburg, undated interview with Deena Rosenberg.

"We tied up the whole show"
Yip Harburg, interview with Deena Rosenberg and Mel Gordon, December 14, 1980.

Harburg's arrival on the musical comedy . . .
"Concerning E. Y. Harburg," *New York Sun*, February 1934. E. Y. Harburg Collection.

p. 91   "Harold was one of the rare guys"
Yip Harburg, "Harburg on Arlen."

Chapter 4

p. 93   a songwriter needed hits . . .
Yip Harburg, in Rosenberg and Goldstein, *Creators*, 149.

p. 94   Your sweet intoxicating clime . . .
Yip Harburg letter, ca. 1930s. E. Y. Harburg Collection.

"socially, we were a refugee colony . . ."
Yip Harburg, in Rosenberg and Goldstein, *Creators*, 149.

"So you've learned to like . . ."
Ira Gershwin, letter to Yip Harburg, January 27, 1935. E. Y. Harburg Collection.

p. 95   [Harold] wrote this beautiful melody . . .
Yip Harburg, undated radio interview with Michael Jackson, KABC.

p. 96   "The juxtaposition of those two phrases . . ."
Yip Harburg, undated interview with Deena Rosenberg.

p. 97   "goes far beyond the boundaries . . ."
Wilder, *American Popular Song,* 266.

"Maturity" (poem)
Yip Harburg, unknown newspaper, ca. 1928. E. Y. Harburg Collection.

p. 98   "is to be transported . . ."
Stephen Holden, "The Lyrics of Yip Harburg," Introduction, *The Yip Harburg Songbook* (EMI, forthcoming, 1993)

"[Because] you're standing *there*"
Harry Warren, in Jablonski, *Harold Arlen,* 106.

p. 100   "It was a great period"
Harold Arlen, in Wilk, *They're Playing,* 156–57.

I went there and sitting . . .
Saul Chaplin, in Wilk, *They're Playing,* 209.

"I am now getting together . . ."
Vincente Minnelli, telegram to Yip Harburg, April 11, 1936. E. Y. Harburg Collection.

p. 101   When the curtain came up . . .
Lahr, *Notes,* 163–65.

p. 102   Fussing with his wig . . .
Lahr, *Notes,* 164.

p. 103   "Bert is precisely the opposite . . ."
Yip Harburg, in Lahr, *Notes,* 163.

"the best little actor . . ."
Yip Harburg, in Jablonski, *Harold Arlen,* 109.

p. 104   It was about a funny inventor . . .
Yip Harburg, interview with Deena Rosenberg, November 1980.

p. 107   "I shuttled to New York . . ."
Yip Harburg, in Rosenberg and Goldstein, *Creators,* 149.

p. 112   "It's not a very good tune . . ."
Dana Suesse, interview with Ernest Harburg, Arthur Perlman, and Brad Ross, May 1, 1985.

p. 115   "Harold Arlen's felicitous score"
John Mason Brown, *New York Post,* December 2, 1937.

"A leisurely contemplation . . ."
Sidney Whipple, *NY World-Telegram,* December 4, 1937.

p. 117   "It's a sophisticated country song . . ."
Wilder, *American Popular Song,* 268.

"That song"
Harold Arlen, in Wilk, *They're Playing,* 155.

Chapter 5

p. 119 "*You* got the job?"
Jerome Kern, in Jablonski, *Harold Arlen,* 118.

"There were plenty of other major . . ."
Arlen, in Wilk, *They're Playing,* 156.

"Once a year"
Yip Harburg, in Aljean Harmetz, *The Making of "The Wizard of Oz"* (New York: Alfred A. Knopf, 1977), 19.

p. 120 "Arthur had sensed my love of whimsy"
Yip Harburg, in Harmetz, *Making,* 73–74.

"Harburg had a great sense . . ."
Arthur Freed, in Lahr, *Notes,* 190.

p. 121 "He was a flag waver . . ."
Yip Harburg, in Harmetz, *Making,* 73.

p. 122 "I have been making believe."
L. Frank Baum, *The New Wizard of Oz* (Indianapolis: Bobbs-Merrill Company, 1903), 147.

"accepted the integrated concept . . ."
Yip Harburg, in Harmetz, *Making,* 74.

p. 124 "Harburg supported Langley's versions"
Harmetz, *Making,* 54.

"In the end"
Noel Langley, in Harmetz, *Making,* 74.

it was an acrostic . . .
Yip Harburg, undated interview with Studs Terkel.

The story and characters, of course . . .
See Bernard Rosenberg and Ernest Harburg, *The Broadway Musical* (New York: New York University Press, 1993), chap. 4.

"Songs seem simple"
Yip Harburg, in Harmetz, *Making,* 87.

"I knew how to change plot . . ."
Yip Harburg, interview notes by Aljean Harmetz for Harmetz, *Making,* spring 1975.

"Harburg's only screen credit . . ."
Harmetz, *Making,* 57.

"Harburg had been allowed . . ."
Harmetz, *Making,* 85.

p. 125 Although he received no screen . . .
Micheal Patrick Hearn, "Introduction," in Noel Langley, Florence Ryerson, and Edgar Allen Woolf, *The Wizard of Oz: The Screenplay* (New York, Delta, 1989), 23.

"I wanted Buddy very much"
Yip Harburg, in Harmetz interview notes.

"Harburg promoted Lahr . . ."
Lahr, *Notes*, 190.

I wrote this scene for W. C. Fields . . .
Yip Harburg, in Rosenberg and Goldstein, *Creators*, 151.

p. 126 "The trouble was"
Yip Harburg, in Harmetz, *Making*, 75.

"What makes the unity?"
F. Scott Fitzgerald, *The Last Tycoon, An Unfinished Novel* (New York: Charles Scribner's Sons, 1941), 72.

Love Me Tonight achieved . . .
Harmetz, *Making*, 88.

p. 129 You always have trouble writing a ballad.
Yip Harburg, "Lyrics and Lyricists" series, December 20, 1970.

"a song of yearning"
Yip Harburg, in Harmetz, *Making*, 77.

"I can't tell you the misery . . ."
Yip Harburg, "Lyrics and Lyricists" series, December 20, 1970.

He and Anya had decided . . .
Jablonski, *Harold Arlen*, 120.

p. 131 "He called me"
Yip Harburg, "Lyrics and Lyricists" series, December 20, 1970.

"I ran to meet him at home"
Yip Harburg, "Harold Arlen, 'Over the Rainbow' and Me: The Man Who Wrote the Melody as Seen by the Man Who Wrote the Words," TV *Guide*, February 24, 1973, 28.

"For two weeks after"
Yip Harburg, "Lyrics and Lyricists" series, December 20, 1970.

"We'd instinctively give each other . . ."
Yip Harburg, in Harmetz, *Making*, 80.

p. 132 "The girl was in trouble"
Yip Harburg, in Harmetz, *Making*, 80.

p. 134 "What makes Harold Arlen, and a few . . ."
Yip Harburg, video interview with Deena Rosenberg, November 1980.

You have to work for sound . . .
Yip Harburg, undated interview with Studs Terkel.

p. 135 "This little girl . . ."
Yip Harburg, in Harmetz, *Making*, 80–81.

"rainbow hustler"
Yip Harburg, video interview with Deena Rosenberg, November 1980.

"I loved the idea . . ."
Yip Harburg, in Wilk, *They're Playing*, 224.

p. 152   "I am always disappointed . . ."
Yip Harburg, radio interview with Paul Lazarus, WBAI, March 2, 1980.

p. 153   "The picture didn't need . . ."
Yip Harburg, in Harmetz, *Making*, 57.

In Baum, the Wizard has provided . . .
Yip Harburg, in Harmetz, *Making*, 57.

"I devised the satiric and cynical . . ."
Yip Harburg, in Harmetz, *Making*, 58.

p. 155   unbearable . . .
Yip Harburg, in Harmetz, *Making*, 81.

"Mr. Fleming walked into the office"
Yip Harburg, "Lyrics and Lyricists" series, January 27, 1980.

p. 156   "Rainbow"
Harold Arlen, in Jablonski, *Harold Arlen*, 121.

"magnificent sets and costumes"
Newsweek, August 21, 1939.

"a Broadway spectacle"
Time, August 21, 1939.

"The Wizard of Oz" was intended . . .
Otis Ferguson, *The New Republic*, September 20, 1939.

p. 157   "a stinkeroo . . ."
Russell Maloney, *The New Yorker*, August 19, 1939.

Not since Disney's "Snow White"
Frank S. Nugent, *New York Times*, August 18, 1939.

p. 158   "I hadn't realized what an impact . . ."
Yip Harburg, in Harmetz interview notes.

p. 159   "Harold Arlen and E. Y. Harburg's . . ."
Ethan Mordden, *The Hollywood Musical* (New York: St. Martin's Press, 1981), 156.

p. 160   "I think that the pervading idea . . ."
Yip Harburg, in Harmetz interview notes.

"When I wrote *Finian's Rainbow*"
Yip Harburg, in Harmetz, *Making*, 20.

"I knew 'Over the Rainbow' was a strong . . ."
Harold Arlen, in Wilk, *They're Playing*, 160.

"We were just doing work . . ."
Yip Harburg, in Wilk, *They're Playing*, 224.

Chapter 6

p. 161   "I've worked with some of the greatest . . ."
Yip Harburg, "Lyrics and Lyricists" series, December 20, 1970.

p. 163   "I tried to get as near . . ."
Yip Harburg, interview with Deena Rosenberg, June 1978.

"Harold went off with Johnny Mercer . . ."
Yip Harburg, in Wilk, *They're Playing*, 226.

"old-fashioned musical comedy"
Time, September 23, 1940.

"He had a great appreciation . . ."
Burton Lane, interview with Ernest Harburg and Bernard Rosenberg, April 11, 1983.

p. 164   "At the end of the show . . ."
Burton Lane, interview with Ernest Harburg and Bernard Rosenberg, April 11, 1983.

p. 167   "It was never a hit"
Burton Lane, interview with Deena Rosenberg, April 29, 1985.

p. 169   "one of the funniest musical plays . . ."
Brooks Atkinson, *New York Times*, September 12, 1940.

"At about 11:10"
John Mason Brown, *New York Post*, September 12, 1940.

"I have heard from many sources"
Ira Gershwin, letter to Yip Harburg, December 23, 1940. E. Y. Harburg Collection.

"The power of Jolson . . ."
George Jean Nathan, *New York Journal American*, September 12, 1940.

p. 170   "A dreary lyric . . ."
Yip Harburg, song inscription, E. Y. Harburg Collection.

He avoided clichés like the plague . . .
Burton Lane, interview with Deena Rosenberg, April 29, 1985.

p. 171   Jerome Kern was not a very good player.
Yip Harburg, undated radio interview with Jonathan Schwartz.

I don't think it was on purpose . . .
Burton Lane, interview with Ernest Harburg, Arthur Perlman, and Brad Ross, July 10, 1984.

p. 174   I had trouble all the time . . .
Yip Harburg, in Wilk, *They're Playing*, 227.

p. 176   Vernon Duke had written a beautiful score.
Yip Harburg, undated radio interview with Studs Terkel.

"the Negro-est white man"
Ethel Waters, in Jablonski, *Harold Arlen*, 68.

Arlen's hallmark is his synthesis . . .
Yip Harburg, in Rosenberg and Goldstein, *Creators,* 146.

p. 179 Harold had a tune.
Yip Harburg, "Lyrics and Lyricists" series, December 20, 1970.

p. 181 "There was something I tried to do . . ."
Yip Harburg, "Lyrics and Lyricists" series, December 20, 1970.

Chapter 7

p. 183 "Harold and I have been intrigued . . ."
Yip Harburg, letter to George S. Kaufman, July 1943. E. Y. Harburg Collection.

p. 184 Could the [satiric and political show] . . .
Ethan Mordden, *Broadway Babies* (New York: Oxford University Press, 1983), 147.

p. 185 No other writer has appreciated . . .
Stanley Green, *The World of Musical Comedy,* 4th ed. (New York: Da Capo Press, 1986), 186–87.

"the perversities of Fashion . . ."
Dan James, "Writing 'Bloomer Girl,'" *The New York Review of Books,* vol. 31, no. 17, November 8, 1984, 52.

Lilith James had come across a costume . . .
Yip Harburg, interview with Deena Rosenberg, June 1978.

p. 186 "It failed to satisfy our lyricist . . ."
Dan James, "Writing 'Bloomer Girl.'"

p. 187 "the indivisibility of human freedom"
Yip Harburg, letter to "George and Nat," October 14, 1965.

"There were so many new issues . . ."
Yip Harburg, interview with Deena Rosenberg, June 1978.

p. 188 was never concerned . . .
Yip Harburg, interview with Deena Rosenberg, June 1978.

It's quite a different medium . . .
Yip Harburg, undated interview with Deena Rosenberg.

To write a song . . .
Yip Harburg, lecture to Buddy Kaye class on lyric writing, February 7, 1971.

p. 190 "namby-pambies"
Yip Harburg, letter to "George and Nat," October 14, 1965.

Bloomer Girl's score . . .
Mordden, *Broadway Babies,* 124.

p. 197 "an amiable hymn to freedom"
Mordden, *Broadway Babies,* 124.

p. 199 "My favorite lyric line"
Stephen Sondheim, radio interview with Jonathan Schwartz, 1977.

"A good lyric writer has ideas . . ."
Yip Harburg, "Lyrics and Lyricists" series, December 20, 1970.

p. 201 "Ira wouldn't write any straight . . ."
Yip Harburg, interview with Deena Rosenberg, November 1980.

p. 204 "the finest combination of spectacle . . ."
John Chapman, *New York Daily News,* October 6, 1944.

p. 205 "That number could go on all night"
Lewis Nicols, *New York Times,* October 8, 1944.

"It does not advance . . ."
Burton Rascoe, *New York World-Telegram,* October 9, 1944.

p. 210 "a serious ballet . . ."
Agnes de Mille, in Jablonski, *Harold Arlen,* 125.

p. 211 At the end of the showing . . .
Agnes de Mille, *And Promenade Home* (Boston: Little, Brown, 1958), 196.

"Goddammit!"
Yip Harburg, in de Mille, *Promenade,* 202.

p. 212 "If it has a weakness"
Louis Kronenberger, *P.M. New York,* October 16, 1944.

The soul and heart of the play . . .
Yip Harburg, letter to "George and Nat," October 14, 1965.

p. 213 "Both are so curious . . ."
Arthur Pollock, *Brooklyn Daily Eagle,* October 15, 1944.

p. 214 a Southern white cracker . . .
Earl Robinson, interview with Ernest Harburg, Arthur Perlman, and Brad Ross, December 9, 1985.

p. 215 "was pretty much a guy . . ."
Earl Robinson, interview with Ernest Harburg, Arthur Perlman, and Brad Ross, December 9, 1985.

"We both agreed"
Earl Robinson, interview with Ernest Harburg, Arthur Perlman, and Brad Ross, December 9, 1985.

p. 218 "If I had been able to write tunes"
Earl Robinson, interview with Ernest Harburg, Arthur Perlman, and Brad Ross, December 9, 1985.

p. 219 "As a collaborator"
Yip Harburg, interview with Deena Rosenberg, November 1980.

"When you stop working . . ."
Yip Harburg, interview with Deena Rosenberg, November 1980.

Chapter 8

p. 222 "I remember more or less . . ."
Yip Harburg, Northwood Institute lectures, 1978.

"I never like to write a play . . ."
Yip Harburg, undated radio interview with Studs Terkel.

"Two years later"
Yip Harburg, Northwood Institute lectures, 1978.

p. 224 "All man has left"
Yip Harburg, Northwood Institute lectures, 1978.

p. 225 "Yip got angry . . ."
Burton Lane, interview with Ernest Harburg and Bernard Rosenberg, April 11, 1983.

"Yip was the one in control"
Burton Lane, interview with Ernest Harburg and Bernard Rosenberg, April 11, 1983.

p. 226 I met Yip through Ira Gershwin . . .
Burton Lane, interview with Ernest Harburg and Bernard Rosenberg, April 11, 1983.

p. 227 I met Yip when I was sixteen . . .
Burton Lane, interview with Ernest Harburg, Arthur Perlman, and Brad Ross, July 10, 1984.

"Rainbow Valley is as mythical . . ."
Yip Harburg, Northwood Institute lectures, 1978.

p. 231 The show has three or four . . .
Yip Harburg, Northwood Institute lectures, 1978.

p. 232 "It was going to be the first . . ."
Burton Lane, interview with Deena Rosenberg, April 29, 1985.

p. 234 "You know the Irish . . ."
Yip Harburg, in Burton Lane, interview with Deena Rosenberg, April 29, 1985.

p. 235 "This pixilated little man . . ."
Yip Harburg, Northwood Institue lectures, 1978.

p. 239 "How to write a love song"
Yip Harburg, Northwood Institute lectures, 1978.

"There's a little bit of witchcraft . . ."
Yip Harburg, Northwood Institute lectures, 1978.

p. 241 "strangely constructed."
Yip Harburg, in Wilk, *They're Playing,* 229.

"You give him a piece of music . . ."
Jule Styne, interview with Ernest Harburg, Arthur Perlman, and Brad Ross, November 16, 1984.

p. 242 I had written a song . . .
Burton Lane, interview with Deena Rosenberg, April 29, 1985.

p. 245 "You'd be Kinda Grandish" (lyric)
Yip Harburg, worksheets, E. Y. Harburg Collection.

"When I first got involved . . ."
Burton Lane, interview with Deena Rosenberg, April 29, 1985.

p. 251 Finian plants the gold . . .
Yip Harburg, Northwood Institute lectures, 1978.

p. 255 "Is it necessary for the idle rich . . ."
Yip Harburg, Northwood Institute lectures, 1978.

p. 256 What happens in this country . . .
Yip Harburg, Northwood Institute lectures, 1978.

p. 258 "Michael Kidd staged a ballet . . ."
Mordden, *Broadway Babies,* 231.

p. 259 People of the soil . . .
Yip Harburg, Northwood Institute lectures, 1978.

He happens to meet . . .
Yip Harburg, Northwood Institute lectures, 1978.

p. 260 "I don't like villains . . ."
Yip Harburg, Northwood Institute lectures, 1978.

p. 262 He's hit by one of the most . . .
Yip Harburg, Northwood Institute lectures, 1978.

p. 264 "The title of the song"
Burton Lane, interview with Deena Rosenberg, April 29, 1985.

p. 265 Yip would get very excited . . .
Burton Lane, interview with Deena Rosenberg, April 29, 1985.

"agonizers . . ."
Burton Lane, interview with Deena Rosenberg, April 29, 1985.

p. 266 Suddenly, he's undecided.
Yip Harburg, Northwood Institute lectures, 1978.

p. 268 "I was dying to be teamed . . ."
Burton Lane, interview with Deena Rosenberg, April 29, 1983.

"For the first time . . ."
Miles Jefferson, "The Negro on Broadway," *Phylon* (1947) 8:2, 149.

p. 269 Prejudice is brought to trial . . .
Review, no byline, in Scrapbook, E. Y. Harburg Collection.

"Gilbert naturally aside"
George Jean Nathan, *New York Journal American,* January 27, 1947.

"It puts the American musical stage . . ."
Brooks Atkinson, *New York Times,* January 11, 1947.

"This is a mere note . . ."
Cole Porter, letter to Yip Harburg, January 13, 1947. E. Y. Harburg Collection.

"Dear Yip, I love you . . ."
Oscar Hammerstein, telegram to Yip Harburg, January 11, 1947. E. Y. Harburg Collection.

"Hammerstein and Harburg made Broadway . . ."
Mordden, *Broadway Babies,* 152.

Finian's Rainbow was . . .
Peter Stone, interview with Ernest Harburg and Bernard Rosenberg, October 13, 1982.

Chapter 9

p. 271   "Yip had an arrangement . . ."
Burton Lane, interview with Deena Rosenberg, April 29, 1985.

p. 272   "I got a call from Metro's lawyer . . ."
Yip Harburg, radio interview with Celeste Wesson, WBAI, 1976.

I am a Franklin Delano Roosevelt . . .
Yip Harburg, letter to J. Robert Rubin, December 25, 1950. E. Y. Harburg Collection.

"In a new society . . ."
Yip Harburg, letter to Dr. Samuel Rosen, January 7, 1953. E. Y. Harburg Collection.

"the leading Popular Front . . ."
Larry Ceplair and Steven England, *The Inquisition in Hollywood: Politics in the Film Community, 1930–1960,* (Garden City, N.Y.: Anchor Press/Doubleday, 1980), 218.

p. 273   "They didn't want anything"
Yip Harburg, radio interview with Celeste Wesson, WBAI, 1976.

"For the birds" (poem)
Yip Harburg, *Rhymes,* 59.

"A vivid example of one . . ."
Victor Navasky, *Naming Names* (New York: Viking, 1980), 94.

"I don't think Yip . . ."
Burton Lane, letter to Yip Harburg, November 1950. E. Y. Harburg Collection.

"even Dore Schary . . ."
Yip Harburg, letter to Burton Lane, April 5, 1953. E. Y. Harburg Collection.

"I was also blacklisted . . ."
Yip Harburg, radio interview with Celeste Wesson, WBAI, 1976.

p. 274   "*Flahooley* . . . is the most . . ."
Ethan Mordden, *Broadway Babies,* 149.

"The only adaptations that . . ."
Yip Harburg, *New York Herald Tribune,* May 13, 1951, sect. 4.

p. 275   "showing how the economy works . . ."
Yip Harburg, radio interview with Celeste Wesson, WBAI, 1976.

p. 277   "It came at a very bad time"
Yip Harburg, radio interview with Celeste Wesson, WBAI, 1976.

"In the course of an evening"
Brooks Atkinson, *New York Times,* May 15, 1951.

"His social prescriptions . . ."
Mordden, *Broadway Babies,* 147.

p. 278 "Fred was always in the background . . ."
Burton Lane, interview with Ernest Harburg and Bernard Rosenberg, April 11, 1983.

"I think I've been very lucky . . ."
Yip Harburg, in Wilk, *They're Playing,* 229.

p. 287 "something of *Babes in Toyland*"
Robert Garland, *New York Journal American,* May 15, 1951.

"*Flahooley* . . . should become . . ."
Unsigned review of *Flahooley.*

p. 288 "Easily the most original . . ."
John Chapman, *The Daily News,* May 15, 1951.

"Although Mr. Fain's music . . ."
Brooks Atkinson, *New York Times,* May 15, 1951.

"It is this over-all . . ."
George Jean Nathan, *New York Journal American,* May 28, 1951.

One first-nighter was overheard . . .
Robert Coleman, *Daily Mirror,* May 15, 1951.

E. Y. Harburg and Fred Saidy . . .
Louis Sheaffer, *Brooklyn Daily Eagle,* May 15, 1951.

"*This* doll . . ."
Cheryl Crawford, *One Naked Individual: My Fifty Years in the Theatre* (Indianapolis and New York: Bobbs-Merrill, 1977), 175.

p. 289 "commanist"
Burton Lane, interview with Deena Rosenberg, April 29, 1985.

"After I was blacklisted"
Yip Harburg, radio interview with Celeste Wesson, WBAI, 1976.

p. 290 it was killed, according to John Canemaker . . .
See John Canemaker, "Lost Rainbow," *Print* 48, no. 11 (March-April 1993): 62–121.

"It was never only one thing"
Yip Harburg, radio interview with Celeste Wesson, WBAI, 1976.

p. 293 "Organization Man" (poem)
Yip Harburg, *Rhymes,* 71.

"A Saint . . . He Ain't" (poem)
Yip Harburg, *At This Point in Rhyme: E. Y. Harburg's Poems* (New York: Crown Publishers, 1976), 41.

"simple island boy . . ."
Jablonski, *Harold Arlen*, 199.

p. 309 The work of librettists . . .
Jablonski, *Harold Arlen*, 205.

The show, like every creation . . .
Yip Harburg, letter to *Harold Arlen*, August 1, 1952. E. Y. Harburg Collection.

Harburg, serving as spokesman . . .
Jablonski, *Harold Arlen*, 208.

p. 310 "*Jamaica*"
Brooks Atkinson, *New York Times*, November 1, 1957.

"Can you make a whole show"
Walter Kerr, *New York Herald Tribune*, November 1, 1957.

no fewer than four . . .
Kerr, *New York Herald Tribune*, November 1, 1957.

p. 311 "when Josephine Premice sang . . ."
Lena Horne, interview with Deena Rosenberg and Ernest Harburg, November 20, 1992.

I did not come in for the opening . . .
Yip Harburg, letter to Maurice Essex, November 19, 1957. E. Y. Harburg Collection.

Chapter 10

p. 313 "Even though we are the same . . ."
Yip Harburg, letter to Arthur Freed, May 23, 1957. E. Y. Harburg Collection.

p. 314 "the Village Blacksmith idea"
Burton Lane, letter to Yip Harburg, March 1, 1956. E. Y. Harburg Collection.

"I can't think of a composer . . ."
Lane, letter to Harburg, March 1, 1956.

"The story lost all . . ."
Lane, letter to Harburg, March 1, 1956.

"Every idea you worked on . . ."
Lane, letter to Harburg, March 1, 1956.

these youngsters are not producing . . .
Yip Harburg, as told to Gerald C. Gardner, "The Young Composers," unpublished piece, 1961. E. Y. Harburg Collection.

p. 315 "We wanted to use tunes . . ."
Yip Harburg, in John Keating, "Yip's Labor of Love," *New York Times*, April 2, 1961.

p. 316 "An Atom a Day Keeps the Doctor Away" (poem)
Yip Harburg, *Rhymes*, 28.

p. 324 "Yevtushenko?" (poem)
Yip Harburg, *Rhymes*, 41.

p. 326   The songs I'm hearing today . . .
Yip Harburg, "Lyrics and Lyricists" series, December 20, 1970.

Here's my little tirade . . .
Yip Harburg, undated interview with Studs Terkel.

"Yip said, 'It needs more' "
Earl Robinson, interview with Ernest Harburg, Arthur Perlman, and Brad Ross, December 9, 1985.

p. 329   Where are the bards that pleasured me . . . (poem)
Yip Harburg, unpublished poem. E. Y. Harburg Collection.

p. 331   "Yip said, 'I want . . .' "
Burton Lane, interview with Deena Rosenberg, April 29, 1985.

p. 332   "Yipper was the right man . . ."
Jule Styne, in Theodore Taylor, *Jule: The Story of Composer Jule Styne* (New York: Random House, 1979), 259.

p. 336   "I knew this was . . ."
Jule Styne, interview with Ernest Harburg, Arthur Perlman, and Brad Ross, November 16, 1984.

p. 337   "I wrote music first . . ."
Jule Styne, interview with Ernest Harburg, Arthur Perlman, and Brad Ross, November 16, 1934.

p. 340   He's a very easy fellow . . .
Jule Styne, interview with Ernest Harburg, Arthur Perlman, and Brad Ross, November 16, 1984.

"He was an art collector"
Jule Styne, in Taylor, *Jule,* 261.

"The strange thing . . ."
Elliot Norton, *Record American,* December 21, 1968.

p. 341   "his self-congratulatory chuckles . . ."
Walter Kerr, *New York Times,* February 11, 1968.

"All I can say . . ."
Kerr, *New York Times,* February 11, 1968.

"The ones that hurt the most . . ."
Jule Styne, interview with Ernest Harburg, Arthur Perlman, and Brad Ross, November 16, 1984.

p. 343   "History Lesson" (poem)
Yip Harburg, *At This Point,* 46.

"The Enemy List" (poem)
Yip Harburg, *At This Point,* 48.

p. 345   "the feeling that life . . ."
Yip Harburg, undated interview, "Only a Paper Moon," Harburg Archive video.

A songwriter is really . . .
Yip Harburg, undated interview, "Only a Paper Moon," Harburg Archive video.

p. 346   "The show is a chronicle . . ."
Yip Harburg, interview with Deena Rosenberg and Mel Gordon, November 14, 1980.

p. 347   Yip always wanted . . .
Phil Springer, interview with Ernest Harburg, Arthur Perlman, and Brad Ross, May 9, 1985.

I decided to come out . . .
Yip Harburg, "Lyrics and Lyricists" series, 1980.

p. 349   "Yip was searching . . ."
Phil Springer, interview with Ernest Harburg, Arthur Perlman, and Brad Ross, May 9, 1985.

Not to have known Jimmy Durante . . .
Yip Harburg, video interview with Deena Rosenberg, November 1980.

"The aim of a song . . ."
Yip Harburg, video interview with Deena Rosenberg, November 1980.

p. 350   "the world seriously, but himself lightly"
Noel Langley, in Harmetz, *Making,* 54.

"Gerontology or Springtime for Senility" (poem)
Harburg, *At This Point,* 17.

Epilogue

Taken from the following sources:
"Lyrics and Lyricists" series, Ninety-second Street YM-YWHA, December 20, 1970.
Rosenberg and Goldstein, *Creators and Disturbers.*
Northwood Institute lectures, 1978.
Interviews with Deena Rosenberg, 1978 and 1980.

Selected Bibliography

Alvarez, Max Joseph. *Index to Motion Pictures Reviewed by Variety 1907–1980*. Metuchen, N.J.: Scarecrow Press, 1982.

American Film Institute. *The American Film Institute Catalog of Motion Pictures: Feature Films 1961–1970*. New York: Bowker, 1976.

———. *The American Film Institute Catalog of Motion Pictures Produced in the United States: Feature Films 1921–1930*. New York: Bowker, 1971.

American Society of Composers, Authors, and Publishers. *ASCAP Biographical Dictionary*. 4th ed. New York and London: Jaques Cattell Press and Bowker, 1980.

———. *ASCAP Index of Performed Compositions*. New York: American Society of Composers, Authors, and Publishers, 1963.

Ashley, Sally. *FPA: The Life and Times of Franklin Pierce Adams*. New York: Beaufort Books, 1986.

Atkinson, Brooks. *Broadway*. New York: Macmillan, 1970.

Best Plays series, various editors. Boston: Small, Maynard, 1920–25; New York: Dodd, Mead, 1916–87; New York: Applause Theatre Book Publishers, 1987—.

Bloom, Ken. *American Song: The Complete Musical Theatre Companion*. New York: Facts on File Publications, 1985.

Bordman, Gerald. *Jerome Kern: His Life and Music*. New York and Oxford: Oxford University Press, 1980.

Burton, Jack. *Blue Book of Hollywood Musicals*. Watkins Glen, N.Y.: Century House, 1953.

Ceplair, Larry, and Steven Englund. *The Inquisition in Hollywood: Politics in the Film Community, 1930–1960*. Garden City, N.Y.: Anchor Press/Doubleday, 1980.

Cooke, Deryck. *The Language of Music*. Oxford: Oxford University Press, 1959.

Cowley, Malcom. *Exile's Return: A Literary Odyssey of the 1920s*. New York: Viking, 1969.

Crawford, Cheryl. *One Naked Individual: My Fifty Years in the Theatre*. Indianapolis and New York: Bobbs-Merrill, 1977.

Croce, Arlene. *The Fred Astaire and Ginger Rogers Book*. New York: Galahad Books, 1972.

de Mille, Agnes. *And Promenade Home*. Boston: Little, Brown, 1958.

Duke, Vernon. *Passport to Paris*. Boston: Little, Brown, 1955.

Film Daily Year Book of Motion Pictures: 1918–1970. New York: Alicoate, Film TV Daily.

Fricke, John, Jay Scarfone, and William Stillman. *The Wizard of Oz: The Official Fiftieth Anniversary Pictorial History*. [New York]: Warner, 1989.

Gershwin, Ira. *Lyrics on Several Occasions: A Selection of Stage and Screen Lyrics Written for Sundry Situations; and Now Arranged in Arbitrary Categories*. New York: Knopf, 1959.

437

Green, Stanley. *Encyclopaedia of the Musical Film.* New York: Oxford University Press, 1981.

———. *Ring Bells! Sing Songs! Broadway Musicals of the 1930's.* New Rochelle, N.Y.: Arlington House, 1971.

———. *The World of Musical Comedy.* 4th ed. San Diego and New York: A. S. Barnes and Co., 1980.

Harburg, E. Y. *At This Point in Rhyme.* New York: Crown, 1976.

———. *Rhymes for the Irreverent.* New York: Grossman, 1965.

———. *The Yip Harburg Songbook,* Tom Roed, ed. Miami, Fla.: CPP/Belwin, Inc., 1994.

Harmetz, Aljean. *The Making of "The Wizard of Oz."* New York: Knopf, 1977.

Hirschhorn, Clive. *The Warner Bros. Story.* New York: Crown, 1979.

Howe, Irving. *World of Our Fathers.* New York: Harcourt, 1976.

Jablonski, Edward. *Harold Arlen: Happy with the Blues.* Garden City, N.Y.: Doubleday, 1961.

Kimball, Robert, and Alfred Simon. *The Gershwins.* New York: Atheneum, 1973.

Lahr, John. *Notes on a Cowardly Lion: The Biography of Bert Lahr.* New York: Knopf, 1969.

Langley, Noel, Florence Ryerson, and Edgar Allan Woolf. *The Wizard of Oz: The Screenplay.* Edited by Michael Patrick Hearn. New York: Delta, 1989.

Mordden, Ethan. *Broadway Babies.* New York: Oxford University Press, 1983.

———. *The Hollywood Musical.* New York: St. Martin's Press, 1981.

The Motion Picture Guide: 1927–1983. Chicago: Cinebooks, 1987.

Navasky, Victor. *Naming Names.* New York: Viking, 1980.

The New York Times Film Reviews, 1913–1968. New York: New York Times and Arno, 1970.

Notable Names in the American Theatre. Clifton, N.J.: James T. White, 1976.

Robinson, Lennox. *Killycregs in Twilight and Other Plays.* London: Macmillan, 1939.

Rodgers, Richard. *Musical Stages: An Autobiography.* New York: Random House, 1975.

Rosenberg, Bernard, and Ernest Goldstein. *Creators and Disturbers: Reminiscences by Jewish Intellectuals of New York.* New York: Columbia University Press, 1982.

———, and Ernest Harburg. *The Broadway Musical: Collaboration in Commerce and Art.* New York: New York University Press, 1993.

Rosenberg, Deena. *Fascinating Rhythm: The Collaboration of George and Ira Gershwin.* New York: Dutton, 1991.

Shapiro, Nat, ed. *Popular Music: An Annotated Index of Popular Songs.* New York: Adrian Press, 1964—.

Stephens, James. *The Crock of Gold.* New York: Macmillan, 1922.

Terkel, Louis [Studs]. *Hard Times: An Oral History of the Great Depression.* New York: Pantheon, 1970.

Theatre World. Daniel Blum, ed. 1945–64; John Willis, ed. 1965—. New York: Blum, 1945–48; New York: Greenberg, 1950–57; Philadelphia: Chilton, 1958–64; New York: Crown, 1965—.

Thomas, Tony, and Jim Terry, with Busby Berkeley. *The Busby Berkeley Book.* Greenwich, Conn.: New York Graphic Society, 1973.

U.S. Copyright Office. *Motion Pictures, 1912–1939: Catalog of Copyright Entries.* Washington, D.C.: U.S. Library of Congress, 1951.

———. *Motion Pictures, 1940–49: Catalog of Copyright Entries.* Washington, D.C.: U.S. Library of Congress, 1953.

——. *Catalog of Copyright Entries. Part 3: Musical Compositions (1906–1946)*. Washington, D.C.: Government Printing Office. Published monthly, 1906–45; annual, 1946.

——. *Catalog of Copyright Entries. Part 5: Music. 3d series (1947–1977)*. Washington, D.C.: Government Printing Office, n.d.

[U.S.] Library of Congress. *Motion Picture Broadcasting and Recorded Sound Division. Three Decades of Television*. Washington, D.C., 1989.

Variety Film Reviews (1907–1980). New York: Garland Publishing, 1983.

Who's Who in the Theatre: A Biographical Record of the Contemporary Stage. 8th ed. London: Sir Isaac Pitman and Sons, 1936.

Wilder, Alec. *American Popular Song: The Great Innovators, 1900–1950*. New York: Oxford University Press, 1972.

Wilk, Max. *They're Playing Our Song: From Jerome Kern to Stephen Sondheim—The Stories behind the Words and Music Generators*. New York: Atheneum, 1973.

Zimmerman, Paul D., and Burt Goldblatt. *The Marx Brothers at the Movies*. New York: G. P. Putnam's Sons, 1968.

Index

Page numbers in **boldface** refer to captions and tables. Page numbers in *italics* refer to complete or extensively excerpted light verses and song lyrics.